THE CINEMA OF BARBARA STANWYCK

Women's Media History Now!

Series Editors
Kay Armatage, Jane M. Gaines, Christine Gledhill, and Sangita Gopal

This series is global in scope and investigates the significance of women's contributions to film, television, broadcast, audiovisual, print, digital, and social media history. Taking advantage of archival discoveries and new materials, the books in the series explore women's media histories through a variety of lenses.

A list of books in the series appears at the end of this book.

THE CINEMA OF
BARBARA STANWYCK

TWENTY-SIX SHORT ESSAYS
ON A WORKING STAR

Catherine Russell

**UNIVERSITY OF
ILLINOIS PRESS**
Urbana, Chicago, and Springfield
www.press.uillinois.edu

∞ This book is printed on acid-free paper.

Library of Congress Cataloging-in-Publication Data
Names: Russell, Catherine, 1959– author.
Title: The cinema of Barbara Stanwyck : twenty-six short essays on a working star /
    Catherine Russell.
Description: Urbana : University of Illinois Press, [2023] | Series: Women's media
    history now! | Includes bibliographical references and index.
Identifiers: LCCN 2022040967 (print) | LCCN 2022040968 (ebook) | ISBN
    9780252045042 (cloth) | ISBN 9780252087172 (paperback) | ISBN 9780252054310
    (ebook)
Subjects: LCSH: Stanwyck, Barbara, 1907–1990—Criticism and interpretation. |
    Women in motion pictures. | LCGFT: Film criticism. | Essays.
Classification: LCC PN2287.S67 R87 2023 (print) | LCC PN2287.S67 (ebook) | DDC
    791.43/028092—dc23/eng/20220922
LC record available at https://lccn.loc.gov/2022040967
LC ebook record available at https://lccn.loc.gov/2022040968

For Marco

and

All the Women of Choeur Maha

CONTENTS

ACKNOWLEDGMENTS

MY RESEARCH INTO the life and films of Barbara Stanwyck has been an exciting journey that would never have gone anywhere without the strong support of many people, most especially Daniel Nassett at University of Illinois Press. Danny thought this book was a great idea before I really knew what I was doing, and he has been a constant enthusiast since we first began talking about it many years ago. Many thanks go to those who read drafts at various stages, starting with my good friends Ivone Margolies and Joe MacElhaney, who gave me completely opposite advice on a draft of the first few chapters, which really helped me find a method in the madness. Hollywood scholars Jon Lewis, Stephen Cohan, and Emily Carman were each very encouraging as I launched myself into a new and crowded subfield of film studies. Julie Grossman read a nearly complete draft and generously offered substantial critical and supportive feedback at a key moment in the development of the project. The readers who were invited by the press, including Veronica Pravadelli and two anonymous scholars, provided excellent and insightful feedback for which I am extremely grateful. Many thanks also go to Jane Gaines for her continued support of the project over the years.

The project benefited greatly from the assistance of graduate students at Concordia University, including Dominic Leppla, Meredith Slifkin, and Muxin Zhang, who made important research contributions and helped me organize my files, a bigger job than one might imagine. The students who took my graduate seminars in Stanwyck studies in 2012 and 2018 also deserve thanks for their patience, their enthusiasm, and their insights into what a female-centered history of Hollywood might look like. Oksana Dykyj and Charlie Lessard-Berger at Concordia University provided invaluable help with locating over a hundred Stanwyck DVDs and making them available to me and my students over the years.

A few chapters of this book have appeared elsewhere in revised form, and I would like to thank the editors of those books and journals for their help in shaping the material: Marcie Frank for "*The Barbara Stanwyck Show*: Melodrama, Kitsch and the Media Archive," *Criticism: A Quarterly for Literature and the Arts* 55, no. 4 (2013); the editors of *[In] Transition* as well as Maria Pramaggiore and Jacob Smith for my video essay "Barbara Stanwyck Rides Again" (*[In] Transition* 8, no. 3 [2021]); Gary Crowdus at *Cineaste* magazine for running my reviews of three biographies of Stanwyck (Fall 2014 and Summer 2012) as well as DVD reviews of the Frank Capra box set (Summer 2013) and *The Lady Eve* (Winter 2020); Allyson Nadia Field and Jennifer Bean for "The File on Theresa Harris: Black Star of the Archive," in *Feminist Media Histories*; and Mark Johnson for "Gambling Ladies: The Games That Barbara Stanwyck Plays," in *The Casino, Card, and Betting Games Reader: Communities, Cultures, and Play* (Bloomsbury, 2021).

I am hugely indebted to the many archivists who helped me along the way, including Genevieve Maxwell at the Margaret Herrick Library, Peggy Alexander at the University of California Los Angeles Library, Brett Service at the Warner Bros. Archive at the University of Southern California, and Piper Marie Thompson and John R. Waggoner at the American Heritage Center at the University of Wyoming.

In Montreal I have had the great pleasure of working with several creative collaborators. Shannon Harris's video editing expertise and critical eye were instrumental in completing the video essay, and Paul Litherland finessed the frame grabs expertly to produce the best illustrations I could hope for. Two Boys TV (Aaron Pollard and Stephen Lawson) were an early inspiration for seeing Stanwyck differently. Finally, I am eternally grateful for the original and meticulous book design work provided by Jennifer de Freitas and Rodolfo Borello at Associés Libres Design.

It can be painful sometimes to complete a project and let it go. Working on this Stanwyck project has been an enormous pleasure, particularly because I could and did share the films with many friends and family members over the last ten years. My greatest debt of gratitude is to all of those who watched one or more Stanwyck films with me, confirming my cinephilic attraction to one of the most dynamic screen queens of the twentieth century. First among those friends is my partner, Marco Leyton, who has come to love her just as much as I do. Other avid Stanwyck viewers include Philip Lewis; my parents, Peter and Sue Russell; my brother Alex; and Penelope Buitenhuis, who was also a great companion during my time in Los Angeles. The wonderful women of Choeur Maha in Montreal have been fellow travelers in the continual reinvention of feminism since 1991, and singing with them has been a constant source of inspiration.

THE CINEMA OF BARBARA STANWYCK

INTRODUCTION TO STANWYCK STUDIES

I think of feminism as a building project: if our texts are worlds, they need to be
made out of feminist materials. Feminist theory is world making.

—Sara Ahmed, *Living a Feminist Life*

BARBARA STANWYCK WAS AN ACTOR who had many ways of making
herself appear larger than she actually was. She had an enormous voice, with
distinctive Brooklynese speech patterns; she had a long stride, with swinging
arms; and she early on adopted a stance with her hands on her hips, chest
forward, with which she could hold a room, a film, a crowd. She also
mastered the art of the close-up and how to make her face a virtual map of
emotional subtlety and range; she wore heels and rode horses with equal
grace. Although her longtime publicist Helen Ferguson insisted that she was
5'4", other reports put her at 5'3", and she maintained a tiny waistline
throughout her sixty years in front of the camera. In making cinema, she
made her own world, her own cinema in her own image, a world and an
image full of contradictions.

Barbara Stanwyck's story has been told many times already, a process that
started shortly after her career began with the tale of her poor beginnings as
an orphan named Ruby Stevens on the streets of Brooklyn. The mix of fact and
fiction that characterizes the star biography is instrumental to the Hollywood
game. Stanwyck's brand was that of a tough dame, an independent woman, and
a hard worker, sexy when she needed to be, and with a great talent for
emotional expression. She may or may not have been gay, but she nevertheless
has become a gay icon, as if the only independent, willful-but-sexy women are
necessarily gay. Scant evidence exists that she was a lesbian, although she
unquestionably challenged the gender conventions that dominated in every
decade of her sixty-year career, and she survived the doctrinal misogyny of the
American film industry with her bank account intact.

The Stanwyck tales that I tell in this book map the view from the
present, in the multimedia worlds of the twenty-first century, where her
name still sells pictures to new audiences. She is back among us, in regular
Turner Classic Movies (TCM) broadcasts and in YouTube mashups. Even
though many younger people don't know who she is, many others are newly
attracted to her original brand. At this point in time, when we are able to
watch almost every Stanwyck movie on DVD or online somehow, she is not
exactly the same star she was for those audiences who saw her movies and

TV shows when they first appeared, from 1927 to 1986. Her contemporaries saw her age before their eyes, and she aged well. One of the remarkable things about Stanwyck was her ability to keep working into her seventies. For audiences today she has an archival presence; she embodies the history of American cinema over five and a half decades. It is this Stanwyck that I am interested in—the woman who changed and whose career enables us to tell a woman's story about Hollywood. Her multiple personas belong not only to her but also to American cultural history, in which she played a fundamental role, mainly by working so hard not to be herself but to play the many parts she was given.

Stanwyck had many important women contemporaries, and I do not want to suggest that she was the greatest Hollywood star or the most talented. She was not the first or last small-statured actor to make a big impression. She is special but not necessarily always exceptional, and to this extent her career is indicative of the challenges facing women in the culture industries and also representative of the roles available to women that changed so much during her lifetime. As a sexy bad girl in the early 1930s, she certainly had her match in Mae West, and there were many other incredible stars during that era, including Marlene Dietrich, Greta Garbo, Loretta Young, Katharine Hepburn, and Bette Davis. In the 1940s Stanwyck became a femme fatale and a paranoid wife, but so did Ingrid Bergman, Joan Fontaine, and Ida Lupino. In the '50s Stanwyck began to stand out from the crowd as she turned to the western and assumed the matriarchal role that was epitomized, finally, in *The Big Valley* TV show, which ran from 1965 to 1969. Her main exception to the rule of women in Hollywood is her longevity.

My approach to Stanwyck's oeuvre as an archival cinema is that of the fan and the collector. My investment is in this sense a variation on the women of the 1920s and '30s who made scrapbooks out of clippings from newspapers and publicity photos, or the women whom Jackie Stacey interviewed for her book on movie stars.[1] Stanwyck has become a kind of a friend and a familiar face who can brighten up the most dreadful of Hollywood fare, and I almost feel as if I know her, but of course I don't know her at all—certainly no better than the women of the past who might have been lucky enough to get her autograph on a publicity photo. Like Barbara, I am a white working woman, and maybe this explains something of the attraction—and the privilege. Unlike Stanwyck, I am a feminist, and my attraction to her cinema is, admittedly, because she offers a strategy of unpacking the structural misogyny of the industry in which she worked.

Women cultural heroes can be doubly challenged in being belatedly celebrated because they cannot necessarily meet the feminist expectations

Barbara Stanwyck on the set of *The Lady Eve* (1941). From the Core Collection Production Files of the Margaret Herrick Library, Academy of Motion Picture Arts and Sciences.

of twenty-first-century historians. Stanwyck's avowed Republicanism made her an exemplary American patriot but makes it difficult to align her story with the progressive agenda of feminist historiography. This critical contradiction underscores my investigation into Stanwyck as an icon of liberal individualism as well as a campy queen. Moreover, her story intersects with many marginalized Americans, and the productive contradiction of Stanwyck's own legacy sheds a critical light not only on other women actors but also on racialized identities within the fabric of American studio history.

The main reason for Stanwyck's very long career is that she worked hard and worked well with directors, crews, and fellow actors, developing a great reputation as someone who was easy to work with. From the outset, in the 1930s she negotiated her contracts with vigilance and never signed an exclusive contract with any studio, managing to remain a freelance actor for her entire career. For that reason, she worked for almost all the major studios and with many of the best directors. In the 1950s she began to be called "Queen" by the Hollywood community, as well as "Missy" and "Stany"; she mentored younger actors and developed an excellent understanding of the craft and the business of filmmaking. She was also a good business-woman and remained a wealthy woman throughout her career, supporting a handful of philanthropic enterprises. However, this book is not about the real Barbara but about the many Barbaras that she performed on-screen and off.

Cinephilia signals a return to film texts and film criticism in light of the recognition that movies are deeply embedded in industries, technologies, and cultural practices that frequently need to be reviewed beyond their aesthetic appeal. Cinephilia thrives on detail and diversity and is not always preoccupied with the masterpieces of art cinema, which is not to say that Stanwyck did not perform in some of the "best" movies of the studio era, including *Baby Face* (1933), *Stella Dallas* (1937), *The Lady Eve* (1941), *Double Indemnity* (1943), *There's Always Tomorrow* (1955), and *Forty Guns* (1957). She also appeared in a lot of lesser-known films and some real clunkers, although she also rejected many scripts, enough to have been suspended twice from studios for being too fussy.[2] She managed to work into the 1980s by successfully transitioning to television, doing so more successfully than most women of her generation. Critical cinephilia entails a consideration of films as archival documents, crammed with details, many of which are legible only in the afterlives of their original release.

The question of how to talk about films and TV shows in detail, and how to make them relevant, is for me a pressing one if film criticism should remain a central pillar of the field. To describe movies as historical documents may be a strange thing to say about fiction films, which are more often contrasted with documentary films as fantastical and as false. And yet American cinema was very much a showcase for constantly changing trends in architecture, costume, cars, and other details of everyday life. It also showcased behaviors and types, new ways of being in the world, new ways of relating to other people, and new forms of identity. In this book "style" refers not only to camera movements or editing patterns but also to fashion and architecture and the modalities of negotiating class, race, and gender in mid-century America.

The critical engagement with Stanwyck's films that I am doing here is in keeping with the critical-historical approach to women's film history advocated by Jane Gaines and Monica Dall'Asta in their collection *Doing Women's History*. It is a strategy of bridging the gap between then and now and a means of taking the "signs" of a historical figure, dispersed across a wide range of media, to evoke an image of her.[3] Stanwyck was never "lost," as so many overlooked women have been in the writing of film history, but she has nevertheless been undervalued as a creative worker, as have so many other women actors. Christine Gledhill and Julia Knight note that doing women's history entails unorthodox sources of evidence.[4] Gossip, anecdote, rumors, and unreliable memories are necessarily mobilized as pieces of the historical puzzle that, as Gaines and Dall'Asta agree, can add up to multiple narratives and a historical montage.

The renewed emphasis on women in film history has challenged the long-standing assumption that women were absent from the "story." Recognizing the work of women directors from the silent era, who proliferated globally, alongside the "women's work" that has long been hidden within the industry's complex workflows of craft and administration entails a different kind of historiography. The historical turn has shifted the theoretical aspect of feminist film studies away from the psychoanalytic paradigm that dominated the field in the 1970s through to the '90s, and yet as Jane Gaines argues, doing women's film history cannot be "estranged" from theory.[5]

Moving the focus from women-as-spectacle to woman's agency is an important subtext of Stanwyck studies, raising new questions about performativity, genre, voice, and cultural labor that are explored in the context of Stanwyck's career. Acting is a technique of hiding labor, and all actors are workers in plain sight. My objective in this project is to recognize Barbara Stanwyck's fundamental contribution to American cinema. Feminist film history demands new ways of doing film history, as the traditional linear narrative based in auteurism and film style leaves little room for the recognition of women's labor.[6]

A NOTE ON THE BIOGRAPHIES

At least six biographies of Stanwyck have been written, each couched within the different writers' methods and perspectives, all of them, of course, reverent and idolatrous. The only "authorized" biography is by Ella Smith, who published *Starring Miss Barbara Stanwyck* in 1985 with direct access not only to the actor herself but to many of her collaborators as well.[7] Smith's book is richly illustrated with glamourous studio portrait photos of Stanwyck's career and large, glossy production stills of iconic poses and compositions. Axel Madsen's biography, *Stanwyck*, was published in 1994 and fills in some of the background missing from Smith's film-by-film approach.[8] It's the kind of biography that sets scenes and puts words into people's mouths in an effort to bring the story to life. Madsen, like Smith, tends to make rather sweeping evaluative assessments, such as dismissing Stanwyck's entire output of the 1950s as having "little distinction." One could only make such a claim if box office returns were the sole measure of success, as I find the '50s films to be full of surprising visual effects and dynamic plot twists, not to mention fantastic characters. Other life histories by Al Diorio (1983) and Jane Ellen Wayne (2009) are somewhat preoccupied with the star's imagined inner life, projecting onto her the ups and downs of a celebrity life but adding little to our understanding of how the films came to be made.[9]

Dan Callahan's critical biography is organized around Stanwyck's relationships with different directors and genres, including Frank Capra, William Wellman, Billy Wilder, Preston Sturges, and Douglas Sirk, with separate sections on westerns, noir, and other somewhat random groupings.[10] Callahan frames his version of Stanwyck as a story of survival, and he finds this story mapped onto her many Hollywood roles, essentially viewing the actor's life through the prism of her films. "In her case," he says, "she and her work are the same thing," and his book is a curious conflation of Stanwyck's personality with the many melodrama-ensconced characters she played.

Callahan's analysis of Stanwyck's acting is somewhat contradictory. He claims she is a "great artist" despite the dozens of weak scripts she was given, and he recognizes that much of it has to do with her facial expressions and subtle eye movements. She knew how to use her body and her face to fill out characters and make them shine, regardless of their morality. Despite this recognition of her technique, and his acknowledgment that Stanwyck had no "method" training, Callahan insists on rendering her roles as various forms of therapy for a difficult life story. In her five films with Capra in the '30s, she learned how to act without makeup and to literally strip herself down to reveal an inner truth, which Callahan describes as "pornographic." According to Callahan, Capra helped her find an inner beauty because he was hopelessly in love with her, a love that was not returned.[11] More important to my mind than their ostensible love affair is the fact that Stanwyck said Capra taught her the tricks of the trade, including how films are shot and lit and what every member of the crew does. He took her to the prop room and the editing room, demystifying the magic of the movies.[12] These are the tools that served her so well over the course of her long career.

Victoria Wilson's *A Life of Barbara Stanwyck: Steel-True* takes over 1,000 pages to cover Stanwyck's childhood and years in New York and the first portion of Stanwyck's film career up to 1940. To be sure, the last 183 pages consist of appendices listing her complete stage, film, radio, and TV appearances, plus comprehensive notes and an index, making it a valuable reference tool. Wilson's research includes hundreds of trade publications, plus Stanwyck's personal documents, and, most valuable of all, interviews with many surviving friends, relatives, acquaintances, and colleagues, and their children. Wilson has woven anecdotal material about Stanwyck's personal life with production details about all of the films made during this period, with an ongoing narrative about American political history and Hollywood politics.

Wilson methodically deals with every single film title up until *Remember the Night* (1940), with varying degrees of detail about the production, Stanwyck's contributions, and the reception upon release, weaving together the various stages of each film and with Stanwyck's life, including details about the lives and films of Stanwyck's two husbands, Frank Fay and Robert Taylor. Stanwyck had no formal training as an actor, but as Wilson's book documents so clearly, she was drawn to the stage, literally from the wings of her sister's stage. She learned from a long series of mentors and from teaching others.

Wilson's somewhat staggered, fragmented biographical approach allows the complexities and contradictions of character to come through, constructing a star image with imperfections. She provides a complex portrait of a woman making her own way in a competitive industry and situates Stanwyck's biography within a detailed ethnography of show business culture of the 1930s. At the same time, Wilson leaves many questions unanswered, despite her thorough research, and she includes valuable extraneous information about the world Stanwyck inhabited. Ongoing speculation about the star's private life is important, particularly when she was so rigorous about controlling her narrative. Speculative nonfiction, such as the approach developed by Sadiya Hartman in the context of Black American women of the early twentieth century, can help to imagine the field of possibilities in which Stanwyck lived.[13] The fantasies of fans, like the fantasies of film narrative and the fictions of studio publicity, need to be recognized as real elements of the imaginative worlds that Stanwyck still inhabits. The field of Stanwyck studies is thus indebted to both the facts and fictions of biography.

Andrew Klevan's short book on Stanwyck's acting is not a biography but is one of the best books on her work and indeed one of the best studies of the craft of a screen actor in print.[14] Klevan discusses only a handful of films, beginning with *Ladies of Leisure* (1931) and ending with Stanwyck's two films with Sirk in the 1950s: *All I Desire* (1953) and *There's Always Tomorrow*. Klevan may have finally put to rest the mantra that Stanwyck's talent was her "naturalness" by showing through detailed close analysis how she employed craft and technique to create her characters. Analyzing her scenes with Joan Blondell in *Night Nurse* (1931), for example, Klevan argues that she was able to "reciprocate" and "accommodate" her acting partners while at the same time maintaining a strong sense of independence and autonomy. This is a great explanation for Stanwyck's ability to portray "independent women" who were nevertheless deeply engaged emotionally with other characters.

THE ABECEDARY

An abecedary is a collection of short essays, organized alphabetically, and titled according to key words. This method is inspired in part by Robert Ray's *ABCs of Classic Hollywood*, in which he discusses four films, each of which is broken into alphabetized fragments corresponding to details of the films in question; for example, "O is for Overhead Shots in *Grand Hotel*"; "G is for Golden Gate Bridge in *The Maltese Falcon*"; "K is for Ketchup in *Meet Me in St. Louis*"; and so on. Ray defends his methodology with reference to a number of theorists, including Wittgenstein, Roland Barthes, Michael Taussig, and Walter Benjamin, each of whom has deployed an epigrammatic or fragmented structure for critical, theoretical enterprises. Because Ray's objective is to "squeeze" the most out of a very small corpus, he chooses this method in order to focus on details. His summary of the resemblances between the methods of these very different writers is: "The faith in concrete details' capacity to animate theoretical speculation; a poetic approach to critical writing; the taste for fragments and speed; a mild suspicion of abstractions—these dispositions converge to imply a way of working different from that of traditional film studies."[15]

A book on Barbara Stanwyck faces a slightly different challenge than Ray's in that there is an excess of material to work with and it is virtually impossible to be comprehensive. For every one of her eighty-five films there is a production story, a set of relationships, source materials, reviews, intertextual roads to go down, and multiple interpretations. The dozens of TV shows, radio broadcasts, and other media appearances have their own stories to tell; meanwhile, the stories themselves are embedded within networks of genre, censorship, fashion, and film style that present a myriad of openings onto the culture in which Stanwyck worked. Because her story intersects with so many others and covers so many decades of a rapidly changing society, a fragmented, selective approach seems most appropriate. It allows an attention to detail—of performance, mise-en-scène, narrative, and industry—that would otherwise be impossible.

The abecedary method allows for a selective series of investigations in which twenty-six windows can be opened. At the same time, there is something magical and poetic about Stanwyck's persona as an actor that challenges scholarly writing and that the ABC method may be able to capture. Benjamin's method in *The Arcades Project* was inspired by the movies and the aesthetics of montage; he aimed to catalog the many ways in which the promise of modernity ultimately failed to change society.[16] Stanwyck's career likewise charts the failed promise of American cinema in the twentieth century to realize anything resembling gender equity, despite its reliance on women's labor. Ray further defends his idiosyncratic method as a vital means to "penetrate the movies' veil while retaining their hallucinatory quality."[17] The abecedary method of this book borrows, in part, from the films themselves, winding its way through such themes as gambling, jungles, and paranoid women, along with historical players such as Edith Head, Theresa Harris, and Fred MacMurray. Other routes begin with a single film title and trace its links to other titles across the decades, and some routes start with biography and end up in the cinema. Although there are still many roads not taken, it strikes me that such a nonlinear trajectory through Stanwyck's career is the most effective means of revisioning, rereading, and reframing her cinema.

In quite a different use of the abecedary form, James Cahill describes it as "strategic anachronism: a knowing temporal disordering that nevertheless engages with thinking historically."[18] For his account of a YouTube bestiary, the ABC method is a valuable methodological interruption of the accelerated technological imperatives of new media, into which he inserts examples of *actualités* and attractions of early cinema. In the case of Stanwyck's career, strategic anachronism can be a means of revisiting the "independent woman" of the 1930s along with the bad women, the scared women, and the bossy women of later decades. It also functions as a method of "collecting" diverse utterances of such themes as New Deal politics, frontier culture, melodramatic affect, body image, and costume over the middle years of the twentieth century.

Stanwyck's extant output includes many B movies as well as a handful of "classics," so while mine is not the random-selection method that David Bordwell, Janet Staiger, and Kristin Thompson used in their major work on American cinema,[19] there is nevertheless a contingent element to its unpredictable path. In examining Stanwyck's performances within wider cultural frameworks of set design, costume, and landscape, and through social networks of cast and crew members, my approach is more closely aligned to performance studies than to acting studies. While most scholarship on performance studies emerges from the conjunction of theater and anthropology,[20] "performance" provides a focus on the body and enables insight to the scene of the woman's labor on the set, reconstructed from archival documents and the audiovisual texts themselves. Performance studies expand the study of acting techniques to the construction of gender and masquerade. Stanwyck's challenge to gender norms is multilayered and intersects with discourses of reception and genre in ways that the analysis of acting alone cannot accommodate.

Marlene Dietrich's ABC: Wit, Wisdom, Recipes offers yet another example of the abecedary, in the form of a memoir. For Dietrich, the abecedary structure enables her to offer advice to fans on topics ranging from schnitzel and *omelette écume* recipes, to dressing, dancing, and fishing, combined with a commentary on people, places, and things. The openness of the form, akin in her usage to a reference book of idiosyncratic topics, enables her to capture the contradictions embedded in her star image.[21] Unlike many stars, Stanwyck never wrote a memoir and did her best to protect her privacy. The contradictions underscoring her career, between the industry and her agency, and between her conservatism and her gender-bending star image, likewise emerge best from a nonlinear, fragmented structure. Her life and career open critical questions about many issues beyond her own celebrity.

ON METHOD

Within the twenty-six essays of this book, a number of different critical methods are at work, including an interweaving of textual and extratextual story lines. Without collapsing Stanwyck's life into her roles, or interpreting her roles as expressions of her psychology as so many biographers do, it is still possible to frame the films within details pulled from the historical record of Stanwyck's life, including production details from the film shoots as well as reviewers' opinions and publicity materials. Much of this detail is drawn from the biographies, and much of it comes from news clippings, reviews, and fan magazines. Production documents from archives have also helped to provide context and are used in conjunction with a wide range of cultural studies texts on topics such as camp, stunts, critical race theory, and fashion.

The most important Stanwyck archive is the archive of her per-formances, which have become widely available and accessible in digital form. They offer themselves up for interpretation to new viewers all the time as new critical priorities and values come into play, including queer theory, affect theory, and new permutations and revisions of feminist theory. My account of Stanwyck's career includes critical analysis of the roles she played and the characters she created, along with the narratives that all too frequently close down women's potential for autonomy and independence. Lauren Berlant argues for an "unfinished sentimentality" that is attached to melodramas of social despair and loss.[22] Many of the films are characterized by broken families, impossible relationships, death, and loveless marriages. Melodrama theory has enabled us to recognize the affective politics of these narrative strategies and to analyze the films as testimony to the social anxieties of different cultural contexts.[23] Once melodrama is conceived of as a means for society to "talk to itself," then a more anthropological approach to film acting consists of recognizing performance as metonymic of social being, or what Christine Gledhill calls "personification," a central feature of film melodrama.[24]

In accounting for Stanwyck's contributions to American film history, I should stress that I do not want to imply that she was an auteur, although the idea of actor-as-auteur is not a new one. Patrick McGilligan has made this argument about James Cagney, based on such things as Cagney's tendency to improvise, stand up to directors, change lines, and alter characters as he saw fit.[25] For her part, Stanwyck did none of these things. She was a team player, who rarely—if ever—challenged her directors. Her approach to filmmaking was entirely collaborative, especially when it came to fellow actors; the technical crews; and the costume, hair, and makeup personnel, who she knew played crucial roles on any production. Her closest friends were her publicist, Helen Ferguson; her hairdresser, Holly Barnes; and her maid, Harriet Corey. The only thing that Stanwyck shares with Cagney, besides their mutual professionalism, is her mark on the culture. McGilligan cites a *New Republic* writer who wrote of Cagney in 1939, "It is hard to say what our impression of the total American character would have been without him."[26] No one in 1939 said that of Stanwyck, although they could have. However, in the 2000s, with multiple Stanwyck screening series programmed all over the world, it is abundantly true of Stanwyck, who has become an important "brand" in the marketing of studio-era cinema.

The formative feminist film theorists were absolutely right to recognize the misogyny embedded in a formal system built around "the male gaze," and yet they offered few paths out of the psychoanalytic labyrinth of the desiring gaze. Given Stanwyck's pivotal roles in key films such as *Stella Dallas* and *Double Indemnity*, I hope to show the role that she herself played in the

Barbara Stanwyck and Yvette Duguay in *Cattle Queen of Montana* (1954)

history of film studies. At the same time, Stanwyck studies marks a definite break with such deep readings, enabling the texts to become levers for the opening up of so much more than female desire. This is made possible by the instability of texts and the instability of stars, which are transformed over and over again as new viewers come to see them from new angles. As Laura Mulvey has written in her own revisionist take on the new ways of watching, replaying, excerpting, possessing, and delaying cinema, "A different kind of voyeurism [is] at stake when the future looks back with greedy fascination at the past and details suddenly lose their marginal status and acquire the aura that passing time bequeaths to the most ordinary objects."[27]

Among the "marginal details" of studio-era cinema that viewers can now see more clearly is the discourse of race that underscores the spectacle of American culture on the screen. Stanwyck's path frequently intersected with Black, Asian, Latin-x, and Indigenous figures on- and off-screen, and these encounters cannot but situate her whiteness within racialized spaces. She glows with the light of the white woman in Hollywood, a light that is repeatedly absorbed by the racialized subordinate characters around her. Attending to the textual and extratextual dynamics of these racialized spaces, in addition to affective forms of gender and class, is intended as a technique of "reparative reading." Eve Kosofsky Sedgwick has described such an "ethical" approach to texts as one that is "additive and accretive." Countering the intricacies of institutionalized misogyny and racism, a reparative reading position "undertakes a different range of affects, ambitions, and risks."[28]

Looking at the actor as a worker is certainly one way of shifting focus on the past, and it also offers a critical path out of text-based criticism. Combined with close analysis of film style and cultural styles, narrative analysis, including the elucidation of far-fetched plots and the complex characters that Stanwyck created, helps to underline Stanwyck's contributions to American cinema. Her films become "legible," in Benjamin's sense, when opened to new readings that enable an awakening from the dream sleep of Hollywood cinema.[29] Reading against the grain can take many different forms, and given the variety of genres that Stanwyck worked in, her career offers a wide range of approaches. My cinephilia is a critical cinephilia in which every film is a valuable cultural document as long as you look at it as a "document of barbarism" as well as a piece of magic.[30]

Stanwyck's career began during the pre–Hays Code era (1930–1934) when the New Woman became a global commodity, selling sexuality and female autonomy as a mode of Americanism. The anxieties and hypocrisies surrounding this image never completely left her, as she managed to reinvent herself time and time again as a new mode of femininity that rubbed against the grain of heteronormativity. In order to foreground the actor's labor and her historical role in the film industry, new methods of historiography are called for. Archival stardom is not a nostalgic enterprise but an account of the social and economic networks in which the actor worked and, at the same time, a dialectical engagement with a sensory and affective past. Articulating Stanwyck's presence in history as a powerful woman is not only a means of writing feminist film history and rethinking American cultural studies more broadly; it is also a reimagining of the critical, diverse, and indispensable roles of women in studio-era cinema.

ALL I DESIRE
PASTICHE AND PERFORMANCE

The cinema exalts the role at the same time that it destroys the actor.

—Edgar Morin, *The Stars*

STANWYCK MADE TWO FILMS with Douglas Sirk in the 1950s—*All I Desire* (1953) and *There's Always Tomorrow* (1955)—in which she gives two of her finest performances. In both films her characters are loners who interrupt family life, but more than that, they are luminous idealized women who sweep into and over families like forces of nature. And yet both Naomi in *All I Desire* and Norma Vale in *There's Always Tomorrow* are also desiring women who think they may long for family life, but they aren't sure. Unlike some of Sirk's better-known films, these two are shot in black-and-white, with dark shadowy scenes of emotional tension, uncertainty, and despair in which Stanwyck's characters—professional women—remain on the peripheries of family homes.

Sirk remarked in his interview with Jon Halliday in 1972 that although he greatly respected Stanwyck as an actress, in 1953 she was not as big a box-office draw as she previously had been: "In this picture [*All I Desire*] she had the unsentimental sadness of a broken life about her. This was a pre-study of the 'actress' in *Imitation of Life*."[1] Sirk seems to blend Stanwyck's star image with the character of Naomi Murdoch in *All I Desire*, and the parallels between them as older professional women actors open up a critical space, not of identity but of disjunction and pastiche. By recognizing Stanwyck's role in the collaboration, it is clear that far from being "destroyed," as Morin implies, she fully embodies the role. Her performance contributes to the emotional intensity of these films precisely because Sirk gives her the attention of a movie star, subtly underscoring her professionalism as a performer and a star.

In contrast to many of her other roles, with Sirk Stanwyck radiates what Andrew Klevan describes as a "stillness," an attitude of listening, and her emotions are kept largely inside.[2] For Stanwyck, acting was about thinking,[3] and she was said to be "cold" and antisocial on the set of *All I Desire*, retreating between scenes to focus on her character, Naomi,[4] although she also professed real disdain for the picture. She said, somewhat disparagingly, of *All I Desire*, that it's yet another woman trying to make up for past mistakes: "I understand the motives of the bad women I play. My only problem is finding a way to play my 40th fallen female in a different way than my 34th."[5] And yet Sirk understood how she had played the role (or similar roles) many times, and he used her presence as a forty-six-year-old star as a subtle mode of ironic social critique. Her star status was big enough to "sell" the picture but not enough, according to Sirk, to make the film in color.[6] Universal lacked its own stable of stars, and thus Sirk needed Stanwyck's star power to get both films made.

In the mid-1950s Stanwyck was still strongly identified with the woman's film of the 1930s and '40s, despite the fact that she had diversified into several other genres by that time. In the mid-1950s the big stars were older men and younger women; mothers were less exalted and more often demonized, and thus the genre of the woman's film had begun to fade, so Sirk's intervention is a darkly ironic, revisionist take on the genre. For Richard Dyer, pastiche is always historical in its formal language and is often apparent in genre revision. Genres that become self-conscious may be described as "postmodern" parody, but they may well operate more subtly on the level of affect alone.[7] Dyer notes that the production of pastiche occurs in periods "which feel themselves coming at the end of an era" and may signal "the perception by a social group that cultural forms do not speak for them."[8] Because pastiche is not "cerebrally observed but felt,"[9] the term seems particularly appropriate to the late woman's films of Sirk and Stanwyck.

All I Desire was adapted from a novel called *Stopover*, and Sirk himself preferred Carol Brink's original title because of its ironic implications. In his view the film is about a woman who "comes back with all her dreams, her love—and she finds nothing but this rotten, decrepit middle-class American family."[10] As a title, *All I Desire* might mean that the protagonist has everything she desires, or it might mean that she is content with what she has or that she remains unfulfilled. In any case, like *My Reputation* (1946), the first person of the title refers to Stanwyck's character, placing her at the emotional center of the plot (see chapter Y). The posters for *All I Desire* exploited the "desire" reference with a steamy caricatured couple bearing no resemblance whatsoever to either Stanwyck or anyone else in the film, placing it squarely in the "adult" category of 1950s cinema.[11] However, the taglines—"Now he knew her as other men had" and "Now he knew she had known other nights like this"—shift the subject from the desiring woman to the cuckolded man.

Compared to the melodrama that Stanwyck made with Fritz Lang, *Clash by Night* (1952), Sirk's films with Stanwyck are restrained, even if the theme of the single woman arriving in a small town (or suburb) is repeated in all three films.[12] In the Lang film as well, her arrival causes havoc. For Sirk, Stanwyck is already larger than life, and his two films with her are thus already about performance. In *All I Desire* her character is an actress who has left her family to pursue a career on the stage; in *There's Always Tomorrow* she is a professional fashion designer who drops in on an old friend (played by Fred MacMurray) who is married with children. The polarization of family and career was of course of topical concern in the 1950s as women were becoming more entrenched in the workplace, while "domestic life" was at the same time becoming reified through consumer culture. Neither film ends up happily, even if the family "wins" in both cases. Sirk would have preferred to follow the novel and have Naomi cast out at the end of *All I Desire*, free from the trap of the home, but he was obliged by producer Ross Hunter to have Naomi reunite with her family.[13] As Lucy Fischer argues, the narrative thus becomes not a stopover but a makeover "from a showgirl to a bourgeois queen.... Naomi's masquerade as a mother becomes a permanent 'imitation of life.'"[14]

The ending of *All I Desire* is far from satisfying. Among other things, Naomi's husband, Henry (Richard Carlson), a school principal, has a romantic (if platonic) relationship with another woman, Sara Harper (Maureen O'Sullivan), the high school drama teacher, that is abruptly aborted when Naomi decides to stay. Michael Walker argues that, given that Naomi's presence in Riverdale as a spectacle of wanton behavior is strongly repudiated by the patriarchal establishment (Henry's boss), Henry's final acceptance of her constitutes a challenge to the narrow-minded small-town prejudices.[15] This interpretation, however, pays short shrift to the women characters, one of whom is simply cast aside, and the other, Naomi, is enveloped by a shadowy, tomb-like home.

In Sirk's films the look and feel of actions and settings tends to challenge the logic of narrative events and their implications. One of the most striking features of *All I Desire* is that the 1900 setting is represented through costume and transportation (horses and carriages) but is not apparent at all in the behavior or speech of the characters. The home to which Naomi returns in Riverdale may appear from the outside as a Victorian mansion, but inside it looks like a split-level open plan 1950s suburban home, granted with floral wallpaper and period furniture. It functions as a trap with the use of balustrades, shadows, and, above all, overcrowding, and it is full of mouthy teenagers. Naomi's two daughters, whom she has not seen for over ten years, are opinionated and self-possessed, clearly grounded in 1950s America and its burgeoning youth culture. They dance the bunny-hug instead of the bunny-hop, and all the men in the film are clean-shaven, sporting '50s-era short haircuts, rendering the "period" setting extremely thin.

Naomi's husband, Henry, is a helpless weak-kneed pushover who is oblivious to the crush that Sara has on him until Naomi points it out—at the point where she says she's leaving again. Naomi's difference from this small-town community is not only that she is played by a bigger (and better) movie star, but Naomi is smarter than everyone too. Toward the end of the film she explains to her young son that "people you want to be perfect aren't always perfect." She does not ask her son for forgiveness. She is leaving because she has accidentally shot her former lover, Dutch (Lyle Bettger), at a rendezvous in the woods (after giving him a good hard punch to resist his advances). Despite her apparent contempt for characters like Naomi, Stanwyck plays her with dignity, because Naomi is a spectacle, drawing the gaze of all the "ordinary" small-town men and women, even if most of her costumes are buttoned-up, long-sleeved, floor-length frocks. Talking to her daughters about the trials and tribulations of being an actor, she admits that the theater is a jungle: "I have no glory, no glamour, and bruises on my illusions." She confesses that she is not performing the classics on Broadway but rather burlesque vaudeville, soon to be "billed below the dog acts." Stanwyck might have been talking about being cast in what she considered to be a soapy adult film at Universal, but at her age she took what she could get.

The tenuous parallel between Stanwyck's story and that of her character is one anachronism that is legible only in retrospect. In these Sirk films she is precipitating her own legacy as an older woman actor, a woman destined to be perpetually out of sync with the youth culture that was slowly transforming the industry and society at large. She reveals her vulnerability and also that all is not as it appears, which is the key to the Sirkian universe. It is her character alone who can see through the illusions. Naomi's two speeches, to her daughters and to her son, are made as she prepares to leave. The fact that she changes her mind and finally stays in Riverdale changes very little, as she will always be an outsider in her own family. What does Naomi want? She is simply too big for the town. Playing an actress enables Stanwyck to occupy center stage fully, making entrances like a queen, spreading waves of awe and jealousy around her. Naomi's performance in

Riverdale is as the actress she once was or hoped to be, although there is little evidence that she was anything more than a burlesque queen.

The problem *All I Desire* sets out to solve is the reconciliation of such a figure with a reformed housewife, and in 1950s America burlesque is code for sex, but it also conceals another link to Stanwyck's own biography. *Burlesque* is the title of the second Broadway play in which Stanwyck had a speaking part, and it was a key transition from her being a cabaret performer to becoming an actress in 1927.[16] The street-smart, hard-nosed Stanwyck image—embedded in her lingering Brooklyn accent—is tied precisely to her roots as a cabaret dancer. The authenticity of such a woman is furthermore attached to Stanwyck through her role as a singing and dancing, scantily dressed burlesque queen in the 1942 film *Lady of Burlesque*, a follow-up to the 1941 hit *Ball of Fire*, the Howard Hawks film in which she plays a streetwise no-nonsense big-band singer.

Lady of Burlesque, based on the novel *The G-String Murders* by former burlesque queen Gypsy Rose Lee, was made during the war, when Stanwyck was at the peak of her career. She plays a starring dancer in a close-knit vaudeville troupe doing a tired show in "the Old Opera House" on Broadway, which was once the stage for a classy highbrow opera company. Stanwyck's tap dance routine with Bert Hanlon is fantastic, and she shakes her thing quite righteously throughout the film. Showing a lot of leg, she does the splits, a cartwheel, Cossack dancing, and maintains a steady jazzy beat throughout. The theme song concerns the workaday trials of a performer who needs to keep kicking it up "four shows a day." Stanwyck mobilizes the troupe to find the ghost who is haunting them by reminding the girls that they are stockholders in the company and have something at stake in the old theater. "Burlesque" in *Lady of Burlesque* is tied not only to the display of women's bodies but also to community, solidarity, and working-class pride. The burlesque trope in *All I Desire*, in other words, invokes a class difference between Naomi and the bourgeoisie of Riverdale. In their mix she can masquerade as one of them, but her truth is that she belongs outside, along with her vitality, her wisdom, and her ownership of the spectacle. Stanwyck herself was able to harness her burlesque background for her great mid-career comeback in the early 1940s, and for Naomi it is a signifier of her desire, as well as her class difference (see chapter V).

Stanwyck has two voice-over monologues in *All I Desire*: one at the very beginning, in which she sets up the story, and another in which she is in the audience of her daughter's play at the high school theater. She is awestruck by the performance, commenting on how perfect her daughter Lily's gestures are. She is in fact describing what acting is, underscoring her own elegance, which is so at odds with everyone else's stiff awkwardness and breathless delivery. Because Sirk repeatedly cuts away from Lily on the stage to Naomi in the audience—glowing in a white lace gown, feather-edged wrap, and a glittery choker—it is in fact she, not Lily, whom we cannot look away from. On one level, *All I Desire* may be regarded as yet another film that undercuts its own discourse of female autonomy and agency insofar as Naomi does return at the end to the status of what Sirk himself describes as an "unknown woman."[17] However, no character that Stanwyck plays can be an unknown or ordinary woman, especially in the postwar period. She is always a movie star, and Sirk highlights that with his lighting, costume, and editing that lets Naomi steal every scene she is in.

In the case of *All I Desire*, I would like to suggest that although Naomi remains in every way an outcast in her own home, and despite the ostensible happy ending, the "desire" at stake remains critically muted—for the character and for the spectator—because we are watching a performance. Through the performativity of the curious mise-en-scène and the reflexivity of Stanwyck's "star" performance, the film can and should be seen as a pastiche of a woman's film, which is to say a revisionist reflection on the genre. As a form of pastiche, the discrepancy in *All I Desire* between the nominal setting of 1900 and the 1950s styles that I have noted is also a discrepancy within the terms of the woman's film, which by 1953 is showing signs of wear.

Despite the racy poster, *All I Desire* was sold as a woman's film in the trades, where it was described as a "soap opera" that would appeal to "woman folk."[18] It was heavily promoted in women's magazines, reportedly reaching 90 million readers.[19] In *Modern Screen* it is noted that Stanwyck gifted the cast and crew with beautiful gold presents at the conclusion of the shoot (perhaps to compensate for her antisocial behavior, which had also been reported in the press).[20] In the same magazine, when "Barbara" changes her mind about leaving town, it is because "this time, her husband bestirs himself to act like a man." Masculinity is clearly the issue here, even if it is framed as the fulfillment of a woman's desire.

There's Always Tomorrow is arguably a stronger film because of Fred MacMurray's performance as a deeply unhappy man (see chapter M). Joan Bennett plays his wife, who pays more attention to their children than to him and is described by one misogynist critic as "housewife as monster."[21] The poster for the film featured all three actors, suggesting a ménage à trois and, at the same time, strong ensemble acting. Marion (Bennett) never seems to realize that her marriage is threatened by Norma, although her

Barbara Stanwyck in *All I Desire* (1953)

teenage children certainly do. When they confront Norma about stealing their father, she gives them a stern lecture about how they have neglected their father and they need to show him a little love (see chapter V). She then finally breaks up with Cliff (MacMurray) and leaves Los Angeles to return to New York.

Norma Vale is a fashion designer, and Stanwyck's wardrobe is appropriately flashy, elegant, and extravagant. Designer Jay A. Morley uses strong blacks and whites for her outfits, including a luxurious white fur stole, a black high-collared dress, and a harlequin-patterned jacket. The fact that Stanwyck's character is a high-profile designer gives her some agency in creating these outfits, and this arguably extends to Stanwyck's own performance. If Sirk's cinema is all about appearances, here we have a character who is a professional manager of her own and others' looks and is always outsmarting everyone with her "flair." She is visually out of sync with everyone in the film. At one point in the film, Marion visits Norma's studio/dress shop with Ann (Pat Crowley), her son Vinnie's girlfriend. Marion tries on a full-skirted "New Look" dress with a white sequined bodice and a black skirt with a sheen to it, but she refuses to take it home, even on approval, despite the urging of both Ann and Norma. "It's too youthful for me," complains Marion, by which the film draws attention to

Barbara Stanwyck and Joan Bennett (right) in *There's Always Tomorrow* (1955)

how Stanwyck's costumes make her appear more youthful and dynamic than the rest of the characters. In the dress shop and in an earlier scene at a Palm Springs hotel (where she and Cliff have "accidentally" found themselves at the same time), she does a quick little run up a short flight of stairs. At Palm Springs Norma and Cliff go horseback riding—Stanwyck's trademark sport—and she is very much the accomplished horsewoman, while Cliff lags behind. Norma/Stanwyck seems larger than life, as if floating through a film in which everyone else is gray and inert.

Sirk opens *There's Always Tomorrow* with a rather obvious cue to its irony. After the opening title, "Once upon a time in Sunny California," he cuts to a downpour that seems to last most of the film. As a disruptive, destabilizing force, Stanwyck as Norma Vale brings something of her own star power to the film, not only as a woman who knows how to "dress for success" but also as an independent businesswoman. The loneliness of Norma Vale is a freedom that only the character of Ann is able to glimpse from within the diegesis. From the outside, we can see that Sirk's expressive formalism, extended here to the world of fashion and costume design, is closely aligned to the casting of Stanwyck and her ability to be both extraordinarily restrained and extraordinarily alive.

There's Always Tomorrow is also a woman's film, based on a novel by Ursula Parrott, and the sympathetic knowingness between Marion and Norma is symptomatic and indicative of its target audience. But by shifting the focus from thwarted desires to performativity, we can begin to see how these two films are as much about male disappointment and failure as they are about women's suffering. In both films Stanwyck brings a knowingness and wisdom that synchronizes well with Sirk's double-voiced style, acting out Norma's emotions but also lecturing the children on how to feel and how to love. She embodies an authenticity and moral authority that seems to be foreclosed by family life. She is too late for Cliff but not too late for the world and its opportunities.

There's Always Tomorrow did not impress the critics in 1955, and the reviews are indicative of the worn-outness of the woman's film as a genre. It was in fact a remake of a 1934 version by Edward Sloman. Although it was in part treated as a "social problem" film about contemporary marriage, with one theater owner bringing in a marriage counselor to promote the picture,[22] it was also treated as a "tear-jerker" that Stanwyck's female fans would appreciate.[23] Its resonance for contemporary audiences is quite different, due to the conflation of production design and performance that renders the emotional terrain palpable as a social drama and as a historical treatment of the new role of teenagers in American society, who literally gang up on the adults until Stanwyck/Norma talks them down.

My Reputation provides an interesting comparison to the two Sirk films, as it is a more conventional "generic" woman's film. The story anticipates the narrative of Sirk's *All That Heaven Allows* (1955): Stanwyck's character, Jessica Drummond (a name that is recycled in *Forty Guns* [1957]), is a widow who falls for an army major, played by George Brent. Her two sons are against the relationship and cause her grief for most of the film, until the boys finally accept the couple and the major goes off to war. Although she is the top-billed star and completely carries the film, Stanwyck's character blends into the ensemble in terms of performance style. The children in the 1940s are a little younger too and lack the discursive power of teenagers in the 1950s. As "late" woman's films, the two Sirk-Stanwyck collaborations point to the way that performativity is a conceptual place where Sirk's particular mode of irony meets Stanwyck's strengths as an actress. The films perform a strong, if nuanced, cultural critique of the closures of domesticity, but the critique comes from a place of pride on the parts of both director and actor.

While *All I Desire* draws on Stanwyck's star image as a working-class heroine, in the later film Norma Vale is a wealthy single professional,

Barbara Stanwyck in *There's Always Tomorrow* (1955)

widening the gap between Stanwyck's 1955 persona and the "Stella Dallas" figure of her prewar career. And yet there remains an affinity between the actress and the role that is subtly exploited to underline Norma Vale's autonomy, freedom, and independence from the entrapment of family. Toward the end of the film, Norma and Cliff meet at a rooftop bar where he has tracked her down, and he confesses that he loves her, but she demurs, knowing that their relationship is not possible. She tells him to leave, and the shot lingers on her standing with eyes lowered, wearing her white fur stole, with shadows crossing her body. Stanwyck's face and posture evoke a deep sorrow, enhanced by the "Blue Moon" theme music, which is a song essentially about loneliness.

Whether Stanwyck herself was a lonely woman we do not know, but in the popular imagination, an unmarried woman was necessarily lonely. Thus her star image in the mid-1950s evoked a mystique, or what acting theorist Benoît-Constant Coquelin called a "first self." The idea of a first self/second self conception of performance is a useful way to understand "naturalist" performance, which is easily overlooked as a craft.[24] Paul McDonald uses the distinction between impersonation (the second self) and personification (the first self) as a means of recognizing the actor's labor in constructing both levels.[25] A movie star is by definition a familiar face and a known persona—in her "first self"—and thus there is always a tension in star performance between their two identities: the one in the story and the one selling the show. In the Sirk-Stanwyck collaborations they were able to exploit that tension to create complex women who are torn between competing desires, desires that are also signifiers of larger social forces. Stanwyck's performance coincides with Sirk's expressive mise-en-scène to create a subtle, yet deeply moving, critique of the limitations and repressions that are endemic to middle-class American life. While Sirk's style has been appreciated on the level of theatricality and narrativity, Stanwyck's work with him is exceptional on the level of performance.

In both Sirk films, Stanwyck conveys a deep pathos, but it is accompanied by wisdom. She does not fit into these bourgeois families on multiple levels, and that disjunction or slippage can also be read as a kind of asynchrony or a being out of time. In this sense, for twenty-first-century cinephilic audiences who appreciate Sirk's expressive formalism and social critique, Stanwyck's characters are with us, or provide an affective point of entry to the repressive mean-spirited families of the 1950s, imprisoned in their shadowy mausoleum-like homes. These films actually compound and complicate the identification of the actor with her roles. On one hand we can see Stanwyck as the diva she never was, professionally, precisely as the queen of a genre—the woman's film—that indulged in suffering, trauma, and regret. On the other hand she emerges in the mid-1950s, however briefly, as bigger than all of that loss, transcendent and elegant, glowing, as the genre itself dissolves into the drama of masculinity. She is a star who will grow brighter as she fades.

THE BARBARA STANWYCK SHOW
EVERYDAY MELODRAMA

> To *go with* melodrama's modality demands that we refigure the critical
> relationship between its aesthetic dynamics and the cultural materials
> and ideologies it draws into its operations.
>
> —Christine Gledhill, prologue to *Melodrama Unbound*

BARBARA STANWYCK INTRODUCES each episode of *The Barbara Stanwyck Show* (1960–1961) wearing a new gown designed by Daniel Werle (who went by the couturier handle "Werlé"). In these glamorous outfits she sets up the plot of the episode and the character she plays, which vary greatly from one to the next. The episodes are frequently pitched as some kind of melodrama: a melodrama of decision, or a melodrama set in the High Sierras, a dark melodrama, or a comic melodrama. Generically, the episodes borrowed heavily from a variety of film genres, including westerns, film noir, adventure films, the woman's film, and comedy, but the general term "melodrama" pointed at the time to a combination of action (which was how the term was used in the popular press at the time) and emotional tension.[1]

The show was canceled after only one year, no doubt due to financial losses totaling $150,742, which were borne by NBC, home to the show's thirty-six episodes. The series nevertheless survives as excellent archival TV and is best described as an allegory of studio-era cinema, placing on full display its failed promise of gender equity. It also shows how the power of the melodramatic mode to explore social contradictions may be vested in the friction between the body of the star and the characters she impersonates and underscores how melodrama operates in American media as a "genre-producing machine."[2]

Stanwyck had some harsh words for the industry when her show was canceled, along with those of Loretta Young, Ann Sothern, and June Allyson in 1961: "I don't know who 'they' are, but they've decreed no more women on television. The only woman who will be left next year is Donna Reed.... We all had good ratings."[3] This is one of the only times Stanwyck adopted anything like a feminist position in her public statements. She undoubtedly knew that the show had lost money and did not have good ratings, and yet she significantly frames it as a plot against shows starring women. She goes on to say, "As I understand it 'they' want action shows and have a theory that women don't do action. The fact is I'm the best action actress in the world. I can do horse drags and jump off buildings, and I have the scars to prove it." Stanwyck herself won an Emmy for Best Actress in a TV Series in 1961, and even if her show is far from a feminist vehicle, she evidently felt that she had a leading role as a woman in the industry.

As an anthology drama series, each week *The Barbara Stanwyck Show* featured a new thirty-minute story, a new cast of characters and guest stars, and a new setting. The show was directed and written by a rotating series of men, including directors Jacques Tourneur and Robert Florey. But Stanwyck was very much the driving force behind the series, starring in all but two episodes.[4] Stanwyck was a co-owner of the show, through a company called Barwyck Productions, created in 1956 through her agency, MCA, and her business manager, Morgan Maree. As a coproducer she was able to choose the scripts, had a say in the writing and the casting, as well as the publicity, and was entitled to 57.1 percent of the profits—had there been any—on top of her salary as hostess and star.[5]

In retrospect, we can see how her TV show tended to reproduce the historical tensions and contradictions that led to its demise. Although Stanwyck would have liked to do a western series,[6] her agents persuaded her that domestic dramas would be more appropriate. In fact she plays only a few mothers in the series, along with a wide range of working women, including businesswomen, scientists, a lawyer, a couple of sheriffs and bar owners, a journalist, and a fashion designer. Stanwyck had already appeared in several other anthology shows, including four episodes as a guest star on *Zane Grey Theatre* in 1958. The small screen offered many top stars opportunities to restart their careers and to have more control over them, and the professional involvement of A-list actors was instrumental to the aesthetics and standards of the new medium.[7] Later in the 1960s, Stanwyck starred in the long-playing western TV series *The Big Valley* as the widowed matriarch of a family dominated by hardy men. A. I. Bezzerides wrote many of the scripts for both TV series and it was he and Louis F. Edelman, producer of *The Barbara Stanwyck Show*, who created *The Big Valley* in 1965, so the first series arguably planted the seeds for the second.

Most commentators agree that Stanwyck "had trouble being herself" in her introductions, and she does indeed seem somewhat uncomfortable in the role of fashion model reading from a teleprompter. Loretta Young had perfected the gesture of introduction in her long-running series, *Letter to Loretta* (1953-1961), in which she spins into her "living room" and reads a viewer's letter introducing the week's story. Before Stanwyck appears, however, each episode begins with an announcer saying, "Tonight, from Hollywood, *The Barbara Stanwyck Show*," underlining her film industry roots and connections, which were distinct from the New York–based theatrical roots of highbrow anthology dramas. Stanwyck was able to attract many high-profile costars, including Dana Andrews, Joan Blondell, Julie London, Lee Marvin, Dan Duryea, Buddy Ebsen, and Joseph Cotten, as well as a long string of utterly banal no-name male leads to play her various dull husbands.

The Barbara Stanwyck Show was produced at the Desilu Studios in Los Angeles and is distinguished by its expressive lighting effects and fast-paced editing for action sequences. Because so many of the cinematographers, directors, and crew were drawn from the L.A. area, the series was fairly cinematic despite the thirty-minute length of each segment. Stanwyck's "unsteady" introductions are symptomatic of the tension between Hollywood and TV that underpinned this series as well as other series featuring women stars on early TV. As Mary Desjardins explains, the "glamorous" image of movie stars tended to contradict the domestic "everydayness" of television in people's homes.[8] Stanwyck's cultural capital was discursively linked to her star power and status as a spectacle, whereas the success and pleasure of the series itself has much more to do with the storytelling and the characters she plays. Out of character, she is the empty signifier of the star Barbara Stanwyck; when she is "in character," she becomes more fully articulated as a persona. While she still may be doubled as the star and the character in each episode, her star persona provides a historical-materialist anchor for the series, interrupting and cutting across its fictions.

Among the thirty-seven episodes of *The Barbara Stanwyck Show*, three are set in Hong Kong featuring Stanwyck playing the wheeling and dealing importer-exporter Josephine Little. Shot by Jacques Tourneur, with Anna May Wong as Stanwyck's confidante and ladies' maid, the film finds Stanwyck on the frontier of the "bamboo curtain." One of the episodes was singled out in Congress as being an exemplary instance of anti-Communism in an entertainment industry that was seen as being reinfested with Reds.[9] Despite such a dubious endorsement, the proposed series featuring Josephine Little was not picked up, and the three episodes were

Barbara Stanwyck in *The Barbara Stanwyck Show* (1960-1961)

rolled into *The Barbara Stanwyck Show* and feature the only recurring character in the series.

Stanwyck's series was never included in the canon of classic TV, and each episode was broadcast only once, with a handful repeated in the summer of 1961. In 2009 the bulk of the series (twenty-seven out of thirty-seven episodes[10]) became available on DVD published by the Archive of American Television. Its simplicity dictated that *The Barbara Stanwyck Show* would be disposable, doomed to die in the dustbin of history, and yet it is a valuable indication of the role of gender in the industrial transition from film to TV. In 2021 the same twenty-seven episodes were available for streaming on Amazon Prime.

As archival media, the series demonstrates quite clearly how issues and anxieties about women's social roles were dramatized in popular culture in the years leading up to Betty Friedan's *The Feminine Mystique* in 1963. The TV show "failed" because of the lack of industry support and sponsorship, and yet a close look at the show itself enables us to see how the dramas written to contain Stanwyck's many characters failed to contain her powerful image, personality, and star power. She was not able to "come down" to the ordinariness of TV and be herself, nor were the scripts able to follow through on the charisma and authority of her characters.

Barbara Stanwyck in "Shock," *The Barbara Stanwyck Show*, season 1, episode 22 (1960–1961)

Christine Gledhill has suggested that "personalization" is the primary strength of melodrama and is one of its central features as an "umbrella genre" of Hollywood genres.[11] Personalization entails the fusion of the social and the individual when they are embodied in actors playing roles that are less about individualized psychology than the exteriorization and language of emotion. Gledhill and Linda Williams have proposed that melodrama be recognized as the ur-mode of popular fiction so that continuities between different media, such as film and TV, are understood as expressive forms of social problems.[12] In their understanding of melodrama, the emotional charge of storytelling and performance is not in excess of reality but is incorporated into the representation of social life. The heightened effects of performance, combined with the mise-en-scène and music, are significant as emotions, embedding the feelings of social contradictions within the contours of everyday life. The various forms of melodrama may be considered different genres within studio-era cinema, but they are all important "repositories of emotional knowledge,"[13] a designation that the term "classical" has tended to preclude, precisely by denigrating melodrama as unstable, excessive, and feminine.

The Barbara Stanwyck Show is a good example of melodramatic effects and dramaturgy being brought to bear on real-world issues of everyday life. Even if the plots often feature quite unlikely scenarios, they dramatize the social anxieties of the time. In the episode called "Shock" (season 1, episode 22, March 6, 1961), Stanwyck plays an atomic scientist who goes into a catatonic shock when she learns of her young daughter's fatal accident precisely at the moment she is supposed to convey an important formula to the office. The drama of coincidence transforms the scientist/mother conjunction into a nightmarish contradiction, and Stanwyck pivots on a dime from professional expert to mother suffering with debilitating emotional pain.

The cultural role of melodrama is its ability to enact ideological conflicts and to engineer symbolic confrontations. In its proximity to everyday life and the emotional issues facing historical subjects, melodrama should not be opposed to realism but recognized as what E. Deidre Pribram describes as an expressive language of real emotions grounded in real "socio-emotional" experience.[14] *The Barbara Stanwyck Show* was sponsored by a gas company and a cosmetics company;[15] thus, it exhibits tropes of soap opera, familiar from decades of radio serials that would have appealed to women viewers, as well as noir and western genres that would have appealed to male viewers. The hair products that were advertised are not soap but instead belong to an industry of glamour and image, and the show certainly foreshadows the prime-time series such as *Dynasty* and *The Colbys* that Stanwyck appeared on in the 1980s. In soap opera everything is out in the open as characters talk unstoppably about their problems, while in melodrama a great deal lies beneath the surface, and *The Barbara Stanwyck Show* manages to do both.

The combination of melodrama and soap opera on which *The Barbara Stanwyck Show* draws means that, on the one hand, everything is crystal clear, and at the same time, in its use of lighting effects and crime stories, many episodes are uncanny and incomplete, perpetuating the ambiguities of film melodrama. Gledhill notes, "We are not supposed to find melodrama and soap opera satisfying; but, frequently, even, we find pleasurable on one level what on another is objectionable to us."[16] It is precisely this doubling effect that is potentially foregrounded in archival media viewed in digital form decades after its production.

Another way of seeing the idiosyncratic melodrama/soap opera combination of *The Barbara Stanwyck Show* is as "fallen" examples of Hollywood cinema, which is not to say that they are pale imitations, because they are clearly conceived for a very different medium. They are fallen from the big-budget utopian promise held out by the movies to something more ordinary and everyday, and yet in its star power and cinematic mise-en-scène, the show bears traces of Hollywood's glamourous aesthetics. The stories are allegories of Hollywood, utilizing its melodramatic language of expression. Following Walter Benjamin's theory of allegory, the series, in its archival form, becomes a melancholic text of unrealized possibility. "The profane world," which would be material history, is at once devalued and elevated in allegory.[17] As a failed cultural enterprise, the TV show constitutes a kind of ruin, which for the allegorist/critic becomes rich with significance: "It becomes the key to a realm of hidden knowledge; and he reveres it as the emblem of this."[18]

A good example of this kind of allegorization is an episode called "Confession" (season 1, episode 20, February 20, 1961), which is introduced as a "melodrama in the manner of *Double Indemnity* [1943]," unabashedly playing off one of Stanwyck's most famous film roles. Lee Marvin plays a divorce lawyer, to whom Stanwyck's character, Paula, turns to help her escape an unpleasant husband. The episode is framed with Paula confessing to a crime, not unlike the opening of *Mildred Pierce* (Michael Curtiz, 1945). She wears widow's weeds (black clothing) and is surrounded by policemen and their recording equipment. Flashback to her fur-coated, bejeweled life with a husband (Morgan, played by Kenneth MacKenna) who is rude and jealous of her ladies' bridge games. Marvin, as lawyer Jud Hollister, convinces Stanwyck to frame her husband for murder, which she does, falling in love with Jud, with appropriately sinister lighting. Stanwyck/Paula stages her own death and then hides out in Jud's apartment near the beach, but as the murder trial drags on, the music of a nearby merry-go-round starts to drive her mad. Wearing slacks and smoking heavily, she paces anxiously while her erstwhile lover is out lawyering every day. Finally, Morgan is accused of the murder, but before Paula and Jud can escape to Brazil, Paula's former neighbor shows up, having tracked her to Marvin's address.

The neighbor, Betty Galloway (Josephine Hutchinson), senses something amiss, and Paula breaks down and confesses, vowing to save her husband after all. Marvin scoops up the bonds that they stole from Morgan and tries to convince her to flee with him, but Paula shoots him instead, once she realizes that he was more interested in the money than in her. The episode ends with her wrapping up her confession in the police station. Compared to *Double Indemnity*, the gender roles are reversed, as it is the woman's confession, not the man's, that frames the story; it is the man who is duplicitous and who is shot. While the noir-inflected lighting of "Confession" and the steaminess of the affair evoke the 1944 film, the TV show inevitably lacks the witty innuendo-laden dialogue. But the biggest shift is the woman's inexplicable change of heart and her willingness to return to a husband she started off vowing to divorce.

This kind of capitulation happens all too often in the series and is an example of what melodrama critics refer to as "containment"[19]—an ending that conveniently restores patriarchal order. But in this case it clearly cannot completely erase the memory of Stanwyck being slapped and threatened by her husband, or the electricity of Marvin and Stanwyck's brief liaison, or her ability to change personas with a change of clothes. The musical setting of the fairground is a familiar melodramatic motif, offering a context of ambiguity, discontinuity, and excess in which everyday life can be disrupted and displaced.

Given the reference to *Double Indemnity* and our recognition of Stanwyck in a similar-but-different role, the text is doubled as an allegory of another film, one in which Stanwyck's character is assertive and totally in control of her own destiny (see chapter C). In "Confession" the idea that a woman may leave an unloved husband is "symbolically" represented; ideological contradictions are enacted but not resolved. For audiences in the twenty-first century, the text is "legible" as a dramatization of the gender anxieties of 1960. The madness provoked by the merry-go-round is precisely the madness of a woman imprisoned within her own home. Stanwyck closes the episode with a directive to the viewer: "Let that be a lesson to you. If you ever commit a crime, don't hide out over a merry-go-round." TV is never afraid to offer lessons, and if this one seems to miss the mark of the episode's real significance, we can see now how the melodrama of film noir is domesticated as TV, only to strip the woman of her power. But Stanwyck arguably wrests it back by towering over the production as its historical inscription, and the trappings of genre swirl around her.

The underlying theme of *The Barbara Stanwyck Show* is Stanwyck's own power within the TV industry, and in several episodes the question of a woman's corporate power is directly addressed. Stanwyck introduces "Big Career" (season 1, episode 19, February 13, 1961) with the following:

> Are women fitted to take their place in the higher executive positions in American business? And what if a woman's success in business is bought at the price of her husband's failure? These are the questions examined dramatically in our story tonight.... I play the role of a high-powered woman executive who could make decisions in her office, but not in her home.

In the first scene following this tantalizing intro, it is evident that Stanwyck's character, Harriet Melvane (be-furred and bejeweled again), is married to a two-timing lush who clearly doesn't deserve her. They live in an opulent home with a Black maid (Amanda Randolph) who eavesdrops on Harriet's behalf, and the husband comes from a good family, whereas Harriet has working-class roots. She feels guilty about his unhappiness and announces her resignation as a department store executive, vowing to be a good wife instead. The delinquent husband is conveniently hit by a car and dies, in a noir-lit urban street scene. Harriet is about to leave town to accept a job in New York when her late husband's mother tells her she should forget about her no-good son. The two women have a heart-to-heart talk, after which the mother-in-law convinces Harriet's boss to date Harriet because "she doesn't want a career. She wants what every woman wants."

The moralizing tone of this episode may be offensive, and the triumph of the old lady over the younger one is somewhat regressive; and yet because Stanwyck is utterly convincing as a corporate executive, and states her desire to resign with neither regret nor passion for her husband or any other man, the episode itself remains inconclusive. She clearly made a bad mistake in marriage, and the episode warns women to stay away from hard-drinking frat boys who grow up to be losers. The second love interest, Harriet's boss, respects her career, and they develop a professional bond that becomes romantic. "Big Career" stops short of the utopian solution of a woman possibly being successful in both work and marriage, but in dramatizing the dilemma, it addresses real-life issues for women of the time.

The elderly mother-in-law is a recurring figure in *The Barbara Stanwyck Show*, frequently setting up obstacles for Stanwyck's characters. Their encounters and power struggles are a dramatization of domestic authority, although in keeping with Hollywood fictions of social mobility, the elder woman is often defending her class. The mother-daughter relationships of the Hollywood woman's film, which Stanwyck emblematically dramatized in *Stella Dallas* in 1937, are largely absent from *The Barbara Stanwyck Show*. Most often Stanwyck is a single woman, either widowed or divorced, or wedded to her career. Her male suitors are an indistinguishable sequence of dull middle-age men played by second-string actors, who never seem to deserve her spunky hardworking characters.

In the thriller episodes, Stanwyck's characters tend to get mixed up in criminal activity by accident and have to find a way out.[20] In this sense she sustains the trajectory of the adventure heroines of silent film serials, such as Pearl White, and she never plays a genuinely bad woman. Stanwyck presides over the series as a glamourous icon of Hollywood celebrity. In her stilted introductions, she uses the same vocal intonation as many of her characters but lacks any narrative context other than her own celebrity to pull it off. Despite the diversity of characters and roles in the series, Stanwyck's performance style tends to be consistent, if not mannered, as a self-possessed professional woman. The consistency of characterization is underscored most clearly in one of the very few episodes in which she wears a wig. In "Frightened Doll" (season 1, episode 29, April 24, 1961) she plays

Barbara Stanwyck in "Frightened Doll," *The Barbara Stanwyck Show*, season 1, episode 29 (1960–1961)

a bar-room floozie with a black wig and heavy makeup for most of the episode, but when she needs to escape a bad situation (involving a gangster dying in her room), she disguises herself by shedding the disguise and becoming Barbara Stanwyck. The plainly dressed middle-age woman with white-blonde hair heading home to the Midwest is the first and only time in the series that Stanwyck achieves ordinariness. The gangsters don't even notice her leaving.

Precisely because it disappeared for fifty years, *The Barbara Stanwyck Show* is not nostalgic but, rather, melancholic, presenting a view of unrealized possibility. As Celeste Olalquiaga—following Benjamin— describes melancholic kitsch, it "revels in memories because their feeling of loss nurtures its underlying rootlessness."[21] This manner of kitsch is allegorical rather than symbolic: "Melancholic memories are shattered and dispersed, referring only to the process of loss that constitutes them, their mythical quality enhanced by this ungraspable condition."[22] In this type of kitsch the intensity of experience is preserved or glimpsed in fugitive form and not fossilized into symbolic, nostalgic form. *The Barbara Stanwyck Show* offered an alternative view of women, but it was quickly sidelined and forgotten. To claim it now as a cultural "memory" is thus a critical act of melancholic kitsch.

By 1960–1961 Hollywood was competing with more critical and more explicitly modernist aesthetics of art cinema, foreign cinema, and independent cinema, and TV culture began to take over the role of melodrama as a form of negotiating social dilemmas. The anthology programs were more or less pitched at the boundary between film and TV, preserving the Hollywood idiom not only in their dramatic narratives but also in the pantheon of movie stars who acted in them and hosted them. *The Barbara Stanwyck Show* was one of the last anthology drama shows on the air. Economies of scale and the conservative power of sponsors cautious of the unpredictability of anthology writing forced broadcasters and TV producers to abandon the format in favor of serials with recurring characters.[23]

One of the last episodes of *The Barbara Stanwyck Show* is called "A Man's Game" (season 1, episode 36, July 3, 1961). Stanwyck assumes the role of sheriff in a western frontier town. As a parody of the genre, it has all the requisite iconography, but Stanwyck warns us in the introduction not to take it too seriously. She provides commentary in her distinctive no-nonsense voice while the drama is paused at climactic moments. When she has the episode's chief bad guy in her sights, she pauses: "Will she pull the trigger? Is she a big tough sheriff or just a woman after all?" As it turns out, she can't do it. Her erstwhile lover, who has effectively set up the situation she finds herself in, arrives for the final shoot-out with the bad guy. She resigns her post, he becomes the sheriff, and order is restored. But what if we were to take such an episode seriously? What if Stanwyck is more than a cross-dressing comedian? What if we are disappointed in the inability of the writers, directors, producers, and star to follow through on the role reversals that are promised but not delivered? The way Stanwyck carries herself in the role of a sheriff with her power stride is evidence enough of her rightful place in the fictional dreamworld of the Old West.

From the perspective of fifty years later, *The Barbara Stanwyck Show* is a ruin of its promise to create new myths for new subjectivities thrown up on the crest of American cultural history. It is a melodrama of missed opportunity and too-lateness. Stanwyck may get her man at the end of "A Man's Game," but is that what she really wanted? At the end of "The Assassin" (season 1, episode 32, May 15, 1961), she and Peter Falk are both led off to jail: he for attempted murder and she for embezzlement. In comedy she is allowed to be bad; in melodrama she is repeatedly locked into romantic situations, such as her remorse at the end of "Confession," that may affect the viewer fifty years later with a pathos unknown at the time of production.

The Barbara Stanwyck Show exemplifies the role of melodrama in popular culture, not as a regime of excess and artiness but as "the form by which timely social problems and controversies can be addressed."[24] The discontinuities of the story lines, with their abrupt accidents and revelations, together with the expressive lighting and detailed set design bring the expressive style of American cinema to the new "domestic" medium of TV. Stanwyck's presence as the personification of the professional woman "personifying" so many women caught between competing social pressures constitutes a rare embodiment of gender anxieties of the early 1960s, making them not only legible but "sensible" and emotional—affective—as well. Condensed into the collectible format of the DVD and digital archive, the program offers a unique view of the older woman challenging the industry to meet her halfway, on the threshold of a new medium. This is kitsch of the highest order, offering a glimpse into the dreamworld from which, as Benjamin insists, we need to awaken.

CRIMES OF PASSION
A DESTRUCTIVE CHARACTER

The destructive character knows only one watchword: make room.
And one activity, clearing away. His need for fresh air and open space
is stronger than any hatred.

—Walter Benjamin, "The Destructive Character"

FOR WALTER BENJAMIN, the destructive character was necessarily male. He was a figure, like the gambler, the flaneur, and the ragpicker, who embodied the unrealized potential of modernity. The destructive character "has no interest in being understood."[1] The openness that Benjamin assigns to the destructive character is closely aligned to the aleatory experience of gambling, the fragmentation of time, and the politics of fate. In his essay "Fate and Character," Benjamin points to comedy as the place where fate can be properly recognized as freedom, precisely because character itself is a sign within which the individual acts. It is the exterior—the face, the gesture—not the interior, that reveals the individual who acts.[2] Benjamin's gambler was also indisputably male, a man who gambled with women as if they were commodities. None of these figures had a future, because in the destruction of time in Benjamin's modernity, the future emerges from the interstitial shocks of ruined dream-wishes. For the feminist critic, such a conception of modernity may provide a valuable conception of character through which we can return to an emblematic performance in American film history. Barbara Stanwyck as Phyllis Dietrichson is neither the first nor the last Hollywood anti-heroine, but from the perspective of her afterlife in the twenty-first century, she is undoubtedly a destructive character: one who "reduces history to rubble—not for the sake of the rubble, but for that of the way leading through it."[3]

In 1943 Billy Wilder famously asked Barbara Stanwyck if she was a mouse or an actress,[4] challenging her to take the part of the murderer/

adulteress Phyllis Dietrichson in *Double Indemnity* (194). Stanwyck was Wilder's first choice for the part, and she was at the peak of her career at this point, said to be the highest-paid woman in America.[5] She was thirty-six years old, and the industry was about to turn a corner into the postwar era of Cold War anxiety and studio disintegration. *Double Indemnity* set the stage for the development of much more complex female characters in American cinema and enabled Stanwyck to reinvent herself as a "new New Woman" a decade after the new women of the 1930s had become a distant memory (see chapter I).

Double Indemnity has been analyzed to death, every scene picked apart from every angle, and yet most accounts of the film privilege the director, writers, and the film's influential style. Stanwyck's performance has most often been demonized as the quintessential femme fatale, rendered mythic rather than historical. As many feminist scholars have come to realize, film noir was not simply the terrain of male production personnel and audiences, and many key titles merged the female gothic with noir to feature women stars. Women producers were instrumental in developing the noir cycle, and the popular press profiled them extensively.[6] Likewise, Stanwyck's gamble was appreciated by her fans. She was praised in some quarters for the courage it took to assume such an "unsympathetic" role,[7] and in 1948 one fan magazine claimed that her "violent" roles were "stimulating" her career.[8] In this chapter I want to look at Stanwyck's role in *Double Indemnity* from the perspective of performance, character, and costume in order to highlight the features of the new New Woman—the newly invented destructive character—of the 1940s that she created with this role.

Double Indemnity is a watershed film partly because it won approval from the Motion Picture Production Code Administration (PCA), and it did so mainly because Wilder and Raymond Chandler's adaptation expanded the role of Barton Keyes—the Edward G. Robinson character—to give the film a moral center, and they cut out the extensive backstory of Phyllis's prior evildoings that James M. Cain had included in the original novel. At the same time, their revisions brought Walter Neff (Fred MacMurray's character) emotionally closer to Keyes, such that most critics agree that theirs is the real love story in the film.[9] All that remains of Phyllis's past is a tale told by her stepdaughter, Lola, about her possibly having caused the death of Neff's first wife, but Neff is not sure whether to believe this story or not, and consequently the viewer is free to believe it or not. The rumor renders Phyllis not only destructive but also anonymous, opaque, and on the outside.

Stanwyck was always looking for good scripts, and whenever any interviewer asked her about acting, she insisted that memorizing the entire script, including the other actors' lines, was essential. She wanted to understand characters and their motivations, and toward the end of her career, she confirmed that *Double Indemnity* was the best script she was ever given. Once she accepted Wilder's challenge, she crossed over to the side of violent women, and her characters became, above all, untrustworthy. They need to prove themselves and their desires while maintaining the dignity of a movie star.

Several reviewers claimed that Phyllis reminded them of Ruth Snyder (the woman on whom Cain based his original tale), even though there is absolutely no physical resemblance between Stanwyck and Snyder. While such claims simply reinforce the evil associated with this very new figure, it is also true that critic Bosley Crowther praised the film for its realism.[10] Stanwyck's "hard-boiled" performance—which Crowther describes as "refrigerated" in its imperviousness and opacity—is in many ways more realist than the histrionics of melodrama and the "affect" she created for so many of her previous and subsequent roles. And yet *Double Indemnity* has become known for the stylistic flair of John Seitz's cinematography. Along with the slants of light through shaded windows, Seitz created a dusty haze that Stanwyck claims was a huge help in creating her character.[11]

Andrew Klevan describes Stanwyck's performance in *Double Indemnity* as "minimalist."[12] Her restraint makes the character difficult to read, and it is indeed the lack of passion or emotion that critics at the time found strangely amiss.[13] Phyllis's lack of emotion, her opacity, is rendered explicit when she wears sunglasses in the supermarket for her rendezvous with Walter. This mask, along with her platinum wig, should alert us to the irony of Stanwyck's performance style in *Double Indemnity*. Klevan has pointed out in some detail that Phyllis Dietrichson has become the iconic femme fatale because she has been demonized by critics rather than by the noir films themselves. Not only are there very few characters who really fit the definition of a woman who seduces a man to his death, but those who do, like Phyllis Dietrichson, are arguably staging a new mode of independence and autonomy.

Julie Grossman has argued for a more contextual reading of the female characters in film noir in order to recognize how this cycle of films profoundly destabilized gender roles. "The predominance of the idea of the femme fatale," she argues, has kept us "from recognizing the complex levels of female subjectivity" at work in these roles and has become a self-perpetuating idea, repeatedly trapping women in social roles.[14] As an example of how the femme fatale mystifies performers as well as characters, take this quote from Scott Snyder that Grossman cites: "Barbara Stanwyck, the 'undisputed first lady of noir,' had a scornful, taut face and voice. Her posture was tight and defensive in keeping with a tough screen presence."[15] Once we recognize that this posture and tautness are part of a performance that Stanwyck could turn on and off, the critical misogyny at the heart of the femme fatale figure is evident. Understanding *Double Indemnity* from the point of view of the actor, who took the part as a challenge that enabled her to adopt an entirely new vocabulary of performance, is precisely the kind of contextualization for which Grossman advocates.

Elisabeth Bronfen has challenged the femme fatale stereotype by arguing that she is often a tragic figure. Women such as Phyllis Dietrichson embody tragic destiny precisely by challenging "American optimism that sees individuals as masters of their own destiny, with a right to pursue happiness at all cost without paying the price."[16] Bronfen uses *Double Indemnity* as her key example, citing the shooting scene as the moment when Phyllis understands and indulges in her own death as inevitable—while Walter remains in denial. In this scene Phyllis breaks down very briefly after she shoots Walter and throws herself into his arms, saying, "I've never loved you or anyone else. I'm rotten to the heart… until a minute ago when I couldn't fire that second shot." Here her eyes are expressive as she reveals her vulnerability. Walter doesn't buy it but she doesn't care. "Just hold me," she says, but he sticks to the script and says, "Good-bye, Baby," and with the gun out of frame, presumably squeezed between their bodies, he kills her and leaves, surviving long enough to tell the whole story to Keyes into the Dictaphone back at the insurance office.

Bronfen credits Billy Wilder for the series of close-ups in which Phyllis's growing anxiety invokes pity, while crediting Stanwyck for her "skillful performance of Phyllis's contrived gestures of seduction,"[17] but we could also credit the actor for creating a character who is at once seductive and deeply anxious. The penultimate scene may be a deus ex machina of sorts, as Hollywood scripts so often resort to. It opens a space for empathy with Stanwyck's character, but unlike many forced endings, it has been entirely earned by the performance and Stanwyck's ability to withhold emotion.

Bronfen asks us to see the women in film noir as separate from the fantasies of the noir hero and describes the famous banter between Phyllis and Neff when they first meet as a collision of two fantasy scenarios. He fetishizes Phyllis's body, while she assesses his capacity for crime. The two fantasy scenarios do not coincide in the opening exchange, and in fact they never do. For Bronfen and Grossman, the sexuality of the femme fatale and her capacity to lure the noir protagonist into her web is not only a rare

Barbara Stanwyck in *Double Indemnity* (1944)

scenario; it is also only one feature of a more significant recasting of women in American cinema.

Phyllis Dietrichson undermines Walter Neff's fetishism by acknowledging her own vulnerability and takes responsibility for her own actions. She chooses death as a critical statement of her impossible and unlivable situation as a trapped housewife, but more than that, she turns the inevitability of fate (the trolley car that takes them right down the line) into her responsibility. Stanwyck's gamble with this character enabled her to become a player within the contingency of studio politics, staking out new ground for female agency in cultural production.

Wilder's directions to Edith Head for dressing Stanwyck, along with his choice of the blonde wig, were to make the character as "sleazy" as possible (see chapter E). Of course one of Stanwyck's best-known roles prior to *Double Indemnity* was Stella Dallas, a character whose taste in clothes is at the center of the film. Critics can debate ad infinitum about Stella's consciousness about her wardrobe, but it is Stanwyck who created any doubt we may have (see chapter S). As Phyllis Dietrichson, her "look" is entirely under her control. She knows her clothes and knows how to use them. Moreover, the wig, the sunglasses, the anklet, and the pom-pom pumps, even her widow's veil, are highly performative accessories that point to the irony that lies at the heart of this performance. Phyllis puts on a show for Neff, which he finds highly entertaining, a diversion from the tedium of office work, and he makes little effort to lift the veil until it is too late.

The tight sweater over the bullet bra has become the outfit featured in twenty-first-century publicity for *Double Indemnity*. The original posters featured the couple in an embrace, with Stanwyck/Phyllis wearing a long yellow gown. When TCM rereleased the DVD in 2012, the sweater girl image was on the cover, tinted pink, and thus Stanwyck's body is aligned with the more modernist imagery of 1950s adult cinema and streamlined cars. The other iconic image from the film that has been popularized in the afterlife of *Double Indemnity* is Stanwyck with sunglasses in the supermarket. This is key to her figuration of a new New Woman who refuses the entrapment of commodity culture, or who is at least disturbed by it, unsettled by it, anxiously planning her escape.

Stanwyck's sexy image had already been created, in collaboration with Edith Head, for *Lady of Burlesque* and *Ball of Fire*. In both films she wears revealing showgirl costumes, showing a lot of leg with tight-fitting bustiers, off-stage as well as on. The sweater look differs in its status as fashion rather than costume. The real game-changing film before those two was *The Lady Eve* (1941), in which Head created the silhouette that Stanwyck sustained for much of her subsequent career. The costumes she wears for Jean, the con artist in *The Lady Eve*, are usually described as glamorous, but compared to Jean's alter ego, Eve, they could also be described as trashy, if not sleazy. It is very likely that this trio of films, in which Stanwyck flaunts a working-class sexual confidence, inspired Wilder to cast her in *Double Indemnity*.

Before the war, Stanwyck appeared in a number of films in which she wore little makeup, such as *The Purchase Price* (1932) and *So Big!* (1932), or was made up to look much older than she was, such as *Forbidden* (1932) and *The Great Man's Lady* (1941). The "natural look" epitomized in the finale of *Stella Dallas* was promoted in Stanwyck's endorsement of Lux soap, but with the release of *Double Indemnity* she appeared in Max Factor ads for lipstick, capitalizing on Phyllis Dietrichson's exaggerated crimson lips. The new New Woman no longer needs to strip away her makeup, or assert her inner honesty, but flaunts her painted face in the recognition of her commodity status.

After *Double Indemnity*, Stanwyck starred in a number of noir films in which she is more victimized than demonized, including *Sorry, Wrong Number* (1948), *No Man of Her Own* (1950), and *Witness to Murder* (1954), so she by no means always plays dangerous characters in film noir. On the other hand, she throws a pair of scissors at her future stepmother in the noirish western *The Furies* (1950) in a weak moment for an otherwise strong character who harbors a vicious burning rage (see chapter F). That violence is also evident in several film noirs, such as *The File on Thelma Jordan* (1950), *The Strange Love of Martha Ivers* (1946), and *Crime of Passion* (1956), as well as the westerns *The Violent Men* (1955) and *Blowing Wild* (1953), in which her characters die violent deaths, like Phyllis in *Double Indemnity*.

Stanwyck's postwar bad girls have important precedents in the pre-Code era, with *Baby Face* (1933) and *Ladies They Talk About* (1933) in particular, as well as her great con artist in *The Lady Eve*, and these films also demonstrate her capacity for irony—a critical strategy for making immoral characters sympathetic. After 1944 her bad girls are not redeemed but die tragically. Her transition to complicated, duplicitous roles parallels her emergence as an older woman, whose sexuality has become a kind of force field. She is neither victimized nor punished but finds her own way to spin her desire into the ambiguous terms of closure in Hollywood narratives.

By becoming untrustworthy, the characters in *Blowing Wild*, *Strange Love*, and *The Violent Men* become expendable, and yet these women also choose their own deaths. Repeatedly draped in flowing capes and gowns, they seize their deaths as rebukes to the corruption they have become aligned with—and also as rebukes to a social system in which women are denied power. Stanwyck's eye movements at moments of critical tension point to a thinking being within the trajectory of doom. She is, after all, the star of all of these films, billed equally with her male costars. The alignment of bad women with sexual desire may take different forms in each story, but by choosing death, Stanwyck's characters are not necessarily "punished." They choose death almost as a sexual act, which is most explicit in *Strange Love*, when Martha helps draw Walter's gun to her sequined belt and places her finger gently over the trigger.

Stanwyck's final role as a criminal is in *Crime of Passion*, in which her killer instinct is closely tied to a critique of middle-class suburban society and its circumscribed gender roles. She starts out as a very successful journalist named Kathy Ferguson, who explicitly rejects marriage as a boring and restrictive institution but is nevertheless persuaded to marry the irresistible Sterling Hayden and give up her career (see chapter W). Bill Doyle (Hayden) is a police detective who lacks ambition, so Stanwyck seduces his boss, Tony Pope (Raymond Burr), in order to win him a promotion. When Burr doesn't fall for it, she decides to shoot him. The scenes in which she steals the gun from the police station, commits the murder, and returns home to bed are dominated by a full-length, light cape-like coat with an Edith Head–like elegance (although Jack Masters is credited for costume

The Strange Love of Martha Ivers (1946)

design). She conceals the gun in its capacious pockets. In this outfit she seems to flow through scenes like water, and the crime seems like a necessity for Kathy, as if she were in a trance. Finally, she literally comes out of a dark tunnel, driving home and slipping into bed. Like so many of her postwar bad girls, Stanwyck's performance in *Crime of Passion* has a sense of being driven by forces beyond her control, even while she is absolutely in control. Kathy in *Crime of Passion* is a tragic hero, whose fate is bound to her role as a housewife.

Crime of Passion is not subtle in its critique of middle-class complacency, and Stanwyck's performance edges into hysterical shrieking as she sees Bill's chances of promotion slipping away. Once again the man and the woman completely fail to know or recognize each other. Deep dissatisfaction with the life of a housewife is rendered tragic in this film, and Kathy is clearly doomed as soon as she gives up her career. Stanwyck in *Crime of Passion* is exemplary of what Elisabeth Bronfen describes as the film noir woman who "by ultimately facing the consequences of her noir action, comes to reveal the fragility not only of any sense of omnipotence that transgression of the law affords, but, indeed, of what it means to be human."[18] As a late film noir, when the competing discourses of power and paranoia are thrown into relief in the late 1950s, it is the woman whose actions posit a freedom beyond the closures of a dysfunctional society.

Despite its bizarre twists of fate, *Crime of Passion* casts the female killer as a violent rebuke of a misogynist society. Stanwyck is configured as a split personality, but the pieces cannot be put together. She will not make small talk with policemen's wives or cozy up to the suburban neighborhood until she can topple the petty little hierarchy that such a bourgeois clique is made of. As the *New York Times* remarked, "As for Miss Stanwyck's transition from the nice sassy girl in the press room to a maniacal stalker, we don't believe it. Come off it, Miss Stanwyck, once a reporter, always a lady."[19] In 1956 critics might have remembered her spunky journalist role in *Meet John Doe* (1941), but by 2006 it is the violent Stanwyck that sold the film. A *Village Voice* reviewer promoted the film with "Hell hath no fury like Stanwyck scorned,"[20] suggesting how her capacity for violence remained a selling point decades after the end of the postwar noir era.

Suicide was proscribed by the Production Code, and in these films Stanwyck's characters do not, strictly speaking, die by their own hand. Their deaths are, however, spectacular and even in *The Violent Men*, where Stanwyck's Martha Wilkison is shot by a rival, they are tied closely to unrequited and impossible love affairs (Kathy Doyle might not die in *Crime of Passion*, but she symbolically dies by being irrevocably imprisoned). Their deaths are crimes of passion against themselves, against their impossible desires, and in this sense they are heroic deaths. For Walter Benjamin, suicide "represents the great conquest of modernity in the realm of passion,"[21] and I would argue that Stanwyck, who continued to play sympathetic, morally upstanding characters alongside these murderers, played her postwar bad girls as heroes. They heroically accept their destiny within the terms of a social contract that limited female ambition to a discourse of sexual desire, a contract implicitly challenged by their suicidal actions. Men and women completely fail to understand each other, and Stanwyck's characters are like angry adults in a children's world. Her passion is precisely what makes these films adult fare.

Stanwyck's affectless performance in *Double Indemnity* arguably inaugurated a new New Woman who had learned the art of masquerade, with which to deflect the misogyny that was built into the studio system. By learning how to create such a dangerous character, Stanwyck was able to extend her talents as a comic actor. "The immense complexity of the guilty person," Benjamin argues, tends to be enslaved in mystified figures (such as the "femme fatale"), and it is character that provides freedom from the tight bonds of social mores.[22] As woman's film history has begun to write different narratives of mid-century America, Stanwyck's creative role as a murderess and adulterer who nevertheless helped to sell the game-changing *Double*

Indemnity with her name needs to be recognized as a critical turn for gender roles in American cinema. Her gamble put her body and her fame on the line, high stakes that she managed to capitalize on precisely by both producing and empathizing with the commodity.

DION THE SON AND BARBARA
THE BAD MOTHER

"She threw me away like so much garbage."

—Anthony (Dion) Fay, in Barbara Sternig,
"Barbara Stanwyck's Adopted Son"

BARBARA STANWYCK'S MARRIAGE to Robert Taylor dissolved in 1950, after which she became ripe pickings for Hollywood gossipmongers. Her publicist, Helen Ferguson, maintained a rigorous narrative of Stanwyck as a no-nonsense, rags-to-riches career woman, but the star did not manage to completely evade the "poison gas of gossip."[1] In the latter part of her career, Stanwyck's role as a single woman failed to fit the discourse of normative heterosexuality, and she was accused of being a bad mother. Speculation concerning Stanwyck's sexual orientation continues to circulate today, and her biographers Dan Callahan and Axel Madsen have certainly fanned the flames despite a lack of evidence.[2] Stanwyck herself vehemently denied being gay, and in Boze Hadleigh's interview with her for his book *Hollywood Lesbians*, she comes off as far more homophobic than gay.[3]

In the late 1960s Stanwyck's public profile became aligned with those of Joan Crawford and Bette Davis as the victims of vengeful offspring. Stanwyck's tale is somewhat less well-known than those of Crawford and Davis, who each saw their estranged children publish revelatory books about them, complicating their celebrity legacies. Nevertheless, the parallels between their public narratives are striking, suggesting that these stars provoked another mythology—one of ambivalence and waywardness. Lauren Berlant has defined "unfinished sentimentality" as a kind of "ordinary restlessness" coming from within consumer culture.[4] In the "archive of women's culture," she argues, normative femininity relies on expectations of emotional reciprocity. In the sentimental worldview, family constitutes the dominant space of sociability, and for those who remain outside the family, their challenge to normative femininity remains within the "folds" of potentiality. Berlant seeks to derive "critique" from within these folds, rather than from a more conventionally feminist challenge or refusal of norms, and thus to recognize affective social relations "as something other than a failure to be in politics."[5]

Stanwyck's abnegation of the maternal role may help to understand her role in what Berlant describes as the "intimate public," where affect is a social practice.[6] Her relationship with her estranged son, Dion, came to haunt her in the 1960s, just as she was embarking on a TV career and remaking herself for the latter part of her career as an older woman. Dion remained separated from his mother from 1952 until his death in 2006. His story of neglect became fuel for the tabloids and a source of speculation regarding her relationships with the young actors in *The Big Valley* (1965–1969). The relationship between mother and son became part of her star image at this key turning point of her career, precisely when she needed to become "something else besides a mother."

This is of course the title of an important essay by Linda Williams about *Stella Dallas* in which she argues that the female spectator of one of Stanwyck's best-known melodramas need not identify simply with Stella's maternal sacrifice. Williams argues for a more complex viewing experience in which the contradictions exposed by the movie become recognized and legitimized as a form of knowledge (see chapter S).[7] Likewise, the tabloid gossip surrounding Stanwyck's own role as a mother not only challenges her fixed identity as a model citizen and woman; it also further complicates her idealization as a celebrity. As a self-made woman, single since the age of forty-three, perhaps she had a flaw after all. The melodrama of her life, in other words, can be read as a mode of "female complaint."

In Lauren Berlant's notion of the female complaint, the institutions of intimacy, of which celebrity gossip is a key example, constitute an ideology of heteronormativity that tends to operate as a discourse of disappointment "but not disenchantment."[8] Beyond melodramatic reversals and allegories, Berlant urges us to recognize that "sometimes feminism is not sentimental and does not bank on the association of femininity with the authenticity of true feeling."[9] In much the same way, Stanwyck's name is frequently included among those of "top Hollywood lesbians" as a strategy of recuperating her for a progressive agenda, but she does not conform to ideals of feminism or lesbianism any more than she does to motherhood. The scandal of her bad mothering, therefore, needs to be read not as her deviation from a generic norm but as a means of recognizing her identity as a construction of collective fantasy and as a woman whose story may in fact be what Berlant describes as "unfinished sentimentality."

The story of Dion's adoption is not pretty by any stretch of the imagination. Stanwyck adopted the infant in 1932 against the wishes of her first husband, Frank Fay.[10] Many stars adopted children, either because they could not, or would not, risk losing months of work due to a changed figure. Fay was an abusive alcoholic who Stanwyck propped up long after she should have. Victoria Wilson's biography suggests that she could not have children herself because of a botched abortion following a rape by a family friend when she was fourteen.[11] The marriage was rocky even before the adoption, but it deteriorated further with the child in the home due to Fay's excessive drinking. Wilson reports violent arguments, frequent calls to the police, and Stanwyck appearing on sets with unexplained injuries. Fay also reportedly urinated on Stanwyck's guests, uttered obscenities at his son, and at one point threw the three-year-old Dion into a pool.[12]

Stanwyck and Fay's custody battle over Dion in 1937 exposed a great deal of their private lives in court, and Stanwyck's performance in the courtroom was widely praised. She was described as a "Hollywood mother" who was "very much like other mothers the world over. They want their children—and when they start fighting for them, they won't listen to anyone."[13] The story quickly shifted to Barbara's romance with Robert Taylor, which had already blossomed in 1937, and the unhappy marriage to Fay more or less faded away until it reappeared in the gossip magazines in 1966 and 1967.[14] A *Photoplay* feature in 1967 even included affidavits documenting Fay's abuse against Dion, but the abuse of Stanwyck herself was not reported.[15] Despite the evidence against him, in 1938 the judge ruled in favor of Fay's request for visiting rights, although he rarely used them.

As a single mother, Stanwyck became extremely overprotective and possessive, and when Dion was only six, she sent him to Raenford Military Academy, a boarding school not far from Stanwyck's ranch. Part of her motivation may have been to protect Dion from Fay, who she believed was driven to kidnap him, but Dion remained in boarding school, followed by a military academy, and then joined the army in 1952. The story that has emerged from the many biographies of Stanwyck is that she had high expectations that her son would be a hardworking person like herself and that she did not want him to take anything for granted. Dion repeatedly got kicked out of the schools he was sent to, and he may have been overweight in Stanwyck's opinion. She said that she "resisted the temptation to shower him with gifts" and restricted his total Christmas allotment to five presents: "Dion needs preparation for the problems he will face as an adult. How could

The man who ruined
  Barbara Stanwyck's
    chance to keep her
      son's love...
(Please turn the page)

Photoplay magazine, August 1967

he develop values?" In the same *Screenland* article, titled "What I Believe,"
she says that being orphaned at age four, she had a rough childhood and took
nothing for granted. She gave Dion an allowance of twenty-five cents a week,
and "to earn extra money, he cleans the back yard or clips the hedge, delivers
newspapers, or works as [a] pool boy at a nearby hotel."[16] In Dion's account
he never lived with his mother, even in the summers, after the age of six.[17]
Dion may well have been a difficult child, beyond Stanwyck's abilities to
manage. Speculation about the boy's bad behavior attributed it to the damage
done by the chaotic relationship between Stanwyck and Frank Fay.[18]

In 1960 Dion was arrested for selling pornography to teenagers. When
reporters discovered that he was Stanwyck's son, the story broke in the *Los*

Angeles Daily Mirror by journalist Paul V. Coates in his "Confidential File." Dion confessed that he was broke and had not seen his mother since 1952. She had not gone to his wedding or seen her grandson. Dion said that he had disappointed her by being a poor student, and he takes the blame for their separation.[19] (According to some sources, Dion sold his story for money in 1959 or 1960 to *Confidential* magazine, although I have not been able to confirm this.[20] In fact, Stanwyck herself is remarkably absent from *Confidential* magazine altogether, thanks, no doubt, to the vigilance of Helen Ferguson.) When Frank Fay passed away in 1961, Dion attended the funeral, although Stanwyck, conspicuously, did not. Dion was not mentioned in the will, although he eventually managed to claim an inheritance. Barbara and Dion reputedly did not meet again at all after Dion's departure for military school in 1952, despite the fan magazines' futile attempts to bring them together.

The story more or less disappeared until 1966, after Stanwyck had reestablished herself as a major TV star in *The Big Valley*, when the fan magazines became somewhat obsessed with her role as a mother on- and off-screen. *TV Picture Life* ran a story in 1967 featuring a picture of an open door of an apartment and the caption: "Dear Barbara. Your lost son steps over this threshold every day. He is living in New York City, in this run-down, gloomy, old building."[21] This story is typical of the speculation surrounding Dion and the longing for Stanwyck to conform to the maternal ideal of her screen roles. Stanwyck often referred to her *Big Valley* costars as the family she never had. As Victoria Barkley, Stanwyck ran the family ranch like a corporate enterprise—a maternal figurehead in a macho universe in which she held little real power over her gun-toting all-American sons.

Lee Majors claimed that she offered him a great deal of maternal advice, taking him under her wing as she had so many young men before, including Robert Taylor, William Holden, and Kirk Douglas (see chapter H).[22] Other gossip about the series suggested that the men had an increasingly difficult time with "Missy" Stanwyck and complained about her top billing.[23] Her role as a matriarch in *Big Valley* and the "family" context of the show generated a great deal of speculation about her maternal instincts, including the role of guardian she took on for her friend Peter Godfrey's three girls when he was hospitalized with Hodgkin's disease (although she was too busy to actually care for them and passed them on to other guardians). Stanwyck may have supported three Native American children through school as well.[24]

Dion sold his story to *National Enquirer* in 1984, when Stanwyck was seventy-six years old, and at that point he did not hold back, with a title screaming, "She Threw Me away Like So Much Garbage."[25] In the tabloid language of scandalous transgression, he says, "She Never Touched, Kissed or Held Me Except When Cameras Flashed." Dion changed his name to Anthony and went by Tony; he died in 2006. Victoria Wilson says she met him multiple times while researching her massive biography, of which only the first volume (to 1940) has appeared. He was an important source for her detailed descriptions of the domestic scene in the 1930s and for Stanwyck's relationship with Bob Taylor. They became quite close, she says, and Wilson ultimately describes Tony as a "loving man who managed to triumph over difficult, dark years."[26]

Stanwyck's maternal trials, like those of Crawford and Davis, were symptomatic of a culture of anxiety over mothers' responsibility for social stability. Mothers in postwar America tended to take the blame for everything, and the term "Momism" was coined by Philip Wylie to reify the psychoanalytic misogyny of the times.[27] For Wylie, women had become fetishized as ideals while also gaining emotional power over men through popular Freudianism. Mothers assumed authority in the home, the workplace, and as patriots, and he compares them to tyrants, the pope, and Hitler. Monstrous mothers appeared in Alfred Hitchcock's films and became a familiar film caricature, although Stanwyck more or less evaded that particular fate. Instead she took numerous roles in which she is simply out of sync with mothering.

The comic version of Stanwyck's character being a bad mother is Elizabeth Lane in *Christmas in Connecticut* (1945), a farcical tale of a cooking columnist who can't cook (see chapter 2). Lane finds herself having to enact her fictional domestic role, complete with husband and baby, as part of a wartime publicity stunt. She is hilariously inept at everything, referring to her baby as "it." In fact the boy baby is on loan from a mother working in the war plant and is replaced by a girl baby just to compound the silliness. This film most clearly distinguishes the professional woman from the domestic woman, resolving the discrepancy through the war effort as Lane is finally paired with the soldier whom she was enlisted to entertain. But not all of Stanwyck's roles as mother-who-is-not-a-mother are quite so funny.

Despite Stanwyck's iconic role as Stella Dallas, and her reputation as a star of the Hollywood woman's film, her mother roles after 1937 are few and far between. In *Always Goodbye* (1938), which is really the last of her maternal melodramas, Stanwyck's character (a governess) ironically protests when another character (her lover's new wife) wants to put a six-year-old boy in a boarding school.[28] The child of course is hers, as she has given the boy up only to insinuate her way back into his life and ultimately rescue him from a life in boarding schools. *Always Goodbye* is actually an iteration of the narrative of *Forbidden*, which Stanwyck starred in in 1932. The story of a mother whose child is raised by a wealthy man who she more or less stalks in order to stay close to the child is a classic women's tale of suffering and victimhood, which ends with a murder in 1933 and a happy resolution in 1938.

Examining Stanwyck's maternal roles in light of the gossip about her own failures as a mother takes us to some of the more abject films in her career, such as *The Gay Sisters* (1942), a film that revolves around a rape (see chapter P). *The Gay Sisters* is a kind of perverse remarriage comedy. The child, Austin, is first introduced as Stanwyck's ward, not her son, and she treats him with the tough love of a drill sergeant—in keeping with her designation as filling the patriarchal role of her deceased father. Eventually it is revealed that the boy's father is Charles Barclay (George Brent), whom Stanwyck's character, Fiona Gaylord, is fighting in court. She keeps the child who is produced by this liaison a secret until he becomes a pawn in their court case. The drama of abduction during their custody battle echoes Stanwyck's own fight with Frank Fay a few years earlier, but in the movie the family is finally reunited and the couple is reconciled. *The Gay Sisters* is a genuinely disturbing movie and was considered so even at its release, described by one critic as "gay in name only."[29]

In *My Reputation* Stanwyck plays a widow with two young sons who protest strongly against her relationship with an army major (George Brent again), a theme that reemerges in *There's Always Tomorrow*. In these films the children function as a repressive trap, turning the nuclear family into a noose around the necks of potential lovers. *No Man of Her Own*, based on the Cornell Woolrich novel *I Married a Dead Man*, is a strong noir film, but Stanwyck's pretense of maternity is decidedly perverse. Her character assumes the identity of a pregnant woman killed in a train wreck in order to give her own child a good home. Stanwyck's character professes loads of love for her infant, but in the few scenes in which the baby appears, Stanwyck holds the oversized docile child as if it were a pet that might give her fleas (see chapter N). In *Titanic* (1953) the children are more developed than the pawns of the previous examples, but the film can be read as another example of the failures of mother love. As the great ship goes down, Stanwyck's character watches as her young son, Norman, goes down on the ship with his father, who is not really his father.

Stanwyck's final maternal role is the very strange western *Trooper Hook* (1957), in which she plays the very unlikely part of a captive white woman who is rescued from the Indians with her half-breed son by Joel McCrea as the eponymous Trooper Hook. The child in this tale is little more than a pawn, and the maternal role stands in for a critique of racism and a defense of miscegenation, neither of which can actually be named. Stanwyck's performance is so awkward and out of place that the ethics of the film are

Barbara Stanwyck in *No Man of Her Own* (1950)

equally contrived and unconvincing. When Stanwyck, as Cora, says, "I got used to being his squaw," we know we are in a deeply troubled ideological space (see chapter J).

Even if they are not all technically "melodramas" in the generic sense, these films use the melodramatic mode to pry apart the demands and expectations of motherhood. For Agustín Zarzosa, melodrama is a mode through which suffering can be ameliorated through its spectacularization.[30] Zarzosa points out that rather than seeking to establish a "moral occult," film melodrama more typically dramatizes a moral investigation in which different social ideas are tested in different historical milieux. In so many of Stanwyck's films, motherhood is revealed as a social role that can be played in any number of ways, but the various performances repeatedly fail to alleviate the injustices of the worlds in which her characters find themselves.

One of the recurring themes of the melodramatic mode as it evolved from nineteenth-century literature and theater is the question of true parentage as the key to identity.[31] These various examples of Stanwyck's maternal roles in the studio era suggest that the theme of true parentage remains pertinent, but it needs to be read within a web of competing social ideas, including gender roles, class, and race. In many of these films the deus ex machina endings follow teary dramas of the failures of mothers to properly love their children. Stanwyck's characters are frequently single mothers whose relationships with men are out of sync. Read against Stanwyck's own parental failures, the problem of parenting turns out to be a problem of servitude to an ideal of parenting. In fact, as Zarzosa explains, even *Stella Dallas* poses the question, Is Stella a good mother? The film reveals "the social gap between social mores and individual happiness."[32] When Stanwyck's own life was suddenly laid bare and revealed for all to see, it was immediately read as a melodrama in which her role was that of the woman outside the family. Her status as a single woman constitutes an ambivalence that undermines heteronormativity precisely on the level of affect and reciprocity.

Perhaps because Stanwyck refused to engage with it, the gossip about Dion and his escapades never amounted to a scandal. It was more like background noise to Stanwyck's career, and in an unlikely way it may have served the reinvention of her star image as a tough, powerful, wealthy older woman. The banner headline in the *Enquirer* over Dion's story refers to Stanwyck as a "superstar"—an '80s term, perhaps, but probably the first time she earned it. Throughout the 1960s, starting with *The Barbara Stanwyck Show*, she starred as a kind of benevolent authority figure,[33] a softer version of the phallic women played by actresses like Judith Anderson in the 1950s (the original Mrs. Ivers) but nevertheless strong enough to stand alone outside the family system and the affective regime of public discourse, with its limited options for female characters and celebrities.

The fact that Stanwyck's relation to the maternal was consistently out of sync with social norms of behavior becomes an unusual patriarchal narrative of public/private taxonomy within the context of the intimate public. Berlant argues that a discourse of disappointment tends to be attached to the constructions of femininity on the unstable ground of public discourse, and it is important to examine the tensions between aesthetic conventions of popular culture and revelations of social behaviors, desires, and belonging. Gossip about Stanwyck's troubled relationship with her son underlines just how much she was able to hold back and how much privacy she was able to maintain throughout a very long career as a public figure, even while that privacy marked her difference and uniqueness as an individual.

How do we account for the many parallels between Stanwyck's private life and the roles she played as an adoptive parent, a role-playing parent, a parent in denial, or even—in *These Wilder Years* (1956)—the head of an adoption agency? Perhaps the most pathetic example of this parallelism (which is to say the most melodramatic) is an episode of *The Barbara Stanwyck Show* called "High Tension," which was broadcast on March 27,

1961. In this half-hour episode of the anthology drama series, Stanwyck plays a bejeweled and fur-draped matron who wants to return her son to the adoption agency because he is deaf. After getting trapped in an electrified bus during a spectacular storm, with high tension wires sparking and shocking throughout, she is persuaded by the other passengers to save her son's life. As mother and son are reconciled, one of the passengers delivers the "message" that "a woman needs to suffer to have a child."

In the semaphoric language of TV drama, the failures of poor mothering are laid bare. Is it coincidence that Stanwyck played so many failed mother characters? No doubt themes of adoption and parenting were endemic to Hollywood during the studio period, and to TV drama as it took over the task of melodramatic storytelling in the 1950s and '60s. However, in these Stanwyck films and TV shows, the revelation of identity occurs not for the child but for the mother. The children are almost always small boys who get shunted about like props, while Stanwyck's characters explore a multitude of mothering roles, which are in turn frequently marked by class and—in the case of *Trooper Hook*—race as well. In light of the gossip about her own son Dion's exploits in the porn business, these rather abject films, many of which have been otherwise forgotten, about mothers who have so much trouble filling their roles as mothers underscore the failures that so much role-playing seeks to obscure.

Stanwyck's problems with her son, which provided revealing gossip during her big comeback on *The Big Valley*, should also be read against her "problematic" Republicanism, which did not entirely conform to her characterization until that particular series. Despite being a favorite of many feminists and cinephiles, Stanwyck was complicit with the House Un-American Activities Committee (HUAC) and a devotee of Ayn Rand. The gossip surrounding her sexuality, her family life (or lack thereof), and her rigorous attempts at privacy constructed a far more complex figure than most stars of her generation. Her inability, or refusal, to be a mother in the 1960s coincides with her playing against younger men who she once may have dated. Just as the popular press at the time begged her to be a good mother, contemporary fans today wish she had been a feminist or a lesbian. Tracing Stanwyck's public image through this period highlights how a narrative of depression, anxiety, and disappointment needs to be recognized as part of the "affective range of sentimentality" that marks women's culture. Stanwyck's public role as a bad mother should be recognized as a proxy for her status as a single woman.

EDITH HEAD
CLOTHING MAKES THE WOMAN A WOMAN

There are those who stand before the mirror, absorbing each minute adjustment.
Barbara Stanwyck is the one who stood with her back to the mirror!

—Edith Head, The Dress Doctor

EDITH HEAD WAS RESPONSIBLE for Stanwyck's costumes for twenty-four films, most of them between 1940 and 1950. Their collaboration began in 1937, with *Internes Can't Take Money* at Paramount, where Head was under contract. Like Stanwyck, Head had a great deal of control over her own career, especially once she became chief designer at Paramount in 1938. Stanwyck and other stars, including Ginger Rogers, Joan Fontaine, Loretta Young, Ingrid Bergman, and Bette Davis, were able to secure her services for films at other studios, and after the 1950s Head became a successful radio and TV personality, advising women on fashion.[1] Stanwyck was one of the first actors to recognize Head's talents, and Head helped Stanwyck to become "glamourous," which is to say a spectacle, an image, and an icon, and much more than an actor selling films. Head's costuming enabled Stanwyck to balance an appropriately "feminine" silhouette with roles that frequently challenged the norms of womanly behavior.

Stanwyck's deep ambivalence about playing the fashion model became highly apparent in her awkward introductions to episodes of *The Barbara Stanwyck Show*. Fashion for Stanwyck, as for Head, was subservient to character until she realized the necessity of dressing like a star and creating an off-screen character for herself. After an unnerving experience of being unrecognized and barred from entry to a preview of *Stella Dallas* because of her "severe" outfit, Stanwyck hired Head to design her personal wardrobe. Their collaboration coincided with her marriage to Robert Taylor, a period when she was regularly photographed at public events, perhaps more so than

Barbara Stanwyck in *Remember the Night* (1940)

at any other time of her career. Stanwyck's collaboration with Head was very much responsible for Stanwyck's successful transition into the cinema of the 1940s. However, despite becoming the highest-paid woman in America, the films themselves tended to trample all over the independent woman label that she had embodied through the 1930s.

Head's first assignment with Stanwyck came about because the chief designer at Paramount at the time, Travis Banton, did not think Stanwyck was important enough (glamourous enough) to warrant his attention, so he passed on the job to his assistant, Edith Head, who did not get screen credit for the production. *Internes Can't Take Money* features Joel McCrea as Dr. Kildare, who doesn't take money from gangsters, even if it means helping Stanwyck's character, Janet Haley, find her daughter (who has been kidnapped by gangsters). Janet is not a wealthy woman, but thanks to Head she is stylish. She sports a dark hat with a drooping brim and a patterned scarf with a dark, loose-fitting tailored skirt and jacket. In one of the later scenes, she wears a dark fur-edged jacket with white ribbons. Stanwyck describes these outfits as "feminine" and claims "they did something for me."[2] Indeed, Head's perspective was always tied to the character, and she helped Stanwyck and many other actors literally "inhabit" their characters, even if that meant contradicting their working-class identities.

Head also designed costumes for *Remember the Night* (1940), another Paramount film, in which Stanwyck plays a kleptomaniac named Lee Leander. Fred MacMurray is the benevolent prosecutor who takes her home for Christmas during a recess in her trial, and although she is a homeless thief, Lee wears a mink coat throughout the first half of the film and a tailored skirt and jacket with a fine print and white collar when her trial resumes at the end of the film. Her stylish cocked hats with white trimmings announce her status as a willful woman even if the outfits seem disproportionate to her social status. In the pre-Code years, many of Stanwyck's characters wear glamourous gowns, especially Lily in *Baby Face*. The prestige designer Orry-Kelly dressed her for that film, and he designed her costumes for eight films altogether, seven of them before 1935. *Lost Lady* (1934), a poor adaptation of a Willa Cather novel, was dismissed by critics as nothing but a constant series of wardrobe changes, as the Orry-Kelly gowns tended to overwhelm the story line. In the mid-1930s, without the sensational scripts and ambitious social climbing, Stanwyck's wardrobe lacked "class," and in many of these films she was down-dressed to the point of being "plain," which was described at the time as "natural." By becoming glamourous in the late 1930s, both Stanwyck's characters and her star image became less "ordinary" and more exceptional. The transgressive edge of glamour is in the self-possession and assertiveness gained by women challenging norms of domesticity,[3] and thus the "independent" label shifted from being an outspoken working-class heroine to being proud, confident, and stylish.

With the Paramount film *The Lady Eve*, Head really helped Stanwyck hit the glamour high notes. Because Stanwyck plays a character, Jean, who plays another character, Eve, who the love interest (played by Henry Fonda) does not recognize as "the same dame," costume is particularly important. The sexy Latin-inspired cruise ship wardrobe that Jean wears is very different from the elegant lady's clothing of "Lady Eve Sedgwick," and the evident flair of couture prompted reviewers to designate Stanwyck repeatedly as "glamourous" (see chapter L).[4] In fact, Stanwyck had been doing photo shoots since she first arrived in Hollywood, as Ella Smith's "authorized" biography loaded with glossy black-and-white photographs clearly demonstrates.

Edith Head's contribution to Stanwyck's star image was, above all, to find and showcase her figure. The bare-midriff outfit in *Lady Eve*, shimmering with black beads, showed off her slender waist, and the bolero-like top would become a recurring feature of Stanwyck's on-screen outfits. It hangs off her shoulders and disguises her long back and large buttocks. High-waisted skirts and large belts had the same effect. The low-cut necklines

Barbara Stanwyck and George Brent in *My Reputation* (1946)

silhouette that would remain popular for the next decade. The alignment of women's breasts with technology was symptomatic of a culture of "streamlining" in which aesthetic form took precedence over function, which in the case of breasts meant nurture.[11] Pinup culture and sweater girls thus rendered women's bodies as technologies: less maternal and more stylish. For Stanwyck, this arguably enabled her to transition away from the role of mother and into the more complex, dubious, and untrustworthy figures of film noir. In *My Reputation*, in which she plays a widow considering remarriage, her sweaters are critical elements of her wardrobe—not only because they signal availability but also because they cancel out her status as a mother.

In *Double Indemnity* Edith Head managed to take Wilder's direction for a sleazy housewife and create idiosyncratic costumes that contribute a great deal to the success of the film.[12] In Walter Neff's apartment, Stanwyck as Phyllis wears a white sweater with a high-waisted skirt, maintaining a semblance of elegance alongside the new profile, and she said at the time that being a sweater girl was to date "her most spectacular experience." At age thirty-seven it was a welcome boost to her career (despite having stripped down to nearly nothing in *Lady of Burlesque* the year before).[13] At the same time, she didn't hesitate to challenge the wolf-whistling by whistling back at servicemen. The *L.A. Times* reported that she completely broke up a military parade with her disruptive behavior. Publicizing the 1944 Paramount film, she added a plug for the "ski sweaters" in the upcoming *My Reputation* at Warner Bros., indicating her ability to capitalize on the trend for her own career.[14]

Many of Head's dress designs exaggerated the size of Stanwyck's bust, and her silhouette became markedly different from that of the flat-chested waif of the 1930s. *Christmas in Connecticut* is the Stanwyck film most closely associated with the war, featuring a soldier on furlough (Dennis Morgan) for whom Stanwyck's cooking columnist character has to put on a show of domesticity that she is completely unequipped for. Head dresses Stanwyck in a series of elegant outfits that exaggerate her figure, including a white fur-trimmed bolero over a long black dress. This journalist may be more feminine than Ann Mitchell in *Meet John Doe*, but she is also more upper-middle class.

Stanwyck wears some of her most "masculine" outfits in films that Head was not responsible for: *Golden Boy* (1939) and *Meet John Doe*. Head's costumes favored elegant lines and drapings, featuring high-waisted skirts that swing with Stanwyck's distinctive walk and with accessories and trimmings that signaled femininity. In Head's advice columns, she emphasized function over glamour, advising women to stay within their means and to definitely stay away from clothing that is too tight or revealing. She recommended slacks only for certain occasions—and never with patterns or stripes.[15] For both Stanwyck and Head, a clear distinction exists between fashion and costume design. Characters on the screen, for the two women, lived on the screen and had little bearing on everyday life. Certainly this is true of the Head-designed costumes in *Lady of Burlesque* and *Ball of Fire* (in the latter, Stanwyck is dressed in at least half the film in a dress that shimmers and glows, literally, like a ball of fire), and of course the period films such as *The Great Man's Lady* and *California* (1947), for which Head designed some fabulous hoop-skirted gowns.

According to Robert Gustafson, who surveyed women's magazines through the 1940s, none of Head's designs significantly penetrated the retail market, which underlines how she designed for specific actors in specific roles.[16] Stanwyck's versatility and ability to work in a wide range of genres also meant she did not become associated with a specific style that translated to the retail market. However J. E. Smyth claims that the Latin-inspired outfits that Head designed for *The Lady Eve* "set the fashion trends for the next few years."[17] Smyth also compares the Stanwyck-Head collaboration with that of Katharine Hepburn and Adrian, a high-profile designer at MGM, to claim that Stanwyck's wardrobe was more "sporty" and "outdoorsy."[18] The discrepancy between these two reports is no doubt due to their different research sources and is symptomatic of how Stanwyck's star image is harder to pin down, particularly during this period from 1937 to 1950, than that of a star attached to a studio with publicity machines that consolidated their celebrity profiles.

As she edged toward a more glamourous and wealthier persona, Stanwyck's "ordinariness" was stressed in publicity that featured her lack of pretension. During the 1940s Stanwyck acquired the nicknames Stany, Missy, and "Queen," and the fan magazines ran many stories about her friendliness, good humor, and generosity. She was constantly giving extravagant gifts to cast and crew members. In addition to the testimonials as a down-to-earth woman, constantly downplaying her celebrity status, Stanwyck and her publicist successfully constructed an image of a benevolent star who was not ordinary but extraordinarily ordinary. As Richard Dyer argues, the hard-won label of "ordinariness" produces a further paradox when the "specialness of stars may be then that they are the only ones around who are ordinary," and yet Stanwyck was close to angelic in her ordinariness, actively working against the glamourous "unnatural" icon that she had become. In one article in *Good Housekeeping* in 1954, "Ruby Stevens" wrote an article about Stanwyck's life "as told to Margaret Lee Runbeck," with the conceit that she was always lurking within "the Queen" and that finally they are together again.[19] Given the repeated iteration of her biography as the Brooklyn orphan who became a movie star, Hollywood publicity constructed Stanwyck as a character in her own life.

In the late 1930s, when Stanwyck's growing reputation as an independent contractor challenged gender norms, Head's designs helped to promote—if not sculpt—the "feminine" qualities of Stanwyck's star image. In 1936, after her divorce from Frank Fay, she told a reporter that she was now "living dangerously." She said, "I am free. I am my own man. And it's dangerous because no woman can live in marriage this way."[20] She had stayed by her man for far too long, holding on to a fantasy of domestic life that Fay was clearly not capable of living up to, but if freedom could only be coded as masculine, she clearly needed to craft new ways of being in the world that would enable her to remain a woman. Various commentators have suggested that Stanwyck was not typically "glamourous." Richard Dyer describes her "tough face" as pointing to "sexual ambiguity,"[21] a dangerous transgression that Edith Head helped her manage with the cloak of glamour.

Dress designs and fashions were definitely an important way in which female viewers as consumers were inspired by Hollywood stars and their on- and off-screen wardrobes. It is also true, though, that actors such as Stanwyck presented different ways of being in the world in the characters she portrayed, different behaviors and styles, in which clothing played an important role. During the mid-century years of her career, gender norms were constantly being challenged and debated. Westerns feature numerous instances in which the criteria and definitions of "real men" and "real women" were repeatedly tested, including through the image of a woman wearing pants (see chapters F and K). At the same time, screwball comedy was also a genre devoted to the negotiations between men and women in a changing world, and Stanwyck appeared in pants in that genre too.

In addition to *The Lady Eve*, *Ball of Fire* might be considered screwball, as could *Remember the Night* and *Christmas in Connecticut*, but *The Bride Wore Boots* (1946) is definitely screwball, if not one of the more memorable examples of the genre. The title points to the role of sartorial style in what Stanley Cavell has dubbed the "comedy of remarriage." In screwball comedies of the 1930s and '40s, men and women had to relearn what marriage is in a new world order of uppity women and emasculated men (this is not quite how Cavell puts it). Cavell argues that "in questioning the legitimacy of marriage, the question of the legitimacy of society is simultaneously raised, even allegorized,"[22] which is not to say that the films are not also about the relations between men and women. Stars like Stanwyck and Katharine Hepburn, who were great talkers, excelled in this genre, which played with language perhaps more than with images, as the settings tended to be consistently luxurious. Stanwyck's characters frequently find themselves pitted against extraordinarily inept and inadequate men.

The Bride Wore Boots, costume-designed by Edith Head, lacks Preston Sturges's wit and Fonda's brilliant straight-man performance, but like *The Lady Eve*, the wife holds all the cards in a rocky relationship. Stanwyck is a high-profile horse rider and breeder, while her husband, Jeff (Robert Cummings), is a Civil War historian who hates horses. When he is pursued by the flirtatious girl next door, and Sally (Stanwyck) sees too much of an old beau and fellow horse breeder, they divorce. Jeff is eventually persuaded by his Black stable boy (Willie Best) to ride an unpredictable horse in the local steeplechase competition, and although he keeps falling off and loses to the overconfident beau, Sally is so impressed with his efforts that the couple is reunited.

In both *The Woman in Red* (1935), in which Stanwyck plays a jockey, and *The Bride Wore Boots*, Stanwyck wears jodhpurs in all the riding and stable scenes. In the 1935 film (which, being in black-and-white, never accounts for the title), Stanwyck's character wears a variety of pants in other

Wallace Ford, Thomas Gomez, and Barbara Stanwyck in *The Furies* (1950)

scenes as well. As the bride who is said to wear boots in 1946, however, outside the horsey world of stables and paddocks, Stanwyck consistently wears elegant gowns and dresses. The pants here are merely a passing thought on Head's part. In *The Furies*, however, Stanwyck wears the pants boldly and with confidence, standing on the porch of the ranch house that she battles her father for. The next and last film that she and Head collaborated on was *Roustabout* in 1964 with Elvis Presley, in which Stanwyck wears jeans and slacks in almost every scene. The collaboration was noted in all the press about the film, and Head boasted on Stanwyck's behalf that she used the same dress dummy for "Missy" as she had in 1950 for *The Furies*.[23]

In *Clash by Night*, Marilyn Monroe, as the younger factory-working woman, wears jeans, while Stanwyck, as the older woman, wears dresses. However, Stanwyck's emergence in the 1950s as the queen of westerns enabled her to buck the trend and wear pants throughout the decade as an action star. Edith Head and Barbara Stanwyck were both fundamentally conservative when it came to sartorial style. Nevertheless, as the star began to transition during the war years from a working-class heroine to a mature, duplicitous, postwar woman, Head's outfits gave Stanwyck the confidence and authority on which she could build to create women who lived differently in the world, women who spoke their minds and moved with deliberation, grace, and style. Their collaboration was a critical contribution to the way that women's images evolved during this turbulent period.

Both *The Furies* and *Roustabout* were shot at Paramount, where Head was still in charge of the costume design department. Their collaboration dropped off in the 1950s precisely when Stanwyck's leverage as a star began to decline and she was less likely to be able to negotiate for Head's expensive services in her freelance contracts. Edith Head won eight Oscars, none of them for a Stanwyck film, while Stanwyck notoriously never won one, despite four nominations and a lifetime achievement honor in 1982. This was undoubtedly the price Stanwyck paid for being a freelance artist without the backing of a studio.

FORTY GUNS AND *THE FURIES*
ANGRY WOMEN

[Stanwyck's] form or class or appeal or whatever you want to call it stems from
tremendous sensitivity and thousands of closeted thoughts she can select at will,
at the right moment, for the exact impact.

—Sam Fuller, quoted in *Starring Miss Barbara Stanwyck*

THE FURIES (Anthony Mann, 1950) and *Forty Guns* (Samuel Fuller, 1957)
are both black-and-white westerns by auteur directors and starring Barbara
Stanwyck. Both are distinguished stylistically and have been endorsed by
the critical establishment as highlights of the genre as it evolved in the 1950s
into an introspective examination of frontier mythology. The two films
bookend the decade for Stanwyck, a decade in which she made twenty-two
films, seven of which are westerns. *The Furies* and *Forty Guns* have both been
recognized as precursors of Sergio Leone's stylized westerns of the early
1960s for very different reasons—*The Furies* for its psychological extremes
and *Forty Guns* for its campy excess.[1] Stanwyck's contribution to both of
these films is critical, as she realized the potential of these projects by
directors who were eventually recognized, at first by French critics, as key
auteurs working within the industry.[2] Her roles are dissimilar in the two
films, but both feature performances of tough, dynamic women who open
the films up to interpretation of the gender politics of the western genre.
Analysis of Stanwyck's performances in these two remarkable westerns
demonstrates how gender politics intersect with discourses of race and
power in the deconstruction of frontier mythology.

The 1950s were a challenging decade for women actors of Stanwyck's
generation. Fewer and fewer good roles were available to women, and as
Emily Carman has demonstrated, their salaries lost parity with men of their
age.[3] Stanwyck managed to keep steady work in movies until 1957 partly

because of her experience as a freelancer, which became a necessity as the studio system gradually ended its contractual relations with actors.[4] Audience demographics shifted to a younger male audience, and studios responded with stories featuring older men and younger women, in addition to a crop of new young men.[5] Joan Crawford made only thirteen features during the 1950s, and Bette Davis starred in only ten, although, like Stanwyck, they had also become active in television. Not only did Stanwyck continue working in Hollywood, but by the end of the decade she was a millionaire, whereas many of her colleagues had fallen on hard times.[6] During these years she became an expert in western-themed literature and was an expert horsewoman, assets that both Anthony Mann and Samuel Fuller drew on for their noirish myth-busting "horse operas."

"The Furies" is the name of a vast ranchland owned by T. C. Jeffords (Walter Huston), and it is also a Greek myth about the vengeance of women. Barbara Stanwyck plays Vance, T. C.'s daughter and heir apparent to the ranch. She is in every sense the hero, struggling with her conflicting desires to love her father, to triumph over him, to love and lose the Mexican squatter who lives on T. C.'s land with his family, and, finally, to marry a banker/gambler who slaps her and swindles her. *The Furies* is set in a permanent dusk. Mann's noirish lighting for exteriors as well as interiors creates a pattern of silhouettes, rendering the figures iconic, mythic, and discursive. Stanwyck is posed repeatedly with her hands on her hips, legs spread, and head high—the image of a hero.

Jacques Rancière says of Mann's westerns that "the film fable is a thwarted fable."[7] Narration and storytelling are challenged by the visual style, so while the "fable" of *The Furies* may be about land ownership and succession, the movie is about much more than this, including the openness of the landscape and its promise of a new social order, as well as the power of angry women. For Rancière, the "visual order" of Mann's cinema tends to outstrip the director's control,[8] and in this case it's possible that Stanwyck outsmarted her director, because in 1957 Mann said that "women do not have much importance in westerns," as they just get in the way, apparently forgetting or dismissing his work with Stanwyck.[9] Women became increasingly important in postwar westerns as cues to the deep contradictions in the genre, and Stanwyck's contribution is critical in this respect. In *The Furies* her power is further underscored by the parallel powers of other angry women who help her along the way.

Vance's triumph at the end of the film is to win the ranch, as well as her father's love and respect; she sacrifices her independence, though, while the corruption and racism that has secured the landholding remains firmly in place and the status quo upheld. Indeed, Rancière's summary of James Stewart's character at the end of *The Man from Laramie* (1955) fits Stanwyck's at the end of *The Furies*: "Although they were once masters of the game, they will all fall, as the story nears the end, before this man who embodies neither the law nor the land, nor the paternal image: this man whose whole secret is to know that the door of the house is closed for good and who passes by coming hither and going thither, tormenting their dreams with the mute jingling of the expropriated."[10]

Rancière does not discuss *The Furies*, and in fact, like Mann, he dismisses the question of a female hero by noting that the heroine constitutes "an eternal problem of Western narration."[11] The opening titles of *The Furies* likewise obscure Stanwyck's role by celebrating T. C. as the "king" who "wrote this flaming page in the history of the great Southwest." And yet it is Vance who appears in every scene and whose actions propel the narrative, and she meets all of Rancière's criteria for a Mannian hero who is not a moralist but one who acts: "And that's it. He does some things."[12] She may not seem to be the one who arrives from elsewhere (that's her brother who enters and abruptly vacates the movie in its first few scenes), but she is from another time, which is postwar America, revisiting the "period of the end of the Western, that moment when its images were being severed from its beliefs and put to use in a new game."[13] Rancière says that Mann does not play games but, rather, explores the "potential" of legends, the means by which a myth becomes a fable. Here the fable is nevertheless a game of "what if" a woman were to inherit everything, and we learn that the problem of narration is precisely the problem of the hero's success ("the hero's success is the success of the film"), because while she wins the ranch, her son will bear the surname Darrow, her father's nemesis, and thus her victory is compromised—or perhaps it is only the patriarchal law of succession that is the problem.

Stanwyck's "psychological" performance is accomplished by assuming different tones in her various relationships and by changing tones abruptly within scenes. She has said that working with Walter Huston was one of the highlights of her career, and in their scenes together she teases him and pleases him, unruffled by his bombast and meeting his gaze with laughing eyes. In a nod toward the Electra complex, Vance haunts her dead mother's bedroom, dons her wedding dress, and coddles luxurious gifts from T. C. She scratches his back just the way he likes it, and T. C. scoffs when they discuss a potential husband for her. He says it will be hard because "I've spoiled most of them for you," which at least one critic has misquoted to say that she is the one who is spoiled.[14] In the universe of Anthony Mann, the

Barbara Stanwyck and Gilbert Roland in *The Furies* (1950)

slippage is entirely legitimate. Everyone is "spoiled" by T. C.'s patriarchal capitalism, especially the Spanish-speaking squatters.

Vance's relationship with Juan Herrera (Gilbert Roland) is especially charged with dangerous passion. Their rendezvous out on the frontier are intercut with her scenes with Rip Darrow (Wendell Cory). Vance and Juan share a ritual of breaking bread together, as they have been "best friends" forever, and yet their kiss suggests much more than friendship. Vance nevertheless turns on Juan abruptly, shifting from lover to master, intoning her father's feudal logic, before kissing him. Despite her conflicting emotions, these are daring images of miscegenation, and the passion of their meetings belies the ostensible limits to their transgressive relationship.[15] Vance's empathy for the Herrera family points to a more modern, utopian vision of the American frontier that is violently crushed by her father. When she flees from T.C., she joins the Herrera family in their fortress perched on top of a rocky hill in the desert, strangely medieval in appearance. Their vengeance is archaic, mythic, and revolutionary, standing up to the feudal landowner, but the scene ends with the hanging of Vance's erstwhile lover. Juan asks her not to beg for his life and she doesn't. Instead she turns with rage against her father, vowing to bring him down.

Vance's vengeance takes the form of smart business dealings, another instance of Stanwyck's character triumphing through intelligence. She buys back T. C.'s debt, with the help of Darrow. She then manages to find a way to buy T. C.'s cattle with the fake money that T. C. has distributed as "T.C."'s (IOUs paid to Hispanic laborers, for the most part) and is able to pay off the mortgage to the Anaheim family's bank. Rip Darrow owns a gambling house called the Legal Tender, which doubles as a bank, accessorized by showgirls—who Vance sends packing with a quick put-down. Banking and gambling are thus conjoined, as is bluffing and courting. Vance is tricked by Darrow early in the film, and she essentially learns to play his dirty games. Wendell Corey, as Rip Darrow, can barely crack a smile. His laconic style is mismatched with his rigid backbone, and he is in every way a man not to be trusted. Stanwyck's Vance is at first desperate for the love of a white man, even though she says several times that marriage would be like a bit in her mouth. And yet her wounded pride and love of freedom does not stand in the way of making the conclusive business arrangement of marriage by the end of the film. Her final words to Darrow are that he might have bit off more than he can chew, putting the bit firmly back in his mouth.

In addition to Vance, three other key women characters loom large in *The Furies*, and while they can hardly be said to be a "team," as they never even meet each other, they can be said to be the furies that finally drive T. C. to his grave—and the Old West with him. Judith Anderson plays Flo, Vance's nemesis, who T. C. brings home as his new wife. In an impulsive frenzy, Vance throws a pair of scissors in Flo's face, right in her dead mother's bedroom. This act of violence raises Stanwyck's character to the status of psychological hero with untapped wells of anger, registered in her wide-open eyes and the physical charge of her thrust. The disfigured stepmother finally refuses T. C. a bailout when he really needs it, so she strikes her own blow against the patriarch.

Another "fury" in T. C.'s decline is the banker's wife, Mrs. Anaheim (Beulah Bondi). Vance plays a woman's game with her, refusing a date with Mr. Anaheim and expressing sympathy for a woman with a philandering husband (as T. C. flagrantly deceived Vance's mother when she was alive). Stanwyck turns on a different kind of charm here, although she is still trading on her sex appeal, agreeing *not* to use it in exchange for Mrs. Anaheim persuading her husband to extend T. C.'s mortgage. At age forty-three, Stanwyck is playing a woman in her twenties or thirties, and Vance is clever enough to push the buttons of older women. The mortgage is extended, and thus Vance's gamble pays off. She still has the mortgage to pay, though, and T. C.'s workers are still shafted with worthless "T.C.'s," although neither consequence is noted in the film. Her empire remains a precarious one, as written in the dark sky over her return to the Furies, passing under the wrought-iron sign pictured backward with writing in reverse.

The most furious fury in *The Furies* is Juan's mother, Mrs. Herrera (Blanche Yurka), who finally shoots T. C. in the back and kills him. With his last breath, he compliments her on her marksmanship and then announces the end of an era: "There will never be another like me." Referred to repeatedly over the course of the film as "the witch," Mrs. Herrera is the embodiment of all of those who have been disenfranchised and broken by western expansion and imperialism. She and Vance cross paths only once in the film, and Juan mediates between them to convince his mother to cease her attack on T. C. as the assault on the hilltop escalates. Vance's presence in the fortress saves her father the first time, only because Juan speaks for her. She is, for once, silent, but her whiteness nevertheless speaks power. "Mother witch," Herrera cackles loudly while shooting at the ranchers, howls when her son is hanged, and laughs hysterically at her own crack shot when T. C. falls. Vance swears at the hanging that she will take T. C.'s world away from him, and she does, with the help of these other women.

The Old West is dead, again, as it would repeatedly die over the course of the decade. Stanwyck always wished she had made a film with "Duke" Wayne, but she didn't need to. The point is made here that the West inherited by women and those who have crossed the white patriarch is not the mythical West of the open frontier but a violent terrain of ethnic cleansing, misogyny, corruption, and sex trafficking. Of all the women-centered westerns made during the studio era, *The Furies* is perhaps the darkest. Mann's fable of a man's last stand is indeed thwarted by the vengeance of those whom he has wronged. The promise of the open prairie is crushed by capitalist patriarchy despite the violent vengeance of the women of the range. Walter Huston's death shortly after the production wrapped served to obfuscate the film's deep-seated counter-myth in favor of the great actor's passing.

Sam Fuller's extreme style in *Forty Guns* is completely different from Mann's mythic formalism. Fuller uses kinetic editing, extreme close-ups and long shots, slow dissolves, special effects, extra-long tracking shots, and musical interludes within a cinemascope framing that seems to have its own inner violence. It is not as dark as *The Furies*, but it is nevertheless darkened with passing clouds and a full-blown tornado. The working title, "Woman with a Whip," was retained by the theme song and crooned repeatedly by Jidge Carroll, who also plays the owner of the town bathhouse. As Jessica Drummond, Stanwyck has a fabulous entrance, galloping across the landscape on a white stallion followed by forty men riding in formation, just like Marlon Brando and his biker gang enter *The Wild One* (1953). Dressed all in black, she does actually whip a man later in the film, although she also commands through her swagger and her husky voice. Jessica Drummond is larger than life, a caricature of a powerful "baroness"—or landowner—lording it over her forty guns and the whole neighborhood, and yet Stanwyck inhabits this woman with her usual authority, rendering her charming and vulnerable as well as tyrannical and fearless.

John Ericson and Barbara Stanwyck in *Forty Guns* (1957)

The image presented by Jessica Drummond is nothing if not a dominatrix, and *Forty Guns* is first and foremost a campy fantasy of female empowerment. Its satirical flavor and ironic display of western iconography, language, love, and gender is yet another incarnation of the myth of the last western, but it also initiates a new cycle of arty and somewhat satirical westerns insofar as Fuller's stylized excess is taken up by Sergio Leone and Akira Kurosawa in the 1960s. Fuller's collaboration with Stanwyck built on her status in 1957 as the queen of the western, earned over the previous decade, and establishes her as the wise older woman of the West, who recognizes and embraces the end of an era. He insisted on casting Stanwyck, despite the fact that Marilyn Monroe wanted the part and was under contract with Fox.[16] Even if *Forty Guns* is comedic and satirical on one level, it enables Stanwyck to engage with a dynamic, performative character. It's not only Fuller's flashy stylistic techniques that makes *Forty Guns* an important transitional film from "Classical Hollywood" to the modern independent cinema of the post-classical era; it's also Stanwyck's "knowing" characterization of a western performer.[17]

Fuller's script was rejected by Darryl Zanuck in 1953 because, as Lisa Dombrowski puts it, "multiple and diffused story lines, overly powerful women, and castles and caviar simply had no place in a Fox western,"[18] so Fuller produced it independently. Distributed by 20th Century Fox, it played as a B movie and as popular drive-in fare but was not released as an A-list film. Jean-Luc Godard nevertheless paid homage to it in *Breathless* (1969), which ensured the film's—and Fuller's—longevity. The main story involves the arrival of federal marshal Griff Bonell (Barry Sullivan) and his two brothers in town to arrest a man named Swain, one of Jessica's forty guns (aka thieves, aka dragoons, aka sheriff's deputies). Jessica's brother Brockie (John Ericson) is a "wet-nosed" juvenile delinquent who creates havoc in town by carelessly killing the blind marshal (Hank Worden, in a reprise of his role as Mose Harper in *The Searchers*).[19] Griff locks up Brockie and Jessica gets him out; Griff picks up Swain peaceably from Jessica's long and laden dinner table—attended by her forty men—after which she clears the room with a wave and a couple of glances, and the hero (Griff) and the star (Stanwyck) proceed to flirt and conduct their business.[20]

In their first scene together, Jessica asks if she can "feel it"—Griff's trademark Colt revolver—and he reluctantly hands it over. She flips it expertly in her hand, and he warns her, "It might go off in your face." The film is riddled with such sexual innuendo, delivered in deadpan, along with casual references to violence and guns. She offers him the job of sheriff, saying, "A popular killer like you is sure to be elected." Griff, like Johnny Guitar, is another "retired" gunslinger, haunting the West with unconvincing pacifism, which Fuller pretends is a critique of violence but is actually only a joke. With the help of his brothers, Griff gets his man, plus another along the way, but then his brother and "second gun," Wes (Gene Barry), is killed on his wedding day by Brockie, so he has to kill Brockie, which, eventually, he does.

Within and among this litter of bodies, the romance between Griff and Jessica evolves as if between a king and queen, whose power is comparable, even equal. They each have authority over their siblings, who in turn make them vulnerable, and they each sit upon massive reputations. And yet the discourse of power is nevertheless bolstered by the detail of subordination and vulnerability, beginning with the blind sheriff, who tries and fails to sneak out of town when Brockie starts threatening him. Warden acts mentally impaired, but like Mose Harper, he bears the burden of truth in his blindness. A "half-breed" woman knocked up by Brockie is dispatched by Jessica with a handout, because power needs subordination. A group of Native American bystanders witness the killing of Wes. The lady gunsmith Wes is married to for thirty seconds is literally the target of a series of misogynist jokes comparing her to a gun (although she gets hers when she says to Wes after their first kiss, "Any recoil?").

Jessica's overwrought mansion, fronted by columns and hung with heavy curtains and chandeliers, converges around a foyer table on which stands a dark-skinned figurine dressed like an outlaw, slung with gun belts. This is not a typical example of what Henry Gates Jr. calls "Sambo Art," although it does appear to be what he calls "racist memorabilia,"[21] and it is

Barbara Stanwyck and Oakie the stunt horse in *Forty Guns* (1957)

a curious object to find in the middle of the film. Perhaps it is a symbol of the role-playing and posturing that enables the inversion of gender and racial norms. It gets knocked over in a brawl and is fondled by the lawyer who brings the news about the end of Jessica's reign. The point of all of these marginal figures is to underscore Griff's and Jessica's underlying empathy and humanism. They profit from violence, but they have the "power" to be caring people nonetheless. Griff, for example, says he asks forgiveness from those he kills, like an Indian does to an animal before the slaughter, a non sequitur that underlines the contradictions within their "humanism."

The theme song for *Forty Guns* analogizes the woman with a horse that needs breaking, parking its misogyny in the middle of Stanwyck's bravura performance, and the ending likewise sees Jessica capitulate to domesticity. She runs after Griff as he leaves town, proving the song right—that she's "only a woman after all." Fuller says that the ending was forced on him by the studio, although it was exactly the way he wrote it in his original and revised scripts.[22] It is a disappointingly generic ending to what Dombrowski calls "a very untidy and problematic plot."[23] Griff has just wounded Jessica as she tries to shield her brother. He walks by her prone body, saying, "She'll live," which would have been another place to end the story, more in keeping with the "untidy" plot. However, Jessica's surprising resurrection proves within the logic of the film that she's "big enough to forgive," but it also means she's spared the fate of Phyllis Dietrichson and avoids becoming martyred for the crime of power. She has already lost everything by paying her debt to Uncle Sam for withheld taxes, so the couple riding off into extreme long shot suggests that maybe a woman in charge does not necessarily entail the end of everything but the beginning of something else.

Stanwyck certainly hoped that *Forty Guns* would kick-start a new stage in her career. She routinely said that she was born to be a stunt rider and she longed for a chance to do action scenes with horses (see chapter R). She notoriously did her own stunts in *Forty Guns*, insisting on being dragged by a horse for three takes as Fuller and cameraman Joseph Biroc adjusted their lenses. She may have been bruised, but she nevertheless proved that age is not an obstacle for a performer who really cares about her role. It did not really work out, though, because except for two episodes of *Wagon Train* (1957–1965) and a couple of scenes in the 112 episodes of *Big Valley*, she saw little "action" in her subsequent TV westerns, where she is mostly housebound.

Nevertheless, Stanwyck's dominatrix performance is very much the climax of the cycle of woman-centered westerns of the studio era, and she pulls it off with the panache of a drag queen. Stanwyck's cross-dressing does not render her masculine but simply intimidating. She fully inhabits the paraphernalia of the western outlaw, including the black hat, boots, studded belt, and leather whip; she rides fast and straight and delivers her orders in the commanding voice that she mastered decades earlier. Her stride and her gestures are deliberate and directed. Her stylized performance in the action scenes, however, is balanced in her romantic scenes with Sullivan, in which she relaxes into a more confessional mode that nevertheless retains a high level of witty innuendo. In a long monologue, lying on her back in a shack where she and Griff have taken shelter from the tornado, Jessica recounts her many accomplishments. Stanwyck's voice is throaty and terribly relaxed. She holds Griff's hand and finishes by telling him that the frontier is closed, it's all over, so he should "throw in" with her because she needs a "strong man to carry out my orders." When he replies "and a weak one to take them," she says her throat is dry and kisses him to cut him off. The off-screen lovemaking presumably continues.

If the old men of the West, like John Wayne, John Huston's T. C. Jeffords, and even Barry Sullivan's Griff Bonell in *Forty Guns*, get tired as they become iconic, Stanwyck's Jessica Drummond and Vance Jeffords are women with a new kind of energy. Despite the metaphor of the wild horse that needs to be tamed, the new woman of the West comes alive in her iconicity. She cracks her whip in anger, but she offers a new kind of authority that is not afraid of loving. Stanwyck's performance can be called "camp" because it is role-playing of the highest order. And yet it is not simply empty style as Susan Sontag's famous definition of camp implies, because as David M. Halpern argues in *How to Be Gay*, camp "enables us to see identities as compelling acts of social theater, instead of as essences."[24] He claims that camp as a mode of viewing and aesthetic appreciation is "the foundation of a political strategy of social contestation and defiance."[25] Likewise, the curious Sambo art in Jessica Drummond's mansion offers another image of role-playing that is a sleight-of-hand gesture of civil rights activism hidden in the decline of the Old West. The next stage of Stanwyck's career was that of a gay icon, whether she liked it or not.

GAMBLING LADIES
PLAYING GAMES

On gambling. There is a certain structure of fate that can be recognized only in money, and a certain structure of money that can be recognized only in fate.

—Walter Benjamin, *The Arcades Project*

The game [of poker] exemplifies the worst aspects of capitalism that have made our country so great.

—Walter Matthau

GAMBLING IS SAID TO BE A METAPHOR for the American Dream because it offers the opportunity for anyone to succeed, regardless of pedigree.[1] At the same time, there is little doubt that gambling is a male domain, which makes it less than a level playing field for all Americans. A poker player in Barbara Stanwyck's 1949 film *The Lady Gambles* tells Stanwyck's character, Joan Boothe, flatly that "women and gambling don't mix." Aaron M. Duncan cites one of the few professional women poker players as saying that the sexism that is endemic to the game can actually help her, as men doubt her skill.[2] And yet women have never been entirely absent from the "scene" of poker and have long played a critical role, especially in films about gambling, in which they never simply blend into the scenery. In Stanwyck's gambling roles, the stakes are always high, as it is her body on the line. Her characters bet their social status and play to escape from the social roles to which they are assigned. As a gambler in Hollywood, she kept ahead of the game by taking risks and keeping her cards close.

Stanwyck made two movies in which she stars as a gambler: *Gambling Lady* (Archie Mayo, 1934) and *The Lady Gambles* (Michael Gordon, 1949). Comparing these two films indicates that gambling served women well in the conjunction of cinema and modernity in the first part of the twentieth century, in pre-Code Hollywood. However, in the postwar period, any potential in assigning a woman the role of gambler was radically curtailed. Stanwyck also plays gamblers in other films, especially westerns such as *California* and *The Great Man's Lady* and, of course, in the screwball comedy *The Lady Eve* (see chapter L). Why are women gamblers referred to in these titles as "ladies"? Is it because a lady is a woman who performs a social role and gambling is a performance art?

Stanwyck's particular affinity for the role of the gambler pertains to the duplicity of her acting style. She very frequently "plays" her leading men, posing as something she is not. Characters such as Phyllis Dietrichson in *Double Indemnity* and Thelma Jordan in the film of that name lead the viewer, as they do the duped lover, into believing in one face of a two-faced woman. If Stanwyck's performances can be considered to be duplicitous, we could further describe her acting in these roles as a form of play, as a poker player bluffs his or her opponent.

In playing role-playing characters, Stanwyck's acting is frequently aligned with the gambler's performance in the playing of games. The notion of play, or *Spiel*, is a central concept for Walter Benjamin, for whom the gambler is a critical figure in that he sustains an archaic mode of experience within modernity: living for the moment, experiencing the "innervation" of chance, a heightened receptivity, and a "bodily presence of mind."[3] Miriam Hansen has convincingly unpacked this conceptual theme in Benjamin's work, to claim that the term *Spiel*, with its linked connotations of performing and gambling "allows Benjamin to imagine an alternate mode of aesthetics that could counteract, at the level of sense perception, the political consequences of the failed ... reception of technology."[4] Film thus comes to serve the crucial function of a possible site for the recovery of experience in technological modernity. Acting itself may not have been a gamble for Stanwyck, as she had great confidence in her abilities, but signing onto any picture in Hollywood was necessarily risky, given the contingencies of studio production methods. Nevertheless, given her rags-to riches narrative, she embodied the social mobility that gambling promised, and her method was precisely in her performativity. When she plays a gambler, which she doesn't do nearly enough, she plays a subject with agency who is perpetually imperiled by the rigged game of narrative cinema.

After July 1934, when the Production Code began to be enforced more rigorously, one sees much less gambling in American films, with a few notable exceptions, such as the films discussed here. Although gambling per se is not specified in any iteration of the code,[5] it was very likely considered to be among those subjects lowering the moral standards of the audience. On the "analysis" forms that the PCA censors completed

Barbara Stanwyck in *The Great Man's Lady* (1941)

for each film, one line is specifically to indicate gambling and how much of it is seen in the film. If the gambling concerned "unsympathetic characters," then it might be condoned, but, then again, exceptions abound, including *The Lady Eve* and *The Lady Gambles*. As the epigraphs to this section indicate, the morality of gambling is complex, given that financial capitalism is but a slight variation on games of risk. However, the debate, as one scholar has put it, is "never about gambling: it is about different ways of being in the world."[6]

One curious Stanwyck film in this respect is *The Great Man's Lady*, based on several stories by women writers and directed by William Wellman (see chapter Y).[7] The so-called great man (played by Joel McCrea) manages to become a heroic town builder only because his wife, played by Stanwyck, helps him every step of the way. One of her first triumphs is to win back the house and livestock that he loses in a poker game to the local gambler played by Brian Donlevy. She crosses paths again and again with the gambler and even works in his casino for a scene or two, but no actual games are played on screen. As a saloon girl, Stanwyck has an opportunity to wear an elegant full-skirted dress in a film where she is also seen in chaps. In *The Great Man's Lady* gambling is an important story element, but the games themselves are made completely invisible in a film that crams eighty years of western history into ninety minutes of screen time. Stanwyck's gamble with one of her favorite directors, William Wellman, did not pay off in this case.

The saloon girl is of course a mainstay of the western genre, serving as counterpart to the moralistic Eastern women who bear the "civilizing" mandate of domesticity, religion, and family in frontier culture. In his analysis of poker and the frontier myth in *My Darling Clementine* (1946), Aaron Duncan claims that "the empowered feminine motif does not fit the requirements of the Frontier myth."[8] He claims that the few strong female characters are "not true women" and that western women are either good and virginal or bad and sexual. In fact, I would argue that the frontier myth and the western genre provide fertile ground for the emergence of women who successfully challenge gender stereotypes. Even within *My Darling Clementine*, the saloon girl Chihuahua, played by Linda Darnell, is not entirely an unsympathetic character, even if she cheats and lies. As Duncan also points out, she is a tragic figure.[9] The "prostitute with a heart of gold" in the West is also a woman making it on her own, through card playing, performing, and often owning or running a saloon in extraordinarily harsh and violent conditions, radically challenging the conventions of Victorian morality and ladylike behavior (see chapter Q).

Women are commodities themselves in frontier culture, and unlike frontier wives, they are virtually communal property,[10] provoking conflict among sex-starved men. Once behind the roulette wheel or the blackjack deck, though, they gain a certain power over men in the other world of the saloon. Typically in the western narrative, the women are well protected by owners and staff who value their enticing presence. In stories of the Old West, most of the legendary gambling women are themselves heavily armed.[11] In Stanwyck's second film, *Mexicali Rose* (1929), she plays a saloon girl with loose morals who gambles with men and loses them one after another. The Mexican setting of a casino called the Gold Mine (*Mina de oro*) enables her to play a wisecracking strong-minded woman on the margins of "society," but in the end her life is worth even less than those of the Mexicans. She dies off-screen, presumably by suicide, her body found at the bottom of a cliff by fishermen. Stanwyck is top billed but not yet big enough to be bad and survive the ending, and Mexicali Rose is a woman who dies of bad luck.

Women gamblers in any Hollywood genre are unusual in that they tend to play both sides of the morality game. Frowned on by some elements of society, they are nevertheless flamboyant and smart and thus seductive as spectacles and as characters, challenging the easy division between good girls and bad girls. In the pre-Code era, before the Hays Code was rigidly enforced, everyone got away with a lot more in Hollywood movies than they did after 1934.[12] One of Stanwyck's last pre-Code movies from this period is called *Gambling Lady*, in which gambling serves as an ideal mechanism for social climbing. As in *The Lady Eve*, made a few years later, "love" is the alibi for social mobility; so while the women in each film are accused of gold digging, the 1934 film conflates love with honesty in a culture of deceit.

Stanwyck plays Lady Lee in *Gambling Lady*, the daughter of a professional poker player (whom she calls Mike and embraces like a lover). He commits suicide in the face of his debts, and she tries to clear his name with a gambling syndicate by working for them herself, but she insists on playing straight. The deal is that she attracts big-stakes gamblers but beats them through sheer smarts, although she eventually gets caught up in a sting operation when it is revealed that the "bodyguard" provided by the syndicate is rigged with cheating devices hidden in his clothes. In the process of the arrest, she falls in love with wealthy playboy Garry Madison (Joel McCrea), who is so innocent and naïve that he accidentally exposes the gambling den to the cops. Madison's father tries to buy Lady Lee off, but they cut cards for him and she wins.

Gambling Lady is in many ways a routine genre film, albeit with a good pace, advanced by quick cutting and newspaper headlines to move the plot along, such as "Girl Gambler in Crooked Game," with a photo of Lady beaming in her white fur coat like a movie star. The film combines elements of the crime film with gangsters, bookies, and cops, and elements of the romance genre. Stanwyck and McCrea, working together for the first time, are destined to fall in love, and in pre-Code Hollywood a gambling lady was able to survive the finale and successfully climb the social ladder. The narrative twists and turns of this story—which even critics of the time found to be too much[13]—are symptomatic of the aleatory mechanisms of melodrama. Coincidences, abrupt turns of luck, accidents, and deus ex machina endings are typical of melodrama and of Hollywood screenwriting more generally. Chance has long been recognized as constitutive of the melodramatic mode.[14]

Lady is warned that "society is only a game, and a racket," and her every move is tracked by newspaper headlines as reporters constantly swarm her. Lady's success at cards can only be attributed to her self-confidence, skill, and ability to dress the part and intimidate her opponents and, of course, luck (although this apparently runs out, which is why the syndicate sends in the loaded bodyguard). Her hands in the game Twenty-One are shown to be consistently perfect: two faces and an ace face. Lady's role in the syndicate is primarily to look good and to attract men to the table. The story

C. Aubrey Smith, Bob Montgomery, and Barbara Stanwyck in *Gambling Lady* (1934)

line follows her ability to secure a place in this social scene, which is to say her ability to gamble her way up the social ladder without compromising her integrity.

Lady's status as spectacle is not incidental to this achievement. From the moment she starts working for the syndicate, and throughout her society marriage, Lady is adorned with stylish gowns designed by Orry-Kelly. *Gambling Lady* exemplifies the social mobility of the New Woman characteristic of pre-Code Hollywood. The dead animals drooping off her shoulders are in keeping with the fur styles of the period, although the foxes' heads signify the underlying cruelty of this competitive society that Lady is inducted into. Stanwyck falls back on her Brooklyn accent to deliver crack lines of "poker argot" securing her role in the high-class salons through her knowledge of the game, without moving Lady Lee too far from her working-class roots.

Lady finally manages to get her husband back but not without a few well-played bluffs along with some trademark card plays. She plays the society game on Sheila's terms when they bargain for Garry's alibi for a crime he probably didn't commit. Sheila (Claire Dodd) wins the first round, and Lady agrees to a divorce. Leaving the courtroom, she "leads with her ace" and insists to Garry that she is happy to be free, meanwhile clearly crying, in one of Stanwyck's trademark "I say one thing but mean the opposite" performances. Her bluff is transparent, but her playacting in this case is consistent with her expressive performance of an honest woman. Peter Madison, Garry's father (C. Aubrey Smith), who has a peculiar affection for Lady, sees her crying and helps his son win her back by bluffing Sheila. In the final reconciliation scene, Lady reaches out to Peter to include him in the couple's embrace, which is kind of creepy, especially given her rather close relationship with her father, Mike, in the opening scenes—of whom Peter was a fan as a fellow card player. The overabundance and proximity of fathers in *Gambling Lady* functions as an ideological buffer for Lady's triumphant social climbing, as the fathers implicitly authorize the class mixing that card play enables. But Lady wins the heart of a rich man by "playing it straight," which means playing a good honest game.

In 1949 Stanwyck played a very different gambling lady in *The Lady Gambles* (dir. Michael Gordon). The cycle of films that became known as "social problem films" were promoted as serious "prestige" films tackling real social issues. Well-known titles such as *The Lost Weekend* (1945, about alcoholism) and *The Man with the Golden Arm* (1955, about heroin addiction), and even *On the Waterfront* (1954, about labor unions) and *Pinky* (1949, about anti-Black racism), are counted among the many social problem films that emerged in the postwar period. As Chris Cagle has pointed out, the rise of this cycle closely coincided with the rise of sociology as an academic discipline.[15] While many such films adopted a functionalist sociological approach, shifting the focus from the individual to the society at large, many of them also incorporated a psychoanalytic approach in which the "sick" person is cured through a narrative analysis and their pathology is "explained" by family drama.

The press book for *The Lady Gambles* stressed the documentary realism of the set, including a replica of the Flamingo Club in Las Vegas (called the Pelican Club in the film), and the coaching supplied by a professional gambler. Magazine articles of the time underlined the recognition of gambling addiction as a psychological disorder.[16] However, the *New York Times* dismissed the film as an "exploitation of a picturesque pastime" and a "rehash of *The Lost Weekend* with dice instead of liquor and a woman in place of a man."[17] Unlike Stanwyck's 1934 gambling film, details of the card games being played are withheld, presumably to respect the "high moral standards" prescribed by the Production Code.

The Lady Gambles starts out with a sociological framework but concludes with a psychoanalytic explanation for Joan Boothe's gambling addiction. The film is structured through flashbacks narrated and strung together by Joan's husband, Dave (Robert Preston), while she lies comatose in a police hospital ward. She has been beaten up in an alleyway over a crap game with loaded dice—the scene that opens the film. Dave tells his story of her descent to a doctor, starting with an introduction to the glittery city of Las Vegas. He had taken her there because he had journalistic work to do at the Hoover Dam, a monument of New Deal infrastructure, of which we see several grand stock shots. It is precisely this liberal, positivist, scientism that sociology and psychoanalysis promised in postwar America and that Hollywood adopted as a means of elevating the industry beyond mere entertainment.

Shortly after arriving in Las Vegas, Joan meets a casino boss named Corrigan (Stephen McNally), who gives her some house chips to use while she takes "candid" photos of gamblers while her husband is off doing his research. Her amateur journalism is quickly abandoned when she starts to win, and Corrigan hires her as a shill until she starts working at poker games in addition to the house games such as roulette and dice. She dips into the family money in the casino safe, loses it, wins it back, and from there on seems to be addicted. Joan's ups and downs include poker and dice and also horse racing (a favorite occupation of Stanwyck herself). When Corrigan hires her to pose as a racetrack owner for his syndicate, she foolishly bets on their carefully planned long-shot horse, the bookies notice, the odds drop, and Corrigan finally kicks her out. In *The Lady Gambles* Corrigan and his syndicate of thugs represent the evils of gambling, and they are much more malevolent than the syndicate in Stanwyck's 1934 film, in which the syndicate operates almost like a corporate board, implicitly linking capitalism to corruption, which was a popular theme in the 1930s.

Stanwyck is dressed in this film once again by Orry-Kelly, and she becomes more elegantly attired as she becomes more immersed in the casino scene. Corrigan wants her to "dress up" the games in his poker den, but her role in the film, and in the game, is less as a lure than as a troubled specimen of the dangers of gambling. The doubling that takes place in *The Lady Gambles* is between Stanwyck's housewife persona, which really does not sit well with her, and the trance-like state she assumes when she becomes energized at the craps table. In several instances her eyes light up before she winds up to throw the dice. She leans over the table with fire in her eyes, coming alive with the energy and excitement of the game, a lone woman among a crowd of men. Her passion with the dice far surpasses any passion with her husband (who actually pushes her away in one scene) or with Corrigan, whom she spurns repeatedly. At one point during a brief hiatus, the Boothe

Barbara Stanwyck in *The Lady Gambles* (1949)

couple retreat to a cottage in Mexico so that he can write, but when he leaves for a research trip, she is left alone with her housework and her demons. She restlessly folds laundry until she cracks open the box with their life savings, suggesting that part of her problem is simply with being a housewife.

Despite Corrigan's declared attraction to Joan, theirs is less a love affair than another masochistic act on her part, as he is clearly using her for his own ends. As an object of desire, she is strangely abject and unsexy. At the age of forty-three, Stanwyck was still getting regular parts, although she was also transitioning into roles playing middle-age women (into which she was frequently able to inject some passion and sexuality), but here her sexuality is evident only at the bottom of her fall, when Joan may even be turning tricks in those small towns, where she is finally found in a coma by her husband. When she is consorting with Corrigan and gambling behind her husband's back, men comment on her poor manicure and hair, not because she looks especially bad but because she uses hair and manicure appointments as alibis for her gambling. (Ironically, when she is finally down and out, her hair has become blonde.)

Joan's real problem, as determined by the doctor to whom Dave tells the whole sordid story, is her sister, Ruth (Edith Barrett), who from the outset comes between Joan and Dave. She seems like an overbearing mother, constantly nagging Joan, until it is finally revealed that Ruth accuses Joan of killing their mother, who died during Joan's birth. Thus the pathology of Joan's habit is explained as her self-loathing and self-punishment, a masochistic addiction to losing. However, this explanation does not entirely explain the web of gazes that have her so caught up, starting with the surveillance in the casino that quickly caught her trying to take her own photos of gamblers. *The Lady Gambles* is not only a social problem picture; it is also a woman's film—of the variant categorized by Mary Ann Doane as the "medical discourse" in which a male doctor paternalistically treats a woman's psychic suffering through narrative explanation.[18] The medical discourse in *The Lady Gambles* is overlaid with the investigative journalism of her husband, which is in turn conjoined with the documentary voice-over of the sociological film narrator, whose discourse lifts her individual problem onto the level of society at large. Montages of cityscapes accompany Dave's tales of her travels through the small towns and gambling halls of America.

Clearly, we are a long way from the utopian aspirations and triumphs of the gambling ladies of the 1930s. The adoring fathers Mike and Pete in *Gambling Lady* have been replaced by the containing and controlling discourses of scientific representation and explanation. Benevolent fathers have given way to the dangers of "Momism" (see chapter D).[19] Nevertheless, Stanwyck's performance of gambling inscribes a resistance within the film, offering a counterpoint to the dead world of the journalist's wife.

The Lady Gambles echoes Benjamin's remarks on gambling most closely and is suggestive of the contradictory and conflicting effects of feminizing the gambling subject. After a long night of poker, the professional gambler Horace Corrigan offers a short treatise to Joan on the pleasures of gambling. Against her objection, in the presence of her sister, that gambling is "noisy, confusing, and just a little dirty," Corrigan assures her that it is really about the scene and the room itself (dressed up with her presence): "the game, the fight, the fear, and the peace that comes with licking that fear, even when you lose." She reluctantly agrees, after which he adds, "I'm right about a lot of things," joining the ranks of the paternalistic voices in the film. And yet Stanwyck's performance at the craps table invokes the kind of intoxication that Benjamin embraces and, in the context of this rather abject film, a point of resistance. Benjamin links gambling to rites of passage and thresholds, of which he notes there are few in modern life: "We have become very poor in threshold experiences."[20] For Benjamin, the "heroic" component of gambling is in the reflexive, instinctual behavior that defies reason and speculation—precisely the trance-like stare that Stanwyck's character assumes at the craps table.

The reliance on chance may make gambling a parodic critique of capitalism,[21] but here it can be read as a critique of postwar rationalized society and its subjectification of women as pathological. In this sense, Stanwyck's curious regaining of her sexuality at the bottom of the pit of her social addiction is also a sign of life in an otherwise dead world. A couple of times, she is asked by a gentleman to "kiss 'em, baby," because she brings good luck. She does so as a ritual offering, as if the dice might one day let her tell her own story. She acts a part, but the game in 1949 has less to do with social mobility than with escape from patriarchy, domesticity, and the network of gazes that has her so entrapped. In fact, the promise of social mobility for a woman is lost, along with her agency—outside the drama of the game. The fire in her eyes at the roll of the dice signals a spark of resistance and a regaining of her gaze after the instigating loss of her camera. She is at a threshold that, decades later, we can perhaps help her cross.

Stanwyck's gambling films may not be representative of all the lady gamblers in studio-era Hollywood, but they are certainly indicative of the ways that gambling intersects with the genres, cycles, and styles of films of the 1930s and '40s. Once the woman crosses over from being solely aligned with the spectacle that lures the gambler to the table and becomes a gambler herself, the terms are going to be slightly inverted. She not only becomes a player, but she owns the scene as well. In the 1930s female characters had extraordinary latitude in what they could accomplish, especially in the pre-Code period, when their sexuality could be flaunted. At the end of that era, and at the cusp of the more "contained" and controlled films of the 1940s, *The Lady Eve* uses gambling as a particularly subversive social critique, precisely through the playful use of performance. By the late 1940s, only a subversive reading can salvage the sociological discourse that blames women for all the sins of the world.

WILLIAM HOLDEN
MAKING MEN

Hollywood knows that it is a sex symbol for the world
and does its best to live up to the reputation.
In Hollywood, sex is regarded as a means of getting ahead,
a form of excitement and fun, a function of power.

—Hortense Powdermaker, *Hollywood: The Dream Factory*

WILLIAM HOLDEN AND BARBARA STANWYCK appeared in only two movies together, but they established a relationship that lasted several decades. Tracking that relationship provides valuable insight into Stanwyck's ability to negotiate the gossip machine in tandem with her film roles, her work on sets, and her status as a single woman after 1950. While rumors abound regarding the two of them having had an affair, little evidence exists.[1] In fact the only testimony of her sexual relationship with anyone outside her two marriages is with Robert Wagner, who wrote about it in his autobiography. He says that their affair ended after four years because "I would always be Mr. Stanwyck, and we both knew it."[2] Wagner and Stanwyck met on the set of *Titanic* when Wagner was twenty-three years old and Stanwyck was forty-six. She was eleven years older than Holden, twenty-three years older than Wagner, and four years older than her second husband, Robert Taylor. The reasons for her breakup with Taylor are speculative, but underlying their relationship was the perception of him, too, becoming "Mr. Stanwyck."

The fact that Stanwyck was attracted to younger men takes us beyond the realm of gossip when we consider it in light of her role as tutor and mentor to these men. When we talk about "production culture," we mean the networked relationships that sustain the industry. Studies of Hollywood by theorists such as John Caldwell and Sherry Ortner use interviews and textual analysis to explore the "social interactions and professional rituals" that define the spaces of production.[3] Victoria Wilson's biography of Stanwyck likewise relies a great deal on interviews with Stanwyck's surviving colleagues, friends, and relatives and provides a valuable ethnographic account of a woman at the center of the Hollywood machine.

The first anthropology of Hollywood was written by Hortense Powdermaker in 1951, based on extensive fieldwork and interviews in Los Angeles with sources whom she kept anonymous by nicknaming them things like "Miss Enterprise," "Mr. Prestige," "Mr. Newcomer," and so on. Using this method, she was able to drill down to the inner workings of the industry that the studios left out of their own extensive self-promotion. For example, on the basis of interviews with actors at all levels of the industry, she points to the paucity of training and how infrequently directors offered creative, imaginative coaching for actors. Powdermaker, however, had little insight into the different experiences of men and women in the industry.

An ethnography that draws on biography and celebrity journalism is inevitably compounded by the performative element of such writing. Nevertheless, the palimpsest of texts that encase Stanwyck's relationship with Holden and other men might be conceived as a mode of industrial ethnography. As Sherry Ortner describes her ethnography of independent Hollywood in the early 2000s, "It is an open-ended set of strategies for getting at how people differently positioned than oneself, socially, culturally, and historically, see the world in their own terms."[4] Interpretation of social and cultural texts such as interviews and publicity documents cannot completely reveal the social and political dynamics within the world of studio-era Hollywood, but they can help to paint pictures of that "scene" as it evolved over several decades. Caldwell's "culture as an interpretive system" approach is one that must always be seen as "fully embedded in the play of power and politics."[5]

In the case of Stanwyck, the story of her liaison with Holden allows a glimpse of her role on set and off as an older woman with knowledge and wisdom in Hollywood. A related anecdote from the set of *The Strange Love of Martha Ivers* about Stanwyck's mentoring of Kirk Douglas, nine years her junior, points to a pattern of behavior. Producer Hal Wallis said, "I knew I was taking a risk pitting a newcomer against that powerhouse Stanwyck, … but she was extraordinarily considerate and played unselfishly with him in every scene."[6] Stanwyck and Holden's relationship is simply one more fairy tale among thousands, as the "facts" remain somewhat obscure, and yet it is nevertheless a vital piece of the networks and rituals of the studio era.

Stanwyck and Holden first met on the set of *Golden Boy*, directed by Rouben Mamoulian, based on a play by Clifford Odets, who was closely associated with the New York–based Group Theatre. The play about a young Italian boxer whose father wants him to stick to violin playing, while he is tempted by the money and spectacle of boxing, had a successful Broadway run in 1937–1938, but by the time it got to the screen, it had lost some of its edginess. Screenwriters Lewis Meltzer and Daniel Taradash changed the ending from a tragic car crash, in which Joe Bonaparte and his girlfriend, Lorna Moon, die in a downward spiral of despair, to a happy ending, in which they have hope for a new future, free of the corruption and violence of the boxing world. Lorna Moon (Stanwyck's character) is an assistant to Tom Moody (Adolphe Menjou), Joe's manager, and also his mistress, although their relationship is made vague on the screen in order to please the censors.[7] Both Joe—the boxer played by Holden—and Lorna are described in the play as having a "mystical feeling of lostness."[8] Victoria Wilson describes Odets's version of Lorna Moon as "there to serve as a mirror of male virtue, male aspiration, male sensitivity, and conflict."[9] Because Stanwyck was cast before or during the writing of the screenplay, the writers transformed Lorna Moon into a "wisecracking gal" suitable to Stanwyck's image. Unfortunately, she gets in only a couple of wisecracks and is frequently backgrounded by a large ensemble cast.

Columbia Pictures studio head Harry Cohn and Mamoulian gave the inexperienced Holden the opportunity to take the lead in Golden Boy after holding a public search in which they interviewed five thousand young men and screen-tested one hundred of them.[10] He was athletic-looking and could pass as both a boxer and a violinist. Holden began the shoot badly, arriving late, nervous, and possibly drunk. He would have been fired immediately if it hadn't been for Stanwyck, who not only convinced Mamoulian to keep him on but also coached him personally. Thus began their friendship, which Holden paid tribute to by notoriously sending flowers to Stanwyck's dressing room every April 1st to commemorate the first day of their collaboration.[11] In 1978 Bob Hope introduced Stanwyck and Holden as "the Golden Boy with his Golden Girl" to present an Oscar at the Academy Awards. On stage, Holden repeated the story of how Stanwyck "saved" him in 1939, and Stanwyck uncharacteristically broke into tears.[12]

How and what did Stanwyck teach Holden about acting? Stanwyck herself was untrained, except for her intense sessions with Willard Mack in 1926, which are described by Wilson as "grueling." They were preparing for The Noose, a play that Mack had partially rewritten after a failed opening. Stanwyck's chorus girl part had been expanded to give the third act more of an emotional charge.[13] According to Wilson, Mack taught her "how to read, how to walk, what tricks to use and not to use, and how to sell herself by entrances and exits."[14] She in turn taught Holden about stagecraft and timing and modulated her own performance to make him look better.[15] Wilson adds a new twist: "She spent hours digging beneath the surface of scenes to drag out some experience of Holden's that would help him."[16]

The deep-digging psychological method used before "the method" was introduced to Hollywood is what Cynthia Baron describes as "modern acting." Baron distinguishes this from the psychoanalytic perspective of Lee Strasberg: "By comparison, Stanislavsky and other Modern acting teachers saw actors as artists, whose minds and bodies form an organic whole, whose inner lives are necessarily connected to the social world around them, and whose work could be enhanced by gently accessing the rich storehouse of creativity available to all human beings."[17] Stanwyck had no more than on-the-job coaching once she arrived in Los Angeles, but given her compulsive script reading and memorizing, she evidently incorporated her own experience and analysis of the story into her creation of characters, which is very likely the method she imparted to Holden, along with other tricks of the trade she had learned from Mack—and from directors such as Frank Capra and William Wellman, with whom she had often worked productively.

In the resulting production of *Golden Boy*, Holden just manages the role but is completely overshadowed and overwhelmed by the blustery performances of Adolphe Menjou, Lee J. Cobb as his father, and Joseph Calleia as the gangster Eddie Fuseli, who buys the fighter from Menjou's character, Tom Moody. Even the secondary characters are exaggerated ethnic stereotypes, playing theatrically rather than cinematically. It was a lot to ask of a novice actor, and even the romantic scenes between Stanwyck and Holden frequently snap from soft to hard. Lorna first tries to persuade Joe to give up the violin for boxing, seducing him at the request of her boss, to whom she says, "I'm a dame from Newark. I know a dozen ways [to convince him]," but later in the film, once she is in love with Joe, she tries equally hard to persuade him not to be a boxer, as it is a corrupt and violent business. Against a back-projected New York skyline, and later in Central Park, their scenes together stand out only because of the isolation of the characters from the theatrics of the boxing culture and the Italian family home. The critical assessment of the film and their scenes is extremely varied, with some biographers describing their "chemistry" as dynamic and others decrying the hollowness of the characters. To my eye, Holden seems unable to crack a smile, and his character seems as stressed as the actor.

Golden Boy eventually gets to the big bout in Madison Square Garden (with location B-roll shots), where Mamoulian picks out portraits of audience members horrified and glued to the spectacle of violence. Joe

Barbara Stanwyck, Adolphe Menjou, and William Holden in *Golden Boy* (1939)

knocks out "the Chocolate Drop," an African American (played by the uncredited James "Cannonball" Green), who dies in the ring. An encounter with the man's father teaches Joe that "we all have our burdens," as if the Chocolate Drop were a part of Joe himself that he had killed and not a man set up to die for entertainment. Joe and Lorna return "home" to Papa, who embraces them both in a loving threesome, and the film ultimately fits the generic form of the boxing film as an inquiry into the values of monetary success and the spiritual costs of ambition in which the body of the actor is symbolic of the soul.[18] In *Golden Boy* Joe breaks his arm in his final bout, jeopardizing his musical career along with his future as a boxer.

Holden's real opportunity to show emotion is in the dressing room preparing for his big fight, where he cries miserably facedown on the table while being massaged by his trainer. He has lost Lorna to Moody (for the moment), and his father has just witnessed the two managers/gangsters treat Joe as a commodity that is designed to kill in order to make them rich. Stanwyck's best scenes are in the first part of the film, where she literally shadows Menjou as they walk and talk together doing the business of a boxing manager and his assistant. She wears a suit jacket with a skirt and carries a square purse under her arm. She speaks street slang, and although she has few lines, she remains central to the action, as one of the boys. She persuades Tom to take on the management of young Joe and repeats a small gesture of fixing Tom/Menjou's tie, indicating her affectionate control over him and his prodigy.

According to her biographers, Stanwyck was enraged by Mamoulian's tendency to lie to the actors that the camera was rolling when it wasn't. She told him that it was unprofessional, and Holden concurred that the director lost a good performance from Stanwyck, even if his own might have been intensified by the exhaustion. Stanwyck also apparently approved rushes that were Holden's best takes but not necessarily her own.[19] These tales from the set of *Golden Boy* are indicative of the challenges facing Stanwyck and how she rose to meet them, helping a younger actor along the way. In the process, she gained valuable respect and admiration from those on the sidelines and those, like Holden, in the spotlight.

Stanwyck's name "sold" *Golden Boy*, but it is not her film at all. She is stranded among the broad-stroked actors and the young novice. Lorna's relationship with Joe flip-flops with little motivation, and her relationship with Menjou's Moody is equally unconvincing, as the age difference on that side is seventeen years. She fares much better in Odets's *Clash by Night*, in which she is also torn between two men, but her character of a washed-up hard-living cynic is much more clearly defined. Despite the casualty of the film itself (in fact, the film did fairly well at the box office and did garner a few good reviews), Stanwyck's off-screen role in *Golden Boy* played a key part in her career. While many stars might have abandoned the ill-conceived project, she stuck to it and was recognized as having had a hand in its success that went beyond her own performance.

Holden and Stanwyck met again on-screen in *Executive Suite* (1954), a film that is notable in Stanwyck's career because it was the first time she did not receive top billing. In an ensemble cast of ten big names, Holden topped the list in the credits, followed by June Allyson and then Stanwyck. By this point Holden was at the peak of his career, while Stanwyck was pleased to be included in a prestige picture. Directed by Robert Wise and produced by John Houseman, *Executive Suite* is a soft critique of corporate culture, featuring Holden as one of six board members battling for control of a large furniture company. Stanwyck's character, Julia Tredway, is a major stockholder. Her late father co-owned the company with a man named Bullock, whose death initiates the power struggle. Julia is a sad lady, burning a torch for Bullock, with whom she once had an affair. Twice when she visits the eponymous executive suite, nicknamed "the tower" on the top of a skyscraper, she is drawn to the window and the steep drop it offers. In scenes of anguish, she clings to the parapets, contemplating suicide.

Barbara Stanwyck and William Holden in *Executive Suite* (1954)

Stanwyck and Holden have one fiery scene together, in which she blurts out her tale of woe and he calls her bluff, pointing out that her plan to sell out is directed at the dead man, not the company. They struggle in an embrace that is also Holden protecting himself from her blows. Holden is much more relaxed than ten years earlier and easily matches Stanwyck's affective energy. However, as the *New Yorker* reviewer pointed out at the time, "They seem out to prove that women connected with business don't have much fun."[20] It's a small part for Stanwyck, and she had little patience for June Allyson, who plays Holden's character's whiney wife. When Allyson showed up on set unprepared, Stanwyck spoke up and scared her into getting her lines right.[21]

Executive Suite concludes with Holden's character, McDonald Walling, winning control of the company despite being the youngest member of the board. He delivers a passionate speech defending the quality of the products over corporate dividends, championing the pride of workers over the rhetoric of efficiency espoused by his rival for the position. He is an engineer living in a sleek modern house with a tidy wife, a ball-playing son, and a maid. The luxurious lifestyles of the corporate executives foreshadow the decadence of *Dynasty* and *The Colbys* (not to mention *The Big Valley*), and the critique of corporate culture is undermined by the triumphant imagery of skyscrapers and the passion everyone has for the institution, as if it were simply a dysfunctional family. Holden's star image was synonymous at this point with the "man in the gray flannel suit," which he never takes off in this film (unlike some of his later 1950s films when he frequently bares his chest).[22] Despite his wife trying to talk him down, Walling's ambition wins out, and the film's celebration of corporate culture rings far truer than its thinly veiled critique.

Barbara Stanwyck did not like giving interviews, and when she did, she revealed very little, except the same stories of her early years repeated over and over again. One journalist actually invented a story about a lover for her because she felt sorry for the actor.[23] The persistence with which biographers and tabloid journalists seek to find lovers is symptomatic of the search for "truth" embedded in romance within the performance of celebrity. In Stanwyck's case it may also have been an ongoing quest for proof of her femininity. In any case, both Alex Madsen and Jane Ellen Wayne insist that Holden and Stanwyck had an on-again, off-again affair for several decades.[24] Al Diorio suggests only that Holden was the first person to call Stanwyck "Queen."[25] Whatever form their relationship took, we can say that their star images nurtured each other, and another story unfolds within the interstices of fact and fiction.

Throughout the 1950s, after her divorce Stanwyck's name was linked to many younger men, including Rock Hudson, Ralph Meeker, and Robert Stack, as well as Holden. They were rising stars and "selling" more movies than she was. In the Museum of Modern Art file on Stanwyck, a series of typed index cards summarize her mentions in the press from 1950 to 1964. In October 1959 the *National Enquirer* reported that she "was so boozed up at Romanoff's in Hollywood the other eve her four male escorts practically had to pour her into a taxi."[26] The ethnography of celebrity reads like a Hollywood movie. This is one of the only mentions I've ever seen of Stanwyck being drunk, and while the source is indeed questionable, it suggests that she and Holden might have been drinking buddies, as Holden was well known to be a chronic alcoholic.

Beneath the shimmering surface of celebrity biography lies an ever-receding horizon of authenticity and sincerity. These are the qualities that Holden's and Stanwyck's characters need in films such as *Golden Boy* and *Executive Suite*, in scripts that take on heightened moral questions and resolve them through sheer force of character. These are films that pose as liberal critiques of American society but are nevertheless so preoccupied with, and invested in, the spectacles of the boxing bout in 1939 and the cityscape of corporate culture in 1954 that their critical stance is little more than a posture.

The moral and ethical dilemmas are delineated on the actors' faces and bodies, their tortured souls, and their techniques of performance. The life stories, like the movies, often depend on a true-love guarantee of moral sincerity, and for Stanwyck and Holden, the legend of their long-standing relationship, surviving failed marriages, and long-declining careers in the 1980s helped sustain their star images long after many others had faded.

In a 1967 interview (during *The Big Valley* years), Stanwyck expressed her disdain for "petulant" effeminate men and a strong preference for virile, "manly" men. She says, "Lee Majors reminds me of William Holden when he started out in *Golden Boy*. Like Bill, Lee has it. He'll make it. These men have the same masculine quality as a Hank Fonda. It's a completeness, an authority."[27] Her attraction to such men both matched and clashed with her own dominating persona. In a chapter called "The Making of a Man," Wilson details Stanwyck's initial relationship with Taylor, in which she helped him in dozens of ways to gain confidence as an actor.[28] As part of her role in the networks of the film industry, Stanwyck "made men" even if she managed to live well enough without them after 1951. She never ceased to be hounded by the stigma of lacking a man of her own, a lack for which Holden served as a useful placeholder.

ILLICIT

HOW TO BE ULTRAMODERN

Anything hotter than this would call for an asbestos audience blanket.

—*Variety* review of B*aby Face*, 1933

ILLICIT **(1931) IS JUST ONE OF MANY** titles of Stanwyck's pre-Code films that suggests racy content and challenges to authority.[1] Others include *Forbidden, Shopworn* (1932), *The Purchase Price, Ten Cents a Dance* (1931), and *Ladies They Talk About*, each of which alludes to women on the margins of society. *Ladies of Leisure* (1930) and *Night Nurse* (1931) are euphemisms for party girls, women who are "available," fun, unmarried, and exciting. These are the films that launched Stanwyck's career, providing her the opportunity to show off her many talents. In 1929, when she arrived in Hollywood, she had starred in only two Broadway plays (*The Noose* and *Burlesque*), in which she delivered charged emotion with a powerful and distinctive voice, but she also had a good seven years' experience singing and dancing in chorus lines. The New Woman that Stanwyck helped to invent in the early 1930s, epitomized in *Baby Face*, was not just sexy and assertive; she also harbored sufficient moral integrity and authenticity to make her sympathetic, despite her challenge to social norms.

Pre-Code woman's films are crucial intersections of several social narratives, including the survival of the film industry during the Depression years, and new styles of performance designed to suit the new medium of talking pictures. Stanwyck quickly became a media darling because, despite the immoral women she played on-screen, she was said to have a "civilized sense of values." The story of Stanwyck's rise to fame so closely parallels the grand narrative of social mobility in pre-Code cinema that she emerges as "ultra-modern"—sophisticated, smart, and, most importantly, opaque. In both *Illicit* and *Baby Face* her characters "have theories," which does not mean they are educated, but they do have intelligence.

Stanwyck's star rose quickly after her first film with Frank Capra in 1931 (*Ladies of Leisure*), and yet the party-girl image was well balanced with that of the working woman. She made fourteen films during the pre-Code years (1930-1934), in which she consistently earned top billing, and they are in fact incredibly varied. In two films she played a farm girl, without makeup, furs, or elegant gowns (*The Purchase Price* and *So Big!*), although these are the exception to the rule of decadent luxury. Many of her films of the 1930s include scenes of Stanwyck's characters applying makeup and wiping it off, unsure of their need or want of it. Stanwyck wanted to prove herself as an actress, which she did, and at the same time, in the pre-Code films she made a major contribution to the development of the figure of the New Woman in the new medium of talking pictures.

Stanwyck was in good company, to be sure, with other formidable actors of the period, such as Mae West, Joan Crawford, Jean Harlow, Miriam Hopkins, and many more. By looking more carefully at Stanwyck's roles during the period, in conjunction with her off-screen image cultivated by studio publicists and fan magazines, her contribution to the New Woman as a new moral authority should become more evident. The tensions between the culture of pre-Code Hollywood's sensational, tantalizing, and "modern" themes, and the strictures of moral authority that surfaced in the press and were negotiated between censors and studios, make it a critical era of social transformation. Stanwyck's role in this period is exemplary of what Thomas Doherty describes as "the road not taken" by American cinema after 1934. Between 1929 and 1934 almost anything could happen on-screen, as long as it was punished or renounced at the end. Despite the reputation of pre-Code cinema as being a site of "immorality and insurrection," the films were in fact heavily censored. In most of Stanwyck's films, she ends up happily married at the end, usually to a gentleman of the upper class. Before she gets there, though, she has a lot to say.

In many of her pre-Code films, Stanwyck's characters are variations on the "gold digger"—a pejorative term for a very popular figure of the period, a woman who manages to marry "up" in society. In fact the gold digger is almost always a working girl, as Stanwyck proves in *Baby Face*. The corruption of the wealthy, on sensational display during the Depression years in the form of conspicuous, luxurious consumption, is called out by the gold digger, who usually ends up with a healthy piece of it, despite her critique. These are films with no middle class, only extremes of wealth and poverty. Veronica Pravadelli identifies the New Woman as a force of energy in pre-Code cinema, tied to the city and the economic framework of the single woman. She describes the films as a convergence between plots of female emancipation and visual attractions.[2] The promise of sexuality on display in the form of women's bodies is also a sign of their emancipation from "the cult of true womanhood," which is to say Victorian rules of decency and gendered behavior.

Stanwyck's accelerated rise to stardom in the early 1930s was in part due to the reputation and connections of her husband Frank Fay and to the talents and encouragement of Frank Capra. After two lackluster films in 1929 and almost a dozen screen tests, she was ready to give up, but Fay helped her to get a screen test for Capra and persuaded him to take a chance on his wife. Under Capra's tutelage, and working with cinematographer Joseph Walker, Stanwyck quickly learned the tricks of the trade. More than that, she took Hollywood by storm by engaging in a salary dispute with both Columbia and Warner Bros. in 1931. She won herself nonexclusive contracts with both studios and a significant salary boost at a time when the industry was struggling financially and the Depression was starting to hit the industry hard.[3]

Stanwyck's cunning business negotiations were noted by the fan magazines. She was identified as a rebel, but at the same time she was praised as a good worker and "not the temperamental kind who holds up productions and makes things difficult for the studios."[4] Stanwyck was gaining a reputation off-screen as someone who snubbed the "elitist" party scene of the Hollywood establishment. Her freelance career style was linked to her dedication to her profession and to being a good wife who preferred home life over the night life, and she thus gained a reputation for "honest independence."[5] During the early 1930s, Stanwyck emerged not only as a free-thinking independent woman on-screen and off but also as a woman with a morality code, keeping her distance from the decadent culture that had come to characterize the industry.

Of the fourteen pre-Code films that Stanwyck made, *Illicit* does not stand out for its visual cinematic assets. As an early sound film, the sets are restricted to domestic interiors in which the actors more or less huddle around hidden microphones. The story, adapted from a play, is set exclusively among decadent "society" types who spend their lives gossiping, going to parties and nightclubs, and sleeping around; only once do we move outside their over-decorated residences, and then only to the street outside a club. The film is thus indicative of the low-budget fare of the period. Stanwyck plays Anne Vickers, "a woman with theories" regarding what *Variety* called "the free love problem."[6] She believes that marriage is a downer and that she and her fiancé, Dick Ives II (James Rennie), should postpone their engagement and live a little before tying the knot. "We have a whole lifetime to be the Richard Iveses, so little time to be us," she says.

In the opening scene Anne and Dick cuddle on a sofa in Dick's apartment discussing marriage. She says she doesn't want to produce an heir for the Ives family for at least two years. Freedom does not necessarily mean the ability to have affairs; it also clearly means the freedom not to have children. The scene ends with Anne giggling coquettishly about "pussyfooting" and rolling backward into Dick's arms. She has no shame and does not want to be bound by old-fashioned institutions. The story then "tests" her theories with an up-and-down narrative of Dick and Anne getting married, having affairs (although these events are alluded to only vaguely), separating, confronting each other's lovers, and finally reuniting, with Anne ultimately capitulating with the line, "Take me home to the Ives mansion." She is ready to "mother" Dick, who has a cold.

Stanwyck's performance is much looser than those of the other actors, with the exception of her banter with Joan Blondell, who plays one of her socialite friends. She is playful in the love scenes; she twists coquettishly and toys with props. Her character's place in "society" is ambiguous, however, because although she is glamourously dressed and socializes with equally glamourous friends, she tells Dick at the outset that she is "a peasant" with "no neurotic blood" in her. Stanwyck feigns a highbrow accent, but her Brooklyn speech rhythms and vowels remain prominent. Her teeth are still crooked (they are capped in *Ten Cents a Dance*, released a month later), and thus Anne's marriage into the Ives family is a mode of social mobility that is downplayed in the script.

Illicit was not a huge hit. In many states the film was seriously edited, even though the Hays Office approved it. In the correspondence between the Hays Office and Warner Bros., most of the debate has to do with the copious drinking and the use of the Lord's name in vain. Although the producers were asked to delete many lines referring to sex (e.g., Anne: "We're both a riot in our underwear"), many of the edits were not actually made before release. The film was nevertheless banned in several Canadian provinces and cut in several states, including New York, but the studio evidently believed that the titillating sensationalism of the story outweighed the threats of region-by-region censorship. In one letter to Darryl Zanuck, Colonel Joy from the Hays Office notes that "we are on trial" regarding the depiction of conspicuous drinking, indicating that the censors and the studios were essentially on the same team during this period. Nevertheless, he allows that "George," the character played by

Charles Butterworth, can drink as much as he wants because it is "necessary for plot purposes."[7]

Georgie, as he is called in the film, provides the comedic relief as the "society drunk" in *Illicit*. He escorts women to parties, always with a drink in hand or flask in his pocket, uttering bon mots or non sequiturs that tend to fall rather flat eighty years later and sound more like surrealist interruptions to the story now. Referred to at the time as a "nance," a "poof," or a "fairy," these figures were familiar to pre-Code audiences as further challenges to the status quo. No reference is made to George's sexuality, but the character offers another view of life outside the family system, even if it is decadent and stereotyped. Butterworth played many such characters on Broadway before moving to Hollywood, where he seems to have consistently played bachelors. Anne's theories of living the life of a single woman are at once supported by Georgie's alternative lifestyle and undermined by his excessive drinking.

Illicit is based on a play by Edith Fitzgerald, the unmarried "partner" of screenwriter Robert Riskin, and is thus based on her own "theories," or at least on her life experience. (Seven of Stanwyck's pre-Code films are based on original stories by women; five more have screenplays written or cowritten by women.) Despite her final capitulation to marriage, Stanwyck's character represents a distinctly modern view; she and her "boyfriend," Price Baines (Ricardo Cortez), are self-declared "moderns"—until he comes on a bit strong. Her "theories" are entertained and tried, and the failure only proves that "true love" is tested and wins. In the end, she has her cake—and her cocktails—and eats it too, secure in the life of luxury.

The trailer for *Illicit* describes the theme as a "terrific problem," referring to the marriage laws that Anne is transgressing. One reviewer described the film as Stanwyck's triumph as a "great actress" in a "smart sophisticated story of ultra-moderns."[8] Indeed she demonstrates a full range of flirtatious sexuality, strong-minded lectures, and vulnerability, as she is able to stand up to Dick's father (Claude Gillingwater) and state her case. Even when she goes to seek his advice (she sucks up to him in yet another stance of society manners), she says that if she returned to Dick, she would be just "a little wife who saw the error of her ways." Stanwyck's penultimate scene has her on the phone to Baines, saying she is ready to celebrate her freedom after serving two years in the marriage institution, while visibly crying. Her facial expression conveys the opposite of her words, visibly registering the character's "truth" by way of its opposite—a performance that she repeats in *Ladies of Leisure* and *The Lady Gambles*, although in those films her quandary is more of a moral sensibility of not "deserving" her aristocratic love interest.

Charles Butterworth, Joan Blondell, and Barbara Stanwyck in *Illicit* (1931)

Illicit is in the end a somewhat marginal film in Stanwyck's long career, but it illustrates how she was able to jettison "the cult of true womanhood"— the Victorian sensibility of lawful behavior—even while cultivating another image of a new kind of woman, who chooses love on her own terms. Her final retreat to the Ives mansion, which resembles a mausoleum, is perhaps a disappointment to the twenty-first-century viewer, but it was perceived at the time as a woman getting her way. "Her hold strengthened steadily until the finish," concludes an enthusiastic review of the film.[9] As archival media, *Illicit* showcases Stanwyck's disruptive performance style, with which she breaks into high society and its attendant forms of entrapment.

Two years later, when the script for *Baby Face* first crossed the desk of censor James Wingate, he wrote to Will Hays that he saw no explicit code violations, although the "theme is sordid and of a troublesome nature." Nevertheless, he felt that the casting of Stanwyck "will mitigate some of the dangers in view of her sincere and restrained acting."[10] In a subsequent memo, he noted that Warner Bros. planned to devote 20 percent of its planned production schedule to "women's pictures … which inevitably means sex pictures."[11] The censor was indicating that some leniency was required if the studio was to remain competitive and stay afloat during the difficult economic times.[12] In March, after getting Zanuck to make some

Barbara Stanwyck and Donald Cook in *Baby Face* (1933)

changes, he told Hays, "*Baby Face* is in good taste," only to be hit by a barrage of criticism after the film was very briefly released. The story of a woman very literally sleeping her way to the top was not, apparently, in good taste after all.

One trade magazine reviewed the first brief release, noting that it would be controversial and advising exhibitors that it would be a hard sell: "Remember you're dealing with a woman who takes the initiative in every case."[13] The film was pulled immediately and altered so that Lily Powers (Stanwyck) is advised by her mentor Adolf Cragg (Alphonse Ethier) that "a beautiful woman like you can get anything she wants in the world. But there is the right and wrong way—remember the price of the wrong way is too great." In what has become known as the "prerelease version,"[14] Cragg quotes (supposedly) from Nietzsche's *Will to Power*: "You have power over men. But you must use men, not let them use you." Lily is another woman with theories. In the original ending, Lily has a sudden change of heart, curtailing her attempted escape from the fallen bank. She returns to her husband, Courtland Trenholm (George Brent)—the bank president, who shoots himself when the bank fails—with her half a million dollars and stands by her fallen man, despite the fact that only seconds ago she had boasted to her friend and companion Chico (Theresa Harris) that "one day

I'll have the other half." A final scene was added to the end of the censored version in which Lily is "punished" by the board of directors, who send her and Trenholm back to the industrial town of Erie, Pennsylvania, where she started the film. Stanwyck was unavailable for retakes, so a shot of the smoky city stands in for her return.

Despite the changes made by Zanuck to make the film palatable, it was widely banned and further edited in different regions and pulled from distribution altogether in 1935 with the establishment of the Breen Office. The PCA files underscore the complexity of authorship and authority in pre-Code cinema as the industry negotiated the field of discretion, novelty, entertainment, and so-called decency through the early 1930s. In Stanwyck's pre-Code films, this ambiguity of authority is manifest in the many absent fathers. Each of the fathers of her characters in *Shopworn*, *The Miracle Woman* (1931), *Gambling Lady*, *So Big!* and *Baby Face* die at the beginning of the film. In *Miracle Woman* she boldly steps into her father's place, berating his congregation for being corrupt and ungrateful toward her poor dead father, and she immediately gets hired as an evangelical preacher herself. In other films, such as *So Big!* and *Night Nurse*, there simply are no fathers or authority figures around.

Thus the New Woman that Stanwyck embodies in the 1930s makes up the rules as she goes along. At the beginning of *Baby Face*, her father pimps her out before he is killed, justifying to Wingate the censor that "her ruthlessness is at least to be understood though not necessarily to be emulated."[15] It is precisely within the moral vacuum of the pre-Code era that Lily Powers briefly subsisted but was "too hot" to last. Even the cleaned-up version of *Baby Face* was decried as "vulgar entertainment" and "extremely demoralizing" by some and "as the roughest story that has come to the screen" by others, although there was some consensus that it was highly entertaining.[16] Several reviews insisted that the kids be left behind, suggesting that this was very much an adult film, but unlike the adult films of the 1950s, these pre-Code woman's—or sex—films featured women challenging social norms on every front.

Several reviewers allude to *Baby Face* as comedy, but they aren't sure what kind. In *Variety* we are told that the comedy is "seldom intentional.... The Strand audience gave it the snick in the wrong spots, especially after the first quarter, when Lily starts to bowl 'em over with just a look and a flash of the gams."[17] Stanwyck actually had a hand in the development of the screenplay, working with Zanuck to make the first half comedic and the latter section more romantic.[18] Indeed Lily's rise to the top is highly satirical, featuring a graphic move up the New York skyscraper, with each floor

Barbara Stanwyck in *Baby Face* (1933)

designating a different department, from filing, to mortgages, to the final beautiful faux crane shot up to the penthouse, where Lily lounges, glittering with sequins and jewels. Directed by Alfred E. Green, *Baby Face* features dozens of fabulous Art Deco sets and, together with the witty, snappy dialogue and extravagant costumes, is among the most cinematic of the pre-Code era.

Stanwyck's performance is explicitly stylized and tongue-in-cheek, as she puts on a show for each of her conquests in turn. In one scene, entertaining Mr. Stevens in her luxurious apartment, she offers him a drink but says modestly that she never touches the stuff, then in deadpan, "maybe just a sip," and quickly downs a tumbler of liquor. She wears a series of more and more exotic wigs, and Orry-Kelly's gowns become increasingly extravagant in their materials and avant-garde designs, while Stanwyck's Brooklyn drawl is maintained throughout. In the so-called romantic part of the film, when she marries Trenholm, the young "playboy" bank president, she is no less coy ("I've always wanted a 'Mrs.' on my tombstone," she says demurely), and the final declaration of love really does come out of the blue. No wonder she had to be "punished" by the Hays Office.

Stanwyck's portrayal of Lily Powers is hard-edged, manipulative, and cynical, but besides being an accomplished seductress, Lily is also a hard worker, legitimately learning new jobs with each promotion and transfer, including learning French to take up a position in the company's Paris office. Lily is a working woman, and thus, on some level, she has earned her way to the top. Throughout her rise, she retains the service and friendship of her Black maid, Chico, who rises in her own way (see chapter T). Lily consistently outsmarts the men, including an entire boardroom full of doddering executives. In this sense the gold digger narrative runs parallel to Stanwyck's own rags-to-riches story that was already being repeated ad nauseam in the popular press.[19] In several of the pre-Code films, such as *Miracle Woman* and *Shopworn*, her characters also move up the class ladder through show business, reinforcing the star's personal claim to these stories as her own.

Baby Face was preceded by a cycle of "kept women" films and was particularly inspired by the MGM film *Red Headed Woman* (1932), which adopted a comic approach to the scandalous subject. Starring Jean Harlow and written by Anita Loos, in *Red Headed Woman* the wages of sin are triumphantly won by a woman who flaunts her sex appeal. Harlow's performance is more in the register of farce, and the film lacks the sexy banter of *Baby Face* that Stanwyck delivers with high irony. Lily Powers is more manipulative and cunning than Harlow's character, Lil, who frequently loses control and shatters the decorum of high society with a frenzied energy. The redheaded woman ends up getting away with her strategy to marry the richest man in town, while keeping the chauffeur lover on the side. Lily Powers's harsh punishment may be due to the year between the two films or because Stanwyck's performance makes her more threatening to the status quo.

As mentioned above, Stanwyck's characters in *Illicit* and *Baby Face* are both women "with theories." The will to power is a joke on one level, a satire of women's emancipation to be sure, but it is also a satire of corporate corruption, a familiar theme of pre-Code cinema.[20] Stanwyck's embodiment of individualism is not a joke but a real accomplishment. Richard Maltby argues that the "kept woman cycle" was a vehicle for social condemnation of Hollywood's excesses—of salaries as well as spectacle. The cycle was a target of censorship and certainly provoked the enforcement of the Production Code in 1934, but also, as Maltby says, the cycle actually enacted the condemnation in the punishment it meted out to its heroines.[21] Stanwyck's disappearing act, failing to show up for the added-on scene of retribution, is another one of those strokes of good fortune, although this time it occurs off-screen. *Baby Face* is not only symbolic of the contradictions of the Depression and its fetishization of sexuality and consumer desire; the film is also exemplary of the space those contradictions opened up for women to step up and step out.

Pre-Code cinema enabled women to break long-established patterns and to take the flapper culture of the 1920s to the next level, using their voices; at the same time, they helped save an industry from collapse. *Baby Face* enabled Stanwyck to solidify her versatility as an actor, employing her wisecracking wisdom to run roughshod over dimwitted men while maintaining her working woman persona. If few audiences saw the censored version, even fewer saw the uncut version until 2004, when the latter was restored and broadcast on Turner Classic Movies and released on DVD. It has subsequently been included in the Library of Congress National Film Registry and is a staple of film history curricula. This is a clear case of Stanwyck finding her audience decades after the film was made, when the comedy is legible and the performance inspiring.

JUNGLE FILMS / WHITE WOMEN

Things happen differently in Burma, that's all.

—Review of *Escape to Burma*, *Screenland*, July 1955

IN THE JUNGLE, Barbara Stanwyck is whiter than she usually is, which is to say that she is necessarily symbolic of imperialism when she is in a tropical setting. In *A Message to Garcia* (George Marshall, 1936) she plays Raphaelita, or "Lita," the daughter of Cuban general Maderos, who is shot by the Spanish in the opening scenes. In a white safari suit, she leads Lieutenant Rowan (John Boles) through the Cuban jungle of 1897 with a message from President McKinley pledging U.S. support for the Cuban rebels. In *Escape to Burma* (Allan Dwan, 1955), Stanwyck once again prowls through a studio-built jungle, this time in Technicolor. Her character, Gwen Moore, is a teak farm owner overseeing a large staff of Burmese peons. She gets mixed up in the pursuit of a white man (Robert Ryan) accused of killing a prince. Stanwyck's whiteness is equally significant in *Trooper Hook*, a western set in the Mojave Desert. Here she plays Cora Sutcliff, captive of Native Americans and the mother of a half-breed boy, who is rescued from captivity by Sergeant Hook (Joel McCrea) and reintegrated into white society.

In the first two films, Stanwyck has the opportunity to emulate her hero Pearl White. She rides horses, she has adventures, she resolves conflicts between men, and she is inevitably wounded and saved by men as well. In *Trooper Hook*, however, she is tied to her maternal role, holding tight to her child and completely dependent on the men around her. These films are linked by their neocolonial settings and by their journey-based trajectories, which take the characters through indeterminate spaces crawling with the hidden dangers of animals and men. American films in the studio era were frequently set in imaginary foreign lands where the social relations of neocolonialism were negotiated through fiction. Women were often given central roles in these films because a female face of colonialism was a tried-and-true tactic of making empire look "valuable and just" in an era of growing anticolonialism within an imperialist worldview.[1]

Richard Dyer notes that white men and women in imperialist narratives tend to play different roles: "When a text is one of celebration, it is the manly white qualities of expansiveness, enterprise, courage and control (of self and others) that are in the foreground; but when doubt and uncertainty creep in, women begin to take centre stage. The white male spirit achieves and maintains empire; the white female soul is associated with its demise."[2] In the three Stanwyck films discussed here, this demise may seem far off, and yet a close reading reveals that these are broken jungles, lacking the illusionist realism that studio-era American cinema is known for. Within the doubt and uncertainty regarding nature, we find as well a slight shifting of race relations. The stories play out in artificial jungles and deserts, linking the demise of imperialism to the Anthropocene, where "nature" is entirely subsumed by artifice.

Message was shot by Rudolph Maté and *Escape* by John Alton, two of Hollywood's most accomplished cinematographers. The studio sets are atmospheric and deeply shadowed, even though the plants themselves are familiar California greenery, supplied by the "green men" employed by the studios. These fake jungles are matched in *Trooper Hook* by process shots that punctuate the film as McCrea and Stanwyck ride in a stagecoach with Quito, her child, between them. The landscape bounces by outside the coach windows as they stoically receive and deflect the racist sentiments of their fellow passengers. The fakeness of these jungles, combined with the different negotiations of colonial cultures, tends to foreground the role of the white woman in the jungle of shifting and contradictory ideologies. What is her role in these audiovisual texts that are so obviously texts—or tracts—on the possibilities of humanism within colonial social relations?

As Rhona Berenstein has argued, in the pre-Code jungle films of the early 1930s, the white woman typically holds an interstitial place between racialized island people and white male colonizers. She moves between them, either by choice or by force, and articulates the anxiety that underscores racist narratives. Jungle films, according to Berenstein, "suggest a degree of white consciousness, albeit minimal, that the color line is arbitrary, and that it must be guarded, confirmed, and promoted at all times."[3] Stanwyck played a white missionary who has erotic fantasies about her captor in the orientalist *Bitter Tea of General Yen* in 1933, a film that was seriously censored outside the United States for its interracial love affair (see chapter X). In the postwar period, the ambivalence around race was even more pronounced, given the emergent civil rights movement, and certainly westerns began to turn away from the demonization of Native Americans to consider the bigotry of has-been western masculinity, embodied most famously in John Wayne's character in *The Searchers* (1956).

White women frequently function as a means of complicating colonial narratives of exploitation, power, and racial subversion; they also function as glowing sources of light in the mise-en-scène. Richard Dyer has argued that the lighting of white women as glowing "angelic" beings can also be treated as sites of resistance and equivocation: "They suggest both a space for white women to work with and against the image and also the play of resentment, punishment and self-awareness in white heterosexual masculinity. They do not lessen the impact of the image."[4] The implicit contradiction between the white woman as source of light and as angelic fetish is played out in Stanwyck's roles in these jungle movies, in which she is symbolic of virtuous morality; at the same time, she exercises the power of action, agency, and ownership. She is not your average white woman.

The three films in question are each set in specific times and places, however fantastically modified, but all three take place in militarized zones. They each play out a bit differently, of course, although a heterosexual romance undergirds each one. The happy endings, added to the background posses of armed men, ensure that whatever cracks may appear in the façade of imperialism, the house still appears to stand. Even so, the journeys taken in each film tend to be visually circular, returning repeatedly to the same landscapes or the same ponds in the jungle, despite the plot (or the "map" inserts in *Message*) indicating otherwise.

A Message to Garcia is based on a story of Lt. Andrew Rowan, who carried a message from President McKinley to Gen. Calixto Garcia in 1897 promising to send troops to Cuba to help in the insurgency against the Spanish. Rowan's tale was written up by Elbert Hubbard in 1899 in a pamphlet that became an internationally popular tale of obedience, loyalty, and dedication to one's country/employer/cause. The first time the story was filmed, in 1916, it provoked outrage in Cuba because Rowan's heroism completely upstaged Garcia's role in driving the Spanish out.[5] The 1936 version of *A Message to Garcia* was made in the context of the "Good Neighbor" policy that was designed to recast U.S. imperialism in South and Central America as consensus rather than coercion, under which American studios went to some effort to portray Latin Americans in a good light.[6]

Casting Stanwyck as a Cuban rebel princess was instrumental in rendering the story more sympathetic to Cuban audiences and history. The practice of casting white actors as Latinas was standard practice in the 1930s, despite the ready availability of talented Latina actresses. Stanwyck's star status as a selling point trumped her ethnicity, and although her opening lines are in Spanish—"Padre!" as she leaps off her horse to find her father fallen, executed by the Spanish militia—she shifts to a kind of broken English and then shifts again to her familiar Brooklynese when she is with the American characters Rowan (Boles) and Dory (Wallace Beery). Nevertheless, the film was very well received in Cuba. It was promoted as a tribute to General Garcia and the Cuban freedom fighters, and proceeds from its screenings went to fund a monument to the general. Stanwyck's character was praised as a representation of a female *mambise*, or freedom fighter, who teaches the Americans the value of fighting for one's country.[7]

The American reception of the film was mixed, with some reviewers complimenting Stanwyck on her "convincing heroism," comparing her role to the adventures of *Perils of Pauline*, and others saying she was miscast as a Latina señorita. One reviewer noted that the well-known story of Lieutenant Rowan is distorted by the lovemaking, and indeed Lita can be said to distract the messenger from his mission, even if she starts out by leading him to Garcia's hideout. The same reviewer commented on the girl's clothing having "extraordinary powers of mud-resistance."[8] Lita wears a white safari suit with a gun belt and a white hat and is consistently brightly lit within the shadows of the jungle, shadows that were also commented on by American reviewers impressed with the effects created by Maté, indicating that the studio-built jungle was among the assets of the film. The publicity chief of 20th Century Fox had actually invited the press to see Barbara crawling through the backlot jungle, so it's hardly a surprise that they praised the artifice.[9]

In terms of acting, *Message* actually belongs to Wallace Beery, who plays Dory, a mercenary ex-marine full of tall tales of comic misadventure. He sells arms to both sides of the revolutionary war and starts off by double-crossing Rowan and his Cuban senorita. When Lita is wounded, Rowan leaves her with Dory, but she persuades him to leave her to die, saying that her life is less important than "her people." She and Rowan bond over their mutual commitments to their national duties, so she is the moral center of the film, even if it is Dory who has the revelatory change of consciousness to support the Cuban/American cause. The villain in the story is played by Alan Hale as Dr. Ivan Krug, a German spy hired by the Spanish. He tracks the American through the jungle, also dressed in a blinding white outfit with a white hat. In 1936 it was okay to offend the Germans but not the Spanish.[10]

Deep in the jungle, after Rowan and Lita have evaded Krug by hiding in the swamp, their faces glowing white under the palm fronds, they settle

Barbara Stanwyck in *A Message to Garcia* (1936)

down by the campfire. Both of their faces are partially shadowed, but the extreme close-up of Stanwyck's face heavily made up, perhaps to achieve a Latina look, stops the movie in its tracks. The scale is disproportional to Rowan's distance, and the angle does not quite match his gaze, so the shot is more directly presented to the viewer than to the man she is with. The soft-focus glamourous close-up of women is a familiar Hollywood convention, but here it is particularly striking. The woman is so clearly not the Barbara Stanwyck familiar to audiences then and now, and its painterly artifice clashes with the rough shrubbery of the studio jungle. The shots just before this, in which her full body is on display as she heaves her saddle into the bushes and boldly steps into marshy swamp water, simply don't add up to the face glowing like a hothouse flower in the steamy jungle.

Nobody can be trusted in *A Message to Garcia*, and the image is likewise duplicitous. What is Stanwyck's role other than a kind of prop for a contest among men? The message is finally delivered after she has heroically freed Rowan from his torturer, Krug. Dory is shot after killing Krug, and Lita is reunited with her brother (played by an actual Latino actor, Juan Toreno). Stanwyck's masquerade as a Latina is as cunning as Dory's double-dealing. With the spatial disorientation of the jungle setting and the multiple narrative detours, the actual message of *Message to Garcia* is undermined on every level. Given that the message is one of dedication and faithfulness to a mission, Rowan's mission is aided and abetted—as well as sidetracked—by the other characters. As white characters in a racialized setting, they are simply lost, and Lita's embrace of her brother carries more passion than her de facto final embrace with Rowan the American. Cuban audiences were pleased to have a movie star of Stanwyck's status impersonate a Cuban heroine, however fictional she may have been.[11] Her whiteness is exaggerated by her costume, and Lita's commitment to the Cuban people is diffused by Hollywood romance, but her active role in negotiating between American imperialist intervention and the Cuban people is critical.

Twenty years later, Stanwyck is once again in a jungle, which could be a color version of the sets used in *Message*, except that *Escape to Burma* was partially shot at the World Animal Jungle Compound in Thousand Oaks, California, in widescreen Technicolor (Superscope).[12] Stanwyck plays Gwen Moore, the owner of a teak plantation, with a stiff upper back and a power stride, barking orders to her staff of elephant herders and house staff in over-pronounced English. The Burmese respectfully call her "the Gwen Maw." The escape referred to in the title can only refer to the hope that the viewer might escape from the banalities of everyday life in America by indulging in an orientalist fantasy of adventure, romance, and colorful spectacle. Certainly none of the characters in the film escape to Burma, as the *New York Times* critic noted at the time: "Everyone is in Burma, or a back lot decked out to look like Burma, so how can you escape to a place you're already at?"[13] Stanwyck's hair is bright red for the (Technicolor) occasion,[14] and once again she has the opportunity to crawl through a steamy set laden with greenery and shadows and get stranded overnight with two white men fighting off both animals and armed natives.

Stanwyck has a nice scene in which she tracks a tiger with a shotgun in order to prove to her men that it is not a "tiger spirit" killing her elephants but a real tiger. Her new friend Jim Brecan (Robert Ryan) is right behind her, so when she accidentally falls down a cliff and the tiger leaps at her, he fires the fatal shot. Of course the tiger is never in the same frame as the actors, so the sequence remains a fantasy—one in which Gwen Moore is robbed of her prize. She nevertheless hires Brecan to work for her, but he is accused by the Burmese *sawbwa* (hereditary ruler[15]) of killing the prince and stealing royal rubies. The sawbwa sends Mr. Cardigan (David Farrar) to arrest Brecan, and in this setting Farrar looks like he just walked off the set of *Black Narcissus* (1949), which may well have been an inspiration for the colorful tropical art design of *Escape to Burma*. Stanwyck is dressed in khaki jodhpurs for most of the film, with a crisp orange scarf at her neck.

Only when she has a romantic dinner with Brecan does she don a lavender gown that complements the blue-green shades of her spacious home. Within the colonial context of this fantasy, Gwen greets and receives both white men as if they were allies, without fear and without suspicion.

As the three white characters chase each other through the jungle, they are attacked by bandits and become stranded in abandoned buildings, which are decorative ruins of oriental design, flooded with steam and bluish lighting and inhabited by friendly monkeys. Gwen Moore cuddles with the monkeys, just as she has a way of talking to elephants, which seems to be symptomatic of her ability to get along with the Burmese as well. The white woman serves as an intermediary between the white men and the natives. She convinces the sawbwa to let Brecan go and the two of them are happily reunited. Cardigan closes the case "for lack of evidence" (a monkey stole Brecan's pistol) and walks off alone, as is his fate in *Black Narcissus*.

As an action film directed by Allan Dwan, Stanwyck does get into a high-stakes shootout when Gwen and her two buddies, Brecan and Cardigan, find themselves surrounded by the Burmese army (wearing Chinese wushu pants and pointy hats) inside the Gwen Maw's oriental ranch house. They barricade themselves inside and shoot through the holes in the decorative grills as if they were in the Old West. The natives go down like bowling pins until Brecan finally surrenders, fearing for Gwen's life. Cardigan hauls him off to the sawbwa, having just defended him and his lady friend. Gwen describes her sprawling bungalow as her father's pride and joy, positioning herself within a patriarchal lineage of land ownership. The house is indeed spectacular, filled with kitschy orientalist artifacts in a blue-green wash of light, and is embedded in the jungle with a continuum of potted plants and flowering vines. The shootout caps the thematic parallel between this jungle film and the western, including the multiple deaths of anonymous non-whites, and the capitalist power invested in livestock and real estate, symbolized by a sprawling mansion.

Rather than decry the artifice of nature in *Escape to Burma*, we might regard it as a cinematic ecosystem in which nature is subordinate to technology, rendered mute and invisible. Jennifer Petersen has made this argument with respect to *Brigadoon* (1954), suggesting that Hollywood's studio-built landscapes mark the margins of the Anthropocene.[16] The "fakeness" of the stylish pastel palette of the art direction, the remarkable tameness of the animals, who seem slightly drugged, extends to stage hands caught on camera.[17] There is no illusion here. Within this ecosystem, Stanwyck's character is fluidly integrated into the fantastical scene in which white supremacy is "naturalized" by style. She is the queen of the jungle, on

Barbara Stanwyck in *Escape to Burma* (1955)

equal footing with the sawbwa, paralleling his hierarchy with her own. He owns Cardigan as his errand boy, and she ends up with Brecan, who declares himself in the end happy not to be "free" as he kisses the queen. Colonial and patriarchal hierarchies are fantastically inverted at the expense of nature and realism.

The third example of Stanwyck playing the white woman in a strange land is *Trooper Hook*, which is also the bleakest of her westerns and a stark contrast to the exotic fantasy lands of studio-based Cuba and Burma. The bleached-out desert setting creates a minimalist canvas for a story in which as Cora Sutcliff she plays the most victimized of all her characters, the most silent, and the most submissive. One night, when the stagecoach she is traveling on with her escort, Trooper Hook (Joel McCrea); her son, Quito; and a handful of other passengers tips over and crashes, they sit around a campfire, and it might as well be the jungle with the curious sounds of animals (or movie-Indians) in the darkness.[18] Although Cora fiercely defends her half-breed child, and she herself is cruelly mocked and snubbed for having slept with a Native American, *Trooper Hook* is not a pro-"Indian" film by any means. She tells Hook that Nanchez, the chief whom she slept with, treated her fairly but that the squaws were mean until she "became one of them. Looked like them, smelled like them." Trooper understands her because he once behaved like a dog to get food in a Civil War POW camp.

Nanchez (Rodolfo Acosta) is depicted as a savage, executing most of Hook's platoon in the film's opening scene, including his commanding officer. The cavalry responds in kind, killing a bunch of Apache warriors before Hook is delegated to escort Cora back to her husband. Nanchez and his men stalk the stagecoach throughout their journey across the desert, and when Cora finally finds her husband, Mr. Sutcliff is not impressed, rejecting both his wife and her child. His racism, and the film's message of tolerance, seems more inspired by the civil rights movement of the time than by any shifting regard for Indigenous people, who remain stereotyped as primitive savages.

In the climactic scene of *Trooper Hook*, Hook talks with Nanchez while Quito stands on a nearby rock with a cowboy holding a gun to his head. Hook forces Nanchez to decide whether the boy should die or go with his mother. Nanchez fears the child will be scorned by white society but nevertheless gives in. He continues to follow them and attacks the Sutcliff home, where he and Sutcliff conveniently shoot each other. Cora is free to ride off with Hook, whose tolerance and acceptance of the half-breed child and the "leavin's" of an Apache, is the film's ultimate moral lesson. In that climactic scene, though, the geographical and spatial relations between the boy on the rock and the confrontation between Hook and Nanchez are vague. Nanchez glances right, but Stanwyck, standing behind Hook, glances behind her and to the left. The cowboy and the child do not appear in the background of any of the shots, as if they were in a different movie, perhaps, or a different desert. The natural topography of Arizona has in this case been replaced or subsumed by film editing that reconfigures the landscape.

With respect to the location shooting of *Trooper Hook* in Arizona, a curious anonymous document from the archives fills in some detail.[19] The typewritten pages are described as the diary of someone associated with the Thomas Wood publicity agency, who accompanied director Charles Marquis Warren on the shoot.[20] The diary writer comments on the interruption of jets flying over the set: "One sullen Apache turned to Warren and said, 'Those jets sure louse up your sky, can't they?'" The caustic humor also enlivens the image of Warren making a deal with Robert Aldrich, who was shooting *The Ride Back* (1957) just out of sight but within gunshot sound: "As soon as Warren got through killing a few Braves, he'd let Aldrich know it was okay for him to start knocking off some Chinese Reds."[21] Even on location "in nature," untampered nature is hard to find, and we find ourselves once again within the contours of the Anthropocene.

The final shot of Cora, Hook, and Quito riding off into the sunset is the most unsettling of the process shots because they are now seated on a buggy rather than a stagecoach, and the jiggling background landscape takes up much more of the frame. Process shots tend to register a double temporality, and the studio performances can seem almost like a tableau vivant, given the limited movements possible within the setup, which is why Laura Mulvey calls such shots a "clumsy sublime."[22] They are also a

Barbara Stanwyck in *Escape to Burma* (1955)

modality of discontinuity, breaking the realist contract of fiction film. In his book *Hidden Hitchcock*, D.A. Miller describes his search for continuity errors as a method of "too close reading." In the case of Hitchcock, he finds himself playing a kind of game with the director, trying to understand whether the errors are deliberate or not—if they are invitations to the viewer to dig deeper and to mistrust the signs in the mise-en-scène.[23] Miller's method may be one of personal investment and an analysis of authorship, but it proceeds by citing anecdotes about the film's production, because continuity errors inevitably point to that other time and place when a movie was shot. The jungle sets designed by Hollywood "green men" and the "sublime clumsiness" of rear projection likewise open up hermetic narratives to their shadow times of production.

The shadow times are precisely the times and places of actors' labor, working alongside vast teams of workers making "worlds" that invite escape. The shadow times of the 1930s and 1950s are parallel worlds to those of the movies but no less fraught by the challenges of racial segregation. The theme of integration is prominent in *Trooper Hook*—which on some level may be considered a "social problem" film rather than a western—and Stanwyck plays along in her usual good spirits, despite her scorned character. Her performance as a Latina in *Message to Garcia* displeased American critics, but Lita's ultimate union with Lieutenant Rowan might have been a form of integration that Cubans, at least, appreciated. The Cold War context of *Escape to Burma* offers no such alliances, though.[24] The white woman in that instance is simply a woman with power, with Burmese peons substituted for "Indians" in a tale that could just as easily have been set in the Old West, although a woman with such awesome authority is rare in the mid-1950s. Stanwyck's other "queenly" roles of the 1950s, including *Cattle Queen of Montana* (1954), directed by Allan Dwan, do not leave her with so much dignity and authority intact (see chapter Q).

The jungles and the desert of these three curious films foreground the dangerous currents of gender as they intersect with race in the discontinuous terrain of the Anthropocene. Nature has stepped aside for stories about women who are heroic in their own new ways. Stanwyck's characters are cut off from nature; even as a mother she is "unnatural" in the film's vocabulary of racial tolerance. It is precisely the artifice and discontinuity of the films that enables her persona as the tough action heroine that she was to articulate new forms of imperfect race relations.

KATE CRAWLEY

CROSS-DRESSING IN THE ARCHIVE

> Genders can be neither true nor false, neither real nor apparent, neither original nor derived. As credible bearers of those attributes, however, genders can also be rendered thoroughly and radically *incredible*.
>
> —Judith Butler, *Gender Trouble*

BARBARA STANWYCK IS FREQUENTLY LISTED among "Hollywood's top lesbians" on internet lists, and there has long been speculation about her sexual orientation.[1] Dan Callahan sees Stanwyck as a gay icon, although he makes no real claims as to her sexual preferences, while Axel Madsen is a bit more suggestive by pointing to Stanwyck's lifelong relationship with Helen Ferguson.[2] She also had long-lasting close relationships with her hairdresser, Hollie Barnes, and her Black housemaid, Harriet Corey, who lived with her for many decades, although there is no evidence that any of these women were gay. Boze Hadleigh included her in his book on Hollywood lesbians even though she slammed the door in his face.[3] The questions about Stanwyck's sexuality are symptomatic of cultural expectations around normative femininity, which she consistently challenged with her self-determination, agency, outspokenness, and bossy, authoritarian manner on sets. Even her outdoorsy persona, groomed through the 1950s with her many western performances, countered the norms of femininity. As a single "bachelor" woman from 1951 to the end of her life, her insistence on privacy left plenty of room for rumors and secrets.

Regardless of her actual sexual orientation, Stanwyck's star image definitely provides a space for lesbian fantasy. The ambiguities and contradictions within her life story are extensions of the persona constructed across her films, while her physical characteristics, such as her deep vocal range, "strong features" (including a nose that is larger than norms of

Barbara Stanwyck in "The Kate Crawley Story," *Wagon Train*, season 7, episode 19 (1964)

Anglo-Saxon beauty), and her style of walking with determination and purpose, point to other ways of being female. For lesbians looking for such images, she continues to provide them in her archival presence; for all viewers she provides evidence that such images of alternative modes of womanhood existed within the terms of Hollywood culture. As Patricia White has argued, the appeal to women viewers in the studio era through vehicles such as the woman's film, and through stars like Stanwyck whom women viewers felt attached to, contributed to "the social construction of what we recognize today as lesbian identity."[4] This chapter follows this thread to uncover hidden gems in the TV archive, opened up through atemporal recognition, and examines a few instances in Stanwyck's career that enabled both ambiguous and unambiguous lesbian representability.

Kate Crawley is the name of Barbara Stanwyck's character in two episodes of *Wagon Train* (1957–1965) that appeared in the 1963–1964 season, the only time in her career she can be said to be cross-dressed. Kate wears blue jeans, a leather vest, and a cavalry cap that belonged to her father, but more than this, her mannerisms and stance are distinctly masculine, and she runs her own freight business, a dangerous job in the Old West. She owns horses and wagons and employs a handful of men to carry goods across the frontier, crossing paths with the men and boys on the eponymous wagon train who escort groups of pioneers across the plains. Even with her white hair, she is youthful and agile as well as strong-minded and stubborn.

In the second episode, "The Kate Crawley Story,"[5] her transgression of gender conventions is extremely threatening to the small community of the wagon train. In the first episode, "The Molly Kincaid Story,"[6] she is less threatening and becomes something of a social healer by helping a young woman reunite with her family after being captured by Native Americans. These two episodes of the long-running series are testimony to Stanwyck's abilities and range as an actor and are also strangely missing from all the biographies, although they are, at the time of this writing, readily available on YouTube.

The character of Kate Crawley originated in one of Stanwyck's very first TV appearances, on *Zane Grey Theatre* in 1958. In "The Freighter,"[7] Stanwyck as Belle Garrison runs a freight line and dresses in jeans and a bandana, with a conventional Stetson as headgear. Belle is very handy with a whip, which turns out to be Kate Crawley's calling card as well. Both women can instantly break up a fight between men with a single snap, snaring one of the combatants around the ankle and felling them with a crack and a good holler. Kate's entrances in both *Wagon Train* episodes are signaled by a whip-cracking intervention that definitely gets everyone's attention. Kate Crawley doesn't wear a gun but competes on her own terms. Stanwyck's characterization of Crawley is unusual, especially in the context of her late career, because it is so stylized, which is to say performative. The link to the *Zane Grey Theatre* episode suggests that Stanwyck herself had a hand in developing the Kate Crawley character—designed to be tough, if not necessarily butch.

Kate Crawley's outfit and persona are unquestionably inspired by the legendary Calamity Jane, who began life as a real woman named Jane Canary and was characterized in a series of dime novels called *Deadwood Dick* starting in 1877. That notoriety led to a career performing "herself" in Buffalo Bill's Wild West Show starting in 1893. Most recently played by Robin Wiegert as a lesbian in the TV series *Deadwood* (2004–2006) and the 2013 movie of the same name, Calamity Jane turned cross-dressing into a career and something of a caricature. The signature outfit of buckskin trousers and jacket with a blue cavalry kepi cap is tied to her arrival in Deadwood with Wild Bill Hickok in 1876, which caused a media sensation. Even if the real Martha Jane Canary suffered from depression and alcoholism, the legendary Calamity Jane endures as a potent figure of gender fluidity in American popular culture.[8] Stanwyck dons the Calamity Jane outfit of buckskin only once on-screen, in a brief scene in *The Great Man's Lady*,[9] but Calamity is the kind of character to which she was attached, the Pearl White of the western. Kate Crawley is the closest Stanwyck ever came to actually playing the legendary tomboy, with her whip, cap, and bandana as signature accessories.

In each of the *Wagon Train* episodes, Kate Crawley is definitely heterosexual, although in neither one does she end up married or reformed into femininity. She walks out of each episode a free woman, traversing the frontier on her own terms. In this sense she differs substantially from Doris Day's impersonation of Calamity Jane in the 1953 film of that name, in which the narrative arc leads to her marrying Wild Bill Hickok and feminizing her attire. Eric Savoy has unpacked the "incoherence and radical undecidability" of Day's character in a most helpful way.[10] Applying the feminist theory of gender performativity to Day's brazen, joyful, and transgressive screen performance, Savoy points out that we know more than the characters do. That knowledge is not simply the privy of a lesbian spectator but is shared by most twenty-first-century viewers willing to recognize and acknowledge gender fluidity and non-binary sexuality.

One may certainly argue that normative heterosexuality constructs such oppositional figures as Kate Crawley and Calamity Jane as a means of containing and reaffirming the status quo. A binary structure of sexuality can often be said to include "the contaminated other" in its oppositional logic.[11] Savoy notes that Judith Butler herself (who theorized gender performativity as a mode of everyday life, not as a theatrical style) might dismiss a film such as *Calamity Jane* as "high het [heterosexual] entertainment," in which "anxiety over a possible homosexual consequence is both produced and deflected."[12] Against this, Savoy argues that "queer performativity within mainstream cinema is almost always far in excess of the heterosexualizing strategies of containment." Savoy argues that the logic of narrative constraint is trumped by the heterogeneity of spectatorship, particularly within the temporal slippage—which I would describe as an archival slippage—that links queer critique with the queer performativity of the 1950s and early 1960s. The cross-dressing of these films leaves gender identities in suspension, "as ideologically fissuring and problematic."[13] Engaging techniques of dress, behavior, and gesture, this is not simply formal excess but an excess of performance and an excess of the body.

The other key point that Savoy makes that helps to link the narrative strategies of *Calamity Jane* with Kate Crawley is the notion (the act) of shaming, which is a prominent theme of the Doris Day movie as well as the "Kate Crawley" episode of *Wagon Train*. The tomboy in both cases is literally shamed into shedding her "disguise" and dressing as a "real" woman. Dressed in men's clothing, the woman's body is rendered monstrous and inadequate in the eyes of both men and women. Day's Calamity Jane goes through this process of feminization, even if she is somewhat sidetracked by her lovely roommate, Katie Brown (Allyn McLerie). Kate Crawley is rudely shamed to the TV audience, behind her back, by the wagon train community. The woman gossips call her "a goose in gander's clothing," and the men call her "a black crow in a flock of swans." And yet when she is shamed into donning a pink prairie dress and steps out of her wagon, she says to Chris (John McIntire), who plans to marry her, "Do I look as ridiculous as I feel?" The answer from any contemporary viewer would be a resounding "Yes!"

The context of the western, like Doris Day's context of the musical, enables Stanwyck to use her body as a strong performance element that the dress would clearly constrict. As Savoy argues, it is the return to spectacle that enables an application of Butler's theory of gender performativity to screen performance. Within the terms of genre, "gaps and fissures … and risky excesses" may "disrupt the coherence of performance itself."[14] Stanwyck's long stride and swinging arms may be a signature gesture, but here they take on additional weight in the portrayal of self-determination, direction, and agency that is more typically the province of the cowboy in TV westerns. Her performativity, in other words, goes well beyond clothing but is embodied in her mannerisms and her tone of voice. As a movie star, Stanwyck rarely if ever had the opportunity to be a true "character," which is to say the opportunity to play a role in a stylized "overdone" manner, especially in the postwar period. Her character of Sugarpuss O'Shea in *Ball of Fire* might be the closest she came to such a performative characterization, although Sugarpuss's ultra-femininity is quite different from the "masquerade" of Kate Crawley.[15]

It should be noted that Stanwyck's outfit as Kate Crawley includes a bolero-shaped leather vest with leather toggles marking her breasts and a woven flowered belt showing off her figure. In "The Kate Crawley Story" she comes on strong to Chris Hale (McIntire)—the benevolent leader of the wagon train crew—right off the bat. They are old friends, and the episode tracks their negotiation of a possible marriage. Chris's pals in the wagon train seem most afraid of having a woman boss them around were she to join them permanently. She runs her own men in a bossy, belittling way, until she loses both men and wagons in a forest fire that Chris and his men have to save her from. The episode concludes with her almost getting married to Chris, but the wedding is interrupted when some TV Indians come to sell back the horses that Kate lost in the fire.[16] She is so incensed that she cracks her bullwhip, in full wedding gear, unleashing a comic mêlée that upsets food tables and sends the TV Indians scattering without a shot being fired. Kate and Chris are both convinced that "she cannot be a lady"

Barbara Stanwyck and John McIntire in "The Molly Kincaid Story," *Wagon Train*, season 7, episode 1 (1963)

because she isn't one, so she rides off in her familiar jeans and cap, horses in tow, to "talk to the army about a forest fire" and relaunch her freight business (she had been carrying dynamite in her original load).

"The Kate Crawley Story" is in some ways more "transgressive" than its predecessor, "The Molly Kincaid Story," because it is Kate's own story and is "about" the question of her gender—or is it only her manners? However, the earlier episode is in some ways more tolerant of her cross-dressing, insofar as it is a story about tolerance. Molly Kincaid is played by Carolyn Jones (who played Morticia Addams in *The Addams Family* TV series from 1964 to 1966), a woman who was abducted by "Indians" and escapes. Kate Crawley just happens to be in town when Molly and another Indian-dressed man show up on stolen horses. Kate uses her bullwhip to stop the local men from attacking and harassing the two and takes Molly up to her room in the hotel. Molly's face is scarred in a tattoo pattern, shaming her with permanent disfigurement. Her tale of abduction in flashback depicts the scarring ritual as if it were a gang rape, so her fear of reuniting with her family is compounded by monstrosity and violation. Nevertheless, Kate breezily orchestrates a reunion, first with Molly's grown-up daughter and then with her "unmanly" husband, who ran away when the Native Americans attacked their homestead. Kate's role is a womanly one of talking, caring, and female bonding in this episode, and Stanwyck plays a kind of maternal authority figure, although it is primarily a lesson of family values and forgiveness. Tolerance of Indigenous people and disfigurement is merely implied in her successful reconciliation of husband, wife, and daughter.

Kate Crawley sees far less action in "The Molly Kincaid Story," but the character is fleshed out by a love of beer drinking. In the saloon she sits back with a pint, her foot casually resting on a chair with her legs artfully spread below the table. Her masculine masquerade is paralleled by Molly's entrance as a "Comanche squaw," but while Molly is eventually unmasked, Kate's appearance and behavior are never commented on by the other characters. She might as well be one of the boys. She does not carry a gun, but at one point Molly steals a gun from her room, so we know she owns one. Kate is last seen casually saying to Chris that she'll "buy him a beer," leaving the door open for her character's return four months later.

Before playing Kate Crawley, Stanwyck had already done two episodes of *Wagon Train*, playing different women on the frontier—a place where "real" women and "real" men, as well as "real" whites, are constantly being tested, tried, and frequently failing. As Maud Frazer, in 1961, Stanwyck leads a wagon train of women, all widowed on the trail, but greed for gold gets the better of her and she ends up being killed by TV Indians.[17] As Caroline Casteel, in 1962, she plays a woman who has escaped captivity, is rescued by the wagon train boys, encounters the usual prejudices, but defends Indigenous ways against white narrow-mindedness.[18] *Wagon Train* was much like *The Big Valley* in how each episode tackled moral and social issues, attempting to offer neoliberal humanist views on the shifting sands of race and gender norms. Almost one-third of *Wagon Train*'s 284 episodes featured women as guest stars, so despite the frontier setting, it was a show about community and social issues, with a strong appeal to women viewers.[19]

Returning to the character of Kate Crawley, more or less buried in the TV archive, provides some insight into the gender-bending attractions of Stanwyck's star image. Seeing her actually cross-dressing makes visible "the uncertain connection between doing gender and being gendered," in Savoy's words,[20] opening a space of fantasy for the lesbian viewer and indeed for any viewer willing to grant the inauthenticity of gender binaries. As a legendary figure, Calamity Jane indicates that the openness of frontier culture provided a valuable textual platform or scene for the inscription of non-dualist sexuality. Within the slippage of media frames and histories, that figure can continue to register the inherent incoherence of heterosexual frontier narratives.

Kate Crawley might have been Stanwyck's most "boyish" character, and it is not the only role that suggested a fluidity of gender identity. However, Stanwyck's single performance as an actual lesbian is utterly unconvincing. The best thing about *Walk on the Wild Side* (1962) is the title sequence by Saul and Elaine Bass, featuring a black cat slinking through an alleyway with Elmer Bernstein's jazzy score as accompaniment. Stanwyck, billed third, after Jane Fonda and Anne Baxter, plays the madam of a New Orleans "doll house" and is supposed to be sweet on one of her girls, played by the ice queen Capucine. In fact, their relationship is little more than a bossy employer and a recalcitrant employee, and it's pretty hard to tell they have any other kind of relationship. Although the original Nelson Algren novel had great potential for an intense Southern drama, producer Charles Feldman had the script watered down to empty monologues, and the actors fail to connect. Stories from the set indicate a complete mess and clash of personalities, including Stanwyck's anger at young actors showing up late and unprepared, which explains why so many scenes feature over-the-shoulder reverse shots, with the actors clearly not speaking to each other.[21] Among the tensions were the contradictory imperatives to make a sexy, titillating "adult" picture—as advertised—and fears of censorship. Indicative of the challenges of even attempting to play a lesbian character is a review in the *Motion Picture Herald* in which Stanwyck is said to give a "penetrating portrayal of a sick and determined woman."[22]

In the archive of Stanwyck's screen performances, there are many more places to look for clues of a different kind of sexuality becoming visible, including *My Reputation*, in which Eve Arden plays Stanwyck's friend Ginna, to whom Stanwyck as Jessica Drummond pours out her sorrows. This is a woman's film, made just after the war, in which Jessica is widowed with two young boys. She meets a handsome officer, played by George Brent, and faces aggressive social stigma for falling in love so soon after her husband's death, including critical retribution from her two young sons. Early in the film, after an ugly encounter with a man who assaults her, Jessica shows up at Ginna's apartment to cry out her sorrows. Eve Arden wears pajamas and a housecoat. Her husband is upstairs asleep, and she tries to cheer up Jessica by encouraging her to "be herself" and not "Mrs. Drummond." She persuades Jessica to join her and her husband on a vacation and embraces her, saying, "I'm crazy about you!" before taking her upstairs to bed. As they walk up the stairs together, Ginna playfully smacks Jessica's bottom.

Eve Arden is one of the most "butch" characters in the studio system stable whose 5'7½" height and husky voice tend to consistently challenge the nominally heterosexual roles that she plays. She plays the kind of exaggerated characters that Stanwyck so rarely could. Judith Roof has described Arden, along with Thelma Ritter, as "female secondary characters" who play roles akin to the Shakespearean fool. They supply and embody perverse knowledge and provide alternative perspectives. Roof argues that paying attention to characters like Ida (Arden's role in 1945's *Mildred Pierce*) "reveals the perverse multiplicity that resonates through Hollywood film, both as supporting ground and as the suspicion of alternative possibility that is never quite extinguished by the weight, glamour, or luminosity of the normative."[23]

Scenes such as Eve Arden's hand on Stanwyck's buttocks are instances where close readings can become like Freudian dream interpretation, revealing "occluded possibilities" embedded within the systems of censorship and closure.[24] In pre-Code Hollywood the innuendo was let out of the bag in the form of rough comedy such as Stanwyck's sexy repartee with Joan Blondell in *Night Nurse*. In *Ladies They Talk About*, Stanwyck plays a woman in prison, locked up among a motley crew of femininities, one of whom smokes a cigar. Stanwyck's friend warns her, "Watch out for her; she likes to wrestle." By 1946 the sexual innuendo was less overt but nevertheless legible in a film like *My Reputation*. Stanwyck's star image must have had a strong butch appeal for those receptive to such an attraction, and her casting in *Wagon Train* and *Walk on the Wild Side* in the 1960s, when alternative sexualities were being whispered about on the sidelines of popular culture, may have cemented that impression, provoking the rumors circulating through her biographies.

Regardless of Stanwyck's actual sexual orientation, there is little question that she opened up a space for lesbian fantasy during her lifetime. Axel Madsen quotes Dana Henninger as speaking for a "young generation of lesbians" in the 1960s who were inspired by Stanwyck's characterization of Victoria Barkley in *The Big Valley*: "You just *knew*.... There was no male testosterone in her Victoria Barkley. We were all just crazy about her."[25] As a star of the archive, her characterization of Kate Crawley makes visible that which was virtually invisible to her and her collaborators. Perhaps we need to hold on to the provocative imagery of the stealthy black cat in the credits of *Walk on the Wild Side*, whose stride is that of the panthers that Stanwyck studied as a young woman at the Bronx Zoo, where director Willard Mack sent her to study walking.[26] In that movement we can find a body that still refuses to be closed off and tamed. In fact, the longer she walks the screen, the less tamed she becomes.

THE LADY EVE
PERFORMATIVITY AND MELANCHOLIA

The relation between Eve and Jean is not an issue for us, but the nature
of the relation of both Eve and Jean to Barbara Stanwyck, or to some
real woman called Barbara Stanwyck, is an issue for us—an issue
in viewing films generally, but declared, acknowledged as
an issue in this film by the way it situates the issue of identity.

—Stanley Cavell, *Pursuits of Happiness*

WITHIN THIS STUDY OF BARBARA STANWYCK and her movies, I have
tried to articulate a persistent tension or paradox between the achievements
of the star and the entrenched misogyny of the industry. *The Lady Eve*
(Preston Sturges, 1941) is a film that has been championed by the critical
establishment, and yet as a film with one woman in a sea of men, its
notorious "perfection" may be at the expense of that one woman.[1] Screwball
comedy in general features many active, talkative, persuasive women who
challenge their husbands, ex-husbands, lovers, and future husbands on
multiple fronts. Stanley Cavell tracks the genre back to Shakespeare and to
Henrik Ibsen's play *A Doll's House*. And yet what Cavell calls "the comedy
of remarriage" consistently undermines the political stakes of Ibsen's piercing
drama by upholding the institution of marriage against all odds. The forced
closure of so many of these films points to something other than fun and
games, and for all of Stanwyck's agency in creating the hilarious, wacky,
insightful comedy of *The Lady Eve* there remains something amiss.[2]

Sturges's film features Stanwyck in one of the best-written roles of her
career. Because her performance is so reflexive, it offers an excellent site
to pull apart this paradox of performance and narrative, or to grasp the
paradox for what it is—a mode of melancholia. Cavell notes that comedies
of remarriage articulate "the inner agenda of a culture" in which gender
roles are being tried and tested; he also defends his readings as "his own

Charles Coburn, Barbara Stanwyck, and Henry Fonda in *The Lady Eve* (1941)

experience."[3] My experience of *The Lady Eve* differs from his, as does my reading of this "inner agenda"; the identity of the woman is indeed the issue, not as an icon or a star but as a collaborator in the production of the film. Stanwyck's performance in this sense has been critically sublimated to the auteurist signature embraced by Cavell and just about everyone else writing about the film.[4]

In the first half of *The Lady Eve*, Stanwyck plays Jean Harrington, who along with her father, "Handsome Harry," played by Charles Coburn, are con artists traveling on a cruise ship. Both Jean and her father are master cardsharps and show off their tricks to the camera in the privacy of their cabin. Harry (Coburn) says to his daughter early on, "Let us be crooked but never common," indicating their aristocratic pretensions as well as the terms of the farce. Jean lures Charles Pike, aka "Hopsy" (Henry Fonda), an extraordinarily naïve beer-empire millionaire, into a poker game with her father. But Jean falls in love with the mark and vice versa. During the second night of poker, Jean and her father play a wonderful game of cheating each other as he tries to beat Hopsy by sliding cards out of his pockets, and as the dealer she keeps exchanging his hands for weaker ones (each hand is shown to the viewer in close-up). The sleight of hand is completely lost on Fonda, whose innocence and ignorance are as exaggerated as the Harringtons' trickery.

When Jean steps away from the table, her father quickly drives up Hopsy's debt to thirty-two thousand dollars. When Hopsy is alerted to the con by the ship's purser the next day, he confronts Jean and she gives an earnest speech about "bad girls" not always being so bad and "good girls" not being so good. Hopsy doesn't buy it and reneges on his offer of marriage.

The second half of *The Lady Eve* features one of the most remarkable performances in studio-era Hollywood. Stanwyck comes back into Hopsy's world as a completely different woman: Eve Sidwich, the supposed niece of Sir Alfred McGlennan Keith (Eric Blore), one of Hopsy's highbrow neighbors in Connecticut (who is actually another con artist fleecing the neighborhood at bridge). Hopsy does not recognize her, although his buddy Muggsy (William Demarest) does. When Eve has successfully married Hopsy, then told him a yarn about her many previous sexual relationships, and then received a generous settlement offer from Hopsy's father, her own father notes that she is holding a royal flush. She refuses to play it, though, and holds out for love—although her change of heart is communicated not to Hopsy but to his father. The father says that, sadly, Hopsy is unavailable because he is "saying good-bye to his mother." Jean and Harry suddenly, almost magically, resume their previous roles on another cruise ship, where they intercept Hopsy again—who is happy to see her after his ordeal with Eve, and they rush to his cabin to consummate the marriage.

As Robin Wood notes about *The Lady Eve*, the film draws on "certain more or less permanent aspects of [Stanwyck's] persona: toughness, worldliness, lower-classness, a resilience by no means incompatible with vulnerability, possible unscrupulousness, even brutality."[5] Indeed, Sturges wrote the screenplay with Stanwyck in mind, having been impressed with her proclivity for comedy in *Remember the Night*.[6] This is not the only Hollywood film to feature a double performance, as it became a familiar trope in screwball comedy, noir, and the woman's film throughout the 1940s (see chapter N).[7] Jean's part in her father's con game is largely to seduce men to the table, not unlike the saloon girls in the western genre (see chapter G). However, she also manages to upstage her own game by her control of the narrative, and by owning her body as Stanwyck the actress, because the spectator is not duped as Hopsy is. We marvel instead at the actor's masquerade and her talents at deception. Henry Fonda's comic performance, including great slapstick physical comedy as well as deadpan ignorance, is rare in his career, but because he is literally "the fall guy" it does not stand out as a bravura star turn as Stanwyck's performance does.

The many levels of comedy and reflexivity within *The Lady Eve* are perhaps why critics have called it a "perfect film."[8] The sexual innuendo of snakes and the theme of virginity are prominent in the film, but the sexuality is literally displaced onto Hopsy's snake named Emma, despite Stanwyck's seductive performance in some of her early scenes with Fonda. The more critical level of Eve's charade is that of class. The film might be described as a parody of the gold-digging theme that was so pervasive in pre-Code Hollywood, including many of Stanwyck's own films, such as *Ladies of Leisure, Forbidden, Baby Face, Gambling Lady*, and even *Stella Dallas*, which is about the challenges of social mobility if not "gold digging" per se. Stanwyck's own biographical legend, widely reported in fan magazines of the time, situated her as having pulled herself out of poverty, not through marriage but through hard work and talent.[9] In *The Lady Eve* she outsmarts, outplays, and hoodwinks poor Charles Pike and owns her own social mobility, despite the two fathers who become entwined in the relationship. Marriage is not between two people but between two families headed by two large, loud men.

Stanley Cavell has argued that comedies of remarriage raise the question of the legitimacy and authenticity of marriage.[10] As a sacred social institution, such films (including *The Lady Eve*) implicitly challenge the authenticity and legitimacy of society itself. The "happiness" of the ending of *The Lady Eve* is certainly questionable, given Hopsy's persistent denial of his lover's double identity. Cavell claims that the suckered man is a stand-in for the audience,[11] but the viewer is not duped, knowing all along that it is Barbara Stanwyck playing both roles and that Jean and Eve are two sides of one fictional character. It is indeed Stanwyck who leads the viewer on and with whom the viewer may well be said to identify as an actor rather than a character. Her gamble is a bluff within a bluff when Eve tells tall tales to Hopsy on their honeymoon, and the whole film might be viewed as a game in which she holds all the cards.

Why does Cavell suspect that all the films in his "comedy of remarriage" category are ultimately about the "real women" who consistently rise above their fictional characters, as indicated in the epigraph to this chapter?[12] Is this not due to their star status, along with their off-screen notoriety as wealthy and independent-minded women and their accumulated roles playing such women? *The Lady Eve* is an especially good example of the threat of a woman's power, as Sturges bets on his leading lady to upset the social order along with the patriarchy. And yet, despite Stanwyck's bravura performance and centrality to the narrative, reading the critical literature on *The Lady Eve* I was surprised to see how frequently Charles/Hopsy is assumed to be the hero.[13] Contemporary critics noted that it was a familiar story of a man in love with a lady of "unsuspected sin" injected with a high

Barbara Stanwyck in *The Lady Eve* (1941)

dose of wit,[14] and yet despite high praise for Stanwyck's comic performance, her character is recognized neither as a full-fledged subject nor as the hero of her own story. Perhaps her heroism is illegible within the terms of the mythic universes invoked by the film—the book of Genesis and the Oedipal model of patriarchal violence and succession.

In order to dig deeper into this contradiction between Stanwyck's starring role and her precarious claim to "heroism," I propose that her performance in *The Lady Eve* is a performative performance, by which I mean that it is not only ironic, satirical, and doubled but that it is also active and has agency. The first full scene on the cruise ship, in which Jean and Charles first meet, is a good example of this and is a significant cue to how the narrative will unfold. As Charles reads a book while dining alone, Jean frames him in her compact mirror and scans the dining room for female competitors for this newly arrived wealthy bachelor. She dramatically narrates the scene in the mirror to her father (and to the viewer), commenting on the women's ploys, anticipating their moves, and supplying their dialogue, along with Charles's thoughts, in the manner of a sports commentator. Finally, watching Charles approach her table on his way out, she sticks out her foot and trips him, triggering their first meeting.

While Cavell reads this scene as Stanwyck becoming a stand-in for the director, a mirror is not quite the same as a camera, because it shares the same diegetic space as the image and is not entirely outside it as a camera is. Given that there are cutaways to Stanwyck looking in the mirror (from which she is absent), we cannot say that she is "the enunciator," but it is certainly her point of view that is expressly privileged. Taken together with her narration and the fetish of Fonda as object of all the women's gazes, we can safely say that Stanwyck's performance leading up to the strategic trip is in every way an act that is also an active action. Precisely because this act "affects reality" (or at least the reality within the diegesis of the film), we could say that this scene is a directly productive form of language (because this is a text, after all), and, as such, it opens the film up to a feminist reading that can fully appreciate the normative, closed, and routine structuration of gender, alongside its critique.

In a film loaded with peripheral comic figures, filling out a social landscape of nonsense and gags, the coincidence of Eve Sidwich and critical queer theorist Eve Sedgwick is not any more absurd. It is Sedgwick who points to performativity as a strategy of challenging dualistic, essentialist thinking through the dynamic of affect. In her book *Touching, Feeling*, she notes that the term "'performative' carries the authority of two quite different discourses, that of theater on the one hand, and of speech act theory on the other."[15] Performativity in speech act theory refers to the ways that certain words and phrases are causal acts, and not simply words, such as the ritual words "I do" in the marriage ceremony.[16] Her project is not exactly the reconciliation of the referential and the theatrical but to think through the oppositions embedded in theories of representation as continuous of the dualities of other critical forms of thought, including gender and the binaries of power and knowledge. Such a reading position, she argues, "undertakes a different range of affects, ambitions, and risks."[17]

Stanwyck's character in *The Lady Eve* is not in control of all aspects of the narrative of course. Jean's identity as a cardsharp is revealed by Muggsy, who knows everything, even if Hopsy doesn't believe him. When Hopsy shows a certain damning picture to Jean, she says, "I've never cared for that picture." It's a photograph of Stanwyck, Charles Coburn, and Melville Cooper (who plays Gerald, Harry's valet and traveling companion) on a ship's gangplank. In the photo the three actors are outside the diegesis of the film. Stanwyck wears an elegant traveling suit, very unlike the glamourous and revealing outfits she wears as Jean. Only the caption provides "character" for the so-called ring of cardsharps, but it is this deadening still image that stops the film in its tracks, because it causes Hopsy to fall out of love with

Jean. Jean's real despair at Hopsy's obstinacy, when he goes so far as to pretend to have been playing her, is Stanwyck at her finest, offering a radical shift from the cheery, bouncy Jean to a heartbroken woman who also realizes her lover is as dumb about girls as he is about cards. He cannot see the woman for who she is. All he can see is the card tricks, the sleight of hand, and the duplicity.

If we consider Stanwyck to be the hero, we can go beyond the duplicity of all of her performances and see the film from the angle of the daughter, which is to say, Antigone, the sister of Oedipus. Sue Thornham has inquired into the female hero and how she might navigate narrative differently. If the price for Oedipus in the Lacanian model of narrative is the loss of his mother in the accession to the symbolic, Thornham concludes that the woman's price is a perpetual melancholia, specifically a modality of melancholia theorized by Judith Butler in relation to the regulatory power of gender. In relation to narrative agency, melancholia refers to the insight that "if I have agency at all, 'it is opened up by the fact that I am constituted by a social world I never chose.' That 'my agency is riven by paradox' does not, however, make it impossible: 'It only means that paradox is the condition of its possibility.'"[18] Melancholia may seem a long way from the comic playfulness of a film like *The Lady Eve*, but maybe we should take another look at the "happy ending," in which Hopsy and Jean finally retire together to their stateroom onboard ship. He confesses that he is already married (to Eve, Jean's alter ego), and she replies, "Don't worry darling, so am I." She is so far ahead of him that I wonder what kind of happy ending is this?

Instead of a marriage suite, the darkness behind the cracked door might be a tomb. And who sneaks out of the dark space where he must have been waiting for Hopsy, but Muggsy. *The Lady Eve* is a film crowded with homosocial coupling. Jean/Eve is the only woman in the cast with a speaking part, besides Hopsy's mother, who has a few perfunctory lines. Hopsy and Muggsy are a virtual couple, having been up the Amazon together and back. As Hopsy's "bodyguard, governess, and very bad valet," Muggsy also feeds Emma the snake, and, like the viewer, is in on the joke of Stanwyck's performance. Above all, he is threatened by her intrusion into Hopsy's life and is unambiguously jealous. Harry and his valet, Gerald, who is also his partner in crime and his partner at breakfast, form another couple. This is a man's world, in other words, in keeping with the book of Genesis, which assigns Eve to the role of transgressive knowledge.

The paranoid reading of *The Lady Eve* would argue that Jean/Eve, despite her conniving agency, remains a commodity traded between men. She is successfully traded by her poor but loving father into a wealthy family governed by a benevolent patriarch. Her so-called uncle gives her away at her wedding, and her capitulation in the end, choosing love over money is a deus ex machina of astounding proportions, in which she throws out all of her hard-earned knowledge. She ends up with a man who has no idea who she is, while the two fathers are both content with her choice. Hopsy's father (Eugene Pallette) answers the phone as Mr. Pike (which is also Hopsy's name), standing in for his son, who has retreated into silence, and hears Eve's change of heart. For his part, Harry somehow believes that Hopsy will continue to be his stooge, even while married to his cardsharp daughter.

The Lady Eve is one of many films that Stanwyck made in which her character has no mother and is very close to her father—so close that they might be mistaken for lovers (e.g., *Gambling Lady* and *The Furies*). In quite a few films she is tapped to replace her father, to step into his shoes, and either will inherit or has already inherited his power or property (*The Miracle Woman, A Message to Garcia, Union Pacific* [1939], *The Gay Sisters, Executive Suite, Cattle Queen of Montana*, and *Escape to Burma*). Like Athena, she is born from her father's brow, but as an Oedipal woman, she can only be the hero and truly claim her inheritance in the company of a husband. On her honeymoon, Eve says to Hopsy, "I know you'd be both husband and father to me," but she says this as part of her grand performance as the bride with a thousand lovers, and therefore the statement drips with irony.

As a melancholic hero, Jean/Eve/Stanwyck is appropriately fragmented and divided. The second time she takes over the narration, she speaks in Jean's American voice about her prediction for the budding romance between Eve and Hopsy (Charles). She lounges on her "uncle's" couch, playing the "cockeyed duchess" Eve Sidwich, and just as she says to her uncle (and the viewer) "one day," we cut to her riding with Charles, and the images unfold accordingly, until gradually, with a bit of horseplay, the couple's voices are synced up to their faces. Eve leads Charles into a repetition of the confession of love that he made to her as Jean on the boat, only this time her dialogue is on a slightly different, ironic, plane than his. The horses' "nuzzling" interruptions compound the silliness and augment her version of the scene against Charles's naïve seriousness. He is once again the butt of the joke as her performance literally directs the scene. Her voice and body are separated at first, but as the scene evolves, her performative control of the situation is consolidated. Their marriage is a brief interlude, a social ritual performed perfunctorily in a montage without dialogue, and then the honeymoon unfolds exactly as she planned it. She accurately predicts Charles's response to her saga of multiple lovers and manages to shock him right off the train and into the mud, his fifth pratfall of the film.

Barbara Stanwyck and Henry Fonda in *The Lady Eve* (1941)

Thus, in *The Lady Eve* we have a character who is truly disruptive of the status quo, a figure who is able to deceive, to masquerade, and to shape-shift not only as a body but also as a voice with narrative authority. Like Emma the snake, she is a danger—to the class system and to the patriarchy—and like the biblical Eve, she knows the vulnerabilities of man. So why is this not a triumphant "feminist" picture? We could point to Stanwyck's fabulous costumes, which transform her into a fetish object for all the men to feast their eyes on, except that in the real world off-screen, Edith Head's creation of a "silhouette" for Stanwyck in this film gave her a huge boost in the labor market of Hollywood stardom (see chapter E). No, the main reason for my disappointment is the closure of marriage and the tomb to which she finally disappears with a man who does not know who she is.

Despite the final entombment, I would argue that the performative performativity of the actor herself recuperates this film for a feminist reading, not as a utopian moment of women's agency but as a reading of melancholia and incomplete grief, a "debarred feminist discourse."[19] In Sophocles's play, Antigone is buried alive, as is Jean/Eve, retreating into the dark space of the truly fallen man known as Hopsy. That is probably the extent of the parallels between Jean/Eve and Antigone, except that Jean's critique of the patriarchy, which is simply that women are harshly judged as being "good" or "bad"—a fundamental duality of studio-era Hollywood—is in keeping with Butler's claim for the importance of Antigone as a "textual problem": "Antigone emerges in her criminality to speak in the name of politics and the law: she absorbs the very language of the state, against which she rebels, and hers becomes a politics not of oppositional purity but of the scandalously impure."[20] If psychoanalysis had taken the model of Antigone rather than Oedipus, Butler suggests, a very different model of kinship, the psyche, and law would have emerged, which is more than an inversion of the Oedipal model. As a discourse of intelligibility, Antigone functions as a "chiasm within the vocabulary of political norms."[21]

It's almost as if Hollywood had a specific slot, a specific name for women who are neither "good" nor "bad" and who trouble the terms of the social contract. Eve Sidwich and Jean Harrington actually come together in Anne Baxter's character in *All about Eve* (1950). Joanne Woodward stars in *The Three Faces of Eve* in 1957, and Claudette Colbert plays Eve Peabody in the screwball comedy *Midnight* in 1939, all of whom are disruptive women, challenging social norms and laws in a variety of ways. Their disruptive behaviors may be quite different, but they share the insight that knowledge is not incompatible with affect. These "Eves" are women who are multiply divided and whose melancholy may be expressed through ironic dissembling and witty repartee but is nevertheless readily legible in the archive.

Stanwyck's double performance in *The Lady Eve* and her appropriation of the narration in the two instances mentioned above, which I have thus far described as "performative performativity," may in fact be an example of what Sedgwick calls the "periperformative." Unlike the direct "utterance" such as the marital "I do," periperformatives are "about performatives and cluster around performatives," and "they are lodged in a metaphorics of space."[22] For Sedgwick, this modality is most critically staged around the theater of marriage as it occurs in the nineteenth-century novel, when women use language to "sketch in a differential and multidirectional surround that may change and dramatize its meaning and effect."[23] The goal, or desire, of identifying the periperformative at work in *The Lady Eve* is to recognize the woman as hero of her own story, and as Sedgwick says of what she calls "reparative reading," "It is additive and accretive. Its fear … is that the culture surrounding it is inadequate or inimical to its nurture." I see reparative reading as a version of "reading against the grain"—specifically, reading against the historical void of eighty years (between the film's release and my writing about it) as a means of what Sedgwick calls "extracting substance from the objects of culture whose avowed desire has often been not to sustain them."[24] In Preston Sturges's official papers, stored at the

UCLA Library, there is a sad little note from Stanwyck to Sturges and his wife, Louise, thanking them for flowers. She says, "Marion and Zeppo [Marx] phoned me after the preview and they were so pleased and happy. Zep says it's the best so far. Wow Preston, all you have to do is write me another please."[25] Not only does she beg for another great script (which never came), but she also invokes the social context of marriage in which she and everyone else around her was subsumed.

FRED MACMURRAY
KISSING AND PLAYING

In the case of film, the fact that the actor represents someone else
before the audience matters much less than the fact that he represents
himself before the apparatus.

—Walter Benjamin, "The Work of Art in the Age of
Mechanical Reproduction"

IN HIS CRYPTIC NOTES on film performance, Walter Benjamin describes
the actor's work as a "testing" process that is made public. While he grossly
underestimates the ability of film actors to develop roles and full-fledged
characters,[1] Benjamin did underline the stakes of film performance in
modernity. "Estrangement" and "self-alienation" are the terms he uses for
the actor whose humanity and "aura" are given over to the mechanics of
filmmaking. Benjamin defines "aura" here as the presence of the actor "in
the here and now," as on a stage.[2] While Benjamin is concerned with fiction
film generally as a space where the actor is separated from their own image,
I would like to suggest, for heuristic purposes, that of all the gestures and
behaviors on display during the studio era of American cinema, perhaps the
most critical instance of "self-alienation" might be the love scene or, more
specifically, the kissing scene.

The question posed by Benjamin is whether the cult of the movie star
is matched by the cult of the audience (the masses) to reify the "putrid magic
of its commodity character."[3] He offers a strategy of unbinding this effect of
film in the dialectics of semblance and play. In one of the long notes to the
artwork essay, he discusses the imbrication of these two concepts, which can
only be illuminated through historical specificity: "What is lost in the
withering of semblance and the decay of aura in works of art is matched by
a huge gain in the scope for play [*Spiel Raum*]."[4] Acting is by definition a

mode of "playing," but what can it reveal about the actor's self-alienation within an industrial production mode? A close look at some of Stanwyck's kissing scenes, taking into account some of the profilmic details of their production—their historicity—suggests that "play" might be understood as a rejection of the heterosexual "magic" of the cult of Hollywood.

Actors, for the most part, then as now, took kissing scenes in stride, as a requisite feature of film performance. Audiences, however, often indulged in the fantasy of favorite stars loving each other on- and off-screen, and Stanwyck's marriage to Robert Taylor in 1939 certainly fed into such movieland lore. Examination of a small sample of Stanwyck's intimate scenes with male actors complicates Benjamin's assessment and tests it as a methodology. It may be possible to glimpse the lost aura of "presence" on-screen within the reciprocity between two actors—which certainly can be on display on many levels besides kissing, including the whip-smart dialogue of films such as *Double Indemnity* and *The Lady Eve*, among other Stanwyck titles. By isolating the kissing scenes alone, I want to refresh Benjamin's argument, which insists on the inherent shock experience of modernity as the crisis that eclipses the actor's aura, in terms of the gendered landscape of American cinema. For an eloquent argument for the importance of kissing scenes to the greater romance of the movies, I turn to Edgar Morin: "The kiss is not only the key technique of love-making, nor the cinematic substitute for intercourse forbidden by censorship: it is the triumphant symbol of the role of the face and the soul in twentieth century love.... The kiss is not only the piquancy in all Western films. It is the profound expression of a complex of love which eroticizes the soul and mystifies the body."[5]

Because most of her career was subject to the limitations of the Production Code, Stanwyck has very few kissing scenes that are truly reciprocal, but that does not mean she does not know how to play at kissing. Steven Harvey described Stanwyck's long list of leading men as "globs of unleavened dough,"[6] and Andrew Klevan counts Fred MacMurray among them, despite being a "deceptively agile performer."[7] Stanwyck made four films with MacMurray, seven with Joel McCrea, and three with Gary Cooper—all three of whom have said in various places that they don't care much for acting and prefer westerns, where they just have to "be themselves." This was not an option for women actors. Many of the scripts for Stanwyck films feature men who are genuinely moronic—including *The Lady Eve*, *Meet John Doe*, *Banjo on My Knee* (1936), and *The Bride Wore Boots*, among others—of which we can say only Henry Fonda in the first of these titles takes his clownishness seriously.

In Klevan's adept analysis of Stanwyck's acting, he singles out "reciprocity" as one of her signature assets, meaning her responsiveness to other characters. He concludes that section of his book by saying, "Stanwyck achieves integration while still appearing independent."[8] The example that he uses to sustain this argument is a scene with Joan Blondell in *Night Nurse*, which is indeed a lovely scene but one of the very few in Stanwyck's career in which she interacts with another woman, the main exception being *Stella Dallas* (see chapter S). In fact, "reciprocity" depends a great deal on the other actor, as well as the script, and in this chapter I explore both Stanwyck's performance of reciprocity as it pertains to the Hollywood kiss and her relationship with male actors.

Klevan leaves out the fact that Stanwyck's star status and the large salaries for which she negotiated so well actually made it difficult for her to costar with equally well paid actors. Particularly when the industry shifted toward independently financed productions in the 1950s, Stanwyck's name, for the most part, sold films on its own. As Kevin Esch has argued, "distant reading" of performances in studio-era Hollywood are more appropriate than "close reading" by critics like Klevan if we want to incorporate a conception of the industrial factors within an analysis of performance.[9] Where Benjamin saw an abstract mechanism of capitalism and technology, we are now in a position to understand the mechanics of personnel, finance, and technique, with all of their own contingencies, that underpin industrial film production.

Esch's argument for a methodological reconciliation of "inside" the actor and "outside" is couched in a theory of "mythistory," in which the aura of the star is conjoined with a recognition of difference. Film acting, for Esch, creates a mythology that can produce a "dialectical response, at once recognizing our shared humanity and exposing our singular difference, instead of dissolving our difference under the spectacular myth of capitalism."[10] As Benjamin understood in the 1930s, "aura" in film was converted into a cult of personality, and thus, if there is any auratic value to be distilled from capitalist mystification, it will not lie in close analysis of faces or gestures alone. Esch's point that the actor's labor does not occur in a vacuum is critical. He recognizes the value of the "here and now" of performance, and indeed this is where Benjamin's remarks on acting are most valuable: the actor is the most critical interface between humanity and industrial technology. The film actor, for Benjamin, preserves their humanity in the face of the apparatus—which is precisely the practice of the factory worker who goes to the cinema in the evening to see the film performer "take revenge on their behalf not only by asserting his humanity … against the apparatus, but by placing that apparatus in the service of his triumph."[11]

As Manohla Dargis has observed, "There are many flavors of cinematic kisses: seductive, chaste, dramatic, playful, erotic, parental."[12] Stanwyck managed them all but excelled with variations on the forced kiss, which were plentiful in the studio era, as Dargis notes. The big kiss can also be a disruptive blocking-out of faces once the shot moves into a close-up of shoulder and hair, and it frequently dissolves to black, either to start a new scene, now that love has been declared and effectively sealed, or to end the picture with the formation of the couple. The fade to black can also be an ominous sign of the sexualized violence that the forced kiss promises but is carefully elided by the Production Code. Dargis makes this point and significantly includes a comment in her article that "Stanwyck's performances along with her radiant charisma and her humanity convey a fullness of female life that many movies have tried—and still try—to deny."[13] If we inquire how this humanity is revealed in the context of kissing scenes, it may help to reconcile Benjamin's remarks on acting with those on the lost aura lurking within the mechanics of cinema.

Stanwyck's career features surprisingly few genuinely romantic kisses, particularly after 1934. Even in *Baby Face*, where she has some of her most sensual moments, with soft lighting and glowing close-ups, she is playing her paramours for cash and thus "playacting" her kisses. In many scenes through the 1930s and '40s, her eyes indicate that her mind is elsewhere. For Benjamin, it is precisely "play" that points the way back to the lost aura of technological modernity, by way of a second technology: "The origin of the second technology lies at the point where, by an unconscious ruse, human beings first began to distance themselves from nature. It lies, in other words, in play."[14] *This Is My Affair* (1939) ends with a playful back-and-forth between Stanwyck and her real-life husband Robert Taylor as she tries to go onstage to join a dance troupe while he keeps pulling her into the wings for a series of smooches (see chapter V). Reciprocity in this scene literally becomes a dance.

Caught over the shoulder of Taylor in another scene in *This Is My Affair*, or Joel McCrea in *Gambling Lady*, Stanwyck's gestures make the kiss complicated, as there is often something "wrong" with the match. In the former she is attached to another man; in the latter she believes she has wronged him. This is certainly the case with MacMurray in *Remember the Night*, where he is the prosecutor and she is the criminal. MacMurray has been quoted as saying, "I was lucky enough to make four pictures with Barbara. In the first I turned her in, in the second I killed her, in the third I left her for another woman, and in the fourth I pushed her over a waterfall. The one thing all these pictures had in common was that I fell in love with Barbara Stanwyck, and I did too."[15]

MacMurray unfortunately misremembers the order of the films and the details, as they made *The Moonlighter* in 1953, where she falls down a waterfall without being pushed (see chapter R), before *There's Always Tomorrow* in 1955, in which she breaks off their affair and he stays with his wife. The love stories within each of these films play out a bit differently in each case. In *Double Indemnity* their characters are attracted to each other in a sordid, lustful, and dangerous affair. Their embraces and kisses in Neff's (MacMurray) apartment are loaded with tension. He grabs her the first time and she says, "You're hurting me, Walter," before returning his kiss; and in another scene he says, "Shut up, Baby," before grabbing her again. The camera remains each time on his eyes rather than hers, and the tension is in keeping with the fact that they plan the murder while making love. Reciprocity in this case is expressed in Stanwyck's cold, distanced gaze, as if her mind is not on Neff as much as it is on her soon-to-be-dead husband. The insincerity of these love scenes is ironically underscored by a letter from a fan in *Photoplay* magazine complaining that MacMurray's wedding ring was clearly visible in the shot of the kiss, and she claimed it made it impossible for her to believe in his sincerity as a lover.[16]

In a Paramount publicity piece, when MacMurray was asked about the kissing of all the women he had performed with, he said that Stanwyck was deliberate and thorough, as opposed to some others, such as Carole Lombard, who "likes 'em rapturous and enthusiastic."[17] Fred's own preference is said to be aligned with Sylvia Sidney: "A kiss is just a kiss … just a smack and let's get on with it."[18] Perhaps the most "moving" scenes between Stanwyck and MacMurray can be found in *There's Always Tomorrow*, toward the end of the film, but the kiss itself, on a rooftop bar in shadow, is almost incidental. She wears a white stole that softens the lighting, and her face before the kiss is racked with the pain of separation; after it she looks down at the ground, avoiding his gaze. Later in his office, with torrential rain pouring down outside the windows, the two mirror each other's misery in maybe the best example of "reciprocity" between them, produced through lighting and body language, costume and framing (see chapter A).

The Moonlighter, a film shot in 3D that failed at the box office, is not a bad western and is a genre to which MacMurray's relaxed style was well suited; it's also one of Stanwyck's favorites. MacMurray had a way of absorbing the high energy and dynamism of Stanwyck's style into his bulky presence and soft-spoken manner, and their bodies and eyes meet most generously in this film. MacMurray is most relaxed in the guise of a Westerner, like many of Stanwyck's costars. The passion is only a brief interlude in the action-packed western, and the big kiss is an unfortunate

Fred MacMurray and Barbara Stanwyck in *There's Always Tomorrow* (1955)

capitulation for Stanwyck's character from being a sheriff's deputy out to arrest Wes (MacMurray) to becoming his lover after he heroically saves her from drowning in a raging river.

MacMurray, like Stanwyck, had a successful television career, including the long-running series *My Three Sons* (1960–1972), for which he negotiated an astonishing contract that led to what became known as the "MacMurray system." He only had to work sixty-five days a year, during which the crew shot all of his scenes alone, and then they matched them up with everyone else's shots on the other days. As one of the actors said, "It was really hard for everyone," even if he respected Fred for getting such a cushy deal.[19] The "MacMurray system" perfectly illustrates Benjamin's argument about "the apparatus" of film production, and it is a far cry from the give-and-take rhythm of MacMurray and Stanwyck's banter in *Double Indemnity* or their mutual sadness in *There's Always Tomorrow*. Shooting scenes in such a piecemeal way is exemplary of Benjamin's "highly productive use of the human being's self-alienation,"[20] and it is emblematic of the industrial machine at work, favoring the star but cutting him off from any meaningful human relations.

Benjamin imagined that film would one day be free of the fetters of capitalism and that "the masses" would not become the fascist *Volk* but a collectivity of individuals. A distanced reading of acting enables us to recognize the ephemeral, inchoate affect of Stanwyck and MacMurray's rooftop kiss in *There's Always Tomorrow* and their comfort with each other in *The Moonlighter*, along with the understanding that they respected each other as professionals in a difficult industry. MacMurray and Stanwyck were good friends off-screen and shared similar conservative values. Stanwyck would not have performed well in the "MacMurray system," because she did so much more than read her lines to the camera/audience. MacMurray called the viewers "customers" and knew he was peddling wares to them, whereas Stanwyck consistently tried to create imaginary worlds around her characters.

If the Hollywood kiss is the promised utopia of genre cinema, it is most often a commodified form of that payoff. Stanwyck's best romantic scenes are those in which the big kiss is a tortured one or a failed one—and often a forced one—undermining and complicating generic expectations. As filmmakers began challenging the Hays Code in the postwar period and sexuality became a theme of "adult" cinema of the 1950s, the generic kiss gave way to expressions of physical desire that Stanwyck was ready and willing to incorporate into her performance.

Comparing her three films made with Gary Cooper is one way of mapping a shift of sorts in Stanwyck's play with "reciprocity" in the delivery of love scenes. In both *Meet John Doe* and *Ball of Fire*, Cooper plays men who are ignorant of the ways of the world, in need of Stanwyck's handling and training. In the former, their final triumphant kiss should come when she saves him from suicide, but instead she collapses in his arms and he carries her off. In *Ball of Fire*, Stanwyck's character, Sugarpuss O'Shea, is eager to teach the fussy professor Bertrand Potts the ways of the world, so she piles up a stack of reference books to kiss Cooper at his level. Face-to-face, she kisses him once, "here's yum"; twice "and here's the other yum"; and finally, "here's yum yum," at which point she knocks him over with her full weight. She comes on strongly and Cooper takes the rest of the film to figure it out. She comes on strongly again to Cooper's character, Jeff, in *Blowing Wild*, leaning in on him as he lies in bed, but he pushes her away and refuses to reciprocate—partly because she is married to his partner, and partly because he has a new squeeze, and partly because she simply repels him. From comedy to melodrama, she plays against Cooper's built-in inertia to create complicated scenes of desire, working with and against his bulky size and reticent grin.

Several of Stanwyck's postwar films stand out as conveying passion, as she resumed her reputation for "adult" content acquired in the pre-Code years. Both *Clash by Night* and *Jeopardy* (John Sturges, 1953) feature intense scenes of passion in which power and desire become overlayed. Neither Robert Ryan nor Ralph Meeker had significant acting training, but both came to their romantic matches with Stanwyck following Broadway plays directed by Actors Studio stalwarts Lee Strasberg and Elia Kazan. Ryan played the role of Earl Pfeiffer in *Clash by Night* on Broadway, directed by Strasberg, before taking on the role in the film version, directed by Fritz Lang. Meeker took over from Brando in *Streetcar Named Desire* (1951), with Kazan directing for the 1949–1950 season, before playing an escaped convict in *Jeopardy*. These actors gave Stanwyck a lot more to work with than the "unleavened dough" she was more typically offered. Her love scenes with these two actors are charged with danger and desire, as they play unstable, troubled men. The only other comparable scene in her career is her final great scene with Richard Chamberlain in *The Thorn Birds*,[21] in which he—playing a young priest—rebuffs the passionate confession of physical desire by Stanwyck's seventy-six-year-old dowager (see chapter Q). She does not force a kiss, but she pleads her vulnerability in an angry growl: "Kiss me, Ralph. Kiss me on the mouth…. Inside this stupid body I am still young. I still feel. I still want. I still dream, and I still love you."

Clash by Night, based on a play by Clifford Odets, was one of the only Stanwyck films that was produced by a woman—Harriet Parsons. It may not have received great reviews, and Fritz Lang was a bit out of his comfort zone with the melodramatic material, but it is steamy enough and was billed in *Look* magazine as a sexy, scorching film.[22] Stanwyck plays Mae Douglas, a hard-bitten, heavy-drinking woman returning to her hometown on the California coast after a broken marriage. Robert Ryan's character was described as "neurotic" in *Photoplay*,[23] and the two flirt with each other, even though she marries his older and more home-bound friend Jerry (Paul Douglas). After an extended flirtation, Earl (Ryan) suddenly grabs Mae (Stanwyck) in the kitchen and kisses her roughly until she gradually relents and returns his passion. In the hot weather he wears a wife-beater T-shirt (à la Brando), which she slides her hand under as she presses him close to her. The scene is loaded with a push-pull energy as if Mae is drawn to Ryan's energy despite her best intentions. RKO used still images of this scene to publicize the film as "adult" content.[24]

The inner violence of *Clash by Night* is also a performed violence, not only in Robert Ryan's large gestures and loud voice but also in a fight between Earl and Jerry in a projection booth. Mae tries to break it up and gets shoved

Robert Ryan and Barbara Stanwyck in *Clash by Night* (1952)

harshly against one of the large machines. Stanwyck reportedly suffered more bruises than the men during the shoot, and while this may not have been exactly what Benjamin was getting at in his claims that film acting embodies the shock experience of modernity, such a detail opens up the text to a more distanced reading. In Jodi Brooks's analysis of Benjamin's comments on acting, she suggests that he "calls for ... a gestural practice which does not simply document or imitate the structuring experience in modernity, but rather mimetically embraces it as the basis for a new form of transmissibility and narrativity."[25] Film acting, in other words, provides a place where the crisis of experience and inability to grasp more immediate modes of communication (like storytelling) can be foregrounded. Brooks looks to Benjamin for the articulation of "new forms of transmissibility" that may in turn provide "a valuable framework to study the *gestus* of a gendered experience of crisis."[26]

Of all of Stanwyck's "love scenes," the one in *Jeopardy* may be the most significant instance of her "playacting" as a response to the potential nexus of aura and shock in film performance. *Jeopardy* is a very simple film, with very few characters, set in Mexico but shot in Dana Point, not too far from Los Angeles. Stanwyck plays Helen Stilwin, a housewife on vacation with

Barbara Stanwyck and Ralph Meeker in *Jeopardy* (1953)

her husband (Barry Sullivan) and young son. The husband gets his foot trapped under water on a beach, and as the tide gradually threatens to drown him, Helen drives off to find help. She finds Lawson (Ralph Meeker), an escaped convict, hanging around an abandoned garage, but he has other ideas than simply helping her save her husband. He drives her to an empty building in the desert, corners her, flirting, flattering her, and she gradually adopts his relaxed mannerisms, "playacting" her willingness for the sake of his cooperation. She casually removes his cigarettes from his shirt pocket, saying, "I'll do anything for my husband," leaning back on the hood of the car in her T-shirt and housewifey skirt, flicking her cigarette ash toward him. He kisses her roughly, but she does not return the embrace, and the shot dissolves to the husband back in the rising waters. Cut to Helen and her savior coming to the rescue in the Ford. Is this a rape scene? Or a housewife's discovery of passion?

After they successfully free the husband, using great ingenuity and teamwork, Helen coldly sends Lawson off with her husband's papers and clothes to escape the police. In voice-over at the end, she wonders how she will feel when she hears he's been trapped: "I've always wondered if every wife wonders?" Although Stanwyck and Meeker's scene together is hardly a love scene, it is one of the most charged in Stanwyck's career, mainly because she adopts the physical mannerisms of Meeker's "bad boy" character. He is dangerous and the scene is edgy, and although it can certainly be interpreted as a "falling for your rapist" scenario, and is definitely transactional, it nevertheless hints at some other way of being and having sex than Hollywood in 1953 would typically condone. *Jeopardy* did well at the box office and earned Stanwyck some of her best reviews of the decade. Critics described it as a suspense thriller and bemoaned the "unconvincing" happy-ever-after ending,[27] suggesting either that Meeker's escape was immoral or perhaps that her return to her marriage was less than satisfying.

Analysis of kissing scenes cannot be separated from the work of writers and directors, but it is especially interwoven with the work of actors working together. For Benjamin, the potential of screen acting is a glimpse of the human within the technology, and the "love scene" in *Jeopardy* works because of the reciprocity between the two actors, offering a potential view of something hidden within the apparatus. The promised payoff of the big kiss is repeatedly a failure to connect for Stanwyck's characters, and in that failure, something more "human" is conveyed and that "humanism" is precisely one of inequity, gendered power, and anxiety. When she had the opportunity to work with method-adjacent actors, she rose to the occasion, and both *Jeopardy* and *Clash by Night* suggest what she may have been capable of if she had been given more opportunities to work with agile and talented men such as Robert Ryan and Ralph Meeker.

If for Benjamin, the screen actor is always being tested in the studio setting, the failed test provides the conditions for the legibility of the lost aura within the phantasmagoria.[28] As a movie star, Stanwyck always passes her tests, but she also fails repeatedly to fulfill the promised romantic role, and her kisses are loaded with anxiety and doubt—and not always because the kiss is forced or, as Dargis puts it, "rapey";[29] sometimes her characters are simply uncommitted. Given the right circumstances, she plays kissing scenes by "playing" her scene partners, using the generic, predictable gesture as a mode of reciprocal challenge and effectively demystifying the magic of the Hollywood kiss. From the distance of several decades, her play can be read as a kind of message from inside the heart of the beast of studio-era cinema.

NO MAN OF HER OWN
DOUBLE WOMEN AND THE STAR

Feminist critical theory must be attentive to both the temporality of reading
and the historicity of reading.

—Mary Ann Doane, Femmes Fatales

THE THEME OF THE DOUBLE WOMAN was remarkably prevalent in
American cinema of the 1940s. Either one actor played two women, as
Stanwyck does in *The Lady Eve,* or one actor played twins, as Bette Davis
does in *A Stolen Life* (1946) and Olivia de Havilland does in *The Dark Mirror*
(1946). Among the variations on this theme, including split personalities
and moral oppositions of good girls and bad girls, we could include the
"hidden personalities" of characters like Phyllis Dietrichson and Thelma
Jordan. Jeanine Basinger has concluded that in the many films where the
woman is replaceable, substitutable, and replicated, the female character is
reduced to a thing-like object.[1] Often the plot revolves around appearances
that the men cannot see past. Where *The Lady Eve* treats this confusion as
comedy, with the performer in control of the situation, this is not the typical
scenario by any means. Gothic melodramas often end "happily," but not
without someone paying the price, including traumatic experiences and
violent deaths. While each film has its own complicated textual dynamics,
the theme offered great opportunities for the strong women actors of the
period to play two characters in the same film or to hold the secret of one
character within the personality of another. What happens when we see the
woman not as an object but as an actor?

No Man of Her Own was variously described in the press of the time as
an adult melodrama, a woman's picture, a soap opera, and a tearjerker,
although it also looks a lot like a film noir. The crossover between noir and
melodrama and the genre expectations around Stanwyck's star image are

indicated by a reviewer who said, "Barbara Stanwyck without a gun is like Bob Hope without a pun…. It looked like she might go the distance without becoming trigger happy. She didn't quite make it though."[2] In the far-fetched story, adapted from a novel by William Irish (aka Cornell Woolrich) by two women screenwriters—Sally Benson and Catherine Turney—along with Leisen, Stanwyck plays a woman named Helen Ferguson (which is also the name of Stanwyck's longtime publicist, changed from the name given in the novel) who impersonates another woman named Patrice Harkness. Helen is a poor pregnant woman who is abandoned by her no-good boyfriend, Stephen Morley (Lyle Bettger). Helen "accidentally" assumes Patrice's identity in a train accident that she survives and Patrice doesn't. Patrice's unborn child and her husband perish as well, and because Patrice's in-laws had never met her, it is simply too hard for Helen not to play along and give her child a good home. The melodrama edges into noir territory when Helen is blackmailed by Morley and she decides to kill him, only to find that someone else has shot him before her.

Basinger describes Stanwyck's performance in *No Man* as perpetually hysterical,[3] but I would reserve that judgment for *Sorry, Wrong Number* (see chapter P). In this film she carries a great deal of the suspense in her face. She is constantly afraid of being discovered as an imposter, as she trips up repeatedly on the details of her namesake and her dead husband. Leisen frequently leaves the camera on Stanwyck's face for reactions to off-screen events and conversations; she acts silently in other instances as her voice-off repeats phrases like "I can't do it" or "It's not too late," contradicting her actions. In fact, the voice-off in this film has been discussed in some detail by Britta Sjogren as exemplary of the "dissonance" of women's voice-over in Hollywood cinema. Sjogren prefers the term "voice-off" to "voice-over" because it "registers an independent space" that is not a layer over the image but works dialectically with the image.[4]

Sjogren challenges the theorization of women's voice-over proposed by Kaja Silverman and Mary Ann Doane, for whom the split between voice and body posed a perpetual problem for the female spectator. Within the psychoanalytic model of film theory that predominated in the 1970s and '80s, the concern was for a "unified" subject position that seemed always to be male, and the splitting of women's bodies and voices simply compounded that process.[5] Instead, Sjogren proposes that the voice-off provides a critical heterogeneity to the construction of female subjectivity. The voice registers an alternate space to the image-sphere, providing a surplus, and a dynamic space outside the misogynist contours of narrative. She describes women's voice-off not as a "resistance" or a "subversion" of the text but as a digression and a dissonance. Because the voice is so frequently poised as if speaking to other women, it communicates a "feminine politics of sorts": "The specific contradictions of being female in patriarchy … are amplified through the voice-off, in its evocation of a heterogeneous consciousness, of a self that is also other."[6]

Sjogren's argument about the woman's voice-off is very convincing, particularly in the context of films seen decades after they were produced. The psychoanalytic approach tended to imply a spectator who was intricately fixed and constructed by a text that addressed spectators' gender-specific desires and anxieties, whereas contemporary viewers are radically "unfixed" in terms of history, sexuality, and viewing conditions. For Sjogren, the cinematic voice-off is uncanny in the way it "suggests both a double for the body and a possible threat to its coherence."[7] Although I would agree in principle that "the voice resists efforts to image it," I would also point to the critical role of the actor's voice, which is attached to a very specific body.

By 1950, audiences were familiar with Stanwyck's distinctive sultry, smoky, full-bodied voice from the thirty-eight radio programs she had broadcast since 1936 (see chapter V). In *No Man of Her Own*, Stanwyck's Brooklyn accent lingers in her pronunciation of "Caulfield," the name of the town where the Harkness family lives. In her opening words, Stanwyck's voice is a throaty whisper, describing the too-perfect residential street that the camera moves through to a very large, too-perfect house with a square lawn and neat flower beds. Cutting to the inside, the camera floats through the foyer while she describes the satin finish and the smell of wax. Even before we get to the line "but not for us, but not for us," we know from the edge in her voice that it is not all as perfect as it seems. The camera settles on her face as the phone rings and her husband, Bill (brother-in-law to the original Patrice), answers it. Her monologue continues—"This is murder"— as she silently awaits his return, awkwardly cradling an oversized baby in her arms (see chapter D). Both husband and wife fear the police will arrest them for the murder of Morley. In the original Woolrich novel, Bill's mother (Jane Cowl) confesses to the crime in a note penned just before her death, but Bill has altered the crime scene to make it appear like a gangland gambling-scene murder, so he destroys his mother's confession.

In the film, however, the mother's confession is revealed to be a false confession, and the blame is placed squarely on "the blonde" (a woman played by Carole Mathews who has been seen in a few scenes previously with Morley as his new sidekick), presumably out of jealousy. Thus, Helen/Patrice and Bill are free to live happily ever after in their perfect house, with only the secret of her identity between them. Nevertheless, it is hardly a satisfactory form of closure, as the script simply produces another woman as the killer. In at least one critical reading of the film, domestic stability and the overbearing support of a stable and wealthy husband seem to triumph over and "cure" the victimization of the unwed mother.[8] Indeed, the relationship between Helen/Patrice and Bill is less than passionate and somewhat opportunistic on both their parts. Bill sees through the masquerade and leads Helen/Patrice into little traps to prove it but keeps her secret and falls in love anyway—all for the sake of the house and having an heir for the family fortune. *No Man of Her Own* belongs to the gothic genre partly due to this power of the house over its inhabitants. It is not haunted or dimly lit, or even spatially labyrinthine like most gothic houses, but it is nevertheless creepy in its overbearing size and perfection.

The gothic sensibility, with its byzantine plots featuring doubles and mistaken identities, unlikely accidents and atmospheric oppression, brought together the style and narrative obfuscation of film noir with women's tales of disappointment and loss in the 1940s. Helen Hanson has argued that "the gothic narrative drive is more retrogressive than progressive."[9] It deals in partial knowledge and partial vision, withholding critical information from its female protagonists and from its viewer. For Hanson, the potential for social critique in the gothic cycle lies in the cultural anxiety embedded in retrogressive narration—where the secrets from the past hold the future hostage. The genre vividly illustrates the failed promise of the war years for women—their relationships with war-ravaged men, rushed marriages, and the enclosure of the domestic sphere. In *No Man* this retrogression opens onto a kind of void, marked by death, repetition, and duplication.

The original title of Woolrich's novel is *I Married a Dead Man*, which, along with "The Lie," was a working title for the film in production. The shift from first person in the novel's title to third person in the film's title nevertheless retains the "man" in a film about an unwed mother. These cycles of obfuscation are played out in *No Man* in the doubling, tripling, and multiplication of women standing in for each other. Besides Patrice and Helen, we have the blonde murderer and Stanwyck's publicist—and of course Stanwyck herself. In this vortex of identities, no man is included. Moreover, Helen/Patrice arguably have three men between them: Morley, the blackmailer and father of Helen's child (whom Helen is forced to marry under threat of blackmail); Patrice's dead husband, Hugh; and Bill, the brother-in-law whom Helen marries after Morley is killed. This is a film about negation, in which the actor is the last woman standing. Sjogren notes that in Stanwyck's opening voice-off, she starts by addressing the viewer, as if she were telling a story, but then she shifts to address her husband and

Barbara Stanwyck in *No Man of Her Own* (1950)

then the baby. Such shifts in enunciation are typical of the woman's film and less evident in male voice-off narration. For Sjogren, it suggests that "the female subject speaks *through* difference, enunciating a plurality of voices in one."[10] Throughout the film, Stanwyck's voice interrupts her actions, including her saying, "I won't stop here" as she marries Bill. In these instances, she is talking to herself as Helen, reminding us that she remains two people, Helen and Patrice. At one point she realizes (in voice-off) that the family thinks she has amnesia, which is why she can't remember many details about her late husband or her own past.

Stanwyck's hair and makeup in *No Man of Her Own* make her face look wider and rounder than usual, and it works well for all the frontal close-ups in which conflicting thoughts run through the character's mind. It is an understated yet greatly nuanced performance, in which she remains coolly distanced from all the other characters. In her scenes with Morley/Bettger, when he tries to blackmail her, she is anxious and vulnerable, but she never actually steps up to confront anyone in the film. One scene was shot and deleted in which Bettger gives her a good slap, and perhaps she had an outburst that also hit the cutting room floor, although it's hard to know for sure.[11] With John Lund she does all the emotional work, expressing

Barbara Stanwyck and Phyllis Thaxter in *No Man of Her Own* (1950)

nervousness and anxiety while he towers over her, using his body as a tool of protective smothering rather than his face or his voice, which sustains a curious monotone of Anglo-Saxon power and authority. As Helen, before "becoming" Patrice, Stanwyck wears "no makeup"—as the real Patrice notices—and looks appropriately pure of heart. In the scene with Phyllis Thaxter, who plays the original Patrice Harkness, Stanwyck's character is passively in awe of the carefree energy of the young pregnant bride marrying into a wealthy family. The two women are in the train washroom preparing for the night when everything turns topsy-turvy.

Leisen filmed the accident scene by literally turning the set inside a steel drum while the camera rolled so that the women rolled from wall to wall.[12] Of course Stanwyck refused a stunt double and took the bruises herself (see chapter R). One anonymous reviewer in *Cue* magazine, probably a woman, opened their review of *No Man* by saying, "Some day somebody's going to start a Society for the Prevention of Cruelty to Actresses. When they do, they can put Barbara Stanwyck and me both down as charter members." The reviewer goes on to list a number of other recent films in which Stanwyck had recently suffered various punishments, including *Sorry, Wrong Number*; *The Lady Gambles*; *The File on Thelma Jordan*; and *The Other Love*. The reviewer blames William Irish and Mitchell Leisen and commends Stanwyck for suffering "with tremendous fortitude."[13]

No Man of Her Own was one of five films that Stanwyck made in 1950. *The File on Thelma Jordan* was shot in 1949 but held back from release until April 1950. A *Variety* story from January 1951 noted that 1950 marked "The End of an Era for Stars and System." The number of contracts signed with studios reached its lowest level in twenty-five years. Stanwyck was singled out as one of a handful of actors who remained busy, although her top-grossing film of the five was *To Please a Lady* (1950), in which she costars with Clark Gable. *The Furies* and *East Side, West Side* (1949) both did well at the box office, but *Thelma Jordan* and *No Man*, according to *Variety*, "didn't make the grade."[14] Both were marketed as melodramas targeted at women audiences, and Stanwyck was paired with relative newcomers Wendell Corey, John Lund, and Lyle Bettger. It was Bettger's first screen role, and he follows many other young men in acknowledging the help and support that Stanwyck offered to him as he learned the trade.[15] As relatively poorly received noirish melodramas built around Stanwyck's star image at the end of the gothic cycle, *Thelma Jordan* and *No Man* bear some intriguing parallels.

In *The File on Thelma Jordan*, Stanwyck plays another type of doubled character, as the drama gradually reveals that she is not the woman who the district attorney (Corey) and the audience thinks she is but is in fact a gangster's moll. The plot has echoes of *Double Indemnity*, and also *The Lady Eve*, insofar as there is some confusion in Thelma's own mind, as well as Corey's character's mind, as to whether she is a "dame" or if she is a good woman. As Thelma Jordan, Stanwyck wears elegant yet restrained Edith Head–designed outfits, not unlike the clothes that she wears playing Helen playing Patrice Harkness in *No Man*. Thelma's dual identity is revealed by a photograph pulled from the file in the police department: a photo of Stanwyck in a blonde wig, "trashy" dress, and makeup, smoking and drinking in a bar—the kind of character who returns as "the blonde" in *No Man of Her Own*. Like the photo in *The Lady Eve*, it comes from outside the diegesis of the film and functions as "evidence" of the truth behind Thelma Jordan's performance or impersonation of a nice middle-class girl living with her aged aunt (who is killed for her jewelry in the film's central murder plot). Isn't this the same blonde that Stanwyck becomes at the end of her luck, at the end of an alley, in *The Lady Gambles* (see chapter G)?

In *No Man of Her Own*, the lack of photographic evidence of the real Patrice Harkness is what enables Helen to carry out her impersonation, but it also creates a kind of vortex of identity, as she is in fact impersonating a dead woman whose image is (inexplicably) not known to the Harkness

Photograph of Barbara Stanwyck in *The File on Thelma Jordan* (1949)

family. The gothic cycle tends to repeatedly feature a painting of a woman, such as the former wives that Joan Fontaine in *Rebecca* (1940) and Stanwyck in *The Two Mrs. Carrolls* (1947) cannot ever hope to replicate. In *No Man* it is the voice that holds the secret of the woman's identity—but not for the other characters in the film who cannot hear that voice, just for the viewer who cannot separate Patrice from Helen because of the continuity of the voice-off. Not only does the woman Helen/Patrice consistently reveal her fears of discovery and reprisal, but we also know that voice to be Barbara Stanwyck's.

Perhaps because *No Man* lacks any sensuality or humanism—aside from Helen's too-brief friendship with the real Patrice—Stanwyck's voice stands out as the film's principal lure. The murder scene that lacks a murder is filmed with great style and suspense, but it turns out to be a cipher as both Bill and then his mother subsequently become suspects—even though only Stanwyck is seen pulling a gun, and later she is told that the man was already dead when she shot him. We cannot trust our eyes, so we are left to the evidence of the soundtrack for any grounding for this curiously unstable film.

The palimpsest of identities that includes the doubling of Helen and Patrice, redoubled by the gangster's moll and by Stanwyck herself and her publicist Helen Ferguson, and embedded in the narrative's central criminal mystery, is finally held in place by Stanwyck's performance of Helen, whose voice becomes the only shred of evidence that the film is not a vortex after all. What is left after all the masks are torn away is the plight of an unwed mother who sells her soul for a house. Despite the apparent social mobility, the single mother, now doubly wed, is hardly erased by the masquerade and lingers as a challenge to the perfectly manicured lawns and polished wood of the home that has enclosed Helen playing Patrice. The memory of the opening scene and its denial of happiness is hard not to forget when the visuals of that scene are repeated at the end.

All acting is a form of doubling, of course, and these woman's films about doubled women are also films about performance. From our historical vantage point, they can be seen as reflexive treatises on gender codes of the period, the impossible expectations of a patriarchy in crisis, and the contradictions thrown up before women. Stanwyck performs the role of Helen playing the role of Patrice as a modality of "expressive incoherence," which, as James Naremore has pointed out (using Stanwyck as an example), is a feature of many Hollywood roles. Actors are often given the opportunity for their characters to hide something, or to suggest that their character is "subject to division or dissolution into a variety of social roles."[16] In other words, she can make her doubled women coherent or incoherent. Like Phyllis Dietrichson, Thelma Jordan manages her double personalities until she gradually allows them to merge, violently killing her rogue boyfriend and herself in a car accident. In *No Man of Her Own*, Helen fails to fully become Patrice, and Stanwyck manages to sustain the performance beyond the end of the film, as she and her husband are doomed to live the lie of her identity. This is precisely the kind of incoherent female subjectivity that creates dissonance within the "system" of studio-era American cinema, pointing to the impossibility of coherent female subjectivity.

ANNIE OAKLEY

A GIRL AND A GUN

> Connecting to American individualism's imbrications with
> transcendentalism, American melodrama insisted on the certitude
> of basic ethical truths, but then located them in the interior wisdom
> of the individual, an individual who could shed the constraints of
> social orthodoxy and heed an inner call.
>
> —Elizabeth R. Anker, *Orgies of Feeling*

ELIZABETH ANKER'S SUMMARY of the ethos of liberal individualism identifies the spiritual core of the American melodrama of political discourse as it has come to be embraced by the right in the twenty-first century. If she tends to draw on film studies methods to account for the "orgies of feeling" that have come to dominate American politics, it is also possible to read those currents of heroism, self-sufficiency, and individualism back onto American cinema—and not just the melodramas of failure but also those of success. By so doing, we can better understand how Stanwyck became embraced as a national treasure and icon of conservative values, particularly through her association with the western genre.

In 1935 Stanwyck got her first opportunity to do a western, although as a tale about show business, *Annie Oakley* (dir. George Stevens) is not set on the frontier but in circus tents. *Buffalo Bill's Wild West Show* was the biggest and most influential of the many such spectacles that traveled across the globe in the late nineteenth and early twentieth centuries, creating legendary characters to represent the heroism, dangers, and challenges of the American territorial expansion and genocide. The inclusion of Indigenous figures such as Sitting Bull in the show was an ideological effort to mask genocide with gestures of inclusivity and diversity. The inclusion of women such as Calamity Jane and Annie Oakley was part of an effort to reach women audiences, but like the cinema that came after, it was also an exploitation of girls and guns for male pleasure.

Stanwyck saw many parallels between Annie Oakley and herself, including their emergence from impoverished beginnings into international stardom on the basis of their own talents, their show business husbands pushed into the shadow of their wives, and their shared humility and virtue. Oakley's success "didn't turn her head," just as Stanwyck did not see herself as "high-hat."[1] Unlike Calamity Jane, Annie Oakley was respected as being ladylike, with good manners (see chapter K). She remained ultra-feminine despite her skill in a man's sport, and although it was not well publicized, she was a happily married woman. Stanwyck saw herself this way too, even though during the production of *Annie Oakley*, her husband, Frank Fay, became so abusive that she escaped their home with their adopted son, Dion, and moved in with friends.[2] Another parallel between the two women unfolded in the 1950s when Stanwyck was made an honorary member of the Blackfoot Indians during the shooting of *Cattle Queen of Montana* and given the name "Princess Many Victories the Third" (see chapter Q). Oakley was adopted by Sitting Bull and named "Little Sure Shot" as part of the mythology of the *Wild West Show*. Both women came to be called "Missy" by their colleagues and crews.

Oakley, like Stanwyck, was a petite woman and slim. (*Buffalo Bill's Wild West Show* also featured a woman performer named Lillian Smith, who lacked Oakley's figure and girlishness and was therefore largely sidelined despite her comparable shooting skill.[3]) Playing the sharpshooter, Stanwyck wears a calf-length black (or dark) fringed skirt, black boots and white pearl-buttoned stockings, and a dark hat with a strap under her chin. This is a famous costume that became commodified in the 1950s and '60s, following the many movies, plays, and TV series that developed around the Annie Oakley name. It is a girlish outfit that probably accounts for Oakley's own long career as a "youthful" and never matronly woman.[4] The costume enabled young girls to play at gender performance within the terms of mainstream costuming and, separated from the character herself, arguably had progressive potential.[5] In 1935 the Annie Oakley persona lay somewhere between the "New Woman," with which Stanwyck had become identified in pre-Code cinema, and "the Cult of True Womanhood," which had a lingering presence throughout the 1930s. In the film, once Annie is famous, off-stage she dresses in full Edwardian bustles and hats and is carefully disassociated from a character named Vera (Pert Kelton), who "ain't no lady."

In the RKO script by Joel Sayre and John Twist, Annie Oakley is preoccupied with her attraction to sharpshooter Toby Walker (Preston

Barbara Stanwyck in *Annie Oakley* (1935)

Foster), a character loosely based on the husband of the historical Oakley, who performed with her in *Buffalo Bill's Wild West* as well as other shows. Stanwyck's version of Oakley is attracted to Walker's picture on a poster, and she repeatedly sighs, saying how pretty he is, as if her sharpshooter eye were a desiring eye first and a killer's eye second. When the young girl, famous in her own town for shooting quail, is drawn into a competition with Walker in Cincinnati, she throws the match so as not to embarrass him. Stanwyck's Annie daintily accepts a gentleman's arm whenever she walks through the circus camp or town. She shares her country mother's values that women need to mind their subordinate place in society. Oakley and Walker are recruited by Buffalo Bill, and Walker teaches her the tricks of the trade. For the sake of the show, he allows her to outshoot him and claims not to mind, because it makes for a better spectacle and also because he falls in love with her. However, he is injured and semi-blinded, and after he accidentally wounds her doing a stunt, he abandons the traveling show. They are finally reconciled with the help of Sitting Bull, played by Chief Thunderbird, and the film ends with them kissing at a fairground shooting range.

Reviews of *Annie Oakley* praised Stanwyck and the fantastic sets, costumes, and extras assembled to recreate *Buffalo Bill's Wild West Show*, but they denigrated the script and the direction. The *Variety* reviewer noted

Richard Davis (Chief) Thunderbird in *Annie Oakley* (1935

that the film would appeal to "elderly patrons" who remember Colonel Cody and his show, which had toured until 1906, only thirty years earlier.[6] Most disturbing about the reception of *Annie Oakley* is the commentary on Chief Thunderbird, who is taken as comic relief. In his first appearance, sitting in the stands as Sitting Bull, Thunderbird speaks through an interpreter, saying that the show "smells bad." However, when he is introduced to Annie, he is persuaded to join the show to participate in a dramatization of "Custer's last stand" along with other scenes of staged warfare between settlers and Native Americans.

When the show travels, the chief is housed in a hotel, where he is unaccustomed to modern conveniences and his grotesque antics are played for laughs. These humiliating scenes culminate in the farcical ending in which he spies Walker in the stands and disrupts the entire show in order to reunite Annie with her erstwhile lover. The affinities between the girl and the chief consolidate a kind of rebuke to the fantasy of the hyper-masculinized Wild West show, but only for the sake of an alternative fantasy of heterosexual closure that excludes the Native American, who serves the narrative function of a pet. The promise of the film, to showcase an early American celebrity, ends up wasted on formulaic entertainment, with the effect of degrading both Annie Oakley and Chief Sitting Bull as merely cogs in a machine that exploits and celebrates the violence of frontier history. The spectacle of the frontier is ultimately traded in for backlot drama, following the conventions of the musical, as the cinema resumes the mythological project of Buffalo Bill's live entertainment.

Chief Thunderbird (aka Richard Davis Thunderbird) provided a series of memos that have found their way to the "Annie Oakley" file at the Margaret Herrick Library. One of them outlines his own biography as a member of the Cheyenne tribe. His father scorned white men but was convinced of the necessity of assimilation and sent his son to the United States Indian Industrial School in Carlisle, Pennsylvania. In another memo he describes how Sitting Bull, a Sioux, was initiated into the Cheyenne tribe and how the Cheyenne and Sioux together brought down General Custer in 1875. In a third, he describes a secondhand eyewitness account of Chief Joseph's surrender in 1877 after the Battle of Bear Paw. These moving testimonials—in typescript with handwriting, marginal drawings, and Thunderbird's signature—are curious documents. It may be the case that George Stevens and his production team collected them as part of the research for the film but found that they did not fit the story they wanted to tell. Stevens was striving for an authentic recreation of *Buffalo Bill's Wild West Show*, not the history that preceded the mystification designed by Bill Cody. In the archive, they serve as a caustic challenge to the belittling role that Thunderbird plays in the film *Annie Oakley* (if not quite accounting for the equally comic/infantilizing roles of the African American cooks in the Cincinnati hotel who are also featured in the film). In fact, Chief Thunderbird had himself performed in Wild West shows in the first two decades of the twentieth century. By 1935 he had become a de facto leader of the "Hollywood Indians," with a large house in Pasadena that became a central meeting place for the Indigenous community.[7]

The archival documents serve as a reminder of how, in 1935, frontier history was the very recent past. Annie Oakley, Buffalo Bill, and the rest of the Wild West show cast were instrumental figures in converting that recent past into an American mythology. Stanwyck recognized the significance of the woman she played and how she stood out from the many unnamed women who also lived as pioneers and settlers. Stanwyck often spoke about the hardships that women faced and the roles they played in settling the country as homemakers and mothers, although she played very few such women in the many westerns she was cast in for film and TV. Annie Oakley is among those Americans Stanwyck referred to as "our aristocracy."[8] The real-life sharpshooter was a heroic woman who made her own way in a man's world, representing a particular brand of feminism that Stanwyck embraced throughout her life, even when it went against the grain of more collective, activist, and "liberationist" forms of feminism that emerged all around her in the 1960s.

It may be possible to draw a line from Stanwyck's impersonation of Annie Oakley to her passionate endorsement of Ayn Rand in the 1940s. Rand and Stanwyck were both members of the anti-Communist alliance called the Motion Pictures Association for the Preservation of American Ideals, a group of Hollywood personalities committed to defending the "liberty and freedom" of the American way of life against threats of corruption by Communists and fascists. Rand's individualist philosophy aligned well with Hollywood celebrity culture, and she was a key activist in the community in the 1940s.

Stanwyck was so taken with Rand's novel *The Fountainhead* that she personally took the book to Jack Warner in 1943, saying she was born to play the role of Dominique, the book's central female character but not its protagonist. Warner contracted Rand to write the screenplay, but the production was too expensive to shoot immediately after the war, so it was delayed until 1947. When twenty-year-old Patricia Neal was cast as the lead instead of Stanwyck, the forty-one-year-old actress was furious. She wrote an angry note to Jack Warner, breaking her contract—not ostensibly for being usurped by a younger actor but because she considered *The Fountainhead* to be her personal project.[9]

In the Warner Bros. archive, the file on *The Fountainhead* contains a series of notes from angry fans reacting to a news report that Lauren Bacall had been cast as Dominique. The level of vitriol in these letters against Bacall, who had recently visited Washington in a high-profile protest against the HUAC hearings, is staggeringly malicious. Stanwyck, on the other hand, is praised for her all-American values, and her fans felt strongly that she should be cast in the prestige ($2.5 million) production, given how many poor stories were "dished out to her" in the early days at Warner Bros. One writer says, "Three cheers for Barbara Stanwyck. She does not want to breathe the same air as the Bogarts … and we are going to boycott Bogart and his wife's pictures … you know what women can do."[10] Warner Bros. backed out of casting Bacall because of the public outrage of casting a "commie-sympathizer" in a film that promoted the virtue of individual genius over mass culture and public taste.[11]

In retrospect, Stanwyck was fortunate to have avoided the role of Dominique, in whom Rand created a rather dislikable character—although who knows what Stanwyck might have been able to do with her. In the final production, with Gary Cooper playing the self-centered "heroic" architect

Roark, Neal as Dominique is a wealthy and glamourous woman who seems helpless without men propping her up. The sexual violence is extreme, even for the period, and Rand's interference, insisting on long monologues espousing her philosophy of heroic individualism, makes for a muddled and plodding film. Stanwyck's visceral disappointment in being left out of this picture, however, speaks to her own, mainly unarticulated, beliefs. She was not as outspoken as her husband Robert Taylor during the Cold War years, but she clearly clung to a vision of self-fulfillment and competitive individualism that would eventually become known as American libertarianism and neoliberalism. For women, these values meant that success in a man's world remained on men's terms. Collectivity and collaboration were sublimated to individual capacity, tenacity, talent, and work ethics. Despite the fact that Stanwyck worked and thrived in an industry based in artistic collaboration, the hierarchies of studio production meant that her star power was consistently challenged by the capitalist motives of producers and studio heads such as Jack Warner. Losing a part to a younger woman was the first sign of her diminishing cultural capital in a system that she both implicitly and explicitly endorsed.

As a frontier heroine who succeeds in a competitive sport, Annie Oakley may be considered a foundational figure of the kind of American womanhood to which Stanwyck aspired and came to represent for many of her fans at the height of her career. Her depiction of Annie Oakley as a desiring subject, insisting on the prettiness of her opponent Toby Walker, suggests an alignment of the "deadeye" (code for sharpshooter) and the desiring eye and the potential empowerment of her gaze. The 1935 film undercuts that gaze, but in the 1950s Stanwyck had many opportunities to wield firearms in frontier dramas. Some of her best shooting scenes can be found in *The Moonlighter*, where she shoots down Ward Bond (see chapter R); *Escape to Burma*, where she valiantly defends her jungle bungalow (see chapter J); *The Maverick Queen* (1956), in which she is a member of Butch Cassidy's gang of thieves (see chapter Q); and *Cattle Queen of Montana*, in which she defends her land against bad movie-Indians and bad white men, using both guns and political diplomacy.[12]

In *Cattle Queen of Montana* Stanwyck returns to the Annie Oakley outfit. This time she wears the fringed calf-length black dress with black heeled boots, giving it a glamourous edge. Accessorized with a neck scarf, it is no longer a girlish outfit, and the costume designed by Gwen Wakeling has been transformed into culottes that hang like a dress but are more suitable for horseback riding. As Sierra Nevada Jones, she befriends a "good" movie-Indian named Colorados (Lance Fuller) as well as a cowboy named

Barbara Stanwyck in *Cattle Queen of Montana* (1954)

Farrell (Ronald Reagan), who turns out to be a spy for the U.S. Cavalry. Shot on location in Glacier National Park in Technicolor, *Cattle Queen* was Stanwyck's second color film. With Alan Dwan directing and John Alton on camera, they managed some great landscape shooting, despite the somewhat predictable script.

Sierra and Colorados, with the help of Farrell, manage to bring down the rich but corrupt rancher along with the villainous movie-Indians with whom he is aligned. Stanwyck has some great action scenes and wears more Calamity Jane–type outfits, with leather chaps and a green shirt that plays off her red-haired wig very nicely. As Sierra Nevada Jones, Stanwyck defends the land that her father has title to and for which he is brutally killed by the bad movie-Indians in the opening scenes. It is a familiar western narrative of land ownership and the triumph of virtue, achieved through violence and genocide: the land of the "free" is available to those who rise up and triumph over smaller men and women. Sierra Nevada Jones shocks the local townspeople by befriending a Native American. However, her friendship is entirely self-serving, as Colorados helps her to get rid of the bad apples in his tribe. She is a crack shot, although Farrell shoots a pistol right out of her hand in one of their first encounters. Nevertheless, Sierra and Farrell end up riding away, happily ever after, with their friend Colorados "assimilated" to the side of law and order.

Cattle Queen was trounced by the critics as a formulaic genre film.[13] Despite the progressive discourse of "good Indians," the bad movie-Indians are depicted as vicious, drunk, and savage. Stanwyck herself dismissed the picture as "awful," even though the *L.A. Daily News* led off their review with the statement: "We are witnesses, it would seem, to the death of a Hollywood era ... that gallant age when western heroines were a sweet and gentle race."[14] Move over, Annie Oakley; Sierra Nevada Jones is mowing down everything that stands in her way.

The phrase "all you need to make a movie is a girl and a gun" is a theme in Jean Luc Godard's essay film *Histoire(s) du Cinéma* (1989–1999), and *Film Ist: A Girl and a Gun* (2009) is the name of an archive-based compilation film by Gustav Deutsch. Godard claims that the phrase originates with D. W. Griffith, and for him, as for Deutsch, it is a good answer to the question "What is cinema?" as if they were shifting the conversation from technology to the tropes of storytelling. A girl and a gun constitute the thrilling potential of sex and violence in the movies, but the phrase also implies the critical threat of women and power that auteur filmmakers usually seek to contain and control within the frames, structures, and mechanics of their films. Stanwyck's portrayals of characters such as Annie Oakley and Sierra Nevada Jones exemplify the spectacle of a girl and a gun in the studio era, but these characters also pose the question of power and desire. What do these women desire and what is their power? What kind of heroism is it that becomes aligned with the freedom to bear arms, settle the land, and train indigenous people to play along?

The line between *Annie Oakley*, running through the failed project of *The Fountainhead*, to *Cattle Queen of Montana*, concerns Stanwyck's attachment on- and off-screen to the ideology of liberal individualism. For Anker, American melodrama is not democratic but liberal,[15] and although her focus is the affective political discourse of post-9/11 America, she traces its lineage historically through the adoption of melodramatic narrative from its European origins. Anker does not comment specifically on the western genre, but this is a key site where individual heroism becomes aligned with the state in a grand nation-building project grounded in myth and legend, that even the "pro-Indian" westerns of the 1950s clearly continues. In *Cattle Queen*, Farrell and Sierra Jones are exemplary ordinary people who become extraordinary through their moral integrity and mastery of violence. Anker concedes that although such heroism is typically gendered male, "gender norms of melodrama have never been tidy,"[16] which is something of an understatement. Stanwyck and Reagan became lifelong friends after *Cattle Queen*, and it is of course Reagan's America in which neoliberal state power intensified and came to eschew government support of citizens in favor of the mystified "moral core" of American virtue—which, needless to say, includes and is arguably grounded in the right to bear arms.[17]

Finally, we need to account for the alliance between Stanwyck's characters and the Indigenous people in both *Annie Oakley* and *Cattle Queen*. In the latter, Stanwyck herself was so admired by the Blackfoot Indians, who were impressed by her physical endurance on the set, that they adopted her into the Brave Dog Society.[18] As Anker explains it, the affective solicitations of melodramatic political discourse have the effect of eliding the "unequal realms of freedom" and "unequal access to power" that subsists within the inclusion of non-whites and women within the construction of American goodness. The "assimilated," educated, Indigenous figures that are included in these productions are enabled in a sense by the ascension of the girl and a gun to heroic status, even if they remain, like the woman, in the shadows of the embrace of the white man. The proximity of the Western woman to Native Americans, while rare in the studio era, is indicative of Michelle Raheja's observation that "the Hollywood Indian can serve as a kind of ground zero for the multiple nodes of identity, performance, and race."[19] Stanwyck's ascension to the heroic role of frontier woman fighting her way across the frontier is accomplished only at the expense of Native Americans doomed to "red-facing," or playing their ancestors dead and dying in the endless time of the frontier myth.

PARANOIA, ABJECTION, AND GASLIGHTING

> To each ego its object, to each superego its abject. It is not the white expanse
> or slack boredom of repression, not the translations and transformations
> of desire that wrench bodies, nights, and discourse; rather it is a brutish
> suffering that "I" puts up with, sublime and devastated,
> for "I" deposits it to the father's account.
>
> —Julia Kristeva, *Powers of Horror*

THE PARANOID WOMAN'S FILM was a cycle of films that were produced in the 1940s, inspired by the success of Hitchcock's *Rebecca*. Straddling the genres of mystery, melodrama, horror, noir, and the woman's film, the category became recognized as "paranoid" by feminist film critics in the 1980s.[1] The women protagonists of these films, many of them played by leading stars of the era, entered into terrifying relationships with men who become violent, controlling, and manipulative. In many cases the women take on detective-like agency as they try to solve the mysteries of their own marriages, but they inevitably end up either dead or widowed or married to the men who save them. Stanwyck starred in five of these films, or at least variations on the theme as it emerged in the early '40s if we include *The Gay Sisters* (Irving Rapper, 1942). At the height of the cycle's popularity, in 1947–1948, she made four films in which she is "played" by conniving, mysterious, and monstrous men: *The Two Mrs. Carrolls* (Peter Godfrey, 1947), *The Other Love* (Andre de Toth, 1947), *Cry Wolf* (Peter Godfrey, 1947), and *Sorry, Wrong Number* (Anatole Litvak, 1948). Stanwyck also appeared in later variations of the cycle in the 1950s and '60s: *Witness to Murder* (1954) and *The Night Walker* (1964) (see chapter W).

Of these titles, only *The Two Mrs. Carrolls* and *Sorry, Wrong Number* are usually considered exemplars of the "paranoid woman's film," and even these can also be described as film noir. The very idea of a cycle is that, unlike genre, the filmmakers pick up bits and pieces of themes and settings of various popular texts and rearrange them from one film to the next. Product differentiation and product familiarity are critical components of industrial media production. In this chapter I am less concerned with the fitness of the term "paranoid woman's films" as with how Stanwyck's performances were systematically undermined by absurd textual strategies. In the context of Stanwyck's career, these are among the most disappointing texts in that they play on her star status, offering her roles that often begin with a feisty, outspoken, and confident character, only to pull the narrative scaffolding out from under her.

The terrifying scream of a woman confronting impending violence, and toward which these stories tend to veer, has been described by Kaja Silverman as an "infantilizing gesture."[2] While the woman's film as a genre often features a woman's voice-over narrating the story, in these films that voice is inconsistent and not always responsible for the story. For Silverman, the paranoid woman, epitomized by Stanwyck's Leona in *Sorry, Wrong Number*, is characterized by a voice that is "called upon to perform for the male subject."[3] The voice spills over from subject to object as if it were a permeable membrane, as if the woman cannot get outside her own story to tell it. Mary Anne Doane reaches a similar conclusion in her analysis of paranoid woman's films, pointing out that female subjectivity collapses in these films—using *The Two Mrs. Carrolls* as one of her key examples—because the woman's look is perpetually detoured back to her own image. The place where meaning collapses, where neither the woman's look nor her voice can sustain narrative authority or coherence, is the place of the abject.[4] Outside the symbolic order, Julia Kristeva suggests that the abject disturbs and rejects the social order, insofar as it constitutes a ritual impurity.[5] The "disruption" of abjection in paranoid woman's films is not necessarily a resistant discourse but is symptomatic of a breakdown of gender relations, a virtual power struggle on-screen, and a real power struggle off-screen with respect to women's agency and star power that haunts the postwar film industry.

For Doane, following from Kristeva, the abject state of the paranoid woman's film pertains to the subject position assigned to the spectator who has formed a cogent identification with the female protagonist. Doane has little to say about the actor playing the "paranoid" female characters, but as archival texts, many of these films survive and circulate mainly because of their stars, whose names have branded the films. The abject state of the paranoid woman has become more legible as a discourse of power and subjugation than a discourse of subjectivity. As Maggie Hennefeld and

Nicholas Sammond have argued, "The abject and abjection have become pivotal terms in twenty-first-century life."[6] In their work, Georges Bataille features as prominently as Kristeva as a theorist of the abject, because for him, "general abjection" is "imposed on the social body by a sovereign imperative,"[7] which has long been obvious in the case of race (the context in which Bataille was writing) and has become increasingly clear in cultures of misogyny.

Sorry, Wrong Number has been written about extensively, both by noir critics impressed with the film's complex flashback structure and use of "real time" narrative and by feminist critics for whom the tension between voice and image is directly related to the corresponding tension between female and male narrative control—and, by extension, radio and film, as the story originated as a popular radio play.[8] Stanwyck plays Leona Stevenson, a wealthy bedridden woman in a large empty house in New York who spends the entire film in bed on the phone, becoming entangled in a network of voices from known and unknown sources, beginning with an overheard conversation about men plotting a murder. As she tries to locate her husband, it becomes apparent to the viewer that the murder being planned is her own. Henry Stevenson (Burt Lancaster) is a henpecked husband unhappily married to Leona,[9] whose illness is described as a "cardiac neurosis," a self-induced heart condition brought on by arguments with her husband, and Henry has bet on her death to pay his debts. In six instances, Leona's phone conversations unfold onto flashbacks, although as Amy Lawrence points out, even though Leona appears in some of the flashbacks, she herself authorizes only one of them.[10]

The nature of Leona's illness is actually hidden from her, in a typical strategy of the 1940s woman's film. At one point she calls her doctor (Wendell Corey). He tells her that he told her husband two weeks earlier that she was mentally, not physically, ill; she is not about to die, but she needs a psychoanalyst. But then the flashback moves to his office, and a sequence unfolds, narrated by Henry, from which Leona is absent. The doctor's office scenes are then intercut with scenes from the marriage in which Leona appears to treat Henry like a handsome, convenient pet. This bossy version of Leona completely fails to understand Henry's sense of entrapment. Once he learns that she is not terminally ill, he takes out a contract on her life.

Additional subplots and complications make *Sorry, Wrong Number* an extremely fragmented, plurivocal text. Some critics of the period found the film "bewildering and tedious, confusing and morbid."[11] Leona is essentially investigating her own murder, which excited some critics as a novel mystery plot.[12] For some, Stanwyck's performance was outstanding, and she was

Barbara Stanwyck in *Sorry, Wrong Number* (1948)

nominated for an Oscar for it, but for others it was just too hysterical. The most notorious review is Bosley Crowther's in the *New York Times*. He says, "Miss Stanwyck does a quite elaborate job of working herself into a frenzy," and calls the whole plot too far-fetched. The exploitation of telephone technology was, for him, a gimmick that in the hands of an "excitable woman" who "uses it recklessly" can only drive herself and everyone else quite mad.[13] The strength of Stanwyck's intense performance of fear is her expression of complete loss of control, and yet her intensity also works against the sympathy such loss might generate. As an exemplary monstrous-feminine figure, in Barbara Creed's definition, she "speaks to us more about male fears than female desire or feminine subjectivity."[14] Beyond a psychoanalytic reading, we can also see the hysteric as a challenge to narrativity through affective energy and intensity. Leona is identified as the "cough-drop queen" and an extension of her father's power, but she is also trapped in a web of obfuscation and deceit orchestrated by her husband. Stanwyck's performance channels that trauma into a powerful struggle against the well-calculated, time-based murder plot.

The phone is a woman's tool, linked to gossip and chitchat, as well as an audible escape from the home,[15] and the role of Leona was a great opportunity for Stanwyck. She took it so seriously that she and director

Litvak agreed to shoot her twelve key scenes continuously in twelve days with no break, because she wanted to try to sustain the level of anxiety that in narrative time was a continuous two hours.[16] The stress of the shooting contributed to Stanwyck's hair turning gray,[17] and her terrified Leona is indeed an intense performance that carries the performative edge of the film, although the role allows Stanwyck little subtlety in her characterization. Agnes Moorehead, who voiced the very successful radio play, had already been typed as a character actress specializing in bitchy women. Precisely because she was not a top star, she could get away with what Patricia White describes as female difference, even deviance,[18] whereas Stanwyck's performance of excessive femininity was turned against her.

Moorehead's performance did not have to contend with a visual counterpart to the audio track, whereas Stanwyck's voice is systematically undermined by the dynamic visuals of the film version of *Sorry, Wrong Number*. Litvak's camera is in constant movement, panning through the darkness of the house and the shadowy scenes of men plotting shady deals—completely detached from anyone's point of view. Despite her bravura performance, Stanwyck's Leona is not at all in control of the story that unfolds from and around her predicament. She has entrapped her husband in her own psychosis and in her family's corporate greed, but she also possesses the viewer in her hysterical demonstration of fear and helplessness. Henry finally tries to help her, but it is too late and her scream is drowned out by a passing train, exactly as he had planned.

In keeping with the anxieties of postwar American cinema, the abjection of women is not unrelated to the emasculated man in the paranoid woman's film. Sometimes the menacing man makes the woman appear monstrous, as in *The Two Mrs. Carrolls*, in which Humphrey Bogart plays a mad painter named Geoffrey Carroll who marries one woman after another to paint their portrait, poison them, and replace them with a new Mrs. Carroll. Stanwyck plays Sally Carroll in this film, a naïve young woman who finds herself in the clutches of a dangerous man. She does nothing to deserve punishment, and yet as part of the gothic cycle, the film seems to relish in her fear. Her portrait as "the angel of death" seems to strike all those who see it with shock and awe, although it reads now simply as a goth look, with heavy makeup and tight leather bodice. Stanwyck plays paranoia well, and her can-do persona emerges late in the film when Sally finally figures out that her nightly glass of milk has been poisoned. Geoffrey's insanity is never diagnosed but seems to be a manifestation of artistic temperament. *The Two Mrs. Carrolls* was roundly panned, and this time Crowther noticed that Stanwyck was the victim of the scriptwriter.[19]

Painting of Barbara Stanwyck in *The Two Mrs. Carrolls* (1947)

Are the paranoid woman's films of the 1940s a form of punishment for the outspoken, well-paid woman stars of the era? Is it retribution for the femmes fatales of film noir? Is it vengeance against women taking men's jobs during the war and holding on to them afterward? Are such films indicative of women's distrust of men?[20] These are questions of historical causality that don't have direct answers, although the coincidence of paranoid woman's films with social trends of the 1940s is evident. The role of the telephone—including scenes of switchboard operators—and the discourse of psychoanalysis in *Sorry, Wrong Number* indicate the social realism that intersected with the gothic in 1948. The psychoanalytic discourse in and around the paranoid woman's films is clearly a strategy of control and authority through which women's hysteria can be diagnosed and contained. In all of these films, the women can be said to be gaslit, manipulated, and set up to fail. They appear to be in charge of their own stories, but they repeatedly run into terrifying traps.

Gaslight (1944) is the title of a key film in the cycle, starring Ingrid Bergman, and gaslight melodrama is a nineteenth-century theater style that lies behind the gothic cinema of the 1940s. As Cynthia Stark has argued, gaslighting needs to be recognized as a form of misogyny and collective psychological oppression.[21] Thinking about paranoid woman's films in terms of abjection enables a stepping back from historical causality to a recognition of the systemic nature of the misogyny at work. Gaslighting involves "the denial of another person's testimony," based on social identity, or "wrongful manipulation and emotional abuse."[22] It is both psychological and a form of power in social relationships, and for Stark, gaslighting has a "looping effect. … Misogynist practices encourage misogynist attitudes."[23] Paranoid woman's films were made by a variety of directors and studios and were at times written by women. Stanwyck's first TV role, taped in 1953 but not released until 1959, was in "Autolight," Jack Benny's parody of *Gaslight*, so she had her chance to "talk back" to the film cycle. In the fifteen-minute sketch, in which she plays Ingrid Bergman's character and he plays Charles Boyer's, she outsmarts Benny and turns the tables on him. When they take their bows, she thanks his wife, Mary Livingston, for her work on the spotlight, a coy, even proto-feminist gag in the variety-style show.[24]

Several of Stanwyck's paranoid woman's films participate in what Doane has described as the "medical discourse" of 1940s woman's films. The woman's body is pathologized and becomes symptomatic of a diseased interiority that invites a doctor's epistemological penetration. For Doane, the erotics of gendered narrative shift away from the spectacle of the woman's body to "an eroticization of the very process of knowing the female subject."[25] The collusion between doctor and husband in *Sorry, Wrong Number* is typical of the medical discourse. Leona may be responsible for her own "cardiac neurosis," but the psychosomatic symptoms have made her vulnerable to both psychological and physical violence. In her abject state, the boundaries between inside and outside the body have dissolved and she has come to doubt her own body.

The medical discourse is arguably more overt than paranoia in *The Other Love*, in which Stanwyck plays a famous concert pianist (Karen Duncan) who is sent to a tuberculosis sanitorium—although no one ever speaks the name of her disease. Throughout the film she whispers breathily and never really uses her full voice. Karen expresses herself by pounding out piano music, which was actually played by Ania Dorfman, with whom Stanwyck studied the fingering and gestures for the romantic pieces that she performs.[26] Stanwyck throws her whole body into the piano playing to effectively signal Karen's unspoken distress. While at the sanitorium, she has an affair with a visiting playboy played by Richard Conte, who entertains her on the nearby Riviera while she falls in love with her doctor, played by David Niven. Conte leaves once he realizes how sick she is, but Niven's character, Dr. Stanton, persuades Karen to marry him—even though she is clearly dying—but he refuses to tell her how serious her condition is. In *The*

Barbara Stanwyck in *The Other Love* (1947)

Other Love the woman is manipulated into a passive state and "played" as if she herself is a musical instrument, and the strictures of the institution create the impression that Karen's sickness is brought on and worsened by the sanitarium itself.

While Doane argues that the women in these films are de-spectacularized, Stanwyck's characters in *Sorry, Wrong Number*; *The Other Love*; and *The Two Mrs. Carrolls*—all three of which were costume-designed by Edith Head—are bejeweled and spangled. In *The Other Love* she wears glittery ski sweaters; in *Sorry, Wrong Number* the jewelry was so valuable that it needed to be guarded by security men who followed Stanwyck around on set.[27] In *The Gay Sisters* and *Cry Wolf* she wears tailored suits but segues into elegant floor-length gowns in the first, and silk blouses and pearls in the second, and indeed all the films are informed by a class discourse. The plots of paranoid woman's films frequently revolve around questions of inheritance. The gothic theme requires the setting of a large, labyrinthine house with secret rooms, grand staircases, evening dresses, and at least one cranky servant. These old and empty houses are typically underlit with shadowy corners, augmenting the distorted reality of

Barbara Stanwyck in *The Other Love* (1947)

abjection.²⁸ The spectacle of class is certainly de-eroticized, but it remains
tied to the women and their appearance.

The Gay Sisters is set in such a house, and it starts off well with Stanwyck
playing a feisty, outspoken woman, Fiona Gaylord, who fights on behalf of
her two younger sisters and herself, to keep the grand old New York home
that was left to them by their father, killed in the war. Fiona has been named
head of the household, and she completely lives up to the responsibility. Her
nemesis is Charles Barclay (George Brent). He has managed to tie up the
estate in legal knots, but she absolutely refuses to negotiate with him—until
he learns about a young boy named Austin who lives at Fiona's home and to
whom he claims paternity.

Stanwyck narrates only one flashback in *The Gay Sisters*, and she does
so in the mode of a bedtime story told to her adult sisters, a story that reveals
the true parentage of Austin. Her performance in the flashback scenes
alternates between silent scenes with sardonic voice-over and sync sound of
her conversing with Barclay, and the whole story culminates in what she
describes as "my big acting scene." In the story she tells, she sets off to find
a husband in order to fulfill the terms of an old aunt's will. She runs into
Charles Barclay en route to Vermont, and she literally snags him, luring him
into a marriage right there in a local farmhouse. After cutting the wedding

cake, she "totter[s] toward the stairs" and feigns an attack "brought on by stirred emotions." Before she can escape and pay him off with twenty-five thousand dollars, he calls her bluff and says she cannot leave until the morning, and finally, "Don't scream; I'm your husband," as he approaches her in the shadows. Fade to black, and Fiona's sisters giggle raucously.

Perhaps the sisters' reaction sealed the response for some viewers, but in 2022 it looks a lot like a rape scene, even if she did mislead the "attractive sap" with his "spaniel eyes." After telling her story, Fiona betrays some latent maternal feelings for Austin and hides him from Barclay. In the end Barclay gets his way: he gets the girl, he gets his son, and he gets the big old house that he plans to tear down for a big development. Meanwhile, Fiona, who has vowed to her father and herself never to sell the land, sells the land. She has a good cry and continues to hate Barclay with a passion until she finds herself in his luxurious high-rise apartment with her son and inexplicably kisses him. The script by Lenore J. Coffee has some excellent lines and a great monologue that Stanwyck delivers drunkenly alone in the big house just before being whisked away, but her rationale for capitulating to Barclay is purely generic: to be a good mother (see chapter D).

Strictly speaking, *The Gay Sisters* is not a paranoid woman's film, and yet it is an "abject" film in the sense that the woman's story is undercut—by money, by the law, and by the affective conventions of genre. Fiona may be a strict and heartless mother, but she has the child's best interests at heart when she gives up custody. Stanwyck's performance as bossy, literate, and active seems to place Fiona in jeopardy, as if she were overstepping her role as a woman. The question of inheritance and land-owning gentry is obliquely referred to by one of the lawyers as "the end of an era," but it could also be the end of an era of unquestioned paternalistic patriarchal authority—as Stanwyck's star status and Fiona's personality suggest. But the end of that era will be indefinitely postponed in 1942.

If George Brent had more comic lines (and if Brent could deliver them), *The Gay Sisters* could almost be screwball, but instead it is weighted down with heavy furniture, old lawyers, and the law of the father. However, the overlap points to the way the patterns of genre conventions get bent with the changing social climate. The end of *The Gay Sisters*, with Fiona's sudden capitulation, is not only disappointing; it is also haunted. Unlike screwball comedy, when the woman in the paranoid woman's film survives, she survives with the burden of violence, within a marriage that seems to be made under the sign of misogyny. The film does feature some comic gags, such as Fiona repeatedly stomping her feet to bring young Austin into line, but even that gesture, smartly performed by Stanwyck, smacks of discipline and maternal anxiety rather than the gayness of the title. One critic at the time actually noted that some scenes are sordid and repelling,[29] suggesting that my reading of the "don't scream" scene was completely legible to 1940s audiences. The *New York Times* reviewer said it was "one of the more gruesome happy endings devised." Stanwyck brings "bite" to her character but is outmatched by a screenplay featuring a family of neurotics "feeling their way around in the gloom."[30]

In *Cry Wolf*, the third "paranoid" film of Stanwyck's to be released in 1947, Stanwyck gets some good action scenes before she is gaslit by the plot. Playing a recently widowed graduate student, Stanwyck as Sandra Demarest visits the home of her deceased husband, James. The big gloomy house is owned and ruled by James's uncle Mark (Errol Flynn), who is suspicious and cold. Sandra befriends James's sister, Julie, and investigates Mark's secret lab in the big old sprawling house, including scrambling over rooftops and hiding in a dumbwaiter. Julie mysteriously falls to her death from a balcony, and Sandra discovers her husband living in a secret lodge on the property, but he has become a madman. In one of the most disappointing endings of the film cycle, Mark turns out to have been protecting James by declaring him dead, and he and Sandra embrace to live happily ever after. The critics went to town on this one, saying that the character reversals turn the whole film into a trick played on the spectator.[31] Stanwyck's Sandra is "played" and the viewer along with her.

The psychoanalytic accounts of paranoid woman's films published in the 1980s pinpointed the disturbing effects of the inverted gender norms of narrative cinema. Female protagonists are repeatedly set up to fail. The effects on spectatorship are, indeed, cruel once one is drawn to empathize with the paranoid woman. The discourse of the abject may move beyond "the symbolic order of language," and yet for the viewer, the body of the performer remains legible as a discursive effect. The star is also set up to fail. Even in her most bravura performance in the cycle, *Sorry, Wrong Number*, Stanwyck cannot help but push the boundaries until they crumble into a discourse of misogyny. While this discourse was clearly legible to writers such as Doane and Silverman, it arguably takes on another valence in the context of an actor's career. Stanwyck survived the cycle, and it is precisely her vocal presence and physical, embodied performance style that support these films as industrial products. Many critics commented on the let-down of the scripts, implying that she deserved to play women who had more control over the outcome of their own stories.

If we consider paranoid woman's films to be "abject" and not simply paranoid, we might better recognize the discourse of misogyny at work in this cycle of Hollywood cinema. The abject complicates the "productive fantasy of the individual or social body as an agential or sovereign being," and indeed women in Hollywood were always already challenged as agential. But as Hennefeld and Sammond argue, the "collapse of the subject" in notions of networked society need not stop us from calling out involuntary abjection when we see it, especially when "the abject may be summoned and deployed as an *objection*."[32] The productive disruption of the abject might be a case for moving beyond the category of the subject in consideration of the paranoid woman's films and to consider them as evidence of a deeply flawed "social body." The women stars of these films were selling them with their names and their performances of charged emotion, but at the same time, as they were literally gaslit in the films' deep shadows, they were being metaphorically gaslit by the scenarios of abjection.

THE QUEEN

She cussed like the Queen of England.

—Jane Wilkie on Stanwyck, in "A Conversation with Jane Wilkie"

Camp is a rediscovery of history's waste.

—Andrew Ross, "Uses of Camp"

"QUEENLINESS" IS A POPULAR TERM in Hollywood discourse, applied not only to women who rise to the top but also to characters who make spectacles of themselves. "Burlesque queens," "glamour queens," and "movie queens" are terms that denote power but a kind of power that might be superficial and is rarely an omnipotent power. Stanwyck was not the only actor to become known as a queen, but unlike Bette Davis, Greta Garbo, and Marlene Dietrich, she never played an actual queen. She played the title role in two "Queen" films in the 1950s—*Cattle Queen of Montana* and *The Maverick Queen*—around the same time that Joan Crawford starred in *Queen Bee* (1955) in a decade full of bad mothers. Crawford's Queen Bee is as malicious as Stanwyck's matriarchal character Martha Wilkison in the western *The Violent Men*. The 1950s queens gave way to the campy queens of *Whatever Happened to Baby Jane?* (1962), but Stanwyck avoided the grotesquery of Grande Dame Guignol, for the most part, and took another queenly route to matriarchal TV roles in *The Big Valley* and *The Thorn Birds*, which does not mean she was not a camp figure in her own right.[1] Unpacking Stanwyck's queenliness is a means of getting at the double standards applied to female stars as well as the cultural economy of camp.

Among Stanwyck's many nicknames, including "Missy" and "Stany," "the Queen" is the one that crossed over to the popular press most significantly, perhaps because it overlaps with many of her roles in the latter part of her career. Although the name was first affectionately endowed by William Holden in 1939, it was taken up by the fan magazines in the 1940s and sustained well beyond her death.[2] Frank Nugent reported in 1952 that Stanwyck's crews were so enamored of her professional and generous behavior on set that they "unfailingly" presented her with gifts inscribed with "to the Queen" or "to the Queen Bee from her Drones."[3] Nugent visited the set of *Clash by Night*, so the anecdote may be true of her RKO pictures, of which this was the fifth, but it is hard to credit the viability of such a story across all of Stanwyck's sets. Nevertheless, she definitely earned respect from almost all of her co-workers, and the nickname clearly stuck.

Stanwyck's queenliness on studio sets referred to her disciplined approach to the task of filmmaking and also to her sharpness with those whose professionalism she felt to be below par. Countless anecdotes of actors who were unprepared or late to the set receiving sharp words from Stanwyck litter the biographies. At the same time, many collaborators commented on the fact that she did not behave like a diva but knew her place within a production as one worker among many. This may not have been the case at home, however, given that Robert Taylor also called her "Queen," while she called him "Junior."[4]

Stanwyck's other nickname, "Missy," reputedly originated with her Black maid, Harriet Corey, who worked for her for decades and lived with her for some time after Stanwyck's 1950 divorce. The diminutive-sounding name originating with a servant once again denotes the soft power of a woman in charge. Stanwyck's affection for Corey is exemplified in an anecdote from the production of *To Please a Lady*, in which Stanwyck forced MGM to book Corey into an expensive hotel in Indianapolis that did not accommodate Blacks. Stanwyck threatened to stay with Corey in a "colored" hotel if the studio could not make the expensive hotel back down, which of course it did.[5] Few tales of Stanwyck using her star power like this have come through, suggesting that her "Queen" title was indeed earned through benevolence rather than vanity or conceitedness.

Stanwyck's on-screen queenliness was, of course, more complicated and contradictory, although it was consolidated through a series of roles in films, from 1941's *The Great Man's Lady* to her final appearances on *The Colbys* (24 episodes in 1986) as a matriarch installed in a large home overseeing some oversized combination of land, men, and wealth. These titles include *The Furies, Cattle Queen of Montana, The Violent Men, Escape to Burma, Forty Guns*, and the TV series *The Big Valley* (112 episodes from 1965 to 1969), *The Thorn Birds*, and *Dynasty* (4 episodes in 1985) (see chapter F). Stanwyck had a long-standing passion for westerns, and *The Big Valley* was the result of her persistent requests to network executives for a western series. She owned a collection of Remington portraits of pioneer women, and she read voraciously about Calamity Jane and other western stories and novels. She believed that the characters who emerged from the Buffalo Bill show, such as Annie Oakley, were "America's aristocracy," which was a sentiment she borrowed directly from President Eisenhower (see chapter O).[6]

One of Stanwyck's unfulfilled wishes was to shoot a film with "Duke" Wayne, the one true aristocrat of movie westerns, forgetting that she and Wayne did appear together, however briefly, in *Baby Face*, in which Lily Powers stomps all over him on her way to the top. Although Stanwyck was inspired by the women who got down and dirty, building the West with their own hands, it was in fact a leadership role that she ended up filling more often, and most of her western characters were powerful figures, with significant control and authority over lands and peoples. Her rough-and-ready Kate Crawley character in *Wagon Train*, who manages a freight wagon company (see chapter K), was the exception to the rule, and the imperial authority that Stanwyck wields in her matriarchal roles blended well with her status as an aging star in the postwar era.

Becoming a queen, on-screen and off, was critical to Stanwyck's survival as an icon, insofar as camp designates a cultural economy of taste, particularly since the 1960s.[7] Stanwyck's capacity to be bossy is clearly articulated in many of these roles and may have been a part of her off-screen character as well, although it was balanced with a good deal of generosity. Off-screen, Stanwyck wielded power through her relationships with those around her, including family members and friends whom she supported financially. Her benevolence and philanthropy were well known and included a fund for Native American children's education and the Athena National Sorority for young businesswomen.[8] On-screen, Stanwyck's queenly power was supported by her ramrod-straight posture, her determined arm-swinging walk, as well as the costumes and roles that she wore with confidence. Starting in the 1950s, these roles increasingly included women with real authority over land and people and arguably helped her to accommodate a new campy category of taste.

In *Cattle Queen of Montana*, Stanwyck's character, Sierra Nevada Jones, remains something of a girl awaiting to be queen. By the end of the film, she has cleared the way for her land claim, avenged her father's death, and found a heroic white man to be her consort. She wields power for sure, but her character is young and relatively unformed, young enough to trust a "university educated" Native American character. The queen of the title refers more to her star power as a leading lady than to a woman who befriends

Indigenous people. Her outfits are more like those of Annie Oakley than a queen (see chapter O), and above all, she does not own a palatial home. Stanwyck's queen characters achieve their authority and power through their proximity to prime real estate, and the corpus of her westerns indicates that, as a frontier genre, westerns are essentially about land ownership. Becoming the matriarch of a large home and large amounts of land is the more telling mark of American aristocracy than simply becoming legendary.

During the shooting of *Cattle Queen*, Stanwyck was inducted into the Blackfoot Nation and given the honorary title of "Princess Many Victories III," which was the closest she came to becoming actual royalty. This anecdote is widely reported in all the biographies and can be traced back to a news item that cites Stanwyck herself referring to the title in the context of her "warm memories" of the Montana shoot.[9] When I tried to track down the significance of her "adoption," I learned that many movie stars have been so honored, and it means only that they have "a little more spiritual ability to be part of the Blackfeet upon death."[10] If there were a document of her adoption, the title may have been endowed as part of a fund-raising mission on the part of the Great Northern Railway, which sponsored Blackfoot camps where tourists could purchase Native American names, among other things.[11] However, no trace of any document seems to exist,[12] so we have only Stanwyck's word for her royal title. Her pride in that title was consistent with her charitable work on behalf of Indigenous children, which substitutes philanthropy for structural reform for Indigenous peoples and tends to reinforce rather than erase the racial hierarchies with which so many of her films were complicit.

Kit Banion is a legendary western queen, invented by Zane Grey in his novel *The Maverick Queen* as a member of the Wild Bunch who fraternizes with their leaders Butch Cassidy and the Sundance Kid.[13] Stanwyck's entrance in the film version of *The Maverick Queen* is in a window over a saloon called the Maverick Queen Hotel, identifying her character, Kit Banion, from the outset as a landowner. The saloon queen, like the related tropes of brothel queen, dance-hall queen, and burlesque queen, are familiar western epithets, and Stanwyck played many such figures over the course of her career (see chapter G). The saloon queen trades sex for power, and Kit is not ashamed of her career trajectory. However, she is getting tired of it, this being like all 1950s westerns about the lateness of the genre. One of her first lines in the film, barked out to the Sundance Kid (Scott Brady), who embraces her roughly in her upstairs boudoir/office, is "For heaven's sake, take a bath," a line that I have been waiting for a western heroine to say for decades.

Scott Brady, Barry Sullivan, and Barbara Stanwyck in *The Maverick Queen* (1956)

In the Zane Grey novel on which *The Maverick Queen* is based, it is clear that Kit Banion builds her empire by branding calves rustled from other people's herds (where the term "maverick" originates). In the film, that story line is merely alluded to, in favor of Kit's contribution to the end of the Wild Bunch and thus the end of the Wild West. She plans a successful train heist, carried out by the gang, but she falls for a traveling gangster/outlaw (Barry Sullivan) who turns out to be a Pinkerton detective in disguise. She dies in his arms when the law catches up to the Wild Bunch. He ends up with Lucy Lee (Mary Murphy), a cattle queen in her own right. In fact, she might as well have walked right out of *Cattle Queen of Montana*, although she is significantly less active, mouthy, or bossy than Stanwyck in either film. The two women in *Maverick Queen* are, in the end, pawns in a game played between lawmen and outlaws.

Republic Pictures produced *Johnny Guitar* (1954) two years before *Maverick Queen* in their patented Trucolor process. For the Stanwyck film, which shares many plot details with *Johnny Guitar*—including the color technology if not the palette, as well as the female lead, the stranger in town, and a gang holed up in a remote home called "the Hole"—Republic added a new widescreen technique called Naturama for an even more spectacular image that, despite the name, or perhaps due to historical distance, creates a tangible world of artifice. In her indoor scenes, Stanwyck, fitted out with a long red wig, wears gaudy, glittering gowns, one of them with a turquoise feathered fan, that match the baroque gilt of the interior décor. *The Maverick Queen* lacks the rich double-layered dialogue of *Johnny Guitar*, as well as Nick Ray's casual pacing and careful framing, but it can nevertheless be read as camp. In the film's latter scenes, Kit cross-dresses in black pants, a gun belt, and a Stetson, riding and shooting like a true outlaw.

The aesthetics of camp are notoriously difficult to pin down because they arguably involve both performance and spectatorship. As an unfixed cultural economy of taste and production, camp is best apprehended as a critical tool that can help to unpack textual contradictions, particularly around gender coding. In the case of *Johnny Guitar*, Pamela Robertson argues that camp operates in the film as "a strategy of containment and a mark of excess" in relation to the suppression of women.[14] In *Maverick Queen*, Stanwyck's "excess" as a bossy, powerful, splendid, active woman is in the end curtailed by her turn to the law and, finally, her death in a gunfight. Because the sign of "woman" survives in the figure of Lucy, we see a kind of splitting of the female, which is a familiar strategy of containment in Hollywood scriptwriting. The campiness is registered above all in the marketing of the film, along with Stanwyck's star power, and a theme song by Victor Young, all of which make the Maverick Queen the center of the film. Killing her off is ostensibly a sign of the end of the Old West, but at the same time, it undercuts everything the film has promised. The film's publicity features Stanwyck dressed much as Crawford in the *Johnny Guitar* publicity, wearing black pants and bright colors and posed in a power stance.

Axel Madsen claims that Republic Studios owner Herbert J. Yates wanted Stanwyck to play Emma Small (Mercedes McCambridge's part) in *Johnny Guitar* but could not afford two stars of Crawford's and Stanwyck's status.[15] Whether this is true or not, it is difficult to imagine them sharing the screen, especially in their garish western outfits. These queens are ultimately more than the genre can take, as both films capitulate to a heterosexual coupling on the right side of the law. Recognizing the films' campiness is a means of leaving the gender roles unfixed and the women's "outlaw" status secure and indelible in the realm of fantasy.

In contrast with the role-playing exuberance of her 1950s westerns, Stanwyck's performance in *The Thorn Birds* is one of the most passionate of her career, as it was her first chance to work with good writing since perhaps *Forty Guns* in 1957 (she received her third Emmy for the show). As the widow Mary Carson, she is not only rich and powerful but selfish and devious as well, using her position to manipulate her family and her priest, Father Ralph (Richard Chamberlain). Her physical attraction to the young priest is nevertheless an excess of desire on the part of a seventy-five-year-old woman, which was Stanwyck's own age at the time of shooting. The strength of her performance in two particular scenes with Chamberlain is in her eyes that lock onto his, even while he politely tries to resist.

Barbara Stanwyck and Richard Chamberlain in *The Thorn Birds* (1983)

Unrequited love becomes the major theme of the series, but Mary Carson dies at the end of the first (2½ hour) episode, and the impossible love affair is taken up by her niece Meggie (Rachel Ward). The sweeping cinematography of *The Thorn Birds* establishes Mary Carson's power in the lush depiction of her huge estate. Shot in California, the ostensible Australian setting enables a kind of limitless scope to the landscape and to Mary Carson's power, which extends ultimately to the Vatican, as she essentially buys Father Ralph a promotion as her final wish, cruelly cutting her brother and his family out of her will. Stanwyck's portrayal of an older woman with bodily desires makes her much more sympathetic than she might otherwise have been. As a coldhearted queen, her passion unmasks her as human (see chapter M).

Stanwyck's best-known queenly role was no doubt in *The Big Valley*, which is still the context for many people's acquaintance with her in the twenty-first century, and it is still in syndication online. After almost a decade of Stanwyck's cajoling, the series was finally launched by ABC in 1965. Created and largely written by A. I. Bezzerides and Louis F. Edelman, who were also key players on *The Barbara Stanwyck Show* (which featured only two western settings in the thirty-six episodes), the new series centered on a large plantation-style home presided over by Victoria Barkley (Stanwyck).

Her four adult children and dozens of other characters come and go on their adventures, but every episode ends up with a conciliatory sherry by the fire. The Barkley living room, attended by the Black manservant Silas (Napoleon Whiting), is decorated with fresh flowers and busy Victorian furnishings. It effectively stands in for the vast landholdings that the Barkley family own, manage, protect, exploit, and expand. Built largely by Victoria's late husband, this empire, which is supposed to be near the town of Stockton, California, is depicted in piecemeal fashion, as each episode takes the various family members beyond the home.

Each stand-alone episode of *The Big Valley* sees the family engage in some kind of moral drama, often involving people who are less fortunate than themselves. It is full of the usual melodramatic devices of amnesia, misrecognition, and disguise; parents and children reunited; evil characters unveiled and punished; accidents; weather events; and corruption. Stanwyck herself is, from time to time, imperiled and rescued, although she is found far more often at home, doling out advice and taking in guests. Stanwyck disliked her TV series being called "*Bonanza* in drag,"[16] and she seemed to speak out more readily to the press during the series' four-year run. (She graced the cover of *TV Guide* at least three times.) She is said to have insisted that producers respect her as a "tough old broad from Brooklyn." She told them, "Don't try to make me into something I'm not. If you want someone to tiptoe down the Barkley staircase in crinoline and politely ask where the cattle went, get another girl. That's not me."[17] However, it took a few seasons before she shed the high-collared print dresses and appeared regularly in split skirts, black jeans, and occasionally in a cropped leather jacket. In the first season, she and Linda Evans are decked out with long bright-colored gowns that seem incongruous with the men's cowboy attire. Although she did not interfere with the director's control over the set, Stanwyck earned the respect of the actors and crew by doing things like yelling for "Quiet" and by her famous punctuality. In a *TV Guide* article by Dwight Whitney in 1966 called "The Queen Goes West," Stanwyck is said to have had final approval over scripts, guest casts, and directors.[18]

In response to the *Bonanza* comparison, Stanwyck pointed out that Lorne Green, the star of the other popular single-parent western series of the time, "pontificates" and "passes judgement," whereas her TV family worked things out together through dialogue, arguments, and the occasional fistfight. Moreover, she claimed her innate right to the role because "I've had my own ranches. I am a horsewoman.… The west was tough, hell-country, full of fights and wrongs and hardness. Pontifical wiseacres did not survive long out there!"[19] For once, Stanwyck herself seems to have confused her life with her roles, because her Marwyck ranch, which she co-owned for five years, breeding racehorses on the outskirts of Los Angeles, could hardly be compared to frontier living. The West, for Stanwyck, and for the Barkleys, is primarily a place for the exercise of feudal power disguised as liberal humanism and rough naturalism. Her role as queen of the Barkley ranch is to exploit resources and distribute justice to the peons of many colors whose business intersected with her own. This is true American aristocracy, bolstered by Victoria's army of three rough-and-ready sons, plus one pretty daughter/princess.

The Big Valley was in many ways the progenitor of the popular 1980s TV series *Dynasty* (1981-1989) and *The Colbys* (1985-1987), popular sagas of the super-wealthy and their chronic soapy loves, losses, and lifestyles. Stanwyck was a longtime friend of Aaron Spelling, producer of both programs, and had facilitated his meeting with Nolan Miller in the 1950s. Miller became Stanwyck's off-screen designer, as well as her companion and escort to gala events, and eventually became the head costume designer for both *Dynasty* and *The Colbys* series, responsible for hundreds of stupendously outrageous outfits for the queenly characters played by Joan Collins, Linda Evans (whom Stanwyck had mentored as a young actor in *Big Valley*), Diahann Carroll, Heather Locklear, and many others. Stanwyck appeared in only four episodes of *Dynasty* and twenty-four episodes of the first season of *The Colbys*, playing the role of Constance Colby, a rich aunt. Although she did what she could with her meager lines, her domineering "queenly" attitude was not as much appreciated on the *Colbys* set,[20] and her part became less and less prominent until she got written out of the series, and she ended her contract in disgust. It was an inelegant finale to an illustrious career but only because she was persistent in her desire to keep working.

Writers in the 1980s were clearly not able to keep up with the desires of an older woman. Even her star appearance in one *Charlie's Angels* episode, as the omnipotent boss "Toni" of three all-American young men, assigned to "keep an eye" on the Angels, offers very little in the way of character.[21] In each of these shows, Stanwyck is cast in the role of matriarch, even while her powers of performance are gradually reduced to little more than a clothes horse. Nevertheless, Stanwyck's affiliation with these shows, which were exuberantly embraced by the gay community,[22] solidified her enduring queenly status as a camp icon. If camp lies in the eyes of the beholder, Stanwyck's queenliness is precisely what enables her to be embraced as the progressive, gender-bending figure that she most definitely was not.

RIDING, FALLING, AND STUNTS

"No animal was harmed" … serves a taxonomic purpose, separating
the two principal film genres, fiction and documentary…. Why aren't similar
reassurances applied to human beings?

—Akira Lippit, "The Death of an Animal"

AKIRA LIPPIT CONTINUES THIS THOUGHT by reference to the prolific representation of violence against men and women in fiction films and suggests that the "human counterpoint to this disclaimer" is "all resemblances to persons living or deceased is purely coincidental."[1] And yet much violence *is* often meted out against actors on sets—and not simply psychological violence. Stanwyck was frequently injured in film shoots, and she wore it more as a badge of honor than a grudge, as evidence of her hardiness and professionalism. Her body was arguably a site of struggle, as she repeatedly put it on the line as a mark of sincerity and action. Aligning her body with nature, she gained some distance from the glamour of Hollywood culture while challenging gendered conventions of movement and stasis.

Looking at some of Stanwyck's many horseback-riding scenes, it is clear that the strong, dynamic imagery of riding enabled her to rise above the entrenched misogyny of the industry. Certainly, those images have outlasted the culture in which they were produced, offering another image of a woman on the twentieth-century screen. At the same time, the transcendent, enabling, independent image of horseback riding was produced within an industry of illusion and deception. When the spectacle is conjoined with anecdotes and trivia pulled from biographies and industry files, the scene of gendered labor and sexist critical discourse is not so pretty. The pleasures attached to genres like the western need to be unpacked so as to understand that, as Lauren Berlant puts it, "freedom is not freedom, pleasure not

Barbara Stanwyck in *Forbidden* (1932)

pleasure, disavowal not disavowal, but ways we have learned to identify knowledge and sensation."[2]

In an early scene in *Forbidden*, Stanwyck is briefly seen riding a horse on a beach in a dazzle of sunlight. In profile her hair flies behind her as the camera tracks beside her fast-moving silhouette. It's a remarkable image of freedom and transcendence, unique in her career in its speed and cinematic energy. The scene is quickly inserted into a long and rambling story about a fallen woman, and it seems to carry the full weight of the height from which she falls. The scene is supposed to be Havana in the moonlight, where her librarian character, Lulu, has gone to find romance and excitement. She finds only Bob (Adolphe Menjou), who turns out to be married. In this, one of her first films, the novelty of the sparkling image might be seen as symbolic of the promise of Stanwyck's stardom. If so, her career as a rider is studded with falls, which she came to incorporate into her star persona as a wannabe stunt performer.[3] Horseback riding in westerns frequently took Stanwyck out of Los Angeles to shoot on locations and landscapes that she came to love. After her death, her ashes were given to the wind at Lone Pine Desert in the High Sierra mountains—a long way from the streets of Brooklyn.

In fact, the beach scene in *Forbidden* was shot in Laguna Beach in Southern California at sunrise, and a double took Stanwyck's place for the long shots. Shooting the close-up, Stanwyck was thrown by the horse and badly injured, although she stoically completed the picture despite spending each night in traction in a hospital. She had already seriously injured her back when the set collapsed shooting *Ten Cents a Dance* and continued to work with excruciating pain, setting a pattern that would continue throughout her career.[4] Stanwyck was said to be "scared of horses" in her early career,[5] although Victoria Wilson's biography has her romping about Central Park in the 1920s with her girlfriends and hanging out in cafés wearing riding breeches.[6] She is seen on horses in *The Woman in Red* (1935), *Annie Oakley* (1935), and *A Message to Garcia* (1936), but in 1938 she had a clause added to her RKO contract protecting her from riding on camera after her good friend Marion Marx had a bad fall from a horse.[7]

Stanwyck built and co-owned a ranch named Marwyck near Van Nuys just outside Los Angeles with Zeppo Marx and his wife, Marion, from 1935 to 1940, where they raised thoroughbred horses. She and Robert Taylor were frequently photographed at the racetrack during this period, and they did many photo shoots at Marwyck with and without Stanwyck's son, Dion. In this way horses became integral to the "happy family" imagery that Stanwyck managed to orchestrate for a brief period of time. It was probably during the years when she lived at Marwyck that she improved her riding skills and overcame any fears she may have had.[8]

By the 1940s she had gained a reputation as an expert horsewoman. When screenwriter Nivel Busch visited the set of *The Furies*, he complained, "They put Stanwyck on a miserable fat-assed palomino that could hardly waddle." She was a good horsewoman, according to Busch, but they thought she would fall off a more energetic horse and endanger the production. Nevertheless, her rejection of stunt doubles inspired John Houston to do the same, not to be outplayed by a woman.[9]

Stanwyck's repeated claim in the latter part of her career that she wished she had been a stuntwoman is in keeping with her early career desire to emulate Pearl White, an action heroine of the teens. Her horsiness undoubtedly abetted Stanwyck's "tough" image and made her an icon of a so-called powerful woman in the postwar years. A horse makes a small woman appear large, her mastery of the animal is symbolic of control and dominance, the aura of nature cuts through the artifice of glamorous stardom, and the lone horsewoman is iconic of the "independence" label that the actor earned by other means in the 1930s.

Horses eventually became an essential element of Stanwyck's star image, and yet viewing footage of her on horseback, we can't always be sure if it is Stanwyck, as doubles were frequently cast. (For example, cutting from long

Barbara Stanwyck in *Blowing Wild* (1953)

shot to medium shot, is that really her galloping into center stage of *Buffalo Bill's Wild West Show* in *Annie Oakley*, the only time she is seen on a horse in that film?) She insisted on doing her own stunts because she felt that it contributed to the consistency of characterization, as if she distrusted the wizardry of Hollywood effects. As Nivel Busch noted about *The Furies*, doing her own stunts meant that Stanwyck jeopardized production schedules, as an injured lead actress can do great damage to a tight schedule. While there is little evidence of that happening, it is true that she endured many bruises with fortitude in order to respect shooting schedules, contributing to her great reputation as a consummate professional. She never fully recovered from the back injury of 1931 on the Laguna Beach and frequently wore a back brace, which accounts for her distinctive ramrod posture. Still, I wonder how often we are not watching Stanwyck at all but a double, whose injuries would not postpone a shoot.

Perhaps her most dramatic and emotional horse riding occurs in *Blowing Wild*, a film in which her character is something of an outsider in a male community of oil speculators. After being rejected by Jeff Dawson (Gary Cooper) yet again, Stanwyck as Marina Conway rides through the Mexican landscape across streams and under ancient bridges, pounding out her distress until she finally dismounts and collapses in tears on the ground.

Process shots are used for close-ups while she is riding and crying, and the animal is a valuable partner in the scene as her anger shifts to despair. In the same film, she races Jeff and her husband, Paco Conway (Anthony Quinn), with the two men driving in a 1940 Packard Custom Super Eight while she gallops through the countryside, beating them within seconds. The horse gives her a wild edge on the two men and, like many of Stanwyck's riding scenes, creates a spectacle that briefly disrupts the narrative like a song-and-dance number, only with horses and scenery.

After 1940 the American Humane Society monitored studio productions in order to ensure animal safety. One thing that changed in the industry around the same time was the increased availability of horses trained to do stunts, some of whom became well known. For example, Stanwyck's most famous stunt, being dragged by a horse through a tornado in *Forty Guns*, was accomplished with a horse named Oakie, ridden by a stuntman named Ken Lee.[10] You don't need to know a great deal about horseback riding to see that she has the wrong foot in the stirrup. Fuller took three takes before he got it right, gauging the best camera placement—not to authenticate Stanwyck's riding technique but to capture the fear registering on her face. In 1962 and 1973 Stanwyck was honored with awards for her riding, which were in recognition of her contribution to the art of western performance.[11]

One of the conventional mantras about women and horses is that they become sentimentally attached, as played out in films such as *National Velvet* (1944) and *The Misfits* (1961). Stanwyck, however, rarely plays this role and tends to treat her horses simply as transport out in the wilds.[12] In *The Moonlighter*, for example, when her horse is shot and falls (hopefully it is a stunt horse), she simply grabs her rifle from the saddle and leaves the horse without a backward glance. The ensuing shoot-out is one of her best action scenes, although the gendered conventions of the western genre were difficult to overcome. Ella Smith quotes a critic from the *New York Herald Tribune* describing this particular scene: "You might fidget a bit as Barbara Stanwyck, stylishly thin and looking mighty small beside a horse, fights it out with rifles with Ward Bond and wins. This, as anyone who has ever seen a Western knows, is practically impossible. Bond may lose a screen battle here and there but never to a wisp of a woman with rifles at fifty yards."[13]

In the climactic scene of *The Moonlighter*, Stanwyck's character, Rela, who has been deputized as a sheriff, is walking her horse over a rocky ledge, leading Fred MacMurray to justice, when she slips and falls down a waterfall, slipping through rock crevices and bouncing to the river below. Stanwyck performed this stunt herself, apparently because the stuntwoman was not available that day or at that time.[14] It's a great scene, except that after MacMurray saves her,

Barbara Stanwyck and Oakie the stunt horse in *Forty Guns* (1957)

she forgives him for his crimes. The film ends with a repeat of the treacherous crossing, but this time MacMurray is in the lead, and they make it safely to the other side and romp away together into the hills.

The most spectacular stunts tend to involve the act of falling, so there is a kind of inner tension between Stanwyck's affinity for dangerous riding and the tendency for her characters to fall off their horses, just to be saved by men. We know how often her power and independence are curtailed by the requisite happy endings of heterosexual romance, and the act of falling is often the price to be paid for riding high. In *The Maverick Queen* she has a spectacular fall (probably performed by a stunt person) when Sundance (Scott Brady) "bulldogs" her off of her horse. They both roll down a cliff, but she stops just short of a precipice and sends down a log to knock the man off to the depths below. The film ends with her dying in her lover's arms, a heroic death for a woman on the wrong side of the law.

As the *New York Herald* critic of *The Moonlighter* indicates, the appeal to male critics of Stanwyck on a horse in what were primarily B westerns, was her figure. The idealized western hero, male or female, is slim and trim, becoming an extension of the animal in silhouette, exuding the lightness of a jockey despite the heavy leather paraphernalia of saddle and guns. Stanwyck's outfits are often commented on by critics, and she arguably helped make pants sexy on older women as a *Parade* magazine cover from 1955 indicated with her sporting black jeans, cowboy boots, and a black blouse. In 1935, for *A Message to Garcia*, she went on an all-celery diet to

Barbara Stanwyck in *The Moonlighter* (1953)

maintain a figure suitable to the riding breeches that she wears throughout the film.[15] Nevertheless, in films such as *All I Desire* and *The Lady Eve*, Stanwyck rides sidesaddle—a Victorian style of riding that protects a lady's chastity. If women riding bicycles in Victorian times were considered transgressive, women straddling horses in mid-twentieth-century America were likewise titillating. To Stanwyck's credit, she consistently rose above such gender nonsense with her posture and her strong characters. An exceptionally weak character, such as Cora in *Trooper Hook*, never rides horses but sticks to carriages.

A third genre of horseback riding that Stanwyck performs in is the equestrian sport of the faux aristocracy. In *The Woman in Red*, she plays a spunky working-class rider who shows up the rot within the upper class that she marries into. The jumping scenes were all played by stunt riders,[16] while Stanwyck on a horse barely moves. In 1946, in *The Bride Wore Boots*, she is much more accomplished in the saddle, as her character, Sally, is much more proficient than her bookish husband, played by Robert Cummings. However, despite the title, she has few riding scenes in that film. She nevertheless injured herself on set, shooting at the Midwick Country Club, by being stepped on by a horse. In fact, Paramount filed six injury reports for the production of *The Bride Wore Boots*, most of them for uncredited stunt people performing jumps.[17]

Anecdotes of behind-the-scenes injuries are plentiful in production files for studio shoots, providing valuable insight into working conditions. Stanwyck seems to have been particularly pummeled over the course of her career, perhaps due to her propensity for action scenes. She had dislocated her spine on the set of *Ten Cents a Dance*;[18] Joel McCrea accidentally struck her in *Banjo on My Knee*,[19] causing a bad bruise on her forehead; a falling light standard hit her while shooting *Always Goodbye*;[20] and bruises were reported after her bravura stunts in *The Moonlighter* and *Forty Guns*.[21] She frequently went back to the set after injuries, hiding her limp or strained back in order to keep the film on schedule.[22] Some injuries were actually reported by studio public relations departments to promote the action of forthcoming films. One of the more extreme reports appeared in the *Paramount News* for *The Great Man's Lady*, under the title "Barbara Stanwyck Takes a Beating as Pioneer Woman":

> Being the feminine star in an epic picture of the early West usually means that the lady takes a physical beating. Barbara Stanwyck, playing the pioneer woman in Paramount's *The Great Man's Lady*, went through the following: was knocked out of a stage coach by a wall of muddy water, floundered in a river thick with mud and debris, worked two entire nights in a driving rain storm, rode a horse for three days, drove a covered wagon, shot rabbits with a shotgun, did two days work outdoor[s] clad only in a nightgown with a thin cape around it, and toiled through ten days of painful work as a woman of 100.[23]

The lady's punishment seems to blur the line between the hardships of the character and the hardships of the actress, stressing that Stanwyck could handle all the challenges of shooting on location. The woman could take it, but at the same time, men in westerns just played the parts. Implicit in the publicity around Stanwyck's "action" parts is the sense that it is unnatural, or at least unwomanly, to be out of the house playing with animals in bad weather. To her credit, Stanwyck continued to pursue such roles to the end of her career, regardless of the misogyny that tended to undermine her performances. She recognized that as long as she could keep her figure, she could find scripts that made space for older women if they were set outside the comforts of urban life. Stanwyck's character Vance Jeffords in *The Furies* says repeatedly to both of her lovers, the Mexican and the gambler, that she likes a man who "pulls the bit" on her, as if she herself were a horse that needed domesticating. And yet Vance, like so many of Stanwyck's western film roles, would be miserable and out of place in a stable and is far better off without that bit.

In the four seasons of *Big Valley*, Stanwyck's character, Victoria Barkley, is the queen of domesticity and mainly travels by horse and buggy, as would have befitted a lady of her social stature. Her three sons, however, are constantly on horseback as they venture more frequently beyond the Barkley estate. Victoria does have a few episodes in which Stanwyck could show off her riding skills, including "Pursuit" (season 2, episode 5, October 10, 1966), in which she slowly tracks a Native American across the desert. Her stylish black leather jacket is a recurring wardrobe item, at least in the last three seasons of the show. She was proud of her waist-drag—being pulled behind a horse with a rope around her waist—in "Four Hours to Furnace Hill" (season 3, episode 12, December 11, 1967), which she did herself.[24] It lacks the dramatic intensity of Fuller's stunt scene, however, and fifty years later it looks a lot like a sixty-year-old woman trying to prove something to a bunch of brutal men (led by guest star Bruce Dern).

Lauren Berlant discusses the female complaint in terms of the dual prongs of utopian, romantic imaginary and its feminist critique, which come together, she argues, in the intimate public sphere that includes the genre cinema that Barbara Stanwyck starred in through most of the twentieth century. Berlant further distinguishes between the "imaginary," which is the fantastic realm of spectacle and dreaming, "a conventional domain of contestation," and "projects of world-changing agency," or "the scene of the reproduction of life as such."[25] The latter might well point to the off-screen scene of labor that attends film production, as well as the critical discourse that reframes spectacle and dreaming, situating filmic texts within historical frames.

Returning to *Blowing Wild*, a film with two spectacular riding scenes, it is worth pointing out that while many Mexicans die on-screen in this action-adventure film set in the oil fields south of the border, I have found no injury reports from the studio. Off-screen, however, Stanwyck and the other actors were featured prominently in news reports about the production. They were threatened with deportation in retaliation for the imprisonment of Mexican actor Rosaura Revueltas in El Paso. She had been charged with illegal entry to the United States in retaliation by U.S. congressmen against the production of *Salt of the Earth*, alleged to be a "commie" production because it was produced by a labor union and by blacklisted producer Paul Jarrico and writer Michael Wilson.[26] Both films were eventually shot and released, and another news item reported that Stanwyck was a "natural fit" for an oil-well drama, given that she owned wells herself in Texas, Oklahoma, and Mexico.[27]

Stanwyck was made an honorary member of the Stuntman's Association of Motion Pictures in 1982, around the same time that *The Thorn Birds* was being shot in California. The plaque she received reads in part, "In appreciation of your unselfish contribution and the great friendship between you and stuntmen,"[28] suggesting that it was awarded in recognition of her professional generosity rather than her riding skills. She has a few horseback scenes in *The Thorn Birds* in which her matriarchal character, Mary Carson, watches her family work the paddocks from her perch atop a large chestnut mount, and she converses with other riders at a stately walking pace. At the age of seventy-six, the little orphan from Brooklyn still sits tall in the saddle.

In an interview taped during the shooting of *The Big Valley* in 1968, Stanwyck was asked if she had ever thought about directing. She dismisses the idea abruptly: "No. I could help, but I don't know enough."[29] In fact, by some reports, she "ruled everything and everyone" in the production and shooting of the TV series.[30] The fact that Stanwyck was always ready to put her body on the line, by radical dieting practices (steak and coffee in the 1960s) and doing stunts, but unable to imagine becoming a director is emblematic of the precarity of women's agency within the film industry. Like her riding scenes, this inequity highlights the affective claim of fantasy as a deep-seated ambivalence within women's cultural history and Stanwyck's role within the dreamscape of Hollywood. In Berlant's words, it can be thought of producing "a sense of thriving in the consumer's body and sometimes in the mise-en-scène itself."[31]

For Berlant, this "thriving" points to the need for "real life to step up to the plate," and in terms of women directors, in the 2020s the tide is finally beginning to turn, and yet, historically, Stanwyck's horsiness is evidence that, in Berlant's words, "affect is formalism avant la lettre."[32] Over the course of her career, as Stanwyck became more and more comfortable with horses, she contributed to a powerful new image of women in movement, riding with purpose across iconic landscapes. These images remain beautiful rare images that were frequently selling points for many of the films, for all of which she either had top billing or shared top billing with her male costars. Contrary to the deeply misogynist theme song of *Forty Guns*, no one actually took her whip away, precisely because she is a woman after all.[33]

THE *STELLA DALLAS* DEBATES

The eternal is in any case far more the ruffle on a dress than some idea.

—Walter Benjamin, The Arcades Project

STELLA DALLAS (KING VIDOR, 1937) is the single Stanwyck film that has received more scholarly attention than any other. The film lifted her career at a critical point, arguably paving the way for the great films that she made in the 1940s. Many of the debates around the film are interpretive: how to read it, how to interpret it, and what kind of address it offers to different spectators. As a maternal melodrama, the film may have been pitched at women, but many men also confess to having shed a tear, especially at the powerful concluding shots that have become emblematic of the Hollywood "weepie." The film ends with Stanwyck as Stella Dallas out in the rain watching her daughter Laurel (Anne Shirley) get married to a wealthy young man. The scene inside the huge house is lit up like a movie set, with large windows facing the street left uncurtained for Stella's benefit by the lovely lady of the house, Helen Morrison (Barbara McNeil). Stella smiles and cries simultaneously, tugs at a handkerchief, and then strides out of the scene into some kind of invisible space beyond the camera's view and beyond the emotional struggles played out in the film. *Stella Dallas* is a film about appropriate behaviors and appearances and the social codes that Stella fails to observe. Stanwyck's Stella is opaque because her performance is at once fabulous in its performativity and moving in its depth of feeling.

For feminist critics in the 1980s, *Stella Dallas* provided a vehicle for an important debate about female spectatorship. The question of identification centered on Stanwyck's role as Stella. The strength of her performance was noted in passing but not entirely recognized as the reason why this particular text put the question of identification in play in such a radical way. Returning to those debates demonstrates how Stanwyck played a critical role in the field of film studies; at the same time, how a consideration of Stanwyck's star text reframes the debates in terms of feminist historiography. Once *Stella Dallas* is situated within a historical frame of reference, her auteurist agency in the production and longevity of the film can be better recognized.

In E. Ann Kaplan's initial foray in "the *Stella Dallas* debates," she argued (in 1983) that the film "taught" Stella and the female spectator that the "correct place" for the mother in patriarchy is outside the frame.[1] Society functions best without her display of bad taste, and her sacrifice is to walk out of her daughter's life in order to ensure Laurel's access to bourgeois "normalcy." In response to Kaplan, Linda Williams argued in 1985 that the female spectator may in fact be able to see Stella both as a mother and "as something else besides a mother," a line borrowed from the film's script. For Williams, "the female spectator tends to identify with contradiction itself,"[2] a conclusion arrived at through psychoanalytic theory rather than empirical evidence. Williams argues against a monolithic notion of the female spectator and understands the contradiction to be one produced within patriarchy: that women are capable of multiple points of identification even with a patriarchal system. Stella's attempt to reconcile the contradictions of her own social role is described as "heroic," even if she ends up out of the scene, on the street, as a spectator. Williams says that we see the contradictions between "what the patriarchal resolution of the film asks us to see" (the eradication of the mother) and what we as empathetic spectators feel. Because we identify with Stella, Laurel, and Helen, the spectator is bound to feel "the loss of mother to daughter and daughter to mother."[3]

In fact, contradictions constitute the raw material of the melodramatic mode as a means by which society "talks to itself."[4] Victimless dramas of intense pathos emerge within worlds where, as Thomas Elsaesser describes it: "The characters are, so to speak, each others' sole referents, there is no world outside to be acted on, no reality that could be defined or assumed unambiguously."[5] He argues that "the dynamic movement, the full artic-ulation and the fleshed-out emotions … become the very signs of the characters' alienation, and thus serve to formulate a devastating critique of the ideology that supports it."[6] Thanks to Stanwyck's performance in *Stella Dallas*, the film is an important precursor of the Sirkian style of the 1950s that preoccupied film critics such as Elsaesser. The ambiguity of the film is precisely what Williams alludes to in her claim that *Stella Dallas* produced a contradictory and divided address. The level and dimension of "critique" are entirely up to the individual spectator, whom we understand now to be far less determined or monolithic than feminist film theory of the 1980 imagined. It is difficult to accept Kaplan's response to Williams, that it was impossible "to refuse participating in the patriarchal viewing economy."[7]

The next phase of the *Stella Dallas* debates came with Stanley Cavell's essay "Stella's Taste," in his book *Contesting Tears*, in which he argued that the film was exemplary of the "unknown woman" in American cinema. By "unknown" he meant mysterious—and also transformative. His approach to the woman's film from the perspective of Emersonian philosophy was not well appreciated by feminist film theorists at the time, who challenged his right to take on the topic outside the psychoanalytic framework that they had so rigorously developed around spectatorship.[8] In fact, Cavell's text-based approach has in some senses survived better, because by shifting the frame from patriarchy to American culture, his approach opens a space for the recognition of historical women, both characters and actors, as individuals, which is to say heroes. The feminist approach had become preoccupied with theoretical female spectators and had set aside the possible role of actual women in the production of these films; even though the debates were an invaluable challenge to the persistence and determinism of the male gaze. Cavell's Emersonian problematic of "self-reliance and conformity" is arguably a variation on the problematic of desire and repression that had become allegorical manifestations of a recurring psychosocial struggle in mid-twentieth-century American culture. The ethical problem posed by *Stella Dallas* is precisely the role of personhood and self-fulfillment within motherhood, because Stella just wants to have fun, which is set up by the film as inappropriate both for mothers and for upper-class ladies.

One of Cavell's most provocative claims is that Stella is not a fashion victim but is in full control of her quirky sartorial choices. The politics of fashion comes to a head in the critical "Christmas tree" scene that occurs three-quarters of the way through the film. Stella dons an eccentric assemblage of ruffles, furs, beads, bows, and florals and prances through a luxury resort hotel, making her first appearance there a bold statement of her "stacks of style." Challenging Williams's reading, that Stella is "oblivious as ever" to the shocking effect of her appearance,[9] Cavell argues that there is "massive evidence in the film that Stella knows exactly what her effect is there," and he runs through quite a number of instances where she has selected her wardrobe very deliberately.[10] In her performance in the hotel, is Stella deliberately making a scene to push her daughter away? Or is she naively thinking that this is how to impress wealthy people? Laurel and her friends see the woman "dressed like a Christmas tree" in the mirror of a café/drugstore, and Laurel runs away rather than acknowledge her own mother to her new friends. In the next scene Laurel and Stella abruptly leave the hotel, and on the train home they hear some girls talking about the incident. Laurel climbs into her mother's sleeping berth and consoles her without mentioning the incident or the gossip. So much is unsaid that both Williams's and Cavell's readings of the scene are possible, but what strikes me as most significant is that Stanwyck has effectively managed to create a performance that has caused two esteemed scholars to argue about what her character is thinking. Neither considers that Stanwyck has nested a performance within a performance.

Following from an account of this debate, Andrew Klevan has offered an even more convincing analysis of *Stella Dallas* based in a close reading of Stanwyck's performance. He points out that Stanwyck creates a complicated, multilayered persona who performs differently to impress different characters.[11] Her excessive costuming is an important component of this fissured character, who wants at first to "learn" from her husband, Stephen (John Boles), how to be sophisticated but falls back on less highbrow behaviors to express her own desires and personality. The many mirrors in the film should alert us to the fact that this is a drama of appearances, although Stanwyck also uses her voice to articulate a raw, musical working-class drawl; at other times, she purrs with politesse and educated enunciation. As Klevan puts it, "The mirroring is apt because she will be perpetually adopting representations, and struggling against them."[12] Klevan provides a finely detailed account of the subtleties of Stanwyck's performance in the film, which emerged as much from her own understanding of the character as it did from the director and screenwriters. As Klevan puts it, "Our assessment of character may also depend on trying to work out the performer's intentions."[13]

Fortunately, we do know a little bit about Stanwyck's understanding of the role of Stella Dallas. In 1972 she gave a surprisingly detailed account of her thoughtful approach, which was to portray Stella as "two separate women." She said, "There is a point in portraying surface vulgarity where tragedy and comedy are very close; that thin dividing line had to be watched carefully." She added that Stella was "a woman who cheated failure. One who eagerly paid the full measure for what she wanted from life."[14] In other words, Stella comes out ahead in Stanwyck's view. Victoria Wilson suggests that Stanwyck was attracted to the role because she was interested in the performance possibilities available to a character actor that were usually denied to "leading ladies" like herself.[15] Once she had become a star, in 1930s film culture she was expected to play "noble" and dignified characters, not vulgar and poorly dressed women like Stella, whose taste was still perceived as proximate with prostitution.

Barbara Stanwyck in *Stella Dallas* (1937)

Getting the role of Stella was no small feat, and Stanwyck worked hard for it. Although King Vidor wanted Stanwyck for the role, producer Sam Goldwyn was not interested because he felt that she "had no sex appeal" on the one hand, and on the other, that because she was not, herself, an actual mother, she would not understand the part.[16] Many actresses, including Gloria Swanson, were not interested in playing the part of a mother for fear it would age them. Stanwyck was advised against it at first for similar reasons (she was thirty years old), and when Joel McCrea finally persuaded Goldwyn to consider her, Stanwyck at first refused to do a screen test, given her seven years on the screen. She was, however, intrigued and considered Goldwyn Productions to be a prestige studio where she was eager to work, so she consented to a screen test and beat out the forty-eight other women who had also done tests.[17] Playing a character who ages twenty years and becomes significantly larger as she grows older entailed altering her figure and face with padding, which was (and still is) considered brave for a woman. For Stanwyck, it was the definition of acting—to become "unladylike."[18]

Over and above the critical debates around *Stella Dallas*, the film has also generated a number of other readings, starting with its historical contradictions. Anna Siomopoulos argues that the multiple identifications engendered by *Stella Dallas*, including attachments to Helen Morrison and Laurel, should be historicized within the political role of New Deal empathy.[19]

In New Deal America, the ideal of a classless society demanded a new ideology of sympathy for the underclasses, and the deep pathos generated by *Stella Dallas* actually coincided well with liberal ideals of benevolence, although the hardline class barriers between Stella and her estranged husband were less convincing. Olive Higgins Prouty's original story was published in 1923, and Samuel Goldwyn's first adaptation was made in 1925, and it was in many ways a story about a class-bound society that offered little chance for social mobility.

Although the 1937 version performed well at the box office, grossing two million dollars,[20] the reviews consistently noted the datedness of the story. "I cannot believe Stella Dallas anymore," said *Picture Play*. At the same time, Stanwyck's performance was said to be terrific and full of "vitality" and "vigor," and even though the motivations are not always clear, "Vidor smooths them over."[21] For the *Variety* reviewer, Stanwyck's Stella was "crudely vital" and makes "the sordid sublime"—exactly the effect Stanwyck was going for. Even so, this reviewer notes that "social station no longer holds the same implications as Prouty's time."[22] Siomopoulos suggests that the rhetoric of empathy effectively "pacifies" the film's more radical implications of class and gender politics.[23] Rather than contradiction, this divided sympathy generates pity for the woman separated from the world of her husband and child, rather than critique. The Goldwyn Company even used Eleanor Roosevelt's image and discourse to promote *Stella Dallas*, linking her New Deal rhetoric of sacrifice to Goldwyn's maternal melodrama.[24] By 1937 the deep and profound class division that the film dramatizes was no longer convincing. Stanwyck's own legendary rags-to-riches story of social mobility was itself testimony to the permeability of class lines.

Prouty actually disliked both film versions of her book as well as the play that preceded them and the radio series of the same name that ran from 1937 to 1955. She objected to the commodification of the story, because her original novel was intended to be a critique of consumer capitalism, and the adaptations were too "infatuated" with the character of Stella.[25] In the book, the narrator looks down on Stella, whose "sordidness" is far from sublime. She becomes sympathetic toward the end, when seen through the eyes of Helen, but her tragedy for Prouty and presumably her 1923 readers, was that Stella, through the artisanal production of fashion simulacra, was able to reproduce her daughter, Laurel, as an elegant upper-class lady and therefore as someone out of Stella's class. The discourse of sewing and fashion is, for Prouty, a tale of a woman's ability to "manufacture social mobility through fashion."[26] Stella produces her daughter as other than herself, and the novel ends with Stella becoming more and more pathetic, working in a factory and propping up the destitute alcoholic Ed Munn.

For the 1925 version of *Stella Dallas*, Frances Marion wrote the adaptation, and Belle Bennett plays Stella with appropriate pathos and wears equally outrageous outfits. The contrast between Stella's overdone costumes and those of Laurel and Helen is starker in the earlier film, because the other ladies wear solid-colored sheaths. In the early 1920s, this style had recently been introduced as an elegant alternative to Victorian frills and accessories and was widely disseminated in the form of ready-to-wear couture as well as sewing patterns for homemakers. Stella is able to make exact copies from shop window models without even using a pattern, but in the 1925 film she herself wears feathered hats, lacy collars, and ruffled dresses that are "excessive" and also old-fashioned. For Prouty, and for Frances Marion, Stella's affinity for excessive stacks of style, along with "paint" (makeup) and fussy hairdos, is bound up with her class destiny.[27] The viewer is supposed to feel sorry for her lack of taste, which Stanwyck defers in her bold, disruptive performance style.

In the 1937 version of *Stella Dallas*, all the ladies' costumes feature bows and ruffles—often at the neck, as ladies wear had taken on vestiges of feminized menswear at this point—but Stella has far more of them, along with the makeup, sparkly costume jewelry, and large pointy hats and headwear. Belle Bennett's Stella only "puts on a show" toward the end of the film, when she pretends to have taken up seriously with Ed Munn in order to finally drive Laurel away in disgust. Stanwyck's Stella, on the other hand, begins her playacting performance in the film's opening scene when she primly poses for Stephen Dallas as he walks by and then turns around and yells at her brother. The "Christmas tree" scene is built up to in a series of performances that culminate in her false liaison with Munn (Alan Hale). In fact, the critics noticed the performative excess in 1937 and still praised Stanwyck for her ability to make them cry. Frank Nugent in the *New York Times* described the film as "caricature all the way,"[28] while the *Variety* critic said that it "only goes to caricature in one spot,"[29] presumably the scene in the resort hotel.

What we know of the film's production history and reception tends to confirm Klevan's observation that the opacity of *Stella Dallas* is in part because "the film does not know what it is doing with Stella at the resort."[30] The elliptical structure of the film leaves many in-between details up to the viewer's discretion, allowing Stanwyck's complex performance to bear the full weight of meaning. Stella's grand parade through the hotel grounds is interrupted briefly by a pair of golfers. She walks straight through their putting green, and one of the men turns and imitates her walk with a limp-wristed flourish, just in case we missed the campy appeal of her masquerade. Perhaps, on top of everything else, Stella is in drag.

Barbara Stanwyck in *Stella Dallas* (1937)

To sustain Stanwyck's affinity for the role of a suffering mother, fan magazines focused on her custody case over her adopted son, Dion, which unfolded just after the release of *Stella Dallas*.[31] Moreover, a popular anecdote further confirmed Stanwyck's own oblivious relationship to fashion and her departure from the norms of "glamour" associated with movie stars: when she and Robert Taylor arrived at the premier of *Stella Dallas*, she was so dressed down that she was mistaken for one of her husband's fans and consequently hustled out of the theater lobby by a policeman.[32] The implicit contradiction between Stanwyck's own social mobility and the impregnable class barriers dramatized in the film was conveniently downplayed. Audiences and critics in 1937 were ready and willing to overlook the elliptical and dated plot in order to praise the film's pathos. *Stella Dallas*'s ability to draw tears from men and women alike seemed to seal the film's fate as an enduring melodrama, and the deep contradictions within Stella's character were resolved in the praise for Stanwyck's bravura role.

The deepest irony of Stanwyck's performance in *Stella Dallas* is of course her future profile as a "bad mother" that emerged in the 1960s when Dion finally spoke out about his upbringing (see chapter D). Stanwyck's own failure or abstention from motherhood is perhaps the obverse side of Kaplan's interpretation of the film as promoting the "invisibility" of motherhood in patriarchy. In light of this further irreconcilable contradiction arising from *Stella Dallas*, we should perhaps return to Cavell's assessment of the film's concluding scenes, which pose the question of Stella's transformation. She is different suddenly, without makeup or fancy clothes, smiling and striding in the rain. Cavell asks first of all, What is she walking away from? He suggests that after returning the gaze of Helen (symbolically) and the gaze of the movie screen itself—in the form of the plate-glass window in Helen's home—"Stella has the right not to share their tastes."[33]

Indeed, the upper-class lifestyle in *Stella Dallas* is depicted as extraordinarily banal. As Klevan points out, the famous "Christmas tree" scene is an interruption into a longer sequence of clichéd courtship and banal rituals of conformist bourgeois culture. He equates Stella's exaggerated and overdone outfit with the disruptive effect of haute couture in everyday life: style as a modality of rupture, even if style is not seen as such within the closed circuits of the film itself.[34] At the end of the film, Stella walks out of that closed world of appearances into a pictorial space beyond it. Cavell suggests:

> Her walk toward us, as if the screen becomes her gaze,
> is allegorized as the presenting or creating of a star, or as
> the interpretation of stardom. It is the negation, in advance
> so to speak, of a theory of the star as fetish. This star, call her
> Barbara Stanwyck, is without obvious beauty or glamour.[35]

Cavell goes on to point out that, retrospectively, we know she has a future, and the final shot of *Stella Dallas* "entails the promise of return."[36] Stella is the outsider who does not belong in high society, but Stanwyck is the outsider (working-class orphan) who stormed the walls of the Hollywood fortress precisely by speaking in the forked tongues of Brooklyn. Her star image at the time was already attached to a rejection of glamour in favor of family life. The "vitality" she lends to her portrayal of Stella is embodied in mannerisms and speech patterns associated with the uneducated underclass, but that character is nevertheless proud of her identity.

The drama of the outsider barred from entry into society in *Stella Dallas* is also an allegory of racial segregation and passing. Alison Whitney has shown how Laurel's problem as the child of a "vulgar" mother is not unlike the problem of the mixed-race child in America.[37] To pass as white, the black mother needs to disappear, which is of course the story of *Imitation of Life*, originally filmed in 1934. As Whitney points out, the contradictions within Stella's character are consistent with interconnected systems of social stratification including race, class, and gender. Stella uses the "St. Louis

Blues" song in her "performance" of decadence designed to drive Laurel away (see chapter T); she behaves increasingly informally with the three different black maids who work for her and finally takes on the kitchen work herself as if she were replacing her own maid.[38]

The threat of a sympathy deficit runs through all melodramas of misrecognition, and Stella's plight might also be seen as an allegory for the immigrant experience, for parents whose children are able to "assimilate" better than themselves.[39] In all of these allegorical scenarios, the emergence at the end of Stella/Stanwyck's self-recognition and pride and her ability to walk away from the repressive structures of white, bourgeois, Anglo-Saxon culture might be recognized as a valuable and desirable modality of personhood. Because the drama is one of motherhood, all of these other allegorical layers of inside/outside are grounded in the experience of women in patriarchy.

James Naremore singles out Stanwyck's performance in *Stella Dallas* in his seminal book, *Acting in the Cinema*, in the context of "expressive coherence." Unlike a role such as Phyllis Dietrichson in *Double Indemnity*, where Stanwyck conceals the complex depths of her character, in *Stella Dallas* she openly displays "expressive incoherence." For Naremore, Stella "never successfully manages the roles she has chosen."[40] He goes on to say that such characterization usually serves to conceal or repress a character's "sincere feelings,"[41] but the beauty of Stanwyck's performance and the reason it is so hard to definitively read is that she performs her sincere mother love with as much passion and zeal as expressed in her exhibitionist personality. Nothing is hidden, and there is a kind of openness of the character's multiplicity on display, and that unique openness further lends the film to yet more layers of interpretation.

Patricia White has argued that the triangulation of the female gaze between Stella, Laurel, and Helen constitutes a unique expression of homosocial subjectivity in Hollywood cinema.[42] The train car scene in which Laurel and Stella comfort each other in bed can also be read as two adult women sharing "the blind gaze of lovers,"[43] a thought that was not lost on Stanwyck herself, who jokingly said to Anne Shirley that when she finally got a scene in bed with her costar, it was not Clark Gable or Gary Cooper "but YOU!"[44] In the following scene, Stella, wearing another outlandish outfit, visits Helen Morrison and speaks mother-to-mother in a powerfully moving scene in which Stanwyck seems to perform for Helen and also for herself,[45] essentially giving her child away. It is a scene of intimacy that is nevertheless shot through with the difference of class, boldly inscribed in Stella's kitschy wardrobe and Helen's elegant and insipid dress and furnishings. White reads these scenes of female bonding in terms of Stella forging a new identity outside and beyond the tropes of motherhood but within the sphere of a differentiated femininity. The heroine "escapes a maternal destiny while capitulating to a maternal ideology," but in doing so, she forms a new connection "with another woman that limns a new identity."[46]

I would like to conclude by returning to Walter Benjamin's cryptic words about the ruffle on a dress and its relation to "the eternal." *Stella Dallas* is not a film about fashion, but it is a film about costume, appearance, and taste, in which "ruffles" constitute a mark of excess, a disruption, and, above all, a performative statement. For Benjamin, women's fashion marked the temporality of the everyday, another way of marking time as always already mortified.[47] All fashion is dead on arrival because it marks a moment already past. Performance also takes place in time, although we usually forget that fact in the case of movies constructed from multiple takes and watched multiple times. Stanwyck's performance in *Stella Dallas* was just that, something that happened during two months in 1937 in a film that would have made little sense until she stepped into the role.

Stanwyck's Stella emerges at the end a free woman. In fact, Stanwyck was still at the mercy of a merciless studio system, but having accepted the challenge of the role of Stella, she managed to produce a character over which film scholars could argue for decades. It is entirely possible that her performance shocked Samuel Goldwyn himself, transforming the film into something entirely unexpected. Wilson reports that Goldwyn inexplicably fired Vidor and the entire cast after seeing the rushes one day but then called the director in the middle of the night to say it was great and they could continue shooting.[48] What did he see that produced such a shock? Could it have been Stanwyck taking over the picture with her multifaceted performance that embraced caricature as an art form? Was it the New Woman resurrected from earlier in the decade, returning in the guise of a woman who knows herself, precisely, to be something other than a mother?

THERESA HARRIS
BLACK DOUBLE

Rather than conceptualizing race as identity, phenotypic characteristics, or biological inheritance, my reading of race as relation suggests that race itself is an *event*. It is not just a relation, but an event of rela*ting*.

—Christine Goding-Doty, "White Event Horizon"

TOWARD THE END OF *Baby Face*, Stanwyck's character, Lily Powers, has an abrupt change of heart just before her ship sails to France. She yells at her maid, Chico (Theresa Harris), for the first time in the film, demanding that she stop singing "St. Louis Blues." Without another word, Lily bustles out of the stateroom, draped in fur with a case of bonds and jewels, and leaves Chico alone to watch her disappear. Lily has chosen to stand by her man and let go of her luxurious lifestyle, but what about Chico, who has been with her since the beginning? Lily's rise to the top is also Chico's rise in Black society, and the two have been inseparable since they escaped from Erie, Pennsylvania, for the big city. I have always wondered about Chico's fate, left alone on the boat to France. I imagine she might be happier in Paris, where her singing might be better appreciated. I imagine she might be able to make a living without serving white people or playing a woman who serves white people. Perhaps we could imagine something similar for Theresa Harris; perhaps we can imagine her as a star of the archive.

In *Baby Face*, Harris plays Lily's Black double. She encourages Lily in her exploits after sharing her abuse in Lily's father's house. "Where I go Chico goes," Lily says to two different men who would prefer to see her maid fired. Harris does not have many lines, but Chico walks in step with Lily, and when they arrive in New York she chews gum and has aspirations as Lily does, but her dreams start with basics, like getting fed. Lily teaches Chico the social codes of conduct that are more appropriate to the social mobility they

Barbara Stanwyck and Theresa Harris in *Baby Face* (1933)

rapidly attain together. In one of the most striking images in the film, Chico is dressed in a fur-trimmed coat, echoing Lily's outfit. It's Christmas Eve and Chico is going out on the town, leaving dinner in the icebox for her employer, who is left alone with the wise words of Nietzsche's *Will to Power* for company (see chapter I).[1]

The image of Stanwyck and Harris in furs is campy in its excess, and in the ways it pushes the limits of credibility within racist culture. Pamela Wojcik has argued that campy Black maids such as those in Mae West's films, can provide a strategy to "create distance from oppressive stereotypes."[2] The relations between Stanwyck and Harris are not personal but institutional, social, cultural, and deeply embedded in the racial hierarchies of Hollywood and mid-century America, from which twenty-first-century spectators have begun to gain some distance. How can we read Harris's career as an event, something produced within the space of whiteness that nevertheless destabilizes that "horizon" and blurs its edges?

Theresa Harris was born to sharecroppers in Texas only six months before Stanwyck was born. She had more training than Stanwyck ever got, starting with high school in Los Angeles and music training at the University of Southern California.[3] Before getting into film, she performed with the Lafayette Players, an African American theater troupe that originated in

Harlem. She married a doctor and by the mid-1930s, Thomas Cripps claims, she was a "grand dame of the ghetto," a generous and wealthy society lady in South Central Los Angeles,[4] although unlike some of her better-known contemporaries, such as Hattie McDaniel and Louise Beavers, she was petite, like Stanwyck, and had a bounce in her step. From the 1930s to the 1950s, she performed in race movies as well as studio productions and became a star among Black communities nationwide. When movies came to Black neighborhoods in which she had a walk-on part as a maid, her name was on the marquee.[5] She may have had only one opportunity to play the lead, in a lost (or missing) race film called *Bargain with Bullets* (1937, aka *Gangsters on the Loose*), but she continued to appear in film and TV until 1958.

Piecing together Harris's career is challenging, because although she made over one hundred films and TV shows, we know nothing about her industry connections and very little about her biography. In an interview around the time *Bargain with Bullets* was released by Million Dollar Pictures, she was quite outspoken about the injustices of the industry, which is to date her only public statement on record.[6] The archive is not empty, though, because digital media has brought many of her fragmentary performances into view. Just as *Baby Face* has had a bigger audience since 2004 than it had during the year of its original release (see chapter I), the circulation of Hollywood films on the internet has the potential to make Harris, too, a star of the archive.[7] Will Straw argues that film spaces that include the faces and bodies of extras should be considered "as cultural repositories, an archive of a sort."[8] Above and beyond narrativity, media such as Hollywood cinema—particularly in its digitized, readily accessible forms, I would add—constitute "an archive of performance styles and specific faces or bodies."[9]

Following the example of *The Watermelon Woman* (Cheryle Dunye, 1996), a film about a fictional Black lesbian star of the silent era, and inspired by the play *By the Way, Meet Vera Stark*, by Lynn Nottage, ostensibly inspired by Harris's career,[10] I would like to propose a speculative history of Harris, based on the fictions that she appeared in and the characters she created.[11] I am going down this road in order to argue that Stanwyck's whiteness is visible only within what Christine Goding-Doty describes as an "affective horizon," in which race is an event. Film analysis allows us to enter into a relationship with these historical figures and fill in the affective horizon of their performances. Stanwyck and Harris are credited together in only three films and shared the frame only in *Baby Face*. They inhabited parallel universes within one large and sprawling city and within one large and fragmented industry. Jacqueline Stewart analyzes fictional Black characters at the movies in Chicago during the 1930s to better understand how their "reconstructive spectatorship" enables them to reconstruct their lives in the city.[12] This method, guided by affect rather than evidence, is critical when the archive is so sketchy, and when it needs to be broken, transformed, and reimagined in order to better understand the role of a Black woman in an industry in which she was sidelined and largely uncredited.[13] It is precisely because Harris is no longer invisible that her archival traces have become valuable sources for a different kind of historiography. Once she is *seen*, and respected as a presence and a body in the archive, everything changes all around her.

Before *Baby Face*, Harris played a maid named Vera in *Professional Sweetheart* (1933) with Ginger Rogers as Glory, a popular radio singing star who is basically a corporate construction, and the plot follows the ups and downs of Glory's manipulation by managers and sponsors. At one point she runs off to marry a country boy, and Vera is abruptly asked to fill in on the radio show. Harris's sexy voice threatens Glory just enough to hurry back to the microphone. Harris's role is tiny, and she is only briefly on camera, shimmying in sequins when her voice breaks through, but she represents Harlem and its pleasures, which the managers and sponsors are ultimately unable to resist. Many of Harris's roles involve this hesitant transgression of the color line, weakening its hold even while leaving it firmly in place. The Black maid inhabits a liminal zone between two worlds, acting as confidante for white women like Lily and Glory who are otherwise stranded in worlds made by men.

In all of Harris's roles we can easily find the prejudice, the humiliation, and the demeaning stereotypes, but we can also see relationships constructed around the gaze and the body that construct horizons of affect. Perhaps Harris's most important role in this respect was as Josephine in two Jack Benny movies: *Buck Benny Rides Again* (1940) and *Love Thy Neighbor* (1940). She plays a maid in these films, but she is also the girlfriend of Benny's sidekick, Rochester (Eddie Anderson), one of the most prominent Black characters of the era. Rochester was a regular character in Benny's movies; his radio program, which ran from 1937 to 1965; and his TV show, which ran from 1950 to 1965. The Rochester-Josephine relationship serves to parallel Benny's romantic relationships, highlighting their privilege while ostensibly symbolizing the white characters' benevolence. In *Buck Benny Rides Again*, Harris and Anderson have an extended musical number, dancing and singing together. In *Love Thy Neighbor*, Josephine cons Rochester with loaded dice and plays a pivotal role in a convoluted plot. She also has the opportunity to wear several smart outfits, plus a Juliet costume (she and Anderson do a Romeo and Juliet routine), in addition to the tired maid's costume.

Black actors as "doubles" of white actors might have once been described as "shadows," but we can also invert the gaze to see them as the main attraction and the white characters as diversions, just as Black audiences did at the time. In the Benny movies, the performance style of Rochester and Harris has more wit, more energy, and more rapport than any of the other characters' scenes. They are unpredictable and joyful, while most of the scenes in these films, including Benny and Rochester together, tend toward condescension, mock anger, and torrents of put-downs, misunderstandings, and threats. Rochester's character was clearly modeled on stereotypes of Black minstrelsy, and especially in the prewar movies, Anderson's dialect perpetuated a degrading image of Black servitude and backwardness. The writers, however, did incorporate a level of reflexivity, turning Rochester's role at times into a commentary on social expectations of racial hierarchies.[14] As Josephine, Harris does not speak in a Southern dialect and has far more scenes with Anderson than with her lady employers, with whom she is barely seen (in both cases they are Benny's love interest). At the end of *Love Thy Neighbor*, she passes Mary Martin's character—her former employer—in the park, both of them pushing baby carriages. She is smartly dressed and I imagine looks more like Harris herself might have looked in 1940.

When Christine Goding-Doty speaks of an affective horizon that is produced by the event of race, she points to the "malleable instantiation of boundedness itself, that is both imposed upon and engulfs bodies … within the purview of modern power."[15] Goding-Doty's innovative approach to critical race studies is not necessarily designed as a historical method, or as a hermeneutic strategy, but as a means of "catalyzing the emergence and reemergence of race in modern encounters," and I believe that critical textual analysis might be an instance of such an encounter. She writes:

> Without an account of race and whiteness that is built from an account of affect and the virtual, the crisis whiteness is undergoing and the processes by which it is inventing new strategies to sustain itself remain invisible to the analytic resources of critical race and whiteness studies.[16]

In the case of Black bodies in Hollywood, Harris's intersectionality as a singing and dancing Black woman playing ladies' maids points to the emergent body produced within a certain "atmosphere" that extends well beyond her actual performances. Her career cannot be said to "trouble" any limits or boundaries, as she remained invisible in the white world and mostly uncast in lead roles, and yet the "event" of rereading and revising, of bringing the background forward and seeing the double not as a shadow but as an affective horizon, may help to understand how the whiteness of Hollywood, and Barbara Stanwyck in particular, was constructed.

To return to *Baby Face*, as Lily's companion and confidante Chico provides valuable empathy for an otherwise cold and calculating character. Lily's abrupt change of heart occurs upon hearing Chico singing "St. Louis Blues," the song she sings in the opening scene, washing dishes in Lily's father's speakeasy. It's what drives Lily back to be with her fallen man. Harris sings this particular song as background music, humming it under her breath, but along with her companionship it is the only note of regret, disappointment, and pathos that accompanies Lily's spectacular rise to the top of the city.

Peter Stanfield points out that "St. Louis Blues," a popular song of the era, attaches itself to Stanwyck throughout the 1930s, repeated in *Ladies They Talk About*, *Banjo on My Knee*, and *Stella Dallas*. Stanfield argues that "St. Louis Blues" represents a kind of "urban primitivism" that articulates a racial instability attached to women transgressing sexual and class boundaries. Not only does it align Lily with Chico, but also "the song functions as an aural birthmark, a sign of her [Stanwyck's] vulgar beginnings and flawed character that regardless of how much wealth she accrues she is unable to shake off."[17] While I agree with Stanfield that "St. Louis Blues" is an important signifier in Stanwyck's star image in the 1930s, I would add that it signifies a working-class background that is of critical value to her portrayals of virtuous characters in the 1930s. Like the subtle critique of class that is often implied in Stanwyck's Brooklyn-inflected speech patterns, her occasional alliance with Black characters also signifies honesty and authenticity, in keeping with Christian myths of the virtue of poverty.

In *Banjo on My Knee* the "urban primitive" theme takes a decidedly awkward turn when Theresa Harris sings "St. Louis Blues." In this case her appearance is clearly as an emotional extension or appendage for Stanwyck, who, as a white woman, is limited in her scope of expression, which may be a surprising way of describing Stanwyck, but in this case her character, Pearl, is a shy country girl. *Banjo* is best described as a hillbilly film, although generically it could also be classified as a comedy of remarriage. Pearl marries Ernie (Joel McCrea) in the opening scene, only to lose him to a long series of plot twists, misunderstandings, and coincidences for most of the movie. She is left with his father, Newt (Walter Brennan), on a houseboat in the Mississippi and a collection of inebriated "boat people" who disdain city folks and are blissfully happy being poor. When she runs off to New Orleans

Theresa Harris in *Banjo on My Knee* (1936)

to look for Newt, she ends up singing for her supper, along with Newt and "Buddy" (Buddy Ebsen). Brennan plays a "contraption" of banjo, percussion, harmonica, and piccolo with surprising flair. Ebsen does a fair tap dance, and Stanwyck sings "Where the Lazy River Goes By" (see chapter V).

Despite their amateur style, the act by Pearl, Newt, and friends is a hit, at least for the café crowd. The New Orleans of 1936 is depicted in *Banjo on My Knee* as a segregated city. The misnamed Café Creole, where Pearl works and performs, has only white clients and staff, although Blacks are seen walking by the windows as part of the everyday life of the city. When Ernie busts up the café (out of jealousy for his wife, who he has more or less abandoned for months), the crowd of onlookers includes many Blacks along with whites.

In the midst of this tale of coitus interruptus is a musical number set in the port of New Orleans, or a studio version thereof. Theresa Harris sings "St. Louis Blues" as a tale of woe and lost hope, this time with the Hall Johnson Choir in the style of a spiritual with full chorus. The male singers haul sacks of cotton off boats, while the women perform washing on the verandas of a plantation-style set and many additional men, women, and children fill in a "community" of despair. Cutaways to Stanwyck sitting on a wharf suggest that this performance is staged for her. "St. Louis Blues" is a song that features two opposing female types—the temptress and the woman who has lost her man—and in *Banjo* the musical number expresses Pearl's lovesick destitution, as well as her poverty.

"St. Louis Blues" is also the song that Newt is saving for his unborn grandchild, who has yet to be conceived. Clearly, there is some racial confusion going on in *Banjo*. Stanfield accounts for the popularity of the song "St. Louis Blues" in the 1920s and '30s as a cross-racial standard in its symbolization of an urban vernacular "unencumbered by the constraints of modernization" even if its popularity was underwritten by phonograph recordings and Hollywood films.[18] Although he claims that it is a prim- itivism formed "not in the agrarian past of the plantation but in a black urban vernacular," the version in *Banjo* evokes a scene of slavery. In the Hall Johnson Choir arrangement, the song has become a spiritual, expressing the sorrows of enslavement and subjugation. As a Depression-era saga, even Pearl's misery—which is caused as much by lecherous men as by her wayward husband– is awkwardly paralleled with the forced labor and dehumanization of Southern plantation culture.

The suggested comparison between Stanwyck's character and Harris's (uncredited) role as a Black blues singer in *Banjo on My Knee* definitely reproduces a hierarchy of white star and Black character actor, but Harris's expressive singing and the exchange of looks between the two is nevertheless important. In the affective racial horizon of the number, Harris may be segregated by montage, scenography, and studio lighting from the diegetic space occupied by Stanwyck and the other characters, but she is nevertheless individuated as the soloist and protagonist of the song. She has a message, which is not only that she has lost her man but maybe that all men are lost. The Black men march out their choreography of hard labor as if they were mechanical figures, opening up a space to recognize Pearl's plight as one of patriarchal dehumanization. Newt's appropriation of the song as a statement of paternity and patriarchy enslaves Pearl in a system in which she is powerless. For producer Darryl Zanuck, despite Stanwyck being the star, the underlying theme of the picture was "the father doing everything he could to get his son and daughter-in-law into bed so he could have a grandchild."[19]

Harris's performance in *Banjo* introduces a note of disorientation, instability, and questioning that can hardly be described as resistance but nevertheless provides a point of contact that is entirely detached from the narrative diegesis. Pearl takes up her own performance in the Café Creole shortly after the scene on the wharf, as if she were inspired by the spectacle of Black misery, passion, and uplifted voices. We are "doing whiteness" when watching *Banjo*, precisely by following the intersectionality of race and gender. From an industry perspective, one can imagine Zanuck saying to director John Cromwell that the picture needed a good strong musical number, given the musical limitations of the cast—and the mythical setting of New Orleans. (Brennan's accomplishments were a surprise to everyone, including him.[20]) We don't know how Harris got to be in this film as a singer with no spoken lines, although musical set-piece interruptions were not uncommon in the 1930s. It is entirely possible that the scene was cut completely when the film traveled to the South, and it would make little difference to the plot if it were, which is all the more reason to reinstate it here to reinscribe the racial horizon of the film. Harris's single scene reminds me of Mahalia Jackson's surprising appearance at the end of Sirk's version of *Imitation of Life* (1959), speaking emotional truth to a drama of appearances. It may not be as earth-shattering as Jackson's performance, and it is really one more world of appearances, but it serves to destabilize the scene of whiteness and patriarchy.

In the third film in which both Stanwyck and Harris appear, it is even more unlikely than *Banjo* that they actually crossed paths. In *The File on Thelma Jordan* Harris's name appears in the credits, but she has only one walk-on scene, with no lines—a scene without Stanwyck. She plays Esther, who works as a maid for Cleve and Pam Marshall (Wendell Corey and Joan Tetzel), and like most Black domestic workers in studio-era films, Esther seems like a fixture in the house, like a piece of furniture. Pam is overly attached to her wealthy father, and Cleve's affair with Thelma Jordan is unambiguously propelled by his feelings of insecurity in his own home and his wounded masculinity. Esther is in turn a sign of Pam's wealth and authority, as she refers to Esther whenever there is work to be done, as in "I'll tell Esther we'll eat on the patio." The maid is an extension of the big house and signals the wife's freedom from housework.

Esther's single appearance is in a very unusual shot. The family is supposedly at the "beach house" when the phone rings, summoning Cleve back to the city to investigate the murder of Thelma Jordan's aunt. Harris stands in the middle of a cluttered indoor-outdoor space that might be a modern trend in casual living circa 1949. Two children play in the shadowy foreground on a sandy floor/beach while Cleve lies on his stomach on a mattress and Pam reads a magazine. The slatted ceiling is low and the back of the space is filled by a high fence. Potted ferns and furniture further crowd the space. Harris, as Esther, clears away dishes on a tray. The image of family leisure is cramped and crossed with shadows, haunted perhaps by Cleve's secret role in the recent crime but also, we could say, by the presence of

Theresa Harris and Joan Tetzel in *The File on Thelma Jordan* (1949)

Harris and the obfuscation of her face. Her long and baggy maid's outfit obscures her body. She enters the shot with a tray, the phone rings, and she continues her work while Pam rises quickly to get the phone and Cleve rises more slowly behind her, blocking our view of Esther completely.

Since her name actually appears in the credits, I wonder if Harris's role was at one time expanded but later cut. Maybe she simply had a better agent who pushed for the screen credit, and maybe the culture had evolved to make that possible. If film noir can be understood as a revision of domestic melodrama, a challenge to the conformist standardization and role-playing of postwar America (see chapter C), this short scene in *Thelma Jordan* is critical. Stanwyck, as the devious, two-faced criminal, may not be physically present, but her crime and her seduction of the husband Cleve are closely tied to the tensions embedded in this sandy, shadowed room. Its liminality is symbolized in the figure of Harris, who is part of this world of luxury living yet very much excluded from it.

The racial events of Harris's film appearances can be continually modified, modulated, and reframed as we learn how to read the relations that those performances can produce. Harris's characters do not make wisecracks or talk back in the ways that Hattie McDaniel was known for,[21] but they were frequently conduits between Black and white worlds, and like Stanwyck, she was a reliable worker in the industry. We know this because of her 103 lifetime credits in film and TV, credited and uncredited. Often she was little more than an extra, stripped of character as in *Thelma Jordan*. As character actor, walk-on, and extra, she appears in dozens of canonical Hollywood films, including *Lady from Shanghai* (1947), *Out of the Past* (1947),[22] *Cat People* (1942), *I Walked with a Zombie* (1943), *The Women* (1939), *Jezebel* (1938), *Flying Down to Rio* (1933), *Gold Diggers of 1933* (1933), *Horse Feathers* (1932), and *Morocco* (1930). Her career parallels Stanwyck's until the end of the 1950s, a parallelism that creates an event horizon in which one woman is a movie star and one woman is not. Studio-era films are all racial events in which whiteness is constructed over and over again. Black and brown characters circulate on the edges of every single film, on-screen and off, marking the lost possibility of a different cinema, one in which whiteness recedes into the background.

UNION PACIFIC
UNMAKING HISTORY

A sensuous engagement with the past … is the foundation for more than individual subjectivity; it becomes the basis for mediated collective identification and the production of potentially counterhegemonic public spheres.

—Alison Landsberg, *Prosthetic Memory*

DURING THE 1930S, Barbara Stanwyck made a number of films that dealt directly or indirectly with American history. New Deal America entailed a vigorous reimagining of American ideals, culture, citizenship, and democracy. The shift from Depression-era America to wartime America saw public debates waged over the terms of nationalism, socialism, and international cooperation. Hollywood produced a wide variety of narratives of American history and politics that contributed implicitly and explicitly to what Warren Sussman describes as a "complex effort to seek and define America as a culture."[1] Through a discussion of four of these films—*Red Salute* (1935), *The Plough and the Stars* (1936), *Union Pacific*, and *Meet John Doe*— this chapter traces the fate of the New Woman whom Stanwyck had come to embody by the mid-1930s, through the "patriotic" films that followed in the latter part of the 1930s. These curious, contradictory films tend to exploit political currents and place them on display and can thus be regarded as what Alison Landsberg calls "prosthetic memories" of American history, meaning they are neither true nor private. Sussman also notes that during the 1930s, popular media, including photography and literature along with the cinema, took on more of a role than ever before in helping Americans understand what it was to be American, even while the fabric of American society was transformed by New Deal policies and pressures from European wars.[2]

Landsberg's notion of prosthetic memory was developed to challenge the dismissal of popular culture as escapist and ideologically closed.

She wants to understand popular culture texts as experiential and affective points of access to the traumas of history such that they are "lived" and remembered by viewers in the form of memory. Given the wide range of examples she offers, from early Vitagraph films to 1990 science fiction, I think it is fair to use the term in reference to some of Stanwyck's films of the 1930s. These titles enable "ethical" thinking in Landsberg's sense to the extent that these texts are easily cracked open through an examination of their gender and racial politics.[3] Stanwyck's characters tend to be committed to values that vary widely between and even within the films, and yet she is passionate and strong-minded about that commitment.

Veronica Pravadelli has posed a similar question regarding the sexy, independent outspoken women of the pre-Code era and their virtual disappearance by the end of the 1930s. She argues that they are subsumed into what might be called "the flapper marriage," which is best understood as "modernizing male dominance through unions in which vital, modern, yet pliant flapper sweethearts formed relationships with sensitive yet still masterful men."[4] This is certainly true of Stanwyck's historical/political films of the 1930s, and yet they also take this fairy-tale union one step further, in repeated attempts to articulate political and cultural values of "democracy." The films inevitably fail in their idealism and tend to expose the deficiencies and contradictions within their own projects. *A Message to Garcia* would also fit into this group (see chapter J) as a film that failed in its attempt to represent America's contribution to Cuba's late-nineteenth-century war of independence. Its failure is precisely a failure of representation, with fake jungles and a fake Latina heroine (Stanwyck). Hollywood had little compunction about using someone else's war for the sake of entertainment.

When Stanwyck was offered the role of society girl engaged to a "radical" student in *Red Salute*, she had not worked for six months. Reliance Pictures, under the leadership of Edward Small, claimed that it was definitely not a propaganda picture, even though Stanwyck's character, Drue Van Allen, ends up marrying a soldier she nicknames "Uncle Sam" (Robert Young) instead of the radical student. Modeled closely on the very successful *It Happened One Night* (Frank Capra, 1934), *Red Salute* has some excellent comic writing, and Stanwyck's performance is dripping with satire. The film belongs to an early cycle of anti-Russian films that ran from 1927 until Hitler invaded Russia in 1941.[5] It was rereleased in 1948 to capitalize on the renewed anti-Communist crusade after the war, but like the postwar cycle of anti-Communist films, *Red Salute* tries hard to reconcile politics and entertainment, ultimately failing on both counts.[6]

Robert Young and Barbara Stanwyck in *Red Salute* (1935)

The "radical" student in *Red Salute*, Leonard Arner (Hardie Albright), looks and talks American, even though he is a leader of the International Students League. His rhetoric is primarily anti-military but vague on other details, except to recognize his audience as the proletariat, and his final speech is in recognition of May Day. Stanwyck's character, Drue, is attracted to Leonard mainly to annoy her father, General Van Allen (Purnell Pratt), who has such omnipotent power that at the end of the film, he arranges to have Leonard deported, and at the beginning of the film, he kidnaps Drue by locking her into a plane bound for Mexico to separate her from her fiancé. Thus the film's politics may simply be a prop for a familiar patriarchal fairy tale of a rebellious daughter learning to respect her father.

Drue is casually drinking sidecars in Mexico when she meets Jeff, aka Uncle Sam (Young), an enlisted man who inexplicably gets loaded with her, and they end up driving across the country in a caravan with P. J., an amiable henpecked husband (Cliff Edwards, a popular singing star who also contributes a couple of musical interludes) who is fleeing his bossy wife. In the mode of screwball comedy, Drue and Jeff keep putting each other down, and she clings to the hope of reuniting with her radical fiancé. The road-trip part of the film is very funny, and Stanwyck refined her talent for satire in this production, delivering her comebacks to Young with vicious irony.

When they first get drunk together, he asks her why she got him so tight. She answers, "Because you look so much better when I'm tight." Jeff calls her "Red" but starts to notice that she is "not as Red as you make out." When they finally get to Washington, Jeff bullies Leonard off the stage and preaches American patriotism to the students, who are magically persuaded to change sides when he says, "You are all real Americans under the skin, only you don't know it."

The Red-baiting plot is motivated by actual student movements of the period, and the release of *Red Salute* was met with vigorous protests from student groups in New York, Philadelphia, and other university towns. Threats of boycotts and petitions against screenings were also useful publicity mechanisms that theater owners were not above using.[7] *Red Salute* was praised in some quarters for its critical satirical edge,[8] but for the most part the film was panned for its opportunistic exploitation of political activism. James Agee described the "angels" in the film—Drue and Jeff—as "faithfully nauseating" and the film itself as "so flagrant that the dumbest fish would cough at it."[9] To be fair, the military is also subject to some ridicule, through General Van Allen's pompous sense of entitlement and privilege. A recurring motif is P. J., the singing driver, longing for someone to start a war because he has such fond memories of being a soldier in the last war. Jeff responds, "We're working on it," which may or may not refer to the agitprop inside the film or as a premonition of the war to come. Stanwyck's witty Drue is counterbalanced by the misogynistic representation of P. J.'s wife, whose henpecking has driven him to prefer war (and driving cross-country) to marriage. This woman, played by Ruth Donnelly, gets no snappy comeback lines.

Stanwyck playing a Commie sympathizer is ironic, and yet there is a way that Drue's relationship with the radical student presages the counterculture of the 1960s, when radical students against the war exercised political activism against the state. As the empathetic center of the film, whose desire to get back to her radical fiancé drives the narrative, Stanwyck's Drue might be considered a prefiguration of the countercultural woman challenging the patriarchy in the cloak of a peacenik Communist. The combination of New Woman and political activist is a rare and precious figure, however fictional and however fleeting. Stanwyck makes history in *Red Salute* by embodying diverse and contradictory vectors of cultural imagination within the archive of Americana.

The next year, Stanwyck found herself playing another unlikely revolutionary in John Ford's *The Plough and the Stars*. Inspired by the huge success of *The Informer* (1935), which earned him an Oscar for Best Director,

Ford returned to the Irish struggle for independence. In both the 1935 film, set in 1922, and the 1936 film, set in 1916, Ford was more interested in the struggles between men and the difficult choices facing revolutionaries than in the postcolonial struggle itself. Indeed the theme of men divided in their own hearts in the face of violence is a theme that preoccupied him for subsequent decades in the context of the American West. Stanwyck yearned for the role of Queen Mary, which eventually went to Katharine Hepburn (who was also Ford's lover), for Ford's *Mary of Scotland* (1936), and thus accepted the role of Nora in *The Plough and the Stars* as compensation, even though it is a far smaller role.[10]

Stanwyck was bitterly disappointed in John Ford for his mismanagement of the film. She later described his cinema as "old fashioned crap,"[11] by which she may have been referring to the atmospheric moodiness of deep shadows that pervades the film, along with a sentimental melancholy that overhangs the doomed revolutionaries. Her biggest complaint with *Plough* was that she worked hard on an Irish brogue with which to blend with the imported Abbey Players, but during postproduction RKO producers could not understand the dialogue, so she and Robert Preston (who plays Nora's husband, Jack) had to reshoot their scenes together. Ford was off sailing, so the final cut was cobbled together with the Irish actors doing their thing and the Americans doing theirs.

The *Plough and the Stars* is set in the Easter Rising of 1916, when Irish Republicans first challenged British rule in the modern era, igniting the revolutionary period that would endure for many decades. Nora's husband, Jack, is promoted to commandant within the citizen army and participates in the failed seizure of the Dublin post office. She begs him not to leave her, and at every meeting she tries to persuade him to give up his lost cause. She is dressed down and un-made-up, and she forms a bond with the other women in her boardinghouse (the three of them mourn together in identical shrouds), but Nora merely bemoans the weeping caused by revolutionary energies and displays no passion for the cause itself. The uprising is quickly ended by the overwhelming firepower of the British army, and the point of the uprising is completely lost in the misery and poverty that follows. As in *The Informer*, women for Ford are there to hold men back from their follies, and Nora in particular might be considered a counterrevolutionary, given her powerful depiction of sorrow.

Ford significantly changed the tenor of Sean O'Casey's original play (without his permission), in which the futility of the uprising and its cost to urban life was more prominent and where Nora's character has a little more tenacity.[12] Ford's own attachment to Irish nationalism resulted in a contradictory ending that pleased no one. If there is any American allegorical parallel, it could be the American Civil War, which tore families apart for the sake of national goals of independence. Laurence Raw notes the parallels in costuming with Union Army uniforms appearing in *Plough*,[13] but that may be simply a contingency of studio wardrobe options. Stanwyck emotes beautifully in *The Plough and the Stars*, and the film may have satisfied a growing demand for more "important" "political" films,[14] but her tears are wasted on a deeply flawed and fractured film.

Stanwyck's cycle of history films continued a few years later with *Union Pacific*, which she made with Cecil B. DeMille, a director she greatly admired and with whom she had worked quite a bit on radio (*Lux Radio Theatre*). She shared his conservative values and dislike of labor unions. Unlike *Red Salute* and *The Plough and the Stars*, DeMille's "superwestern" celebrated American progress and nationalism in the form of "straight movie entertainment." As one reviewer put it in 1939, the film "presents no arguments, makes no attempt at profundity, requires no thought from its audience …. Villainy is apparent and personalized from the start."[15] In other words, in 1939 this was the "old fashioned crap." Eighty years later, *Union Pacific* is definitely thought-provoking and also difficult to watch because of its overt racism and slaughter of Indigenous peoples, who are literally mowed down in the name of progress (aka manifest destiny). Movie-Indians are shot outside the train window for sport, and although they ingeniously crash a train by knocking down a water tower over the tracks and try to stop the rescue train by burning down a trellis bridge, the Native Americans (played by local Sioux, Cheyenne, and Arapahoe tribes) are depicted as infantile primitives when they sack the train and loot the freight of knick-knacks.

While such racist stereotyping and imperialist historiography was par for the course in prewar westerns, moral dilemmas had begun to be broached in the same year, specifically in Ford's *Stagecoach* (1939). Peter Stanfield has pointed out that the production of *Union Pacific* coincided with Hollywood's war on European dictators and early embrace of a nationalist fervor.[16] Thus the story of America's first transcontinental railway is couched as a tale of democratic nation building in which genocide and racism are among the many "adventures" along the way and certainly not open to debate. Like many New Deal–era films, *Union Pacific* was the subject of a group discussion guide to promote the educational values of the historical film.[17] Among the factoids and study questions embedded in the pamphlet, we are told that the great Union Pacific Railroad "pushed the Indians before it," although students are also asked, "Was the white man fair to the Indian?

Barbara Stanwyck and Joel McCrea in *Union Pacific* (1939)

If not, can the present generation do more than is now being done to atone for the injustices of the past?"[18]

The discussion guide also asked, "Do you ever resent the banal love stories in this type of film?" which is a curious question in light of Stanwyck's central role in *Union Pacific*. She plays Mollie Monahan, a postmistress on the train servicing the "end of track," the last leg of the Union Pacific track that met up with the Central Pacific at Promontory Point, Utah, in 1862. Her character holds together the different threads of the narrative, including her father, the Irish engineer, and her suitor Dick Allen (Robert Preston), who is employed by nefarious parties to slow construction by setting up temporary saloons along the track to distract the workers. Allen's boss is in turn hired by one of the railway investors, who is also "shorting" the company by betting that the Central Pacific line will cover more ground than the Union Pacific line. Mollie is also sweet on Jeff Butler (Joel McCrea), who has been hired to keep law and order during the construction. Stanwyck is able to stick to her Irish brogue this time (the work crews are made up primarily of Irish immigrants), so her performance is somewhat stylized. She also notoriously did all her own stunts, although they are not terribly remarkable and she never gets on a horse. Most of the film was shot on studio backlots with rear projection,[19] but she nevertheless saw the film as an opportunity to exercise her inner Pearl White.[20]

In the climactic scene of a film with many big action scenes (DeMille excelled in crowd scenes with lots of extras and may not have been as interested in the more intimate scenes such as those with Stanwyck[21]), the "Indians" have Mollie and her two love interests trapped in a train car. Mollie actually lives in the train car, decked out like a small cottage, and Jeff is supposed to be hunting Dick, who has stolen the railway payroll. Shortly before the train ambush, Dick has forced Mollie to marry him in exchange for him returning the payroll to the company. Alone together, Dick tries to make good on his marriage, but Mollie pushes him away and she is saved by the Indian attack. Jeff heroically scrambles between feathered arrows to join Mollie and Dick in the train car, and the three of them pick off movie-Indians with rifles and pistols. They rig up a telegraph wire that Mollie knows how to use to signal for help, just like the Lonedale operator of Griffith fame.

Before the cavalry arrives to kill the last Native Americans, Mollie and her two suitors run out of ammunition, except for three bullets. Mollie says, "You won't let them take me alive," and Dick, putting aside his rivalry with Jeff, asks him to "do the honors all around." While Mollie prays with her face turned from her sweetheart and potential assassin, she hears the train whistle announcing their salvation. The "fate worse than death" was a familiar trope of silent cinema that reinforced the racism of threatened capture. As J. P. Telotte puts it, the scenario "offers the audience the gratification of reward for … imagining and acknowledging the only correct response to the transgression of the racial other."[22] Telotte does not note that it is always a gendered scenario in which the woman's virtue (as a symbol of the fate of the white race) is most at stake, and it implicitly codes the woman as property, while the men are offered a heroic role on the threshold of their own imagined death: "The victim's only salvation seems to be death itself, mercifully and lovingly delivered by someone near and dear."[23] Thus Jeff is designated as Mollie's destined mate (which of course is made possible at the end of the film when Dick is shot at the grand opening of the railroad by his former partner), and Mollie is doubly victimized.[24] Telotte notes that in 1939 Ford stages a similar scene in *Stagecoach*, but in that film the "sacrifice" is cast as the prejudice of a single morally flawed character rather than the accepted norm as it is in *Union Pacific*.[25]

The woman's role in *Union Pacific* is, in part, to boost the heroism of her male companions. Stanwyck certainly brings some aspects of the New Woman to the film as a working woman, and Mollie is one of the few literate members of the Irish community. Her careful management of her two suitors on opposite sides of the law essentially transforms the backstory of corruption into one of romance, although her real loyalty is to the railroad company embodied by her father, the engineer. Even the study guide for the film notes that the Union Pacific executives financed the railway using dubious tactics: "It was the Nadir of National Disgrace … but it is perhaps best to forget these financial transactions, for they resulted in the building of a railway against almost superhuman odds."[26] *Union Pacific* was released in Omaha in April 1939, attended by a trainload of movie stars and thousands of citizens dressed in pioneer garb to celebrate the film and the achievement of the railway company in the name of American imperialism and triumph. As Americans debated joining the war in Europe, DeMille provided a grand scene of American unity. Stanwyck flew into Omaha for the afternoon and returned quickly to L.A. to shoot *Golden Boy*.[27]

All the westerns in Stanwyck's subsequent career can certainly be considered history films, and *California* is explicitly about the establishment of the state, but there is one more title from before the war that engages allegorically with American political history. Frank Capra's *Meet John Doe* was made to capitalize on the success of *Mr. Smith Goes to Washington* (1939). Audiences were grateful to Capra for making a "serious" film about American government and its perceived abandonment of "the people."[28] Eric Smoodin's analysis of the fan mail that Capra received for *Meet John Doe* indicates that it was regarded as "important" for its representation of Christian activism, class inequality, democracy, and "unity."[29] In fact, *Meet John Doe* is a complicated and contradictory film in its attempt to negotiate between a democratic institution such as the free press, the utopian "freedom" of hobos living outside the norms of consumer culture, the fascistic power of high-rolling capitalists, the grassroots organizing of neighborhood groups that are vaguely communitarian, and, finally, the romantic possibilities for a hardworking, fast-talking woman journalist (Stanwyck) who intimidates men—especially the man she essentially "creates" like a gender-inverted Pygmalion: John Doe (Gary Cooper).

Stanwyck's character, Ann Mitchell, is a journalist who is fired in the opening scene when a corrupt businessman takes over the newspaper. She saves her job by writing a column about a fictional John Doe who is pissed off at the inequalities of American society. His threat of suicide captures the public's imagination, and she finds an unemployed baseball player (Cooper) to impersonate John Doe. Things spiral out of their control when the capitalist Norton (Edward Arnold) tries to co-opt John Doe's popularity for the creation of a "third" (neo-fascist) party. Ann is a key figure who mediates between the "big men" at the newspaper on the one hand and with the traditions of familial wisdom on the other, and the plot turns on her ability to reconcile the two discourses in herself.[30] She channels her father's words

Barbara Stanwyck in *Meet John Doe* (1941)

in John Doe's big speech about "the meek" people: "the average guys," who really count to make "the character of the country."

Stanwyck's performance of a tough working dame has echoes of Jean Arthur's comparable character in *Mr. Smith Goes to Washington*, and like Arthur's character, Saunders, she knows the ropes and runs the show from the wings, at least for the first half of the film. Once John Doe gets his wits, she recedes a bit and accepts gifts of fur and jewels from Norton without realizing what exactly is going on, and thus the film tracks her transformation and enlightenment, although it's also a story of her being used and then saving the day—and perhaps saving democracy too. In a couple of instances, her performance is somewhat excessive. Dudley Andrew excuses her hysteria as acceptable because in Capra's universe it becomes a register of "authenticity."[31] He argues that Stanwyck is "an emblem of the American personality, for her resourcefulness is checked by a basic sense of values which she is certain will win out in the end and which she feels, unreflectively, that she is pushing forward."[32] Andrew is pointing to something critical about Stanwyck's star image as it evolved in the years leading up to America's entry into the war—her performance of determination and commitment.

Stanwyck's first "hysterical" moment in *Meet John Doe* occurs in the opening scenes when she throws her shoe through a glass window in the

Barbara Stanwyck and Gary Cooper in *Meet John Doe* (1941)

press office as a gesture of disgust at the cutthroat round of firings. She has a mother and sisters to support and cannot afford to go a day without work. The shattering of glass announces the film's protest against class inequality and corporate capitalism (the paper has been taken over by Norton), a theme that the film toys with without quite naming. Her most hysterical scene occurs at the film's conclusion, in an ending that Capra rewrote five times. In fact, Capra himself admitted that he and cowriter Robert Riskin had "written themselves into a corner" with the script and had made it impossible to end.

Ann's hysterics are central to all of the endings that Capra rewrote and re-shot.[33] The problem he faced was that if John Doe does not commit suicide as he had originally threatened in Ann's fictional invention of him, how and why is he talked out of it, given the rise of Norton, who has managed to discredit Doe as a fake, and rally "the people" behind his embrace of the John Doe clubs that had sprung up around the country? Love for a good woman (and Cooper's movie star counterpart, Stanwyck) provided only part of the solution. How is the challenge to corrupt capitalism wrapped up without letting down "all the John Does," which is to say the audience, and how does one save democracy without Doe's promised messianic death? Basically Stanwyck had to wrap it all up in a final passionate speech in which she begs him to live for her sake and for "the John Doe idea" because "somebody already died for that once," with a coded reference to Christ. As Charles Wolfe puts it, "the sheer force of her performance" is what persuades John Doe, including her belabored climb up the stairs of the office building to reach him, dressed in a nightgown and a winter coat.[34] After her big pleading speech, she faints, and a family of "ordinary people" who have driven into town to support John Doe take over the mantra on behalf of everyday Americans and the film's imagined audience.

The role of the New Woman in Capra's two political dramas of "the everyman" pitted against corrupt capitalism is often overlooked, and yet both Mr. Smith (James Stewart) and John Doe are motivated, scripted, and essentially written by strong independent women professionals. Within the conceit of screwball comedy, the men have to learn to adapt to a new gendered landscape, but at the same time, in *Mr. Smith* and *John Doe* the women become figureheads for those typically left out of politics. The films clearly demonstrate how their power is neutered as soon as they are in a position within the industry and within the narrative, to exercise it. The emotional energy of the independent woman is repeatedly exploited in these history films, only to fold that independence into narratives of containment and upholding of the national status quo.

In conclusion, these four very different films have three features in common besides Stanwyck's starring roles. First of all, each of them is "inspired" by another financially successful film. Even *Union Pacific* was spurred on by *The Plainsman* (DeMille, 1936), another historical epic set in the American West. As industrial products, studio-era films tended to cycle through formulas that reproduced stories that were similar and yet differentiated just enough to look like new products. In this sense, we could say that they wear their capitalism on their sleeves, even when they flirt with its critique. Second, each of these films includes crowd scenes, embedding their character-driven stories within a look and feel of "masses" or "the people" who may be affected—or persuaded—by the characters' actions. Third, due to the articulation of the public sphere, Stanwyck's characters have "political" stakes in their emotional commitment to values and ideas. Thus, her appearances in these films potentially open them up to counter-readings invested in other potential histories embedded in deeply contradictory tales of American heroism and political action. The filmmakers tend to use Stanwyck's characters as figures whose passions are strongly articulated but are ultimately used in service of the status quo, despite the challenges and choices thrown up by the narratives and her performances in them.

VOICE, BODY, IDENTITY

We ask the acousmatic question because it is not possible to know voice, vocal
identity, and meaning as such; we can know them only in their multidimensional,
always unfolding processes and practices, indeed in their multiplicities.
This fundamental instability is why we keep asking the acousmatic question.

—Nina Sun Eidsheim, *The Race of Sound*

IN THE LATTER PART OF HER CAREER, Stanwyck's voice became husky,
rich, and very deep, even smoky, if that isn't confusing cause with effect.
Even as a young woman, her voice was lower than that of many women, and
it had a surprising strength and range. She had a melodic style of delivery,
and she was able to move quickly from intimate, velvety tones to a loud and
angry scolding voice, creating melodramatic turns of events that were aurally
as well as visually moving. It is also true that her Brooklyn accent remained
in many roles, even when it was least expected. Film scholars have had
surprisingly little to say about actors' voices. Sound studies have tended to
focus on the role and significance of voice-over and the "acousmêtre," which
poses the question of the person speaking. Michael Chion describes the
voice as an object,[1] and while his work has been a critical intervention,
helping us separate the voice from the speech or language that issues from
it, Nina Sun Eidsheim argues that voice should be apprehended as an event
and a relation rather than a static, knowable object. This seems like a more
useful approach to a consideration of Stanwyck's voice, precisely because the
acousmatic question of "who is speaking" is precisely the question of body
and identity, both of which are fluid and multiple in Stanwyck's case, as they
are perhaps for every screen actor and celebrity.

Feminist scholars have closely examined the role of women's voice-over
in studio-era Hollywood cinema (see chapters N and P),[2] but few have

attended to the gestural effects of an actor's voice, its performative aspects, or the way it can inscribe the actor's body into a film's soundtrack. In the psychoanalytic accounts of women's voice-over, "the body" tends to refer to a conceptual figure shared by spectators and on-screen women, but in a discussion of Stanwyck's voice, we are talking about a very specific body that certainly changes over time but is nevertheless the material source of the sound of her voice. Stanwyck did not have a great number of voice-off parts in her films, perhaps because of the distinctiveness and familiarity of her voice, which unsettles the already destabilizing qualities of the female voice-off. As Britta Sjogren has argued, recognition and analysis of women's voices are critical means by which heterogeneity, contradiction, and plurality are inscribed into the representation and reception of women in studio-era cinema.[3]

The grain of an actor's voice inscribes both the star within the character and the historical figure of the actor within the fiction, thus installing a plural subject within many films with a familiar star. Roland Barthes describes the "grain" of the voice as "the body in the voice as it sings, the hand as it writes, the limb as it performs."[4] While Barthes's discussion of voice is grounded in music, pointing to the role of the performance of the body as it is threatened by recording technologies for the listener, in another essay he proposes that the grain of the voice might be best heard in the cinema because "it captures the sound of speech close up … and make[s] us hear in their materiality, their sensuality, the breath, the gutturals, the fleshiness of the lips, a whole presence of human muzzle … throwing, so to speak, the anonymous body of the actor into my ear."[5] Of course Stanwyck's voice is anything but anonymous, and yet an exploration of the parameters of her vocal performance, using the tools of musicology, shows how a more fluid and multidimensional subjectivity is expressed by her singing voice, her accented voice, and the vocal range of her monologues.

In one of her earliest roles, as the evangelical celebrity Florence Fallon in *The Miracle Woman*, Stanwyck's voice rolls out through the city streets, beckoning the people with the soothing words of a faith healer. She manages to seduce and revivify a suicidal blind man with her voice alone, even though he describes it as the voice of a "coon shouter" (a "repugnant label for a white minstrel popster"[6]). Like a preacher in her radio broadcast, she delivers a sermon, calling herself a "human microphone … broadcasting from station G.O.D., God." Indeed the sound of a "coon shouter" may refer to the technologically filtered voice as much as the color of the speaker's skin. Although the film is based on the story of Aimee Semple McPherson, who preached in Los Angeles in the 1920s, Stanwyck's long vowels and missed *r*'s are distinctively New York. In 1931 Stanwyck was hardly a familiar voice, but her opportunity to come to Hollywood was largely based on her limited Broadway experience at a time when the film industry badly needed actors who could speak. Particularly through the 1930s, her New York accent had important connotations of working-class toughness, which she exaggerated in films such as *Baby Face*, *Ladies They Talk About*, and *Gambling Lady*, for characters who needed that extra edginess, and her accent may also be part of the "coon shouter" reference.

Later in *Miracle Woman*, as Florence gets close to the blind man John (David Manners), they have an intimate scene together in which he plays a wind-up musical toy and Florence sings along. As Andrew Klevan has described it, her tone is "rough-edged, improvisatory ... rudimentary."[7] She is playful, and they giggle together while singing along to the children's song "Farmer in the Dell," but then she wanders off from the tune to land finally on the word "dell" in a spoken tone, not sung, as her voice drops abruptly in pitch. The effect robs the scene of sentimentality and makes it just a bit more serious before a cut to a party scene, where other characters are carrying on in a decadent manner. About this scene, Klevan says, "Stanwyck rarely advertises a superficial fantasy of feminine appearance,"[8] a claim that is perhaps unevenly sustained throughout her career on the level of the image. It could be said to be more consistent on the level of voice, particularly in her subtle resistance or refusal to become a "singer" or even performing a proficient, accomplished singer. Speaking and singing, Stanwyck uses her voice as a gestural expression, playing with her low register, which challenges gender norms, and her accent, which complicates class and ethnicity.

Stanwyck opens the film *The Purchase Price* singing "Take Me Away," leaning into men at café tables as if she were begging them to take her away—but not in the flirtatious way that the film otherwise implies. She handles the tune expertly, even when it ranges up to an F above middle C, which is as high as she ever goes while singing, and then she interjects "take me away" in a spoken voice, turning the song into a cry for help. In *Banjo on My Knee*, she sings "Where the Lazy River Goes By," once with Joel McCrea playing harmonica and the second time with Tony Martin as a duet. Stanwyck's singing is casual and relaxed, in a low register, slightly behind the beat. She manages the song well enough, but it lacks the spark of her usual performance. Despite her rich and flexible speaking voice, her singing voice is hesitant. As a quasi-musical, *Banjo* features much stronger musical performances by Walter Brennan and Theresa Harris (see chapter T). Brennan surprised cast and crew with his mastery of a "contraption" of percussion instruments, harmonica, banjo, and piccolo.[9] Stanwyck's

Barbara Stanwyck in *This Is My Affair* (1937)

character, along with Brennan and Buddy Ebsen, perform in the Café Creole in New Orleans when they find themselves down and out in the big city. Stanwyck also performs a jig with Ebsen, and she seems much more confident in that capacity, given her years of experience dancing in chorus lines in New York.

Perhaps because she proved she could, Stanwyck was cast in another singing part the next year in *This Is My Affair*, a film that was conceived by Darryl Zanuck primarily as a means of bringing Stanwyck and Robert Taylor together on-screen. Their first film together, *His Brother's Wife* (1936), had been very successful, due mainly to fans looking for "real love" to be replicated on-screen in the form of a Hollywood couple.[10] In *This Is My Affair* Stanwyck plays a saloon queen named Lil Duryea in St. Paul circa 1901, and Taylor plays a former soldier working undercover for President McKinley to capture a gang of bank robbers. The first song is Lil's big entrance to the film, and she is alone onstage in a black sequined gown. This is her diva moment, but again her voice is without character. It is deep and sultry, but she carries the scene mainly by walking through the café tables and flirting with the audience. It's the kind of scene in which performers like Marlene Dietrich or Mae West would use the language and phrasing of the song to heighten the effect, but Stanwyck is not really invested in the singing. It is slightly out of sync, revealing the doubled status of the prerecorded song.

Later in *This Is My Affair*, Lil sings a barroom drinking song with a chorus and a barbershop quartet holding it all together as she wanders off key and finally belts out the chorus in a speaking voice. In another number, "Fountain in the Park," she goes flat, and although we can hear her voice in the last verse, her lips don't move as she dances with the men and women of the chorus, who are all dancing and singing at the same time. Stanwyck can clearly carry a tune, but she seems profoundly disinterested in doing it well, and thus her characters—Pearl in *Banjo* and Lil in *Affair*—are likewise defined as amateurs. Lil is the café star, but her real job is to get the men to the gambling tables, and she expresses more authority than sex appeal as a singer (see chapter G). Pearl and Lil are women singing in cafés frequented by lowlifes and gangsters, and in this sense Stanwyck's performances are also strong characterizations of women on the margins who are not professionals but women singing for a living. Indeed Stanwyck herself in 1936 and 1937 was singing for her own living, as she no doubt had to agree to these musical numbers to get these two parts at 20th Century Fox.

In 1942 Stanwyck sang for the last time on-screen in *Lady of Burlesque*, and this time her character's status as a working girl is made explicit. The film opens with a troupe of chorus girls onstage singing and dancing rather distractedly, going through the motions with various degrees of enthusiasm and accomplishment. After a bit of backstage action, Stanwyck as Dixie Daisy is finally revealed as the show's main star. Her song "Take It Off the E-String," again in a low register suiting her voice, is a satire on the burlesque scene itself, with lines like "If this is giving you a thrill, it's happening much against my will," and the repeated line in the chorus, "Four shows a day." She strips off some fur accessories while replying to a wisecracking suitor in the wings, and her dancing is as perfunctory as her singing (see chapter A). In fact, *Lady of Burlesque* is about the showgirls as workers, and Dixie becomes something of a labor organizer over the course of the film, in the context of a murder mystery. The film is by no means a critique of burlesque culture or the business of selling "girls, girls, girls," but as a backstage drama it does manage to put the women's working conditions in some perspective. As in several other films in the early '40s, Stanwyck shows a lot of leg and a lot of midriff in *Lady of Burlesque*, and she retained her slim figure to the end of her career, so we cannot say that she did not advertise some kind of fantasy of feminine appearance. However, her low vocal register and her casual, indifferent approach to singing are key elements of a "hard-boiled" refusal of conventional femininity, a performance strategy that she certainly shared with other stars of the 1940s, such as Lauren Bacall, Ida Lupino, and Lizabeth Scott.

her profile, her stage name, and her own cryptic suggestion that her mother may have been Jewish.[11] While the official narrative, most reliably told by Victoria Wilson, is that Stanwyck's father was from Maine and her mother from Nova Scotia, of Scotch-Irish descent, which is likely the truth, a provocative note is filed in the Margaret Herrick Library that points to a more complicated, unconfirmed story. In 1941 a woman named Miss A. Tisley wrote to Hedda Hopper, noting that neither the address on her stationery nor her name were her own. She claims that she knew Stanwyck as "Frieda Hellwig," in Harlem when she was a baby in 1902–1903 (adding about five years to Stanwyck's age). Her parents were German, and she says twice that Stanwyck and her sisters probably "concealed" their true heritage in order to "save embarrassment," which likely refers to Jewishness. The letter goes on to explain how Ruby Stevens's identity was confirmed by a casual meeting with her sister, around the time Stevens's stage career was taking off in New York. This sister may or may not have been one of the sisters with whom Ruby grew up in the Stevens family—who Tisley says adopted her after her German mother died and her father put her in an orphanage. Stanwyck's biographers have not given this easy-to-find archival document any credence, and indeed without validation it is hard to accept its violation of the well-trodden biographical legend in which the star is of Irish descent. And yet it is part of the archive, as are Stanwyck's films and all the characters she created, and in my view it may be considered one fragment of a multifaceted, fluid identity.

Stanwyck's deep voice is far bigger than her body. In music we would expect such a deep, chesty voice to issue from a larger woman, if not a Black woman, which is not to say that she "sounds Black," but that her voice unsettles expectations of body size and race as well as gender. The sound of a heavy smoker is also a sign of historical experience and a trace of a former way of life when people of many races and classes smoked heavily in North America (Stanwyck died in the end of emphysema, among other complications). This deep voice also helped Stanwyck deliver powerful, commanding, lectures in almost every film. She addresses one or more people at a critical moment and lets them know what's on her mind, usually at a pivotal point in the drama when the characters have to examine their prejudices and their moral compasses.

To take just one example, in *There's Always Tomorrow*, in which Stanwyck plays an elegant, soft-spoken (yet firm) New Yorker in Los Angeles, she turns the tables on her lover's teenage children when they visit her in her tony hotel room (see chapter A). She lectures them fairly harshly about how they have taken their father for granted, ending with "How many years do you think a *real man* would put up with that?" These big speeches have a certain rhythm as well as booming underlined words that endow them with authority. She delivers such speeches to older men and women, husbands and lovers, and to crowds, beginning with *The Miracle Woman*, when she takes her dead father's place at the pulpit and delivers a sermon to the congregation about how they drove him to his death.

Stanwyck's lecture to the kids in *There's Always Tomorrow* is characteristically melodic. Using a notation app, I found that this two-minute, seventeen-second monologue ranges from a G above middle C to a G# two octaves below middle C, for a three-octave range.[12] Often her phrases drop an octave between words, and the rhythmic phrasing is extremely variable, including punchy staccato rhythms and sliding runs. Every time I recorded Stanwyck, the app placed her voice in bass clef, whereas most other women were notated in treble clef. This is not an exact science by any means, as the app was designed to record music not speech, but it indicates that Stanwyck's speech in longer passages like this (which is interrupted only briefly by the teenagers) holds the attention because of its rhythmic and tonal musicality, as well as the actor's diction and facial expression.

Stanwyck performed in forty-nine radio dramas from 1936 to 1954, including twenty-four for *Lux Radio Theatre* and seven with *The Jack Benny Show*. Many of these dramas are based on her own movies, usually with other actors than the originals playing the male lead. She also did versions of other films, including *Dark Victory* (1938), *Wuthering Heights* (1939), *Waterloo Bridge* (1946), and *Undercurrent* (1949)—titles associated with the woman's film cycle.[13] In these dramas the melodic quality of her voice comes through strongly, along with her ability to modulate tone from one phrase to the next, with a full range of fear, delight, longing, sorrow, laughter, and scorn packed into every play.

Nevertheless, I would argue that Stanwyck's radio performances are less vocally expressive than her film performances for a couple of reasons. First of all, because the radio dramas compress a ninety-minute film into a forty-five- or fifty-minute radio play, the scripts are tight, with little room for anything more than moving the story along. They are heavy on music, which provides much of the "drama," leaving little space for Stanwyck's melodic and commanding speeches, which might come across as lecturing the audience rather than other characters. Second, her throaty, velvety tones, which predominate, sound fantastic, but the MP3 recordings in the archive do not register the depth of her full vocal timbre. The radio recordings tend to level out the sound more narrowly than the DVD and video files on which the films of the period have been saved. Her voice is always higher pitched than those of her male costars, and she has very few scenes with other women, so the distinctive depth of her voice is often lost in the archive. Moreover, the Lux broadcasts include the stars gushing about Lux cosmetics in the most sweetly feminine voices they can muster, and the dramas likewise tend to reinforce gender stereotypes much more strongly than their cinematic originals.

The inclusion of radio dramas in Stanwyck's career points to the ways that discussions of voice need to take into consideration the auditor or listener, the technology that intervenes between the voice and the ear that hears it, and the many other ways that a listener receives a voice. For example, the "grain" of the voice, which Barthes defines as a kind of "timbre" and also as an "erotic relation," is very much his own response to a particular singer's voice. Barthes also reveals the way that the listener can interfere in the sound by imposing cultural assumptions onto a voice. In championing his favored singer, Charles Panzéra, Barthes notes that he rolls his *r*'s, "but the roll had nothing peasant-like or Canadian about it."[14] I have characterized Stanwyck's voice more positively as having working-class, wisecracking-dame, and Jewish connotations. And yet Eidsheim has argued persuasively that voice, especially in the category of timbre and grain, should be considered an event and not a knowable entity.[15] The voice is a process that is enabled by a relation of singer/speaker and listener. Moreover, the voice is unable to provide reliable information about the identity of the vocalizer. The stakes for such an argument lie precisely in the kind of cultural values and assumptions that become attached to certain sounds, particularly the idea of sounding white or sounding Black. In the same way we judge being in tune according to a culturally derived system of pitches, "sounding like" any raced or ethnic (or, I would add, gendered) voice is likewise a matter of judging tunefulness.

To return to Stanwyck's singing roles in light of this, we can perhaps better gauge her vocal performances as events that will be heard differently by different auditors. At the same time, Eidsheim helps us understand the fluidity of identity that is embedded in musical performance, both spoken and sung. Stanwyck's voice has not only tremendous range but also a melodic quality that makes "singing" redundant to her star image and acting abilities. Her deep voice carries a wide range of cultural signification that she can call on for any given line in any given role, but in itself its only "meaning" is that it issued from her body as it transformed physically over eighty-three years of wear and tear.

WORKING WOMEN AND CULTURAL LABOR

> The actor as worker is a prerequisite term in formulating
> the actor's subject identity.
>
> —Danae Clark, *Negotiating Hollywood*

OVER THE COURSE OF HER LONG CAREER, Barbara Stanwyck played dozens of working women. The jobs performed by Stanwyck's characters include nurse, secretary, model, librarian, journalist, farmer, office worker, equestrian rider, governess, doctor, postmistress, student, housekeeper, dress designer, hairdresser, and several saloon keepers and showgirls. In the latter part of her career she played executives and managers, ranchers and business owners; and of course she played many wives, mothers, and daughters who were not employed but nevertheless performed demanding emotional labor. She played these working women as competent and, for the most part, proud, thereby helping to popularize, if not normalize, an image of the working woman. Stanwyck herself was one of the hardest-working women in Hollywood, but she was more of a role model than an advocate for working women.

In 1936 Stanwyck was pressured to join the Screen Actors Guild under threat of suspension, and although she was quickly elected as a "senior member" (at the age of twenty-nine), she was never an enthusiastic supporter of organized labor.[1] She may not have had a long-term affiliation with any one studio, but she was on more or less friendly terms with all of them (until she broke with Warner Bros. over *The Fountainhead* in 1943 [see chapter O]). Roy Grundman has argued that in the context of the postwar strikes, "Stanwyck's loyalty was clearly to the studio system."[2] During the shooting of *The Strange Love of Martha Ivers* in October 1945, Stanwyck became a scab, continuing to work after director Lewis Milestone walked off the Paramount set to support the Conference of Studio Unions (CSU), a union for craftspeople in the industry. Their battle with the International Alliance of Theatrical Stage Employees (IATSE), the union endorsed by the studios, erupted in violent street fights at the Warner Bros. and Paramount lots. Kirk Douglas, acting in his first Hollywood production, followed Stanwyck's lead, although he subsequently felt guilty about it.[3] *Screenland* reported that Stanwyck hosted a birthday party for her maid, Harriet Corey, on the set of *Martha Ivers*, and although the lockdown is not mentioned, Robert Taylor's presence at the party is, suggesting that the couple intended to make a statement about their anti-union principles.[4]

Stanwyck, like many movie stars, became a rich woman, aligned with capital, and thus her labor power cannot be analyzed within the class differences of classic Marxism. For Danae Clark, the specific social relations of the film industry mean that "labor power acquires use value (living labor) and becomes a commodity that is transformed into an object of exchange."[5] The question of Stanwyck's labor demands a prying apart of on-screen and off-screen working women, as difficult as that might be. Her on-screen persona included many hardworking women, from Lily in *Baby Face* to carny operator Maggie Morgan in *Roustabout*, and includes both "professionals" in the white-collar sense and "professionals" in the showgirl sense. Meanwhile, her off-screen persona was equally carefully framed as an industry pro, which helped to mask her status as an anti-union advocate.

In Danae Clark's work on actors' labor, she persuasively argues that star studies, as a subfield of film studies, has tended to reproduce the objectification and fetishization of Hollywood actors as commodities. The discourse of "personality," which was particularly prevalent during the studio era, tends to blur the differences between the off-screen and on-screen subject, effectively veiling or masking the labor relations of industrial production. Considering an actor as a worker does not necessarily reveal a "true" identity but can illuminate the agency of the actor within a discursive struggle over labor, image, and the social practices of production, publicity, and cultural value.[6]

As Grundman puts it, Stanwyck's "life-long propagation of the doctrine of self-reliance points to a more pervasive cultural phenomenon. It is connected with the atomizing aspects of social hegemony that tend to undermine most forms of political collectivism—including feminism."[7] Stanwyck's staunch right-wing politics—which became particularly public when she became one of the founding members of the Motion Picture Alliance for the Preservation of American Ideals (MPAPAI), the group that invited the HUAC investigations into Communist-affiliated workers in the industry—makes it even more difficult to align her work with "labor" in the trade union sense. Her work ethic thus needs to be framed within a discourse of cultural labor, in which her subjectivity adds value to cultural products in ways that may be alien to her own belief systems. "Cultural labor" is a twenty-first-century term that is used to refer to a materialist notion of culture in which the production of nonmaterial symbols, texts, and their circulation is made possible by the work of individual subjects.[8]

A recurring theme in Stanwyck's films is the constant wonderment about a woman working, expressed in visual fetishization of her legs or commentary on the peculiarity of her holding such a job. In several cases the basic story line is about husbands who dislike their wives working. In *The Bride Walks Out* (1936), Stanwyck plays a fashion model named Carolyn, who marries a proud young engineer, Michael Martin (Gene Raymond), who insists that "the Martin women never work" and demands that she quit her job. He makes only thirty-five dollars a week, which is not enough for Carolyn to buy nice clothes, so she goes back to work without telling him. Early in the film she protests his old-fashioned attitude, vigorously saying, "It's a new world," but somehow, by the end of the film, she is back in her housewife role, supporting her husband by managing his home office. Despite the title, her walkout is rather brief, and her return is somewhat surprising.

In interviews after her marriage to Frank Fay fell apart in 1935, Stanwyck insisted on her "independent status," as Emily Carman has detailed with reference to multiple fan magazine articles. She warned her female fans away from the dangers of falling in love and, as Carman puts it, "undermined the patriarchal and paternal structure of Hollywood. The actress had no behind-the-scenes man shaping her career, either personally or professionally."[9] The RKO production documents for *The Bride Walks Out* underline the weight of her star power and the value attached to it. She earned $42,000 for the picture, whereas Raymond made only $14,609. In fact, she made more than all the male actors in the film combined, although these figures were not made public.[10] Moreover, RKO internal reviewer sheets, on which company employees were invited to comment frankly on the finished picture, with notes for publicity campaigns, repeatedly stressed that *The Bride Walks Out* should be "sold on Stanwyck's star value," even though most reviewers were lukewarm about the film itself. One anonymous reviewer demurred, confessing to a personal opinion that Stanwyck had a "negative personality,"[11] a comment that conflates actor and character in their mutual challenge to social norms.

Carolyn spends three-quarters of *The Bride Walks Out* insisting that she wants to work, against her husband's obstinate refusals. Their marriage is

Barbara Stanwyck and Henry Fonda in *You Belong to Me* (1941)

not only loveless; it is interrupted by Robert Young's character, Hugh McKenzie, who can clearly keep Carolyn in the wardrobe she desires. She turns him down out of pride and a desire to be self-sufficient and ends up as a poor but happy housewife. How can this story possibly be reconciled with Stanwyck's "value" to the production? Or with her public statements about independence? Such endemic contradictions may be symptomatic of a "negative personality" but were otherwise "managed" or "contained" by an industrial system that cloaked women's work within the fetish of "the star."

A second iteration of the story of the man who does not want his wife to work appeared in 1941 as *You Belong to Me*, in which Stanwyck plays a doctor. Henry Fonda plays a wealthy idiot named Peter Kirk, who falls in love with Dr. Helen Hunt when she rescues him on a ski hill. He and everyone else in the film seem utterly astonished that a beautiful woman could be a doctor, despite Helen's evident know-how and professional demeanor. Once again the working woman marries the old-fashioned, backward-looking man for no obvious reason, and in this case Kirk irrationally and rather cruelly suspects her of cheating on him with her male patients. He cannot imagine how she could be alone with a man who is not aroused by her. The childishness of this film is quite astounding, and at one point Helen even closes down her practice in the hope that she and Peter can

Barbara Stanwyck in *To Please a Lady* (1950)

live on the modest salary of a tie salesman, rehashing the dream of middle-classness that underscores *The Bride Walks Out*. However, in the last five minutes of this Dalton Trumbo–authored story, Peter buys a hospital and appoints his doctor-wife to be the director. The happy ending hardly compensates for ninety minutes of misogynistic, demeaning, and objectifying so-called humor.

The question of a woman working crops up in many other films, most notably *Crime of Passion*, in which Stanwyck as Kathy Doyle gives up her career to marry a police detective but becomes profoundly disappointed with her decision and forces her ambition onto her husband, who fails to meet her expectations (see chapter C). *Crime of Passion* ends badly, with a dead body, but Stanwyck played several other journalists who fared somewhat better, with the exception of *Forbidden*, in which Stanwyck as Lulu kills her boss and unloved suitor, Holland (Ralph Bellamy). Her portrayal of journalist Elizabeth Lane in *Christmas in Connecticut* is very strong, except that, like Carolyn in *The Bride Walks Out*, she is utterly hopeless at domestic work such as cooking and child care.

While the journalist and detective roles are places where a woman character might be expected to have some agency in motivating the narrative by following clues, Stanwyck had surprisingly few such opportunities.

As reporter Regina Forbes, in *To Please a Lady*, Stanwyck dictates her columns while trying on shoes, just to be sure we see enough leg. Regina actually exposes a fraudulent capitalist through her dogged reporting, although this is a mere subplot in the larger story of her "following" Mark Brannan's (Clark Gable) career as a racing car driver. However, she also performs a radio broadcast, announcing her breaking story on the air following a series of "society" items about babies and marriages. Stanwyck's only opportunity to play a detective is in two episodes of *The Untouchables*, in 1962 and 1963.[12] Despite the ongoing skepticism about a woman detective, and her predictable assignment to "women's issues," she makes an excellent investigator and fortunately has few scenes with Robert Stack, who is the series' leading man, playing Elliott Ness. She is assigned to different threads of the cases than Stack, against whose stiff blank façade she provides an excellent affective antidote.

Stanwyck plays working women in many episodes of *The Barbara Stanwyck Show*, and the challenges facing female professionals is a singular theme of the thirty-seven-episode series (see chapter B). *The Barbara Stanwyck Show* was in many ways out of sync with its own time but nevertheless points to a historical undercurrent of female professionalism and independence that has remained virtually unrecognized in 1960s popular culture. When Friedan's *The Feminine Mystique* was published in 1963, questioning the ideals of domesticity for women's happiness, it appeared to come out of nowhere. And although the dominant images of women throughout the 1950s were maternal figures and young ingenues, Stanwyck and several other stars were extremely active in television— working women hiding in plain sight, including Gloria Swanson, Loretta Young, and Donna Reed.[13]

In "Size Ten," episode 15 of *The Barbara Stanwyck Show*,[14] set in New York's cutthroat garment district, Stanwyck plays a fashion designer with her own business. When she finds that someone has been stealing her designs, she accuses all her staff before discovering that the culprit is her fiancé. The strong character actors who play the staff point to the need for reconciliation, so as a story about the abuse of power "Size Ten" redeems Stanwyck's character as inherently virtuous and exceptionally competent. She has learned a lesson about managing staff and protecting herself against men with ulterior motives.

Some of the dramatizations of women professionals in *The Barbara Stanwyck Show* are somewhat extreme. For example, in "Out of the Shadows" (episode 11)[15] she plays a psychiatrist treating a trumpet-playing juvenile delinquent who manages to seduce her, so she needs to be "cured" by another doctor. The noirish shadows and the jazzy soundtrack give the episode a certain cinematic cachet, pitching the psychopathology of the counterculture as a menace to vulnerable women professionals. The woman doctor seems to have an unreliable memory and is effectively gaslighted by her male colleagues as well as the young man.

The gaslighting of working women is a theme of several Stanwyck films of this period. William Castle's *The Night Walker* is perhaps best known as an example of Grande Dame Guignol cinema, a cycle in the 1960s featuring older actresses. Most of these films are schlock-horror parodies of studio-era genres, especially the gothic woman's films.[16] Castle paired Stanwyck with her former husband Robert Taylor to further the exploitation factor in a film that undermines the woman's narrative authority in new and creepy ways. Irene (Stanwyck) owns and manages a hair salon and has a blind husband (played by Hayden Rorke) who secretly records her talking in her sleep to a mysterious lover. One thing leads to another until she feels like she cannot wake up from the dream, unsure of whether her so-called lover (played by Jess Barker) is real or not. Irene moves into a small apartment attached to her salon, where she thinks she is safe, although one of her employees turns out to be in league with the creepy men. Her husband dies early in a lab experiment, and Taylor as the lawyer replaces him as Irene's persecutor—although she thinks he is helping her.

Irene is the last one standing in *The Night Walker*, as Taylor's character follows her husband into the bottomless pit that opens up in the home laboratory and with him goes her dream lover. Irene may survive, but her body in this film is not her own. A dreamy montage of a woman floating through space in a gauzy haze opens the film, featuring a silhouette that is definitely not Stanwyck's. At one point Taylor's character rips apart female mannequins to toss into the pit in the lab, and inexplicably, as he makes his way through the feminized space of Irene's hair salon, he sees a monstrous-looking woman (undergoing a facial maybe). Before her blind husband's death, Irene gives him a fierce talking-to. Standing over him on the staircase, Stanwyck rages that her lover may be only a dream, "but he's more of a man than you!" Grande Dame Guignol is over-the-top truth-telling about the gothic melodrama. Significantly, Irene not only survives the infiltration of her dreams, but she also survives as a small business owner, finally returning to her hair salon to take refuge from the haunted house.

The woman detective often lurks within the paranoid woman's film, even if she is rarely recognized as such within the narratives of men trying to terrorize her (see chapter P). In *Witness to Murder*, a Hitchcock-like noir, Stanwyck plays a single woman who works as an interior decorator named

Cheryl Draper and lives alone in an apartment decorated with her own paintings. Although her professional status is not a significant plot point, the fact that the police do not believe she witnessed a murder, and the murderer himself (played by George Sanders) manipulates her into disbelieving her own eyes, is implicitly tied to her status as a single woman professional. Because the viewer sees the murder along with Cheryl, her attempts to investigate the murder herself are valid efforts to prove herself a reliable witness. She gets committed to a mental health ward and is interrogated by a psychologist about her paintings before the police finally figure out that she is telling the truth—and save her from a devious trap set by the Sanders character. The *Los Angeles Times* critic noted that "the good old gaslighting technique is resurrected here,"[17] whereas *Film India* described *Witness to Murder* as "an ugly, depressing and very demoralizing essay on crime. It should be banned forthwith."[18]

Despite these vicious stories that undermine Stanwyck's professional women characters, a few titles in her career show some respect for working women, even if they are not among the best or most well-known of her films. She plays Anne Dempster, the director of an orphanage, in *These Wilder Years*, a picture that was slammed in the press as "heavy handed, with little conviction," as a "slushy drama" and as a "deluge of soapsuds," although it was also more positively described as a "good adult drama" and "somber and sympathetic," appealing to "matrons seeking a good cry."[19] Dempster protects the rights of adopted children and helps them find good homes. James Cagney plays a man looking for his son, who has bonded with another family and is not inclined to be reunited with his real father. Steve (fifty-seven-year-old Cagney) ends up adopting a teenage mother named Suzie, played by eighteen-year-old Betty Lou Keim. The film was billed as an adult drama because of the taboo social issue of a "teenager in trouble," but the resolution of Steve taking the young woman home is beyond "adult" for contemporary viewers, as it looks a lot like pedophilia. Nevertheless, Stanwyck's role as a hardworking professional, with no romantic liaison with Cagney's character or demeaning remarks about her gender, is refreshing.

In case *These Wilder Years* looked like just too much hard work— emotional as well as managerial—Stanwyck and Cagney did some off-screen swing dancing for the press, as it was the only film they ever worked on together.[20] As Richard Dyer has argued, entertainment provides the utopian antithesis to "work," and it is not only genre that provides alternative realities to mundane principles of scarcity, exhaustion, dreariness, manipulation, and fragmentation.[21] Stars themselves appear not to work but to play, and even a dreary film such as *These Wilder Years* can muster some jazz to counterpoint

Barbara Stanwyck and Elvis Presley in *Roustabout* (1964)

the hard emotional work of the film. Another late film in Stanwyck's career in which she plays a manager is *Roustabout*, featuring Elvis Presley as the musical star who saves the small-town carnival owned by Stanwyck's character, Maggie Morgan, from bankruptcy. Stanwyck has no love interest and fends off creditors, competitors, and an alcoholic employee named Joe (Leif Erikson), who may have once been a lover but is now a volatile liability.

In *Roustabout*, Elvis pulls in crowds of teenagers to the carny and also romances Joe's daughter Kathy, thus helping producer Hal Wallis market his film for teens in turn. In this phase of his career, according to David James, "The King and his music no longer signal generational divide, delinquency … but mainstream values…. The King is disguised as an ordinary guy."[22] In Elvis's films he is always working-class, and *Roustabout* is one of the few films in Stanwyck's late career that, as a struggling owner of a small business, living in a trailer, she is also depicted as working-class. Costarring with Presley, she is finally free from being visually objectified, handing the spotlight over to the spectacle of the young male rock star.

In *These Wilder Years* and *Roustabout*, as in many episodes of *The Barbara Stanwyck Show*, Stanwyck's characters' "work" consists of sitting at desks covered with papers, counting money, and managing her employees with various degrees of bossiness. *Walk on the Wild Side*, in which she plays a brothel owner, is yet another example of this managerial type of work (although she wears expensive clothes that veil the working-girl dimension of this job), as is *The Thorn Birds*, where once again she is seen doing copious amounts of paperwork and bossing people around.

Barbara Stanwyck in *The Purchase Price* (1932)

To find examples of Stanwyck's characters actually doing physical labor, we would have to go back to the pre-Code films, where she is a younger woman, of course, and during the Depression, working-class values were more likely to be celebrated for their own merits. Thus we find her farming in two films that she made with William Wellman: *The Purchase Price* and *So Big!* Contrary to the dominant narrative about the pre-Code era, working girls in these films don't just sell their sexuality. Stanwyck played plenty of party girls, to be sure, and also women on the fringes of the sex industry, such as Barbara O'Neill in *Ten Cents a Dance*, a taxi dancer (dance-hall hostess for hire) with perpetually sore feet. In *The Purchase Price*, a film that announces from the outset that Joan Gordon is a woman for sale, she starts out as a showgirl with a manager who is probably a pimp. After being dumped by a wealthy suitor, she flees to Montreal, where she changes identities with a hotel maid who has been contracted as a mail-order bride by a farmer in the Canadian prairies. Joan follows through with the marriage to farmer Jim (George Brent) and refuses him sex for a while without any real explanation. He is a poor farmer, even though he has cultivated a valuable new wheat seed, and Joan quickly lands on her feet as a farmer's wife, midwifing a neighbor's baby, dealing with bankers and competitors, and finally sowing and harvesting the wheat.

The working title of *The Purchase Price* was "Mudlark," signaling the character's proximity to the earth. Stanwyck and Wellman got along well as outsiders to Hollywood society, preferring outdoor activities and casual clothes to glamour, cocktails, and shop talk.[23] Stanwyck was drawn to characters like Joan Gordon and Selena Peake De Jong in *So Big!* because she felt that working women who wore no makeup and performed menial labor were more "authentic" and allowed her to showcase her acting abilities.[24] In *Shopworn* she waitresses, scrubs floors, and works a cash register in an episodic tale of the trials and tribulations of a showgirl who falls for a wealthy young man whose mother disparages her as totally unsuitable for her son—a plot similar to that of *Ladies of Leisure*. The PCA file for *Shopworn* makes it pretty clear that the original script was completely unacceptable because "prostitution and its rewards are made very attractive."[25] Columbia went ahead and reworked the story line until it was acceptable and "reasonably safe," resulting in an incomprehensible narrative that nevertheless revolves around a woman working hard, including as a showgirl named Kitty Lane, to make her way in the world.

To return to the question of the actor's subjectivity posed by Danae Clark, in the context of an industry that extracts value above and beyond her labor, the endemic contradictions between Stanwyck's roles and her off-screen identity are partially resolved in her star image or brand, as a "tough" working woman who is "independent" but not too good or too haughty for heterosexual love and marriage. When she is older, the brand comes to include the merits of good business management, and her working status is never a real threat to the status quo, even while her "dangerous" roles as a thief and murderer might have been so perceived. Despite her "femme fatale" reputation, she plays a criminal in only six titles, if we discount her sadistic rancher characters and her housewives driven to murder. When Stanwyck's characters are not taking their fate into their own hands, their cultural labor often consists of righting wrongs and helping others see the errors of their ways. As early as 1932, Cecelia Ager, reviewing *Shopworn* for *Variety*, noted:

> "Barbara Stanwyck's temper will never atrophy from disuse. Since it was discovered [that] Miss Stanwyck is what's known as an 'emotional actress' her pictures have always contrived somewhere to have her make a scene. Miss Stanwyck's low combustion point in *Shopworn* may be the inside on how she became a world famous actress. Temper and dramatic temperament have always been closely allied in the public mind."[26]

Stanwyck's powerful speeches do not always get results, but they embody a certain passion and intensity that in turn became part of her brand. Stanwyck's vocal power is only one aspect of her cultural capital, and regardless of the role, the script, or the words themselves, she delivers an emotional intensity that might be best described as cultural labor. We could also point to the many injuries that she incurred on sets (see chapter R), including bad burns from an out-of-control fire while shooting *The Purchase Price* and a bad fall during *Ten Cents a Dance*.[27] She repeatedly returned to the set after each injury, masking her pain to keep the production on schedule, behavior that could be read as enabling the industry to exploit her physically.

The term "cultural labor" has developed in the twenty-first century as a means of recognizing activist labor and thinking of culture not as something outside of material politics but as "understandable through a blend of political economy, textual analysis, and ethnography."[28] As Toby Miller and Richard Maxwell put it, "There are cultural aspects to all that is labor, and there are labor aspects to all that is culture."[29] Stanwyck's cultural labor encompassed her thorough preparation for her roles, including the memorization of scripts, and her participation in publicity campaigns and glamour photography, magazine interviews, and so forth. It encompasses her injuries just as much as her emotional tirades and her ability to elicit tears. It also encompasses her portrayal of strong, independent women. The subjectivity of the star lies in the interstices between her on-screen and off-screen work, the work of her characters and the work she performed for the industry. However, as Miller and Maxwell also note, "Interpretations are made through labor too," so in the case of Stanwyck, it is our turn to produce (by highlighting) the discursive double standards of misogyny in which so much of her labor was embedded and, at the same time, to recognize her discursive modeling of gender alterity.

EXOTICA AND BITTER TEARS

No picture half so strange, so bizarre, has ever passed outward through
the astonished doors of the Columbia studio.

—Philip K. Scheuer, review of *The Bitter Tea of General Yen*

STANWYCK'S CHARACTER, MEGAN DAVIS, in *The Bitter Tea of General
Yen* (Capra, 1932[1]) is not as fiery, active, or independent-minded as some
of her other characters during the pre-Code years, and yet the film stands
out today as an ambitious foray of the American New Woman into Asia.
Critics at the time reveal a contradictory set of expectations that she was
expected to fill as a rising star. Several complained that her costar Nils
Asther, a Swedish newcomer who plays the Chinese general, "steals the
show" from her;[2] another said that she was "a poor fit for a puritan
missionary";[3] and she was also described as "too strident" for the role.[4] The
film itself was described as "distasteful,"[5] and the orientalist spectacle was
pulled from its opening in New York after only six days and was banned or
heavily censored internationally. Nevertheless, *Bitter Tea* is an important
film in Hollywood history for the risks that Capra, Stanwyck, and Columbia
Pictures took on a film about interracial romance. Its luxurious, sensual
setting and its confluence of desire and historical change make it an iconic
example of film melodrama and a film ahead of its time in terms of a
uniquely feminine cosmopolitanism.

Only one critic recognized the potential of imagining interracial love
in *Bitter Tea*: Cecilia Ager, in *Variety*, who noted not only that "Stanwyck
is exactly right for the role" but also that "the dream explains everything."[6]
Indeed, the centerpiece of the film is Megan's fantasy of General Yen barging
into her boudoir, at first attacking her in the guise of Nosferatu, a dark
creature with spiky nails, and then appearing as a masked white man saving

Nils Asther and Barbara Stanwyck in *The Bitter Tea of General Yen* (1932)

her (critics have compared the masked man to both the Lone Ranger and Zorro). Still in the dream, as Megan's head appears to swirl with special effects, the figure dissolves into Yen himself, unmasked, and he leans in for a kiss. Megan reclines on the bed, head tilted back somewhat flirtatiously to catch the softly diffused light, and then she reciprocates and their lips touch. Their full kiss is recapitulated in a flashback a little later in the film. The scene is dynamically edited with dolly shots, process shots, and dissolves that connote fear, pleasure, and a dangerous eroticism to which Megan finally submits before suddenly waking up to find that Yen has entered her room while she was sleeping, simply to talk to her. She berates him for his bad manners.

Ager says that Stanwyck was perfect for the part because she is so direct that her forthrightness makes her "ultimate conversion" credible.[7] Interracial relations were proscribed by the Production Code on the level of casting but not on the level of fiction. One of the posters for *Bitter Tea* featured an image of a Chinese man leaning over a blonde woman (who bears no real resemblance to Stanwyck or to her costume and hair in the film) as if he were ravaging her. She is leaning upside down, practically bare-chested, with her long hair hanging down: an image of inversion, violation, eroticism, and, of course, exoticism. Stanwyck's star image was linked to the New Woman,

Barbara Stanwyck in *The Bitter Tea of General Yen* (1932)

cosmopolitan man educating a naïve young woman. The reception of Capra's film indicated that, for American audiences, miscegenation was much more of a threat than a promise.

Stanwyck's performance was clearly not what audiences expected of her in 1932, and yet her stillness and restraint constitute an important and surprising depiction of listening, learning, and watching. Megan sits in a wicker chair watching the activities of Chinese women and soldiers outside her balcony at Yen's palace-cottage. She begins the film as an action hero, saving children in Chapei, but here she is an observer, absorbing the strange culture in which she finds herself. In fact, the balcony on which she is frequently found, outside a huge window, is a key architectural detail of the exotic bedroom. Designed by Stephen Goosson, the octagonal shape of the window is enormous, framed by baroque chinoiserie, and functions as a kind of threshold, beyond which is the chaotic, stylized, pictorial landscape of China. The window also functions as a kind of screen, through which the "lone ranger" jumps in the dream, to become her savior General Yen, and on which nightscapes and action scenes can be viewed, and by which Megan is drawn into the culture and its aesthetics.

Stanwyck's muteness and stillness, a performance trait that Andrew Klevan associates with *Double Indemnity* and her two films with Sirk,[25] is tied to her gaze in *Bitter Tea*. She looks and absorbs her exotic surroundings. Megan's application and removal of makeup suggests that she is unsure of her place in this world, until she finally succumbs to its pleasures in her final submission to Yen. In one of their last scenes together, he talks to her about his portrait to be designed in a Chinese style of photograms, while she says nothing for two whole minutes before blurting out, "Why do you torture me so?" She starts crying and basically continues to cry until the end of the film, even during her final application of heavy makeup and her return to Yen's room, saying only, "I will never leave you." On the set, Stanwyck had the entire cast and crew in tears, sealing the film's status as high melodrama.[26]

Tears in melodrama have been described as a sign of "too lateness," an expression of powerlessness, and the irreversibility of time. Tears are said to be a sign of wish fulfillment, specifically as a return to innocence and, psychoanalytically, to infantile reunion with the mother's body.[27] Jane Gaines, however, has suggested that tears in melodrama may have a more complex relation to historical time, such that they mark a point of conjunction between past, present, and future: "Melodrama as a modality is obsessed with the problem of the way that the 'former' present (the past) impinges on the 'present' present, which is also the 'former future' of an earlier present now past."[28] Gaines suggests further that melodrama, "in its flawed attempts to rectify past mistakes, to reverse time … might be understood as demonstrating a willingness to buck givens of historical time."[29] Gaines is not entirely clear whether the "now" of a given melodrama refers to the time of its original production and release (January 1933 was the release date of *Bitter Tea*), or the time of its setting (around 1927), or the time of viewing (e.g., 2022). For the sake of argument, let's say that the "present" of the film is 1933, such that one possible future is the one we live in now, when interracial romance is (almost) fully accepted, at least for viewers of this archival film. The tears it provokes now would thus be for its status as "too early" for the romantic dimension of the film.

Bitter Tea is also a film about history, and Yen's death marks the loss of a certain ideal of Chinese empire, which Megan sees crushed not only by civil war but also by capitalism and the colonial culture installed by British missionaries attempting to "save" the Chinese from themselves. (The Japanese invasion is not even mentioned in the film.) In this sense, the geopolitical changes implied by the drama include a fusion of Chinese and Western cultures that remains an orientalist fantasy (as inscribed in the Asian/Art Deco production design) but is nevertheless a nascent form of anti-racist cosmopolitanism.

Stone's novel may be considered a "modern" novel in its depiction of a woman who goes to China out of a deep need for adventure and travel, but it also partakes of a "Victorian" sensibility in its depiction of a missionary culture. Even if Megan learns to doubt some of its precepts, such an outlook was already outdated by 1933, at least for film critics and viewers, and may lie behind the consensus that Stanwyck, an iconic New Woman, was not suited to the part. Victorian literature did, however, launch an important notion of cosmopolitanism that Amanda Anderson has described as a mode of detachment. In her analysis of novels and essays by George Eliot and Charlotte Brontë, among other writers of the late nineteenth century, including Charles Dickens and Oscar Wilde, Anderson unravels an "aspiration to detachment" in which writers and their characters depict a self-reflexive wonderment about the world.[30] They find truths in their situatedness as a mode of observation and distance, dismantling universal truths and erecting the partialness of their own experience as a modern modality of knowledge. Anderson describes this as a mode of cosmopolitanism, which seems fitting to Stone's novel, in which Megan and Yen become "companions" and not lovers.

In the film, Megan and Yen are not actually lovers, and yet the dream sequence certainly suggests that they might be, and this dream is unambiguously assigned to Megan. It invokes her fear and her desire, scored to an Asian melody and instrumentation that segues into a Western romantic theme. The expressionist montage may have been Capra's further aspiration to making an art film, and its powerful dynamics are hard to forget. Indeed, fear and desire are promised in the film's publicity, and the dream scene lingers in the film as an explanation for Megan's repeated return to Yen, bidden and unbidden. Colonialism is likely an element within all forms of cosmopolitanism,[31] but here that colonialism is reconfigured as a woman's passive desire and an affective form of empathy.

To return to the tears, though, the title of Stanwyck and Capra's 1932 film is strongly evoked by Rainer Werner Fassbinder forty years later in *The Bitter Tears of Petra von Kant* (1972). This also is a tale of tortured, dangerous love, set in the claustrophobic, overdecorated chambers of a lost woman with an unconventional love life. Whether or not Fassbinder intended any connection to the out-of-time film from 1932 with a similar title, the "bitter tears" of 1972 seem appropriate to the Columbia production, especially as a means of capturing Stanwyck's contribution. Her uncontrollable sobbing at the end of *Bitter Tea* suggests that even while her honor has been saved by the general's suicide, the fantasy of their romance persists. If the film provokes tears ninety years later, it is for the mistiming. It is "too late" for

Yen to save his provincial empire in the face of civil war, international capitalism, and Japanese invasion, but "too early" for interracial romance. We could also bemoan the ways that the New Woman, going places where few white women had gone before, comes away with her pride shaken, even if her honor is intact.

Stanwyck made two films (including *Bitter Tea*) and two TV episodes about captivity narratives, evidence of the pervasiveness of the theme in American popular culture. While the sensuality of *Bitter Tea* is unmatched in the other works, the death of the racialized man is standard practice. We could also point to the relationship in *The Furies* (1950) between Stanwyck's character, Vance, and the Mexican rancher Jean Herrera (played by Mexican-born actor Gilbert Roland), who is killed by her father (see chapter F). The moral issue in *Trooper Hook* as well as the two episodes of *Wagon Train* that feature captivity narratives ("The Caroline Casteel Story" [1962] and "The Molly Kincaid Story" [1963]) is the question of whether the husbands will take their women back (see chapter K). Captivity tales set in the American West revolve around racial tolerance, not cosmopolitanism. The Chinese setting of *Bitter Tea*, aestheticized and stylized in ways that bring it into alignment with modern design, provides a unique space for the production of a female subject who is drawn into the attraction, including its alternate modes of spirituality and love.

YOU BELONG TO ME
ARCHIVES AND FANS

The very search for what is lost and gone (in an individual past
or a public historical past) alters it, as it goes along, so that every
search becomes an impossible one.

—Carolyn Steedman, *Dust*

THE LIST OF FILM TITLES that comprise Barbara Stanwyck's oeuvre
includes an astonishing number with pronouns and forms of possession,
You Belong to Me (1941) being just one of nine. In only two of them are
Stanwyck's characters the grammatical subject of the phrasing—*My
Reputation* and *All I Desire*—coincidentally two of her strongest woman's
films. The line "ever in my heart" is recited by Stanwyck's character
repeatedly in the 1932 film of that name, until she dies with her husband-
turned-German-spy in a tragic double suicide.[1] In *You Belong to Me*, Henry
Fonda's character, Peter Kirk, thinks he owns his wife, Helen (see chapter
W), and in *This Is My Affair*, the affair in question is Lieutenant Perry's
(Robert Taylor) government-appointed mission (see chapter V). Stanwyck
shares top billing with her male costars for both films, but her subjectivity
is erased in the titles. This structural misogyny raises critical questions of
possession and address that are traced in this chapter, first of all through the
titles and the contingencies of industrial production and then through
Stanwyck's archive and the work of her most dedicated fans.

No Man of Her Own is a title that refers to Stanwyck's character in the
third person, subtly demoting her from the first-person title of Cornell
Woolrich's original novel *I Married a Dead Man*. Likewise, *B.F.'s Daughter*
(1948) and *His Brother's Wife* are formulations that situate the female
protagonist and star in the possession of male characters and costars,
rendering her story into contests between men. The only person who plays

a banjo in *Banjo on My Knee* is Walter Brennan, the father-in-law to Stanwyck's character, Pearl, whose desire for a grandson overwhelms Pearl's story of struggle in the big city (see chapter T). These examples of mistitled films point to the circuitous processes by which films were developed from screenplays, to casting, to marketing by (mostly) men in different departments of the studios. One of the most egregious examples of mistitling is *The Great Man's Lady*, starring Barbara Stanwyck and Joel McCrea.

The file on *The Great Man's Lady* at the Margaret Herrick Library contains a list of possible titles for a film for which the working title was "Pioneer Woman." This was one of Stanwyck's personal favorite films,[2] perhaps because it was directed by one of her favorite directors, "Wild Bill" Wellman, and she executes both action scenes and heartbreak scenes with great panache while aging—with the help of talented makeup artists—from sixteen to one hundred over the course of ninety minutes. Her character, Hannah Sempler Hoyt, tells the story in flashback to an eager young female journalist who looks a lot like Stanwyck's character Ann Mitchell in *Meet John Doe*. Provisional titles for the film included:

"Unconquered"
"Can I Forget You"
"Laurels and the Lady"
"Land of Promise"
"Go West, Young Woman"
"But Go I Must"
"Builders of Empire"
"None but the Brave"
"The Return to Glory"
"The Amazing Pioneer"
"Two Shall Meet"[3]

Two of these titles may refer to Stanwyck's character (if she is the one forgetting her late husband), while three of them, along with the working title "Pioneer Woman," celebrate her spirit of adventure, perseverance, and triumph. It is indeed a tale of an "amazing pioneer" who is a woman. Another memo in the file, signed by Stan Frey, proposes "The Frontiersmen" as a possible title, proof of the detachment of marketing personnel from the production department and the persistence of the cult of masculinity in narratives of manifest destiny and its covert projects of genocide and land expropriation—for which women were apparently nothing more than bystanders.

Barbara Stanwyck and Joel McCrea in *The Great Man's Lady* (1941)

Meanwhile, the release title, *The Great Man's Lady*, which is not even mentioned in the studio memos, can only be interpreted with great irony. The so-called Great Man, Ethan Hoyt, played by Joel McCrea, was described by a *New York Times* reviewer as "not a very praiseworthy fellow. … [He] behaves like a numskull towards his wife.… In short not the sort of fellow to put on a horse in the city square."[4] Two male screenwriters had cobbled together three stories by women authors (Viña Delmar, Seena Owen, and Adele Rogers St. Johns) to create a saga of a woman repeatedly bailing out her rogue husband through wit, hard work, and sharp card-playing. After eloping with him and getting married in buckskin in a thunderstorm, bearing and losing his children, and propping up his political career, which consists of building, settling, and governing a town somewhere "out west" along the railway line, she outlives him only to see him eulogized and celebrated by the people of Hoyt City. The perceptive *New York Times* critic ends their review with "Our pioneer heroes were fascinated by something larger and more breathtaking than the gold in them thar hills."[5] Despite its rambling plot and gross mistitling, *The Great Man's Lady* did surprisingly well at the box office.

The "Lady" of the title may have been a nod to Stanwyck's string of "Lady" pictures, of which this was one of eight,[6] but it remains as one of the most blatantly misogynist of all Stanwyck's titles. Other bits of trivia deposited in the archive point to her status on set. In one memo she is said to have agreed to forfeit her salary for two days of canceled production days caused by McCrea's unnamed illness. Lloyd Corrigan, an actor playing Mr. Cadwallader, Hannah's original "betrothed" and right-hand man to her banker father—who denies Hoyt money for his planned development—is hired for an extra three days ($750) so that Stanwyck can study how to mimic him. Indeed, in her first scene in *The Great Man's Lady*, Hannah playfully mocks the fatuous, stuffy man to entertain her sisters. These memos, in their brevity, provide clues to Stanwyck's relationships and leverage with the cast and crew for this Paramount production.

Such is the trivia of the official archive of the Motion Picture Academy. Fragments of the long story of each production, cryptic notes and memos, and details of publicity campaigns, along with selected magazine articles, are filed by film title and in one "core collection" file on Stanwyck. Many of the details from these files in the archive have been incorporated into this book as a means of filling in the production contexts for her films, but it is worth noting how absent Stanwyck is from the archive. She was not a writer, and she was intensely private. She was not a collector or a hoarder either. Press releases crafted by Helen Ferguson, Stanwyck's longtime publicist, appear repeatedly in the Academy collections, often rehearsing a well-trodden narrative of her poor beginnings and stellar rise to fame, along with her (slightly inflated and never changing) vital statistics: height 5' 4", 110 pounds.[7]

Despite the prevalence of possessive forms of titling, neither Stanwyck nor her characters "belong" to anyone, even though much of the marketing and fan magazine discourse and the cosmetic and fashion sponsorships were addressed to her female fans, particularly during the 1930s and '40s, when she appeared in many "woman's films." In one of the seminal articles of feminist film theory, Mary Ann Doane points out that the term "woman's pictures," allocated by scholars perhaps more than the industry itself, stipulates that "the films are in some sense the 'possession' of women and … their terms of address are dictated by the anticipated presence of the female spectator."[8] She explores what she calls the "sexual specificity" of the female spectator as she is constructed by the textual system, examining the tropes of space, the gaze, and the "economics of subjectivity."[9] Doane's methodology certainly exposes the deep contradictions within the genre, particularly in its 1940s incarnation, in which Stanwyck was indeed one of the most "gaslit" of traumatized heroines (see chapter P), but the "historical spectator" remains an elusive category and outside the scope of her method. In Jackie Stacey's oral history of the Hollywood woman's film, in which she conducted a survey of British women recalling their affinities and attachments to stars of the studio era, Stanwyck appears in Stacey's prompt to jog the minds of her interviewees, but she is not prominent at all in their recollections.[10]

The only trace of Stanwyck's female fan base in the Academy archive lies in a set of scrapbooks compiled by Audrey Chamberlin, described as a film buff who was married to a California movie theater manager. She collected images of stars clipped from fan magazines from 1919 to 1932. Her layouts are carefully composed and arranged, organized by film, and interspersed with clippings of reviews and short plot summaries with casting credits. Chamberlin's pages on Stanwyck's films include the lost silent film *Broadway Nights* (1929) and run to *So Big!*, a film to which she devotes four pages. The account of *Broadway Nights*, in which Stanwyck is an uncredited showgirl, or chorus dancer, is the most comprehensive I have found in any source. The silent film, shot in New York with Broadway stars, is described in an uncredited review in Chamberlin's scrapbook as containing merely a kernel of a human story, the result of poor casting. Miss Lois Wilson, playing the lead, is taken to task, while the production itself is described as "lively"— perhaps due to Stanwyck's contribution in the background. The story bears some small resemblance to Stanwyck's up-and-down relationship with Frank Fay (whom she had not met before making this film): two vaudevillians whose marriage is challenged by the wife's success.

Scrapbooking was a popular pastime for women in the interwar years and a critical means for them to engage with the print technologies and "New Women" of the period. Amelie Hastie describes the scrapbooks of movie stars as "epistemological collections, invested with affect and history and designed for rediscovery either by the subject herself or by a future reader."[11] The "subject" may be a fan, or it may be the actor herself, as in Hastie's example of scrapbooks compiled by Colleen Moore. Hastie parses theoretical differences between the souvenir and the collection to declare that movie star scrapbooks partake of a bit of both, and I would also add that they enact a form of possession. Scrapbooks are means by which fans may become closer to their idols by collecting them in fragments. Likewise, for the star herself, it may be a means of owning the narrative, or at least the fantasy of such ownership, as she knows that it is always out of her control.

Beyond the Academy and the industry's own memorialization, an archive specifically dedicated to Stanwyck is located in the American Heritage Center (AHC) at the University of Wyoming, along with and beside hundreds of men and women, most of whom have some kind of connection to settler culture in the state. The library includes files on many other actors, musicians, and figures associated with the transportation and extraction industries upon which the state was founded, and its subjects tend toward a conservative, patriotic orientation, despite the center's current claim to be dedicated to the "diversity" of the West. Presumably, Stanwyck's fondness for the West and Western culture inspired her or her descendants (nieces and nephews) to deposit her materials in Laramie, Wyoming. The materials were donated by her official biographer, Ella Smith, and by two women who I shall call superfans, given their dedication to Stanwyck's legacy. Although the collection contains twenty-three boxes of scripts, they remain unannotated, so if she ever scribbled in the margins of her scripts, the notations are presumably lost.[12] The AHC collection contains copies of all of Stanwyck's films and TV episodes, although, curiously, some are recorded only on audiocassettes, along with audio recordings of her few TV appearances at award shows and talk shows, most of her awards, and other miscellanea.

One fan named Pat McMath, of Richmond, Indiana, deposited all of her correspondence from Stanwyck from 1950 to 1960 with the AHC, which has to stand in for the thousands of notes that Stanwyck was reported to have written to her fans (or had an assistant write for her) and were usually sent off with a signed photo. Stanwyck's kind but banal notes to McMath are handwritten on embossed notecards and stationery, many with Christmas greetings that changed very little from one year to the next. The collection does not include McMath's notes to Stanwyck, but McMath is thanked for her many gifts, including cheese, a book by James Street, a "white leather set," a clip or brooch, a secret music box, a Christmas book, a little heart, a scarf, and a handkerchief—with thanks for her kindness. A few notes are typed and signed by a secretary, including an ominous one dated August 14, 1950, stating simply that Stanwyck is traveling to Italy. This trip that she took with Helen Ferguson to visit Robert Taylor on the set of *Quo Vadis* (1951) precipitated the end of their marriage when Stanwyck learned the truth about the rumors that he was having an affair with "starlet" Marina Berti.[13] The correspondence does have a personal flavor when the star commiserates with Pat over her mother's illness, comments on her vacation photos, and apologizes for being unavailable when Pat and her family visited Los Angeles. The correspondence also includes index cards with lists of Stanwyck's film titles, suggesting that McMath tried to keep track of her career without the aid of reference tools that we have come to take for granted. One of the cards includes "corrections" provided by Stanwyck's secretary that curiously include titles of unmade films.[14]

It is hard to know whether Stanwyck maintained such intimate, yet perfunctory, relationships with many fans or with only a handful. Surely

McMath could not be the only one. Stanwyck had a house fire in the 1980s, so if there were other traces of fans, their missives have likely been destroyed. A typewritten note from a secretary dated May 2, 1950, reads:

> Dear Mis[s] McMath:
> Miss Stanwyck has asked me to thank you for your letter and for your interest in starting a fan club for her. It is a most generous gesture on your part and appreciated as such. However, because of the innumerable similar requests, Miss Stanwyck has decided that it would not be at all kind to show any favoritism by accepting one or two and not the others. Therefore she has accepted none. This is typical of the straightforwardness which characterizes Miss Stanwyck.

This queenly behavior goes some way to explaining the lack of further evidence of Stanwyck's fans. She would bless them with autographed photos but not indulge their deification of her or honor their tributes. She did not want to be owned.

McMath also deposited some scrapbooks, although which of the six at the AHC are hers is impossible to know.[15] One or more were deposited by Stanwyck herself, along with some by Ella Smith and Suzanne Frasuer— Stanwyck's most dedicated "superfan." While the layout style of collage varies somewhat from one book to another, the predominant theme through all of them is the Stanwyck-Taylor marriage. All six books focus on the 1940s, although one of them includes an ad for *The Bitter Tea of General Yen* in Swedish. One of the books, titled "Second Honeymoon," features many snapshots alongside the clippings, suggesting it may have been Stanwyck's own—although it could also have been assembled by an assistant. The images include publicity stills and posters from Taylor and Stanwyck films along with magazine photos of the couple at home or socializing, effectively blurring on-screen and off-screen personas, transforming their relationship into another movie. Their marriage was forged in 1939 under some pressure from MGM that Taylor be certified heterosexual,[16] but it was a real marriage nevertheless. On display in these scrapbooks is an account of living and loving in public, crowded in by traces of war, Bob's absence, Stanwyck's turn to treacherous characters, young Dion, ads for RC Cola, and changing styles of dress and hats. Scrapbook number 5 contains the only photo I have seen of Stanwyck on a motorcycle. She and Taylor belonged to an "exclusive" motorcycle club along with Howard Hawks and other Hollywood folks. "These characters could really ride," according to William Wellman Jr.,

Scrapbook pictures of Robert Taylor and Barbara Stanwyck circa 1946. Scrapbook 35, p. 12, box 148, Barbara Stanwyck Papers Collection no. 03787, American Heritage Center, University of Wyoming. Stanwyck's certificates appear to be for "Fellowship of the Western" and an Award of Recognition from the "China Relief Legion."

whose parents were also members of the club.[17]

Stanwyck's archive also includes a set of interviews compiled by Suzanne Frasuer, which were actually conducted originally by Jane Wilkie, a fan magazine writer who contributed to *Photoplay*, *Modern Screen*, and *Motion Picture Magazine* in the 1940s through to the 1960s. Portions of Wilkie's interviews with Stanwyck were published in *Confessions of an Ex–Fan Magazine Writer*, alongside comparable intimate talks with dozens of other stars. Wilkie seeks the "real" Barbara Stanwyck and does get a few gems, such as evidence of Stanwyck's tendency to cuss.[18] Loretta Young had a "swear box" installed on her set, requesting a quarter for every swear word uttered. Stanwyck was not in the least intimidated and, with a string of invectives, shoved in a dollar to pay in advance for the day. She told an interviewer once that her father was Chinese, just to "relieve the monotony" of being asked the same questions over and over again. The interview was published and the studio had a fit. Overall, one gets the impression of a very down-to-earth woman who dislikes pretention (such as dyed hair and older women dressing young) and harbors many insecurities. Wilkie's softball questions, however, leave many stones unturned. When she asks, "Do you talk too much?" Stanwyck replies, "At times … particularly when I'm in a group of people talking politics. I get very vehement about it." Wilkie has no follow-up but goes on to the next question—about material things. Stanwyck replies with an anecdote about her 1953 Chrysler, which she recently traded in for a new Thunderbird with "a dashboard like a jet." Like any sixty-year-old, she complained about the newfangled gadgets. In 1967 she said that Harriet Corey was her very dearest and closest friend, even if she had once been her maid.

Jane Wilkie along with archivist and collector Suzanne Frasuer, Pat McMath, and Audrey Chamberlin were historians no less than "authorized" biographer Ella Smith.[19] Stanwyck herself seemed to care little for keeping her own records, and without a memoir, others had to step in. Wilkie and Frasuer both talk about the heavy hand of Helen Ferguson and her blue pencil as well as her attempts to capture Stanwyck's "vernacular" in pieces she penned in Barbara's name. As historians, these superfans have created an archive of memories, taking the form of images and texts collected from their own homes and acquaintances. It is thus an intimate archive and an affective one, even if its subject, the movie star, remains elusive. The scrapbooks tend to merge the woman with her roles, substituting a fairy-tale romance for the misogynist plots that so often victimized, traumatized, and killed off the leading ladies played by Stanwyck in the 1940s. In Chamberlin's scrapbooks, the clipped reviews all use the actor's name in place of the characters she played, effectively blurring the boundaries between the woman and her roles.

As Richard Dyer explains, stars tend to foreground a trope of life-as-theater that infects all social behavior to some extent, but "what is interesting about them is not the character they have constructed but rather the business of constructing/performing/being a 'character.'"[20] The work of Stanwyck's historian-fans may entail new fictions, but as Hastie puts it, "They also point to the reality involved in such work, and the imagination necessary for the recollection of lost histories."[21] Jane Wilkie dared not ask her interviewees questions about sex, politics, or religion, because the answers may not conform to the idyllic character she wanted to construct.[22] The scrapbooking likewise ends when the marriage ends, opening up a blank space for the character of the unmarried older woman.

The star, in the end, belongs to no one, as the film titled *You Belong to Me* ultimately, if belatedly, determines for Helen Hunt, Stanwyck's doctor character (see chapter W). Neither the superfans, nor the biographers, nor scholars like myself have possession of Stanwyck's legacy or truth, even if we enter her archive as if addressed or invited, precisely because we have consumed her and absorbed her through countless viewing hours. Her archive is most accessible through her dozens of performances, most of which have been digitized in the form of electronic records of the characters she created using her body and voice. Sixteen-millimeter copies of the films are stored in the American Heritage Center, but the film archive is now as widely dispersed as her characters, her roles, her body, and her voice. These audiovisual documents have proven to be the most valuable archival documents for an understanding of her life and her contributions to American culture and feminist film history.

Stanwyck's archive is in this sense a vast imaginary space, an archive of potential, or as Carolyn Steedman puts it, a "boundless, limitless space."[23] This archive is not closed but open to absorb new memories and able to produce new histories. For Steedman, once history has become a cultural activity (like scrapbooking and movie-watching), the archive is itself transformed from an impenetrable fortress to become a place of dreams.[24] The trivia and gossip that constitutes the fabric of Stanwyck's life in the archive is of a texture that is similar to that of her performances: fragments that will never cohere into a single tapestry but are linked only by the index of her name. This archive is not closed but open to absorb new memories and able to produce new histories.

ZEPPO MARX
COMEDY AND AGENCY

> When I see Barbara Stanwyck, I know that women are strong. I don't want to
> privilege these responses over analysis, but equally I don't want, in the rush
> to analysis, to forget what it is that I am analyzing. And I must add that,
> while I accept utterly that beauty and pleasure are culturally and historically
> specific, and in no way escape ideology, nonetheless they are beauty
> and pleasure and I want to hang on to them in some form or another.
>
> —Richard Dyer, final words of *Stars*

BARBARA STANWYCK'S ABILITY to manage a freelance career largely
depended on her choice of agents who were able to negotiate excellent
contracts for her. Zeppo Marx acted as her agent from 1935 to 1937,[1] which
may have been only a short time, but it was a critical time, during which she
made twelve films, including *Annie Oakley* and *Stella Dallas*. Exploring the
parameters of her relationship with Marx in this chapter provides insight
into the ethnographic landscape of Hollywood, as well as the terms and
conditions of free agency. "Agency" is a critical term for star studies, as it
poses the question of an actor's personal contribution and control over their
career. Star studies, however, has tended to overlook the question of agency
in favor of a star's cultural significance. If Stanwyck is as strong as she looks,
in Dyer's words, can such strength also be located in her ability to negotiate
and renegotiate her place within the film and TV industry? I propose that
her place in the industry and in cultural history depends not only on her
business sense but also on her comic abilities, among other acting talents,
and what Sara Ahmed calls "willfulness."

Zeppo Marx became a talent agent in 1934, after performing in the
Marx Brothers' first five movies and before that a decade of vaudeville and
Broadway. In a public letter to Groucho in March 1934, he said he would

not be his brother's stooge any longer.[2] His name in later years became a derogatory term for the fifth wheel or weak link in a group, the one without talent and seldom seen, to the point where a satirical group was briefly formed in 2002 called the Society for the Prevention of Abuse toward Zeppo Marx (or SPAZ).[3] He was more or less pushed into joining the Marx Brothers when the eldest brother, Gummo, joined the army in 1918. Zeppo was the youngest, and entering show biz, he said, saved him from a very likely life of crime. As a teenager in Chicago, he was already carrying a gun, although his worst crime seems to have been taking advantage of young women.[4] Like his brothers, he was a lifelong womanizer. He was also a gambler, who in later life, after quitting the talent business in 1949, got mixed up in various lawsuits and shady dealings with gangsters, including the alleged beating of a gangster's girlfriend.[5]

Marx became a wealthy man during the war by virtue of another talent: mechanical engineering. He had worked as a mechanic for Ford Motor Company before his mother pulled him into show business, but his "tinkering" led to his forming a machine company that sold the airplane parts he designed to the armed forces during the war, one of which may or may not have been used to drop atomic weapons.[6] By all accounts, Zeppo was a charismatic and somewhat erratic character. In one anecdote, he punched out an "obnoxious drunk" in a Hollywood nightclub because he was wooing a potential client whom the drunk person was bothering. He boasted to the client that no other agency provided that kind of service.[7] He was an operator who was not only smart and cunning but worked the social scene strategically as well, a key asset for a talent agent in Hollywood.

In Tom Kemper's book on Hollywood talent agents, he singles out Zeppo Marx as one of the most "nuanced" and "rigorous" and points to Stanwyck's contracts at Columbia, Warner Bros., RKO, and Fox in the early to mid '30s as among the most flexible in the business.[8] Stanwyck maintained the right to work for other studios in each of her contracts, enabling her to accept roles of her choice. Compared to other stars, such as James Cagney and Bette Davis, who fought protracted lawsuits over contract disputes, Stanwyck was "exceptionally well-represented."[9] Before she signed on with Marx, she had been represented by Arthur Lyons, an agent with whom she and Frank Fay had started out in New York. In fact, many agents, including Marx, continued to represent both theater and film artists, including writers along with actors. In 1937 Stanwyck signed with Jules Stein, the founder of MCA, which became one of the most powerful agencies in the business. Around 1950 she started working with Lew Wasserman, who had become president of MCA.[10]

Barbara Stanwyck and Robert Taylor in *His Brother's Wife* (1936)

Marx may have been only one of a series of well-positioned agents who helped Stanwyck steer a course through the industry, but in the 1930s Marx and his wife, Marion, also played an important role in Stanwyck's personal life. When Stanwyck finally escaped her abusive husband, Frank Fay, she took her son to seek refuge at the Marx's home. She partnered with them in the Marwyck horse-breeding business and built a home on the Marwyck ranch near theirs. She and Marion became close friends, and she socialized with them in a way that had not been possible with her explosive and unpredictable husband. The Marxes introduced her to her second husband, Robert Taylor, and attended their small secret wedding in San Diego.

Zeppo Marx may also have helped Stanwyck develop her talents as a comedian. It was said that he was the funniest of the Marx Brothers off the stage.[11] He probably convinced her to take the role of Drue Van Allen in *Red Salute*, in which she exchanges wisecracks with Robert Young.[12] And then, in 1936, under contract with RKO, Stanwyck balked at doing another comedy, and so did the studio, until Zeppo convinced both that she could do it.[13] In the resulting film, *The Bride Walks Out*, in which Stanwyck is paired once again with Robert Young, she manages to carry the film despite the weak writing.[14] With the exception of one drunk scene, she gets very few funny lines but provides a center around which a slew of character actors provide the laughs. Her character, Carolyn Martin, cries at her courthouse wedding, protesting loudly about having been coerced into getting married. It may have been intended to be a comic scene, but Stanwyck plays it with so much convincing pathos that few would laugh today.

Nevertheless, Stanwyck was known for her wit off-screen, and with or without Zeppo's support she needs to be recognized as an excellent comedian. Most accounts of Stanwyck peg her as a noir and melodrama actor, but her talent for comedy was a critical component of her career, particularly in the 1940s. Although Victoria Wilson implies that *Red Salute* and *The Bride Walks Out* were Stanwyck's first attempts at comedy, I would argue that *Baby Face* is essentially a comedy (see chapter I), not only because audiences laughed,[15] but also because Lily Powers displays all the skills of the con artist that Stanwyck plays in her most famous comedy, *The Lady Eve*. She plays these women with razor-sharp timing and the expressive coherence of a multi-modal performance, working with scene partners responsively to smoothly create and integrate satirical and ironic situations.

Andrew Klevan has described Stanwyck's comic talent as an ability to "create a world of exquisite deviation and deflection."[16] He points to the "conning scenario" as ideal for her ability to "dramatize the obscurities of attraction and seduction."[17] He describes her "tonal palette" as a resource she draws on to shift the mood and tenor of speech and behavior within scenes: "Stanwyck does not simply tell gags or make ordinary phrases funny (like 'thank you'), she nuances them to complicate tone and address. It is how she opens up her characters while keeping them oblique."[18] This is precisely how she plays Phyllis Dietrichson in *Double Indemnity*, pitching her con game as a type of satire, achieving a slight distance from the character with the aid of the stylized blonde wig (see chapter C).

Christmas in Connecticut is not among Stanwyck's most critically acclaimed films, but this romantic comedy has become among the best known after her death because it has defaulted into the popular genre of Christmas movies that are rebroadcast routinely during the holidays. When it was released in July 1945, critics noted the refreshing look of snowdrifts and generally applauded its high entertainment values, describing the film as a "jolly little thing," a "sophisticated comedy," a farce, and as situation comedy.[19] Only the *New York Times* critic complained that Stanwyck was "not happily cast," perhaps expecting something more melodramatic from her.[20] In fact, I think she does an excellent job of "putting it over," a line spoken in the film and also a familiar Stanwyck line. The key thing that she shared with Zeppo Marx was an upbringing in vaudeville, where the main objective for comedy acts is "putting it over." Even after she had found

Barbara Stanwyck and Sydney Greenstreet in *Christmas in Connecticut* (1945)

success on screen, she accompanied Frank Fay on his continuing vaudeville run, propping him up during his slow decline into alcoholism.[21]

In addition to being a comedy and a Christmas movie, *Christmas in Connecticut* is also a home-front movie. It opens with a ship being torpedoed, stranding a soldier, Jefferson Jones (Dennis Morgan), in a life raft, dreaming of food. In the hospital he reads a cooking column by Elizabeth Lane (Stanwyck), and a nurse manages to persuade the magazine editor, Alexander Yardley (Sidney Greenstreet), to arrange for Jones to spend Christmas with Lane and her family. Stanwyck's entrance as the highly successful and popular journalist is at her typewriter, describing in voice-over the view from her farmhouse window. Cut to an inner-city view of bricks and laundry. She is the scribe of false news. She has no farm, no family, and cannot cook. That chore is left to her restaurant-owner friend, Felix (S. Z. Sakall), who also delivers her lunch in her apartment.

Sakall and Greenstreet have most of the funny lines in *Christmas in Connecticut*, while Morgan is a somewhat anodyne love interest, and Reginald Gardiner plays John Sloan, the man everyone agrees to dislike, including Elizabeth, even though she agrees to marry him. To make Yardley happy and keep her job, she plays the role of housewife in Sloan's quaint farm in Connecticut, dragging Felix along to do the cooking, but she plays the housewife badly. A baby is provided by a neighbor working at the war plant, in the habit of leaving it with Sloan's housekeeper. Stanwyck plays incompetence adroitly, handing the child off to Jones with haste and aplomb, radically recasting the war hero as an expert in diaper changing. In their first flirtation, she pretends to be married and teases him mercilessly, while he plays the straight man, conned by her performance. She flirts with soft tones, switching dramatically from her more pitched, straight, and directed tone that she uses with other characters—except for Yardley, who talks so much that she can never get a word in edgewise, which is how she ends up playing along with the fictional persona that she herself has invented. To up the ante on the comedy, Yardley decides to sample Lane's famous hospitality himself and joins the "family" for Christmas in the quaint but luxurious farmhouse.

As a commentary on journalism, the make-believe behind Lane's column pales in comparison to Yardley's equation of high morals and baby production, with circulation numbers and cash. In a mise en abyme of corporate culture, the Mennen baby oil company sponsored *Christmas in Connecticut*, running ads referencing the film, capitalizing on the playful depiction of baby care.[22] While it may appear that Lane gets the cute husband-in-uniform and gets to keep her job too, in fact she throws the job back in Yardley's face when he proposes a husband-and-wife pairing of columns, even after he has been let in on the joke and knows perfectly well that Lane is not married to Sloan. Stanwyck finally lets loose one of her big speeches, saying to Yardley, "You listen to me. I'm tired of being pushed around, dancing to somebody else's tune, tired of writing your gal-darned articles, tired of being told who to marry. Frankly, I'm tired." The last line is delivered with a flippant tone, but the flippancy is entirely unconvincing. With this speech, the comedy is dropped and the independent woman returns, even though she will give it all away in the next scene with Jones, in which they both reveal, or discover, that the other is free to marry. *Christmas* does not have as much physical comedy as *The Lady Eve* or *Ball of Fire*, although Stanwyck plays one pancake-flipping scene in which Lane is supposed to prove her cooking skills to the obnoxious Yardley, with appropriate trepidation. She plays the role of housewife as if she were an imposter.

Stanwyck was by no means alone in this kind of role, as *Christmas* partakes of a cycle of romantic comedies, some of which were labeled screwball, that were made before and during the war. Many of these films tended to upset gender conventions, repositioning men and women within domestic roles and hierarchies.[23] We can point to Lucille Ball, Ginger Rogers, Judy Holliday, Katharine Hepburn, Rosalind Russell, and Jean Arthur as accomplished comedians, but it is also true that Hollywood cinema tends to incorporate comedy into any and every type of film. Popular entertainment means keeping things just a little light, even when it is achieved only by character actors on the margins. Stanwyck's comic talents sustained her long career and enabled her to make throw-away films like *Christmas* that earned substantial returns at the time and continue to entertain audiences and fill broadcast TV schedules decades later.[24]

Women comedians and comedies about housekeeping were much more prolific during the silent era. Maggie Hennefeld has written about a cycle of films from early cinema featuring "women who spontaneously combust while doing housework."[25] Her definition of comedy is "the attempt to preserve pleasure and mystification against the rupture and historical finitude characteristic of industrial modernity."[26] In 1945 the rupture shifts to the wartime upsetting of entrenched gender roles, and a film like *Christmas in Connecticut* may be seen as a playful treatment of such unruliness, even if the heterosexual romance is reestablished as narrative goal and closure. The woman who cannot cook or change diapers is a novelty character, whose ignorance is overshadowed and excused by her public profile and journalistic prestige. Stanwyck handles this character with pride and dignity, even though her elaborate con goes south as soon as she swoons over the soldier. Her character is at the center of the show that she puts on and directs, a show about a woman who exists outside the boundaries of conventional femininity.

Hennefeld has also posed the question of how to read comedies that offer such brief respite from the normative terms of ideological closure. For some feminists, the carnivalesque experience of disruptive, subversive comedy is a critical upsetting of the power dynamics of gendered society, while for others, "laughing on cue represents yet another coercive mechanism of neoliberal capitalism's mandate to happiness," a variety of Berlant's "cruel optimism."[27] Hennefeld suggests that rather than see these opposed views as an impasse, we could consider their "necessary and possible intersections." One strategy of recognizing the feminist killjoy is to position women's comedy within a historical framework of personal, subjective experience.[28] In this respect, *Christmas in Connecticut* is a war film that shifts the battlefield from the torpedo-ridden explosive ocean to the modern home fashioned in magazines. The idealism of the stylized, systematized home, from insulating panels to menu planning, is effectively blown up in smoke. Elizabeth Lane invented a world of cuisine that is ultimately uninhabitable, and audiences in 1945 may well have appreciated a dose of reality-checked fake news about homemakers, even if they were not in a position to say so.

For Stanwyck, her ability to do comedy was part and parcel of her approach to acting. She was able to create characters within characters and to con other characters just as capably as she conned audiences into staying with her and following her lead. Most importantly, in *Christmas in Connecticut* she is able to invoke the "new New Woman" within the terms of home-front cinema, and her rejection of corporate capitalism along with her declaration of independence is one of her last such monologues in a film with a contemporary setting. The comedy genre enables a playfulness that allows for subtle forms of subversion that get mostly written out of noir and women's films, and *Christmas* is her last strictly comic performance before her alternately dangerous and terrorized characters of the late 1940s. Kathleen Rowe has argued that masquerade need not be a false appearance, as it was considered by feminist theorists past, but can also refer to a "woman's ability to affect the terms on which she is seen," which is on display repeatedly in studio-era romantic comedy. Stanwyck's tendency to play roles within roles is not only a comic technique but also a means of her taking control over her characters, manufacturing them from within the narrative.

According to Victoria Wilson, Stanwyck's resistance to comic roles in 1935 was due to an attachment to "what she called 'the Get Outs,' the point in every one of her pictures where she told someone, 'Now get out!'"[29] Stanwyck, in other words, felt that her strength was in her moral strength and authority: her ability to lecture other characters and state truths, whereas comedy is about game playing and creating convincing untruths. Her outburst at the end of *Christmas* is a great example of her ability to stop the comedy in its tracks and state the truths about her character and others. Whether that truth includes Elizabeth Lane's right to keep her job alongside her marriage we can only speculate, but Jones agrees to take her even without cooking skills. In retrospect it is evident that Stanwyck's longevity owed a great deal to her versatility, and in order to prove such versatility, she needed to move beyond being typecast as a mournful matron, and Zeppo Marx was instrumental to her making this transition.

As a worker in a complex industry, Stanwyck was in need of the men (it seems as if they were all men in the prewar era) who traversed the networks of power to buttress her stardom with projects and financial gain. Agents are mediators, moving between creative and managerial levels, but they are no less members of the industry themselves. In this sense we could describe Zeppo Marx and his successors as Stanwyck's collaborators, helping her to land great roles and also responsible for her ending up with some weak and mediocre roles—films that she regretted making. Marx was also her agent in managing the social scene, which in Hollywood was an important component of a star's career. In the 1950s Stanwyck became close to Nancy Sinatra as they both shared the pain of Ava Gardner's muscling in on their marriages, and it is entirely possible that she met Nancy through the Marxes. Zeppo Marx, a decade later, lost his second wife, Barbara Blakely, to his neighbor Frank Sinatra. Stanwyck's connection to Marx entails a lifelong link to the underside of Hollywood and its circuits of gambling, gangsters, and adultery, a world without which she may or may not have survived, even if it was a world that she ostensibly disdained, in alliance with her network of divorced women.

What can we say, though, about Stanwyck's own agency? To what extent was she the designer of her own career? To be sure, her agency has something to do with friendships, not only with Zeppo but also with figures such as Hal Wallis, who produced seven of her films, from 1932 (*Ever in My Heart*) to 1964 (*Roustabout*), and Peter Godfrey, director of *Christmas in Connecticut* and *The Two Mrs. Carrolls*. She adopted Godfrey's children when he passed away in 1970, and according to Axel Madsen, she became closer to the Sinatra children—through Nancy—than she ever was with Dion.[30] An actor, despite her popularity, her networks, and her reputation as a worker, has little control over the scripts that come her way or how they are filmed. Other than Stanwyck's disappointing adventure with 1949's *The Fountainhead* (see chapter O), which, in retrospect, may have been a blessing, she did not push any particular novel or script into production. She did advocate for more than a decade for a western TV series before she finally succeeded with *The Big Valley* (see chapter Q). Considering its long run and slew of awards, that show should be considered a triumph for the actor in terms of agency.[31]

We may also need to find another term to recognize Stanwyck's contribution to American film culture, because it needs to include the many memorable characters that she created. I am drawn to Sara Ahmed's category of the "willful subject," whose will is dispersed but is nevertheless a force to be reckoned with. Ahmed describes her philosophical treatment of the willful subject as an "archive of willfulness," in that she assembles multiple accounts of willful subjects in order to create a fluid and unfixed figure. For Ahmed, willfulness is not a disposition but a matter of "depositing," and such depositing is "unevenly distributed across the social field." She writes about the "swerve" away from normative tropes of willful individualism: "It is the depositing of willfulness in certain places that allows the willful subject to appear as a figure, as someone we recognize, in an instant. It is this figure that explains why we might hesitate in using the language of willfulness to describe the potential of the swerve. She is a powerful container."[32]

Stanwyck's archive is populated by dozens of willful women, characters manufactured in an industry designed to perpetuate neoliberal ideals of heroism and heterosexual behaviors, and yet many of these women have two faces, or they harbor other women inside them, or they keep secrets in a play of doubles. Thus in her archive we find these ideals dashed across the rocks of misogyny, racism, and class inequities, while the stories themselves are unveiled as sets of roles and games in which the woman, Stanwyck, repeatedly escapes, although not without bruises. The longer she survives as an archival star, the more willful she becomes, and the more agency she acquires in the archives of American cultural history.

NOTES

INTRODUCTION

1. Jackie Stacey, *Star Gazing: Hollywood Cinema and Female Spectatorship*.
2. Stanwyck was suspended from RKO in 1937 for not making a picture they wanted her to make. Emily Carman, *Independent Stardom*, 103; Victoria Wilson, *Life of Barbara Stanwyck*, 678. She was suspended by Fox in the same year. Warner Bros. suspended her in 1934. Wilson, *Life of Barbara Stanwyck*, 843.
3. Jane Gaines and Monica Dall'Asta, "Prologue: Constellations: Past Meets Present in Feminist Film History," 18.
4. Christine Gledhill and Julia Knight, introduction to *Doing Women's Film History*, 6.
5. Jane Gaines, *Pink-Slipped: What Happened to Women in the Silent Film Industries?* 3.
6. Jane Gaines, "Film History and the Two Presents of Feminist Film Theory," 113–19; Maggie Hennefeld, "Film History," 77–83.
7. Ella Smith, *Starring Miss Barbara Stanwyck*.
8. Axel Madsen, *Stanwyck*.
9. Al Diorio, *Barbara Stanwyck*; Jane Ellen Wayne, *The Life and Loves of Barbara Stanwyck*.
10. Dan Callahan, *Barbara Stanwyck: The Miracle Woman*.
11. Wilson, *Life of Barbara Stanwyck*, 265; Callahan, *Barbara Stanwyck*, 24.
12. Barbara Stanwyck, speech given at the American Film Institute (AFI) honorary dinner, May 29, 1987, in "Interviews and Awards" tape recordings, box 50, folder 5, Barbara Stanwyck Collection, American Heritage Center.
13. Sadiya V. Hartman, *Wayward Lives, Beautiful Experiments: Intimate Histories of Riotous Black Girls, Troublesome Women, and Queer Radicals*.
14. Andrew Klevan, *Barbara Stanwyck*.
15. Robert Ray, *The ABCs of Classic Hollywood*, xvii.
16. Walter Benjamin, *The Arcades Project*. See also Catherine Russell, *Archiveology: Walter Benjamin and Archival Film Practices*, for my interpretation of Benjamin.
17. Ray, *ABCs of Classic Hollywood*, xv.
18. James Cahill, "A YouTube Bestiary: Twenty-Six Theses on a Post-Cinema of Animal Attractions," 264.
19. David Bordwell, Janet Staiger, and Kristin Thompson, *Classical Hollywood Cinema: Film Style and Mode of Production to 1960*.
20. Johannes Fabian, "Theatre and Anthropology, Theatricality and Culture," 233–50.
21. Marlene Dietrich, *Marlene Dietrich's ABC: Wit, Wisdom, and Recipes*. Amelie Hastie describes *Dietrich's ABC* as an intersection between glamour and domesticity, expanding on the genre of women's advice manuals to include "the fields of knowledge with which women might be associated." Amelie Hastie, *Cupboards of Curiosity: Women, Recollection, and Film History*, 168.
22. Lauren Berlant, *The Female Complaint: The Unfinished Business of Sentimentality in American Culture*.

23. Christine Gledhill, ed., *Home Is Where the Heart Is: Studies in Melodrama and the Woman's Film*; Agustín Zarzosa, *Refiguring Melodrama in Film and Television: Captive Affects, Elastic Sufferings, Vicarious Objects.*

24. Christine Gledhill, prologue to *Melodrama Unbound*, xxiii.

25. Patrick McGilligan, *Cagney: The Actor as Auteur*, 266.

26. Ibid., 261. McGilligan cites Otis Ferguson, *The New Republic*, 1939.

27. Laura Mulvey, *Death 24x a Second: Stillness and the Moving Image*, 192.

28. Eve Kosofsky Sedgwick, *Touching, Feeling: Affect, Pedagogy, Performativity.*

29. See Benjamin, *Arcades Project*, Convolute N. Also see Russell, *Archiveology.*

30. The phrase "There is no document of culture which is not at the same time a document of barbarism" is from Walter Benjamin, "On the Concept of History," in *Selected Works*, 4: 392.

A. *ALL I DESIRE*

1. Jon Halliday, *Sirk on Sirk: Interviews with Jon Halliday*, 89.

2. Klevan, *Barbara Stanwyck*, 110.

3. Victoria Wilson, *Life of Barbara Stanwyck*, 76.

4. Callahan, *Barbara Stanwyck*, 179.

5. Ella Smith, *Starring Miss Barbara Stanwyck*, 241–42.

6. Halliday, *Sirk on Sirk*, 89.

7. Richard Dyer, *Pastiche*, 131.

8. Ibid., 132.

9. Ibid., 133.

10. Halliday, *Sirk on Sirk*, 89.

11. Barbara Klinger, in *Melodrama and Meaning*, has argued that Sirk's films of the 1950s were largely marketed as adult films.

12. Although I use the term "melodrama" in this book as an "umbrella genre," as defined by Christine Gledhill and Linda Williams (see chapter B), some films, such as the Sirk films and *Clash by Night*, can also be classified as domestic melodramas.

13. Lucy Fischer, "Sirk and the Figure of the Actress: All I Desire," 144.

14. Ibid., 148.

15. Michael Walker, "*All I Desire*," 37.

16. Wilson, *Life of Barbara Stanwyck*, 95.

17. Fischer, "Sirk and the Figure of the Actress," 146, quoting a Sirk interview in Michael Stern, *Douglas Sirk*.

18. Review of *All I Desire*, *Motion Picture Herald*, February 6, 1954, 35. January-March 1954.

19. "U.I's Summer Releases," *Motion Picture Daily*, June 15, 1953; "National Pre-Selling," *Motion Picture Daily*, May 14, 1953.

20. "Hollywood Report," *Modern Screen*, April 1953, 88.

21. Callahan, *Barbara Stanwyck*, 183.

22. "Manager's Round Table," *Motion Picture Herald*, January 21, 1956, 40.

23. *L.A. Examiner*, n.d., *There's Always Tomorrow* Production File, Margaret Herrick Library.

24. Sharon Marie Carnicke, "The Screen Actor's 'First Self' and 'Second Self': John Wayne and Coquelin's Acting Theory," 186–89.

25. Paul McDonald, "Story and Show: The Basic Contradiction of Star Acting," 169–83.

B. *THE BARBARA STANWYCK SHOW*

1. Steve Neale, "Melo Talk: On the Meaning and Use of the Term 'Melodrama' in the American Trade Press," 66–89.

2. Christine Gledhill and Linda Williams, introduction to *Melodrama Unbound*, 15.

3. Christine Becker, *It's the Pictures That Got Small: Hollywood Film Stars on 1950s Television*, 227. Also quoted in E. Smith, *Barbara Stanwyck*, 280. Smith's source for the quote is a column by Joe Hyams.

4. The two episodes that Stanwyck introduced but did not appear in were each a showcase for other stars: Milton Berle and Andy Devine.

5. William H. Wright Collection, f. 96, Margaret Herrick Library. Her partners were producers Louis Edelman and William Wright, and the show was more or less managed through the William Morris Agency.

6. E. Smith, *Barbara Stanwyck*, 271.

7. Becker, *It's the Pictures That Got Small*, 10.

8. Mary Desjardins, *Recycled Stars: Female Film Stardom in the Age of Television and Video*, 20.

9. Madsen, *Stanwyck*, 324.

10. The numbering of the episodes runs from 1:0 to 1:36. The first episode, "Hong Kong and Little Joe," is numbered episode 1.0 and it's not clear that it ever aired. It is currently not available on DVD or for streaming.

11. Gledhill, prologue, xii.

12. Gledhill and Williams, introduction to *Melodrama Unbound*, 1–14.

13. Gledhill, prologue, xiv. Gledhill cites Jane Gaines, "The Genius of Genre and the Ingenuity of Women," in *Gender Meets Genre in Postwar Cinemas*, ed. Christine Gledhill (Urbana: University of Illinois Press, 2012), 18.

14. E. Deidre Pribram, "Melodrama and the Aesthetics of Emotion," 243.

15. The show's sponsors were the American Gas Association and Alberto-Culver hair products. When the show was canceled, Stanwyck complained that they never even sent her any free samples. Madsen, *Stanwyck*, 324.

16. Gledhill," Speculations on the Relationship between Soap Opera and Melodrama." 105.

17. Walter Benjamin, *The Origin of German Tragic Drama*," 175.

18. Ibid., 184.

19. See, for example, Christopher Orr's analysis of *Written on the Wind*, in which he argues that the film cannot "contain" the character Marylee within its "circular structure and hence its ideological project." Orr, "Closure and Containment: Marylee Hadley in *Written on the Wind*," 380–87.

20. "Thriller" episodes include "The Choice" (8.3), "Frightened Doll" (8.1), "The Assassin" (8.2), and "The Key to the Killer" (7.8).

21. Celeste Olalquiaga, *The Artificial Kingdom: On the Kitsch Experience*, 297.

22. Ibid.

23. Becker, *It's the Pictures That Got Small*, 221–37.

24. Linda Williams, "'Tales of Sound and Fury … ' or the Elephant of Melodrama," 205.

C. CRIMES OF PASSION

1. Walter Benjamin, "The Destructive Character," 541.

2. Walter Benjamin, "Fate and Character," 1: 205. For a more nuanced and detailed account of the relations between Benjamin's notions of gambling, fate, criticism, and character, see Robyn Marasco, "It's All about the Benjamins," 1–22

3. Benjamin, "Destructive Character," 542.

4. E. Smith, *Starring Miss Barbara Stanwyck*, 170.

5. Madsen, *Stanwyck*, 216.

6. Shelly Stamp, "Film Noir's 'Gal Producers' and the Female Market."

7. Linda Berkvens, "No Crinoline-Covered Lady," 121, citing "Various articles c. 1944," BS Scrapbook vol. 2, Constance McCormick Collection, University of Southern California, including an article that is probably by Louella Parsons, *Los Angeles Examiner*, n.d.; also found in the clippings file for *Double Indemnity*, Margaret Herrick Library.

8. Berkvens, "No Crinoline-Covered Lady," 105, citing Mary Powers, "She's Murder," *The Photoplayer*, November 13, 1948.

9. For a comprehensive analysis of the anti-heterosexual aspect of the film, see Hugh S. Manon, "Some Like it Cold."

10. Bosley Crowther, "*Double Indemnity*, A Tough Melodrama with Stanwyck and MacMurray as Killers Opens at the Paramount," *New York Times*, September 4, 1944.

11. Madsen, *Stanwyck*, 218.

12. Klevan, *Barbara Stanwyck*, 104.

13. James Agee was particularly critical of the film's chilly lack of passion. See review of *Double Indemnity*, "Films," *The Nation*, October 14, 1944, 445.

14. Julie Grossman, *Rethinking the Femme Fatale in Film Noir*, 25.

15. Ibid., 49, quoting Scott Snyder, "Personality Disorder and the Film Noir Femme Fatale," 162–63.

16. Elizabeth Bronfen, "Negotiations of Tragic Desire," 107.

17. Ibid., 109.

18. Ibid., 105.

19. Review of *Crime of Passion*, *New York Times*, January 10, 1957.

20. Michael Atkinson, "Pickup on Houston Street," *Village Voice*, May 3, 2006.

21. Benjamin, *Arcades Project*, 360.

22. Benjamin, "Fate and Character," 205.

D. DION THE SON AND BARBARA THE BAD MOTHER

1. Gladys Hall, "The Poison Gas of Gossip," *Photoplay*, June 1956.

2. Dan Callahan sees Stanwyck as a gay icon, although he makes no real claims as to her sexual preferences. Callahan, *Barbara Stanwyck*. Axel Madsen is a bit more suggestive, pointing to Stanwyck's lifelong relationship with Helen Ferguson. Madsen, *Stanwyck*, 81–85.

3. Boze Hadleigh, *Hollywood Lesbians*.

4. Berlant, *Female Complaint*, 25.

5. *Ibid.*, 16–26.

6. Lauren Berlant, "Introduction," *Critical Inquiry* 24, no. 2, Intimacy: A Special Issue (Winter 1998): 281–88.

7. Linda Williams, "Something Else Besides a Mother," 2–87.

8. Berlant, *Female Complaint*, 2.

9. Ibid., 233.

10. Wilson, *Life of Barbara Stanwyck*, 30.

11. Ibid.

12. Ibid., 378–432. Many of these details are corroborated in Robert Elliot, "The Man Who Ruined Barbara Stanwyck's Chance to Keep Her Son's Love," *Photoplay*, August 1967, which includes excerpts from court transcripts.

13. Marjorie Driscoll, *Journal American*, July 19, 1938, MOMA clippings file: *Photoplay* collection.

14. Anon., "I Never Stopped Loving You, My Son," *TV Radio News*, June 1966; Jan Bayer, "Why Barbara Stanwyck Has Never—Can Never See Her Grandchild," *Screenland,* August 1967; Helen Martin, "Dear Barbara" (undated clipping in MOMA Film Library). The author wrote for this magazine from September 1967 to March 1968. Anon, "The Real Reasons Why Barbara Stanwyck Can't Talk About Her Son," *Movie Life*, August 1966; Elliot, "Man Who Ruined Stanwyck's Chance."

15. Elliot, "Man Who Ruined Stanwyck's Chance."

16. Barbara Stanwyck, "This Is What I Believe," *Screenland*, January 1945.

17. Barbara Sternig, "Barbara Stanwyck's Adopted Son: She Threw Me Away Like So Much Garbage," *National Enquirer*, January 3, 1984.

18. Bayer, "Why Barbara Stanwyck Has Never."

19. Paul V. Coates, "Barbara Stanwyck's Son Thinks It's Over," *L.A. Mirror News*, April 12, 1960, http://latimesblogs.latimes.com/thedailymirror/2010/04/paul-v-coates-confidential-file-april-12-1960.html; confirmed by Madsen, *Stanwyck*, 383, with reference to *L.A. Mirror News*, April 8, 1960.

20. Although Dan Callahan's biography cites an article from a 1959 issue of *Confidential* magazine for a story of Dion's pornography selling, I have found no evidence of such a story. Callahan, *Barbara Stanwyck*, 85. The clippings files I consulted include the Margaret Herrick Library, the MoMA Film Study Center, and the New York Public Library for the Performing Arts.

21. Jane Quigley, "Dear Barbara," *TV Picture Life* (undated clipping in MoMA Film Library).

22. Anon., "I Never Stopped Loving You."

23. Jane van Dyke, "Barbara Fights to Keep Her Three 'Sons,'" *Photo Screen*, n.d. (MoMA clippings file).

24. Joyce Gilbert, "We Found Them! The Hidden Children in Barbara Stanwyck's Past!" *TV Picture Life*, March 1967.

25. Sternig, "Barbara Stanwyck's Adopted Son."

26. Lara Gabrielle Fowler, "An Interview with Victoria Wilson, author of *A Life of Barbara Stanwyck: Steel-True (1907–1940)*," *Backlots*, October 24, 2013, https://backlots.net/2013/10/24/an-interview-with-victoria-wilson-author-of-a-life-of-barbara-stanwyck-steel-true-1907-1940/.

27. Philip Wylie, *Generation of Vipers*, 184–96.

28. Wilson, *Life of Barbara Stanwyck*, 725.

29. *Hollywood Reporter*, June 2, 1942. The review in the *L.A. Times* describes the film as "repellent and sordid." *L.A. Times*, July 30, 1942.

30. Christine Gledhill, "Rethinking Genre"; Linda Williams, "Melodrama Revised"; Agustín Zarzosa, "Melodrama and the Modes of the World."

31. Peter Brooks, *The Melodramatic Imagination*.

32. Zarzosa, "Melodrama and the Modes" 241.

33. Catherine Russell, "*The Barbara Stanwyck Show.*"

E. EDITH HEAD

1. See David Chierichetti, *Edith Head: The Life and Times of Hollywood's Celebrated Costume Designer*; Kate Fortmueller, "Gendered Labour, Gender Politics."

2. Wilson, *Life of Barbara Stanwyck*, 488.

3. Carol Dyhouse, *Glamour: Women, History, Feminism*, 167.

4. *Photoplay*, "Brief Reviews," July 1941, 19; "The Shadow Stage: Reviewing Movies of the Month, *Photoplay* May 1941, 24; Madsen, *Stanwyck*, 192.

5. Wilson, *Life of Barbara Stanwyck*, 805.

6. *Joey Bishop Show*, June 3, 1968, audio cassette in box 50, Barbara Stanwyck Papers, American Heritage Center.

7. *Omaha Morning World Herald*, April 28, 1939. This advertising campaign in Omaha coincided with the release of *Union Pacific* in 1939.

8. "Thank God I'll never be thirty again," Barbara Stanwyck Interviews, Number 4, collected and compiled by Suzanne Frasuer, folder 1, box 50, Barbara Stanwyck Papers, American Heritage Center. This theme of enjoying her age is repeated in many of the interviews, such as Lloyd Shearer, "Barbara Stanwyck: She's Indestructible," *Parade*, August 7, 1942.

9. Eileen Boris, "Desirable Dress: Rosies, Sky Girls, and the Politics of Appearance," 126.

10. Robert B. Westbrook, "'I Want a Girl, Just Like the Girl That Married Harry James,'" 602.

11. Adrienne Berney, "Streamlining Breasts," 339.

12. Lisa Colpaert has done a breakdown of the shooting scene at the end of *Double Indemnity*, pointing out how the white pantsuit/peignoir that Stanwyck wears works with the overall lighting design. "Costume on Film," 65–84.

13. Edwin Schallert, "Call of Wolf Reversed by La Stanwyck," *Los Angeles Times*, July 23, 1944.

14. Ibid.

15. Fortmueller, "Gendered Labour," 485.

16. Robert Gustafson, "The Power of the Screen," 8–15.

17. J. E. Smyth, *Nobody's Girl Friday*, 190. Smyth offers no sources to back up this claim.

18. This comment is based on a photo published in a Los Angeles newspaper: "Film, Custom Designers to Display Styles Feb. 13," *Los Angeles Examiner*, February 3, 1941; Smyth, *Nobody's Girl Friday*, 191.

19. Margaret Lee Runbeck, "Nobody Knows Barbara as I Do," *Good Housekeeping*, July 1954.

20. Quoted by Carman, "Independent Stardom," 601. From the Gladys Hall file at the Margaret Herrick Library.

21. Richard Dyer, *Stars*, 66.

22. Stanley Cavell, *Pursuits of Happiness*, 53.

23. Harrison Carroll, "Behind the Scenes in Hollywood," *New York and Brooklyn Daily*, March 26, 1964.

F. *FORTY GUNS* AND *THE FURIES*

1. Howard Hampton, "Extreme Prejudice," 51.

2. See articles by Luc Moullet on Sam Fuller on André Bazin on Anthony Mann in Jim Hillier, ed., *Cahiers du cinema: The 1950s: Neo-Realism, Hollywood, New Wave*, 145–57; 165–68.

3. Emily Carman, "'Women Rule Hollywood,'" 21.

4. Ibid., 16.

5. Ibid., 21.

6. Madsen, *Stanwyck*, 349.

7. Jacques Rancière, *Film Fables*, 11.

8. Tom Conley, review of *Film Fables*, *Screening the Past*, November 2006. http://www.screeningthepast.com/2014/12/film-fables/.

9. Charles Bitsch and Claude Chabrol, "Interview with Anthony Mann," *Cahiers du Cinema*, March 1957, rpt. in booklet accompanying Criterion DVD of *The Furies*, 2008, 22.

10. Jacques Rancière, *Film Fables*, 77.

11. Ibid., 73.

12. Ibid., 78.

13. Ibid.

14. Hampton, "Extreme Prejudice," 52.

15. A memo from the Breen office summarizes the PCA's dispute with Hal Wallis over an "open mouthed kiss" that they wanted removed from the film. It is not clear to which kiss they are referring, as in both the film and the memo there are several such kisses, all of which are either cut short or darkened in a compromise solution to the dispute. The subtext of the complaint is that (1) Vance kisses a Hispanic man, and (2) she kisses two different men in alternating scenes. January 25, 1950. MPPDA file on *The Furies*, Margaret Herrick Library.

16. Sam Fuller, "Stuffed with Phalluses," excerpted from Sam Fuller, *A Third Face: My Tale of Writing, Fighting, and Filmmaking*, rpt. in booklet to accompany *Forty Guns* DVD, Criterion Collection 2018.

17. See Joe McElhaney, *The Death of Classical Cinema* for a full account of the transitional aesthetics of late studio-era cinema.

18. Lisa Dombrowski, *Samuel Fuller: If You Die I'll Kill You!*

19. Fuller has said the film was inspired by the theme of juvenile delinquency. Fuller, "Stuffed with Phalluses," 19.

20. The ironic distinction between the hero and the star is Dombrowski's. She writes, "Fox insisted that the star of the picture survive to ride off with the hero into the sunset." Dombrowski, *Samuel Fuller*, 111.

21. Henry Gates Jr., "Should African Americans Collect 'Sambo Art'?" *The African Americans: Many Rivers to Cross* (blog), https://www.pbs.org/wnet/african-americans-many-rivers-to-cross/history/should-blacks-collect-racist-memorabilia/.

22. Dombrowski, *Samuel Fuller*, 111.

23. Ibid.

24. David M. Halpern, *How to Be Gay*, 194.

25. Ibid., 195.

G. GAMBLING LADIES

1. Aaron M. Duncan, *Gambling with the Myth of the American Dream*, 41. The epigraph quotation attributed to Walter Matthau has been made by several writers on poker and gambling, although no original source is cited. See Ole Bjerg, *Poker: The Parody of Capitalism*, 2; and Al Alvarez, *The Biggest Game in Town*.

2. Duncan, *Gambling with the Myth*, 41.

3. Miriam B. Hansen, *Cinema and Experience*, 186. Benjamin's remarks on gambling are found principally in *The Arcades Project* (1999) and "Notes on a Theory of Gambling," 297–98.

4. Hansen, *Cinema and Experience*, 183. An earlier version of Hansen's essay was titled "Room-for-Play: Benjamin's Gamble with Cinema."

5. See *The Motion Picture Production Code*, compiled by David P. Hayes, 2009. https://productioncode.dhwritings.com/multipleframes_productioncode.php/.

6. Jackson Lears, *Something for Nothing*, quoted by Ole Bjerg, *Poker: The Parody of Capitalism*, 2.

7. The writing credits for *The Great Man's Lady* include original stories by Adela Rogers St. Johns and Seena Owen, plus a short story by Viña Delmar.

8. Duncan, *Gambling with the Myth*, 75.

9. Ibid., 87.

10. David Baker and Danielle Zuvela, "Mann and Woman: The Function of the Feminine in the 'Noir Westerns' of Anthony Mann." http://www.transformationsjournal.org/issue-24/.

11. Chris Enss, *The Lady Was a Gambler: True Stories of Notorious Women of the Old West*.

12. *Gambling Lady* was released in March 1934. The Hays Code was established in 1930 but not enforced until July 1, 1934, with the institutionalization of the Production Code Administration (see chapter I). Therefore, this is one of the last of the pre-Code movies of the period.

13. Anon., *Hollywood Reporter*, June 1934.

14. Ben Singer, *Melodrama and Modernity*, 52, 136.

15. Chris Cagle, *Sociology on Film: Postwar Hollywood's Prestige Commodity*.

16. File on *The Lady Gambles* at Margaret Herrick Library.

17. Bosley Crowther, *New York Times*, May 21, 1949.

18. Mary Ann Doane, *The Desire to Desire: The Woman's Film of the 1940s*.

19. "Momism" was a term coined by Philip Wylie in his book *Generation of Vipers*. Popular Freudianism further pushed the discourse of mother hating and mother blaming, and Hollywood cemented the narrative in films such as *The Strange Love of Martha Ivers*, *Now Voyager*, and *Strangers on a Train*.

20. Benjamin, *Arcades Project*, 494.

21. Bjerg, *Poker: The Parody of Capitalism*.

H. WILLIAM HOLDEN

1. See, for example, Madsen, *Stanwyck*, 168. He claims that Stanwyck and Holden had an affair "sometime in the next six years" after the shooting of *Golden Boy*. His source is a conversation with Billy Wilder.

2. Robert Wagner, *Pieces of My Heart: A Life*, 64.

3. John Caldwell, "Socio-Professional Rituals and the Borderlands of Production Culture," 166.

4. Sherry Ortner, *Not Hollywood: Independent Film at the Twilight of the American Dream*, 25.

5. John Caldwell, *Production Culture: Industrial Reflexivity and Critical Practice in Film and Television*, 2.

6. Madsen, *Stanwyck*, 256, quoting from *Starmaker* by Hall Wallis and Charkes Higham, p. 116.

7. David Luhrssen, *Mamoulian: Life on Stage and Screen*, 98.

8. "Review," *National Board of Review Magazine*, October 1939, 11.

9. Wilson, *Life of Barbara Stanwyck*, 768.

10. Frank S. Nugent, "Golden Holden," *Colliers Weekly*, June 2, 1951, 64. Holden had done a screen test at Columbia, which was sent over to Paramount.

11. Madsen, *Stanwyck*, 171.

12. Wayne, *Life and Loves of Barbara Stanwyck*, 184.

13. Wilson, *Life of Barbara Stanwyck*, 76–77.

14. Ibid., 76.

15. Nugent, "Golden Holden," 64.

16. Wilson, *Life of Barbara Stanwyck*, 778.

17. Cynthia Baron, *Modern Acting: The Lost Chapter of American Film and Theatre*, 83.

18. Ledger Grindon, "Structure of Meaning in the Boxing Film Genre."

19. Michelangelo Capua, *William Holden: A Biography*, 21.

20. *New Yorker*, May 15, 1954.

21. Madsen, *Stanwyck*, 304.

22. Stephen Cohan's essay on Holden in *Picnic* (1955) is one of the best accounts of the actor in the 1950s and his negotiation of the spectacle of masculinity. Cohan, "Masquerading as the American Male in the Fifties: *Picnic*, William Holden, and the Spectacle of Masculinity in Hollywood Film."

23. Barbara Stanwyck, "As I See Me," unpublished interview by Jane Wilkie, transcribed by Suzanne Frasuer, 1996, box 50, Barbara Stanwyck Collection, American Heritage Library.

24. Wayne, *Life and Loves*, 7, 118; Madsen, *Stanwyck*, 186, 267.

25. Diorio, *Barbara Stanwyck*, 103.

26. MoMA clippings files, Barbara Stanwyck, index card #101.

27. Bill Tusher, "Barbara Stanwyck Talks about 'That' Touchy Subject," *Movie Mirror*, April 1967, 66. The man she cit es as an exemplary he-man is Brian Keith, with whom she starred in *The Violent Men* (1955).

28. Wilson, *Life of Barbara Stanwyck*, 483–95.

I. ILLICIT

1. "Pre-Code Hollywood" refers to the period from March 1930 to July 1934 when the industry enforced its own production code with a strict set of rules about depictions of sex, violence, and vice that were unevenly applied. In 1934 the government stepped in with a more rigorous application of the code overseen by Joseph Breen, which was enforced until the mid-1950s. See Thomas Doherty, *Pre-Code Hollywood: Sex, Immorality, and Insurrection in American Cinema, 1930–1934*, for a comprehensive discussion of the "parallel universe" of these films.

2. Veronica Pravadelli, *Classic Hollywood: Lifestyles and Film Styles of American Cinema, 1930–1960*, 26.

3. See Carman, *Independent Stardom*, 160–61, for a summary of Stanwyck's contracts through to 1948.

4. Ibid., 98, quoting Adele Fletcher, "The Girl Who Has Hollywood's Number," *Modern Screen*, June 1932, 34.

5. Carman, "Independent Stardom," 598.

6. Sid, "Illicit," *Variety*, January 21, 1931, 17, 30.

7. Memo in *Illicit* PCA file, August 6, 1930, Margaret Herrick Library.

8. Robert Kurrle, review of *Illicit*, *International Photographer*, April 1931.

9. Ibid.

10. Memo from Wingate to Hays, December 30, 1932, *Baby Face* PCA file, Margaret Herrick Library.

11. Memo from Wingate to Hays, February 28, 1933, *Baby Face* PCA file, Margaret Herrick Library.

12. Richard Maltby, "Baby Face, or How Joe Breen Made Barbara Stanwyck Atone for Causing the Wall Street Crash."

13. Anon., "*Baby Face* (Warner Bros.) Sophisticated," *Motion Picture Herald*, April 1, 1933, 24.

14. TCM Classics released both versions of *Baby Face* on DVD, with the "Original Theatrical Version" as the censored version and the "Prerelease Version" as the uncut version, which was found at the Library of Congress in 2004.

15. Memo from Wingate to Hays, March 2, 1933, *Baby Face* PCA file, Margaret Herrick Library.

16. Harrison's reports, July 1 1933; Uncredited review in *Baby Face* PCA file, Margaret Herrick Library.

17. Bige, "Baby Face," *Variety*, June 27, 1933, 15.

18. Wilson, *Life of Barbara Stanwyck*, 338.

19. One of the first major stories was by Jim Tully, "The Waif Who Threatens Garbo," *New Movie Magazine*, 1932.

20. Banks and corporations were widely satirized as the cause of the Depression, and a whole cycle of films starring Warren William made hay of the authoritarian manners of bank directors (e.g., *Employee's Entrance* [1932], *Skyscraper Souls* [1932], and *Beauty and the Boss* [1932]). In *Baby Face*, all the company directors are rendered blathering idiots in the presence of Stanwyck's Lily.

21. Maltby, *Baby Face*, 183.

J. JUNGLE FILMS / WHITE WOMEN

1. Jon Cowans, *Empire Films and the Crisis of Colonialism, 1946–1959*, 55.

2. Richard Dyer, *White*, 184.

3. Rhona Berenstein, "White Heroines and Hearts of Darkness: Race, Gender and Disguise in 1930s Jungle Films," 319.

4. Dyer, *White*, 140.

5. Megan Feeney, *Hollywood in Havana: US Cinema and Revolutionary Nationalism in Cuba before 1959*, 46.

6. Ibid., 75

7. Feeney, *Hollywood in Havana*, 96.

8. T. G., "*Message to Garcia*," *Monthly Film Bulletin* 3, no. 25 (1936): 104.

9. Madsen, *Stanwyck*, 119.

10. Noted in a *Hollywood Reporter* publicity piece for *A Message to Garcia*, July 9, 1936.

11. Feeney, *Hollywood in Havana*, 96.

12. *Escape to Burma* was probably shot at the RKO studios as well as the Animal Jungle, and *A Message to Garcia* was shot at 20th Century Fox, but the ponds in the jungle look remarkably similar.

13. "At the Palace," *New York Times*, May 21, 1955.

14. Stanwyck claimed that she never dyed her hair after *Stella Dallas*, so this may well be a wig styled in her usual short 1950s style.

15. In 1955 Burma had achieved independence from Britain and had democratically elected leadership, as well as Communist insurgencies, neither of which are referred to in the film, which is set in a timeless colonial period.

16. Jennifer Peterson, "Ecodiegesis: The Scenography of Nature on Screen."

17. I haven't actually seen the stage hands yet myself, but the *New York Times* critic noted them on May 21, 1955.

18. I call them "movie-Indians" because they are racist caricatures of Indigenous peoples probably played by Hispanic actors, and have little relationship to any actual Native Americans.

19. *Trooper Hook* production file, Special Collections, Margaret Herrick Library.

20. The transcript is dated Friday, October 21, 1969, and Wednesday, October 19, 1966. *Trooper Hook* file, Special Collections, Margaret Herrick Library. There was a Thomas Wood Publicity Department associated with Paramount Studios in the 1940s, but it is not clear if it is the same one connected to this diary, as *Trooper Hook* was a United Artists release.

21. Anon., *Trooper Hook* production file, Special Collections, Margaret Herrick Library.

22. Laura Mulvey, "A Clumsy Sublime," 3.

23. D. A. Miller, *Hidden Hitchcock*.

24. The misperception and persecution of an innocent man who refuses to speak for himself is a possible allegory for McCarthyism, although none of the writers nor director Dwan were known to sympathize on either side of the HUAC hearings.

K. KATE CRAWLEY

1. David Ehrenstein, *Open Secret: Gay Hollywood, 1928–2000.*

2. Callahan, *Barbara Stanwyck*; Madsen, *Stanwyck*, 81–85.

3. Hadleigh, *Hollywood Lesbians.*

4. Patricia White, *Uninvited: Classical Hollywood Cinema and Lesbian Representability*, 2. White cites Jackie Stacey's book on female spectatorship for evidence of spectators' attachment to Hollywood stars, as a complex relationship of desire ("to be like" and "to love").

5. "The Kate Crawley Story" aired on January 27, 1964. Season 7, episode 19 of *Wagon Train.*

6. "The Molly Kincaid Story" aired on September 16, 1963. Season 7, episode 1 of *Wagon Train.*

7. "The Freighter" aired in January 17, 1958. Season 2, episode 15 of *Zane Grey Theatre.*

8. Catherine Mary McComb, "Undressing an American Icon: Addressing the Representation of Calamity Jane through a Critical Study of Her Costume."

9. During the shooting of *Great Man's Lady*, Stanwyck was photographed wearing buckskin pants and fringed jacket as she danced with William Randolph Hearst, looking more like a scout than the cavalry-inspired outfit of Calamity Jane. See Sandra Schackel, "Barbara Stanwyck: Uncommon Heroine," 45.

10. Eric Savoy, "'That Ain't *All* She Ain't': Doris Day and Queer Performativity."

11. Ibid., 159, citing Diana Fuss, introduction to *Inside/Out: Lesbian Theories, Gay Theories*, 3.

12. Savoy, "'That Ain't *All* She Ain't,'" 181, citing Judith Butler, "Imitation and Gender Subordination," *Inside/Out: Lesbian Theories, Gay Theories* (New York: Routledge, 1991).

13. Ibid., 167.

14. Ibid.

15. Stanwyck described her character in *Stella Dallas* as "noisy and vulgar," unlike her usual, more refined parts, which Victoria Wilson interprets as Stanwyck's attraction to character parts.

16. I call them "TV Indians" because, like those on the big screen, they are racist caricatures of Indigenous peoples probably played by Hispanic actors and have little relationship to any actual Native Americans.

17. The "Maud Frazer Story" aired on October 11, 1961. Season 1, episode 3 of *Wagon Train.*

18. The "Caroline Casteel Story" aired on September 26, 1963. Season 6, episode 2 of *Wagon Train.*

19. Virgil W. Vogel directed the two Kate Crawley episodes, and he later directed forty-eight *Big Valley* episodes, making him the director with whom Stanwyck worked most often in her career.

20. Savoy, "'That Ain't *All* She Ain't,'" 178.

21. Madsen, *Stanwyck*, 327.

22. James D. Ivers, *Motion Picture Herald*, February 7, 1962, clippings file, Margaret Herrick Library.

23. Judith Roof, *All about Thelma and Eve: Sidekicks and Third Wheels*, 19.

24. Patricia White has developed this methodology most substantially in the context of lesbian viewers in *Uninvited*, including an extensive analysis of the relationship between Stella and her daughter in *Stella Dallas*.

25. Madsen, *Stanwyck*, 373. Unfortunately, Madsen provides no source for this quote, and it's hard to know who Dana Henninger is.

26. Wilson, *Life of Barbara Stanwyck*, 74.

L. *THE LADY EVE*

1. Robin Wood deemed *The Lady Eve* to be a "perfect" film, which subsequent critics have taken up like a mantra. Wood, "Screwball and the Masquerade: *The Lady Eve* and *Two-Faced Woman*," 19.

2. A good clue to the film's misogyny is in the opening scene in the Amazon where women are "free" for the taking and the leaving.

3. Cavell, *Pursuits of Happiness*, 7, 17.

4. The privileging of the director's signature is evident in all the supporting materials on both of the Criterion DVD releases of 2001 and 2020.

5. Wood, "Screwball and the Masquerade," 17.

6. Callahan, *Barbara Stanwyck*, 109.

7. See Jeanne Basinger, *A Woman's View: How Hollywood Spoke to Women, 1930–1960*, for an account of the double women roles in the women's film. See Dana Polan, *Power and Paranoia: History, Narrative, and the American Cinema, 1940–1950*, for an account of the unreliable filmic narrative in the 1940s and its relation to contradictions in American culture more generally.

8. Wood, "Screwball and the Masquerade," 19.

9. See, for example, Gladys Hall, "Barbara Stanwyck's True Life Story: Intimate Glimpses of a Glamor Girl who Conquered the Insurmountable in her Rise to Fame," *Modern Screen*, November 1939.

10. Cavell, *Pursuits of Happiness*, 53.

11. Ibid., 66.

12. Ibid., 64.

13. Two essays in particular in which Charles is assumed to be the hero are Irving Singer's chapter on *The Lady Eve* in *Cinematic Mythmaking: Philosophy in Film* and Maria DiBattista, "The Lady Eve and the Female Con," in *Fast Talking Dames*.

14. Bosley Crowther, "'The Lady Eve,' a Sparkling Romantic Comedy, with Barbara Stanwyck and Henry Fonda, at the Paramount—Other Films at Rialto, Miami and New York," *New York Times*, February 26, 1941.

15. Sedgwick, *Touching, Feeling*, 7.

16. The literature around this theory is vast, but the key source is J. L. Austin, *How to Do Things with Words*.

17. Sedgwick, *Touching, Feeling*, 150.

18. Sue Thornham, *What If I Had Been the Hero: Investigating Women's Cinema*, 17, quoting Judith Butler, *Antigone's Claim*.

19. Thornham, *What If I Had Been the Hero*, 17.

20. Butler, *Antigone's Claim*, 5.

21. Ibid., 82.

22. Sedgwick, *Touching, Feeling*, 68. The wedding scene in *The Lady Eve* includes no utterance of "I do," the only expression being uncomfortable eye movements on the parts of Fonda, Stanwyck, and Blore, playing the protagonists of the ritual.

23. Sedgwick, *Touching, Feeling*, 149.

24. Ibid., 150–51.

25. Preston Sturges File, box 83, file number 8, n.d., Special Collections, University of California at Los Angeles.

M. FRED MACMURRAY

1. Because Benjamin describes the work of actors as props in the hands of editors, his theory has been largely dismissed by theorists of film acting. See, for example, Cynthia Baron and Sharon Marie Carnicke, *Reframing Screen Performance*, 2.

2. Benjamin, "Work of Art," 112.

3. Ibid., 113.

4. Ibid., 127n22.

5. Edgar Morin, *New Trends in the Study of Mass Communications*, 179; as quoted by Dyer in *Stars*, 52.

6. Steven Harvey, "The Strange Fate of Barbara Stanwyck," *Film Comment* 17, no. 2 (1981): 36.

7. Klevan, *Barbara Stanwyck*, 10.

8. Ibid., 28.

9. Kevin Esch, "The Bond That Unbinds by Binding: Acting Mythology and the Film Community," 122.

10. Ibid., 129.

11. Benjamin, "Work of Art," 111.

12. Manohla Dargis, "What the Movies Taught Me about Being a Woman," *New York Times*, November 30, 2018, https://www.nytimes.com/interactive/2018/11/30/movies/women-in-movies.htm/.

13. Ibid.

14. Benjamin, "Work of Art," 107.

15. Charles Tranberg, *Fred MacMurray: A Biography*, Kindle loc. 4523.

16. Irma Savin, Neward, NJ, "Speak for Yourself: $1000 Prize: Hide the Rings Please," *Photoplay*, April 1945, 106.

17. Tranberg, *Fred MacMurray*, Kindle loc. 1250.

18. Ibid., loc. 1190.

19. Ibid., loc. 3170.

20. Benjamin, "Work of Art," 113.

21. Richard Chamberlain trained in England during the 1970s in the middle of his TV and film career.

22. Anon., "Clash by Night: Sex and Violence in a Scorching Film," *Look*, June 3, 1962, 106–108.

23. Review of "Clash by Night," *Photoplay*, August 1952, 24.

24. In addition to the photo spread in *Look*, *Collier's* also featured shots of the Ryan/Stanwyck kiss. Frank S. Nugent, "Stanwyck," *Collier's*, July 12, 1952.

25. Jodi Brooks, "Crisis and the Everyday: Some Thought on Gesture and Crisis in Cassavetes and Benjamin," 83.

26. Ibid., 98.

27. Notes from the *Jeopardy* file at the Margaret Herrick Library, including *L.A. Times*, 221–53, and *Boston Evening Examiner*, n.d.

28. Noa Steimatsky makes this point in *The Face on Film*, 223.

29. Dargis, "What the Movies Taught Me."

N. *NO MAN OF HER OWN*

1. Basinger, *Woman's View*, Kindle loc. 1678.

2. Hollywood CN, clippings file on *No Man of Her Own*, Margaret Herrick Library.

3. Basinger, *Woman's View*, Kindle loc. 8252.

4. Britta Sjogren, *Into the Vortex: Female Voice and Paradox in Film*, 6.

5. Sjogren performs a cogent critique of both Silverman and Doane, particularly their arguments in *The Desire to Desire* (Doane) and *The Acoustic Mirror: The Female Voice in Cinema and Psychoanalysis* (Silverman), in which they deploy psychoanalytic theory to argue that the lack of unified subject positions in Hollywood cinema is a problem for the female viewer. As Sjogren points out, Silverman's arguments are predicated on a male-centered theoretical apparatus, in which "the psychoanalytic scenarios themselves are ideological constructions that determine which readings can be made of the films (Sjogren, *Into the Vortex*, 47). She goes a little bit easier on Doane, suggesting that her recognition of the alterity of sound "entails the possibility of exposing an ideological fissure—a fissure which points to the irreconcilability of two truths of bourgeois ideology" (Sjogren, 36, citing Doane from "Ideology and the Practice of Sound Editing and Mixing," in *Film Sound: Theory and Practice*, ed. Elizabeth Weis and John Belton, 54–62 (New York: Columbia University Press, 1985). Indeed, Doane recognizes the spatial dimension of voice-off and its potential interruption/dissolution of diegetic space.

6. Sjogren, *Into the Vortex*, 17.

7. Ibid., 25.

8. Martha May, "From Cads to Dads," 2–8.

9. Helen Hanson, *Hollywood Heroines: Women in Film Noir and the Female Gothic Film*, 35.

10. Sjogren, *Into the Vortex*, 158.

11. E. Smith, *Starring Barbara Stanwyck*, 227.

12. Ibid., 222.

13. Anon., "*No Man of Her Own*," *Cue*, June 5, 1950, file on *No Man of Her Own*, Margaret Herrick Library.

14. Anon., "End of Era for Stars and System: Swanson Cues Comeback," *Variety*, January 3, 1951, 3.

15. E. Smith, *Starring Barbara Stanwyck*, 227.

16. James Naremore, *Acting in the Cinema*, 72.

O. ANNIE OAKLEY

1. Wilson, *Life of Barbara Stanwyck*, 442.

2. Ibid., 443.

3. Sarah Cansler, "Annie Oakley, Gender, and Guns: The 'Champion Rifle Shot' and Gender Performance, 1860–1926."

4. Ibid., 163.

5. Ann McGrath, "Being Annie Oakley: Modern Girls, New World Woman."

6. Review of *Annie Oakley*, *Variety*, December 25, 1935.

7. Nicolas G. Rosenthal, "Representing Indians: Native American Actors on Hollywood's Frontier," 336–37.

8. Wilson, *Life of Barbara Stanwyck*, 443, citing Buck Rainey, *Sweethearts of the Stage*, vii.

9. Madsen, *Stanwyck*, 251.

10. Letter dated February 25, 1948, from Peekskill, New York, *The Fountainhead* file, Warner Bros. Archive, University of Southern California.

11. J. Hoberman, *Army of Phantoms: American Movies and the Making of the Cold War*, 97.

12. As indicated in chapter J, I use the phrase "movie-Indian" to refer to racist caricatures who are played by actors who may or may not be Native Americans themselves.

13. Review of *Cattle Queen of Montana*, *Variety*, November 17, 1954; review of *Cattle Queen of Montana*, *Motion Picture Daily*, November 19, 1954; review of *Cattle Queen of Montana*, *New York Times*, January 26, 1955. The *Motion Picture Daily* reviewer seemed to think it was hard to tell the "good" Indians and "bad" ones apart, so they advised that *Cattle Queen* might be best shown only in areas where "spectators are exacting in their requirements."

14. Roy Ringer, "Gun Gal Role for Stanwyck," *L.A. Daily News*, December 9, 1954.

15. Anker, *Orgies of Feeling*, 26.

16. Ibid., 82.

17. In later life, the real Annie Oakley taught society ladies to shoot, and part of her rationale for this activity was the need for women to defend themselves. She also suggested they could contribute to national defense if necessary (Cansler, "Annie Oakley, Gender, and Guns," 173).

18. E. Smith, *Starring Barbara Stanwyck*, 255.

19. Michelle H. Raheja, *Reservation Reelism, Visual Sovereignty, and Representations of Native Americans in Film*, 37.

P. PARANOIA, ABJECTION, AND GASLIGHTING

1. Doane, *Desire to Desire*; Diane Waldman, "'At Last I Can Tell It to Someone!' Female Point of View and Subjectivity in the Gothic Romance Film of the 1940s."

2. Silverman, *Acoustic Mirror*, 78. Silverman mistakenly says that Leona is strangled with a telephone cord at the end, but in fact the unseen murderer strangles her with his hands (off screen) and then picks up the ringing phone by saying, "Sorry, wrong number."

3. Ibid., 80.

4. "Because female vision is objectless, free-floating, it is more proper to what Kristeva calls the 'abject.'" Doane, *Desire to Desire*, 141.

5. Kristeva, *Powers of Horror*, 92.

6. Maggie Hennefeld and Nicholas Sammond, eds., *Abjection Incorporated: Mediating the Politics of Pleasure and Violence*, Kindle loc. 150.

7. Ibid, 110. The Bataille essay referred to is "Abjection and Miserable Forms" (1934).

8. Both the original radio play and the script for *Sorry, Wrong Number* were written by Lucille Fletcher. The radio play began as an episode of a popular radio program called *Suspense*, which featured stories about women stalked by homicidal men, including their husbands. The biggest difference between the radio version and the film version is that in the original Leona's husband is not given a full voice or character, so the entire play is from her (audible) point of view. See Jeff Porter, "The Screaming Woman," 6.

9. See J. P. Telotte's "Tangled Networks and Wrong Numbers" for an analysis of the discourse of possession in *Sorry, Wrong Number*.

10. Amy Lawrence, "*Sorry, Wrong Number*: The Organizing Ear." Lawrence's essay is expanded in her book *Echo and Narcissus*.

11. Review of *Sorry, Wrong Number*, *New York Times*, September 2, 1948; review of *Sorry Wrong Number*, *Harrison's Reports*, July 31, 1948; review of *Sorry Wrong Number*, *L.A. Daily News*, September 24, 1948.

12. *The Exhibitor*, September 1, 1948, clippings file, Margaret Herrick Library; review of *Sorry, Wrong Number*, *Photoplay*, October 1948.

13. Bosley Crowther, "*Sorry, Wrong Number* Based on Radio Play, at Paramount—Barbara Stanwyck Stars," *New York Times*, September 2, 1948.

14. Barbara Creed, *The Monstrous-Feminine: Film, Feminism, Psychoanalysis*, 7.

15. For Ned Shantz, writing more recently, the "telephony" of *Sorry, Wrong Number* is linked to the play of coincidence that Crowther found so upsetting. Shantz argues that while the film offers up the phone as a way of ending the woman's "gothic isolation" in a big, empty, creepy house, it also turns that instrument against Leona in the end. Nevertheless, the flood of coincidences, like the annoying busy signal that Leona gets from Henry's office, is a "saturation of busyness that worries easy listening in a male key." Ned Shantz, "Telephonic Film."

16. E. Smith, *Starring Barbara Stanwyck*, 211.

17. Ibid.

18. Patricia White, "Supporting Character: The Queer Career of Agnes Moorehead," 100–101.

19. Bosley Crowther, "*The Two Mrs. Carrolls* with Humphrey Bogart, Barbara Stanwyck and Alexis Smith, Arrives at the Hollywood," *New York Times*, April 7, 1943.

20. Andrea Walsh, "Films of Suspicion and Distrust: Undercurrents of Female Consciousness in the 1940's," 1.

21. Cynthia A. Stark, "Gaslighting, Misogyny, and Psychological Oppression," 221.

22. Ibid., 222.

23. Ibid., 229.

24. The broadcast of "Autolight" was delayed six years due to legal wrangling, so in 1959 it might have missed its mark. Guy Barefoot, *Gaslight Melodrama: From Victorian London to 1940s Hollywood*, 5.

25. Doane, *Desire to Desire*, 42.

26. E. Smith, *Starring Miss Barbara Stanwyck*, 202.

27. Ibid., 212.

28. The exception of *The Other Love*, set not in a house but an institution, is nevertheless populated by a large staff of bossy nurses who, like the doctor, divulge nothing to the patient about her own health.

29. Edwin Schallert, "*The Gay Sisters* Augments Filmdom's Americana," *Los Angeles Times*, July 30, 1942.

30. T. S., review of *The Gay Sisters*, *New York Times*, August 15, 1942.

31. *The Brooklyn Eagle, Cry Wolf* file, Margaret Herrick Library; *New York Times*, July 19, 1947.

32. Hennefeld and Sammond, *Abjection Incorporated*, Kindle loc. 490.

Q. THE QUEEN

The first epigraph is from Jane Wilkie, "A Conversation with Jane Wilkie," by Suzanne Frasuer, "The Barbara Stanwyck Interviews," interview #5, box 50, Barbara Stanwyck Collection, American Heritage Center.

1. Stanwyck's camp status is confirmed in two canonical essays on camp: Susan Sontag's "Notes on Camp" (1964), in which she is categorized as a "great stylist of temperament and mannerism" (in *A Susan Sontag Reader*, 109); and Fabio Cleto's introduction to *Camp: Queer Aesthetics and the Performing Subject: A Reader*, where he places her in "the nave of the camp architectural building" (27).

2. At the time of this writing, the most prominent and active fan site is called "Barbara Stanwyck The Queen," https://www.barbara-stanwyck.com/.

3. Frank S. Nugent, "Stanwyck," *Collier's Weekly*, July 12, 1952.

4. Callahan, *Barbara Stanwyck*, 74.

5. Madsen, *Stanwyck*, 271,

6. Ibid., 209. See "Anecdotes," https://www.eisenhowerlibrary.gov/eisenhowers/quotes/for Eisenhower's endorsement of Wild Bill Hickock.

7. Ross, "Uses of Camp," 326. See also Daniel Harris, "The Death of Camp."

8. Unfortunately, few details are available for Stanwyck's support of native children or businesswomen aside from Wilson, *Life of Barbara Stanwyck*, 409; and Madsen, *Stanwyck*, 111, 195. It is unclear how long the Athena Sorority survived or who it actually supported, although Madsen claims it had four hundred members in 1940, with Stanwyck still attached to it. I have found no traces of it after the war. The Frasuer interviews at the AHC include a discussion of Stanwyck's support of her uncle Buck. One of the tasks he performed for her included delivery of anonymous gifts to beneficiaries whose troubles she read about in the newspaper.

9. "Barbara Stanwyck Unable to Attend Premiere," *Independent Record*, Helena, Montana, November 11, 1954.

10. Email correspondence with Aaron LaFromboise, director of Library Services, Medicine Spring Library, Blackfeet Community College.

11. Ibid. My correspondent in Montana favors the latter interpretation.

12. Stanwyck had several house fires, the last one in 1985, so the absence of documentation is not necessarily meaningful.

13. The novel *The Maverick Queen* was published in 1950 after Grey's death. He wrote it in the 1920s.

14. Pamela Robertson, *Guilty Pleasures: Feminist Camp from Mae West to Madonna*, 105.

15. Madsen, *Stanwyck*, 308.

16. "Bonanza in drag" originated with "Syd" in a review of *The Big Valley*, *Variety*, September 22, 1965.

17. Diorio, *Barbara Stanwyck*, 185; E. Smith, *Starring Miss Barbara Stanwyck*, 293; Gary A. Yoggy, *Riding the Video Range: The Rise and Fall of the Western on Television,* 327. Smith probably got the quote from the *New York Journal-American*, 1965.

18. Yoggy, *Riding the Video Range*, 326.

19. Diorio, *Barbara Stanwyck*, 187.

20. Madsen, *Stanwyck*, 358.

21. "Toni's Boys," also produced by Aaron Spelling, released April 2, 1980, was intended to be the pilot for a spinoff series that never took off. E. Smith, *Starring Miss Barbara Stanwyck*, 322.

22. Mark Finch, "Sex and Address in Dynasty," in Cleto, *Camp*, 143–59.

R. RIDING, FALLING, AND STUNTS

1. Akira Lippit, "The Death of an Animal," *Film Quarterly* 56, no. 1 (2002): 11.

2. Berlant, *Female Complaint*, 261.

3. A typical headline from *TV Guide* in 1961, during the run of *The Barbara Stanwyck Show*—in which she doesn't ride any horses—is "Stanwyck, The Frustrated Stuntwoman." *TV Guide,* January 21–27, 1961.

4. Wilson, *Life of Barbara Stanwyck*, 198.

5. E. Smith, *Starring Miss Barbara Stanwyck*, 39.

6. Wilson, *Life of Barbara Stanwyck*, 52.

7. Ibid., 432.

8. An undated photo from Stanwyck's scrapbooks includes a picture of her on a horse, with the caption: "Part owner of Marwyck Stables, Babs has become an equestrienne of considerable note. She is shown riding *Reno*, her prize stallion." Scrapbook 1, box 48, Barbara Stanwyck Collection, American Heritage Center, University of Wyoming.

9. Madsen, *Stanwyck*, 297.

10. Patrina Day Mitchum and Audrey Pavia, *Hollywood Hoofbeats: The Fascinating Story of Horses in Movies and Television.*

11. Stanwyck was given the Stuntmen's Association of Motion Pictures Award in 1962 and the Western Heritage Wrangler Award in 1973. Boxes 43 and 43a, American Heritage Center.

12. The one "sentimental" exception that I have found is Stanwyck's jockey character in *The Woman in Red* (1935), who cares for her horses as if they were pets.

13. E. Smith, *Starring Miss Barbara Stanwyck*, 247.

14. Ibid.

15. Wilson, *Life of Barbara Stanwyck*, 460.

16. Ibid., 411.

17. Paramount Production Injury Reports, *The Bride Wore Boots* production file, Margaret Herrick Library.

18. Wilson, *Life of Barbara Stanwyck*, 197–98.

19. 20th Century Fox press release for *Banjo on My Knee*, production file, Margaret Herrick Library.

20. 20th Century Fox press release for *Always Goodbye*, production file, Margaret Herrick Library.

21. E. Smith, *Starring Miss Barbara Stanwyck*, 247; Axel Madsen, *Stanwyck*, 318.

22. For example, she had a fall at Marwyck during the shooting of *Stella Dallas* but didn't miss a day on set. Wilson, *Life of Barbara Stanwyck*, 633.

23. Paramount News, November 11, 1941, *The Great Man's Lady*, production file, Margaret Herrick Library.

24. "Portrait of a Star," 1968, box 46, Barbara Stanwyck Collection, American Heritage Center.

25. Berlant, *The Female Complaint*, 269.

26. "Hollywood Stars Face Mexican Reprisals," *Daily Mirror*, March 2, 1953, Warner Bros. Archive. This was only one of many challenges met during the production of *Salt of the Earth* (1954), which has been subsequently recognized as an important pro-labor and feminist film.

27. "Oily Role Snug Fit for Stanwyck," *The Herald*, October 22, 1953, Warner Bros. Archive.

28. The plaque is archived in box 43A of the American Heritage Center in Wyoming. Stanwyck also won a Wrangler Award in 1973 from the National Cowboy Hall of Fame and Western Heritage Center, also archived at the American Heritage Center.

29. "Portrait of a Star," 1968, box 46, Barbara Stanwyck Collection, American Heritage Center.

30. Yoggy, *Riding the Video Range*. Yoggy cites Dwight Whitney, "The Queen Goes West," *TV Guide*, February 22, 1966, 6–7.

31. Berlant, *The Female Complaint*, 267–68.

32. Ibid., 268.

33. The song "Woman with a Whip" was written by Harold Adamson and performed by Jidge Carroll in *Forty Guns*.

S. THE *STELLA DALLAS* DEBATES

1. E. Ann Kaplan, "The Case of the Missing Mother: Maternal Issues in Vidor's *Stella Dallas*."

2. Williams, "Something Else Besides a Mother," 17.

3. Ibid., 18.

4. Gledhill, "Rethinking Genre," 241.

5. Thomas Elsaesser, "Tales of Sound and Fury," 56. Originally published in *Monogram* no. 4 (1972).

6. Ibid., 62.

7. E. Ann Kaplan, "Dialogue," *Cinema Journal* 24, no. 2 (1984): 40.

8. See Tania Modleski's response to Cavell's essay on *Now Voyager* in Modleski, "Editorial Notes."

9. Williams, "Something Else Besides a Mother," 14–15.

10. Stanley Cavell, *Contesting Tears: The Hollywood Melodrama of the Unknown Woman*, 201.

11. Klevan, *Stanwyck*, 29–56.

12. Ibid., 33.

13. Ibid., 48.

14. E. Smith, *Starring Miss Barbara Stanwyck*, 99. Smith cites *Movie Digest*, January 1972, for a very long quotation from Stanwyck.

15. Wilson, *Life of Barbara Stanwyck*, 610.

16. Madsen, *Stanwyck*, 143; Jerry Asher, "The Price She Paid for Stella Dallas," *Picture Play*, December 1938, 87.

17. Wilson, *Life of Barbara Stanwyck*, 579.

18. Ibid., 610.

19. Anna Siomopoulos, "I Didn't Know Anyone Could Be So Unselfish": Liberal Empathy, the Welfare State, and King Vidor's *Stella Dallas*," 3.

20. Madsen, *Stanwyck*, 145.

21. Anonymous review of *Stella Dallas*, Barbara Stanwyck file, MoMA.

22. "Film Preview: *Stella Dallas*," *Variety*, July 23, 1937.

23. Siomopoulos, "I Didn't Know," 4.

24. Ibid., 3.

25. Edith Thornton, "Fashion, Visibility, and Class Mobility in *Stella Dallas*," 441.

26. Ibid.

27. Ibid., 432.

28. Frank Nugent, "The Screen," *New York Times*, August 6, 1937.

29. "Film Preview: *Stella Dallas*," *Variety*, July 23, 1937.

30. Klevan, *Barbara Stanwyck*, 49.

31. Siomopoulos, "I Didn't Know," 17.

32. Wilson, *Life of Barbara Stanwyck*, 662; Edwin and Elza Schallert, "Hollywood Highlights: The Bob-Barbara Complex," *Picture Play*, October 1937, 42. The disastrous wardrobe failure at the preview of *Stella Dallas* is what convinced Stanwyck to work closely with Edith Head for her personal as well as professional designer (see chapter E).

33. Cavell, *Contesting Tears*, 217.

34. Klevan, *Barbara Stanwyck*, 47.

35. Cavell, *Contesting Tears*, 219.

36. Ibid.

37. Alison Whitney, "Race, Class, and the Pressure to Pass in American Maternal Melodrama: The Case of *Stella Dallas*."

38. Ibid., 16.

39. Cavell makes this point in *Contesting Tears*, 212.

40. Naremore, *Acting in the Cinema*, 70.

41. Ibid., 71.

42. White, *Uninvited*, 107.

43. Ibid., 104.

44. E. Smith, *Starring Miss Barbara Stanwyck*, 109.

45. Klevan makes this point in *Barbara Stanwyck*, 40. He also notes how Stanwyck pulls away a sofa cushion in mid-sentence as she presses her point with Helen. It is a great example of how she integrates props and gestures seamlessly into her performance.

46. White, *Uninvited*, 107.

47. For Benjamin, fashion exemplified his refusal of the concept of "timeless truth" and was proof of the transience of historical knowledge. Insofar as fashion is always on the cusp of the new, it is the signal for "new legal codes, wars and revolutions." *Arcades Project* 64 [B1a,1].

48. Wilson, *Life of Barbara Stanwyck*, 624–25.

T. THERESA HARRIS

1. See chapter I for a discussion of the two different versions of *Baby Face*. In the "original theatrical release" all references to Nietzsche have been deleted, but in the "prerelease version" it is clear that Lily's mentor Cragg has sent her Nietzsche's *Will to Power*.

2. Pamela Robertson Wojcik, "Mae West's Maids: Race, 'Authenticity,' and the Discourse of Camp," 287–99.

3. Thomas Cripps, *Slow Fade to Black: The Negro in American Film*, 102.

4. Ibid., 109.

5. Cladrite Radio, "10 Things You Should Know about Theresa Harris," *YouTube*, December 30, 2020, https://www.youtube.com/watch?v=Y_W1c7qrzjc/.

6. Fay M. Jackson, "Dainty Theresa in Gang Film," *The Afro American*, August 28, 1937.

7. Despite the paucity of published materials or documents related to Harris's career, several compilations have been made to circulate online: "Theresa Harris, an Overlooked Star," https://www.youtube.com/watch?v=LI2SNw7uAz4/ ; "10 Things You Should Know about Theresa Harris"; TCM promo for *Hold Your Man*, https://www.facebook.com/tcmtv/videos/332390004492001/; and one excellent blog post by Steve Cubine, https://frombeneaththehollywoodsign.com/f/theresa-harris-born-too-soon/.

8. Will Straw, "Scales of Presence: Bess Flowers and the Hollywood Extra," 121.

9. Ibid., 122.

10. Lynn Nottage, *By the Way, Meet Vera Stark*. The published play includes URLs for two websites: http://meetverastark.com/ and https://www.findingverastark.com/, of which only the first remains functional in April 2022.

11. Samantha Sheppard has offered a parallel reading of Harris as she is imagined by Nottage in "Changing the Subject: Lynn Nottage's *By the Way, Meet Vera Stark* and the Making of Black Women's Film History," 14–42.

12. Jacqueline Stewart, "Negroes Laughing at Themselves? Black Spectatorship and the Performance of Urban Modernity," 669. More specifically, she draws on *Native Son* by Richard Wright and *The Bluest Eye* by Toni Morrison, for speculative accounts of Black spectatorship.

13. The ongoing work on revising the archive of Black women in American cultural history is inspired by Sadiya Hartman, *Wayward Lives, Beautiful Experiments*. I am also indebted to Ashley D. Farmer's "In Search of the Black Women's History Archive," among many other sources.

14. Michele Hilmes, *Radio Voices: American Broadcasting, 1922–1952*, 196.

15. Christine Goding-Doty, "White Event Horizon," *Monday Journal* 4, https://monday-journal.com/white-event-horizon/. Goding-Doty's full argument is put forward in her dissertation, "Virtually White: The Crisis of Whiteness, Racial Rule, and Affect in the Digital Age."

16. Goding-Doty, "Virtually White," 9.

17. Peter Stanfield, "An Excursion into the Lower Depths: Hollywood, Urban Primitivism, and 'St. Louis Blues,' 1929–1937," 96.

18. Ibid., 86.

19. Wilson, *Life of Barbara Stanwyck*, 547.

20. Ibid., 549.

21. See Miriam Petty, *Stealing the Show: African American Performers and Audiences in 1930s Hollywood*).

22. Harris's character, Eunice, in *Out of the Past* has attracted considerable scholarly attention because Eunice does not defer to Robert Mitchum's character and is very at ease in her fancy clothes at a Black club—and indeed, this kind of scene and this kind of outfit is exactly what I imagine Harris herself would be like. James Naremore has commented, "The scene as a whole is played without condescension, and whether it intends to or not, it makes a comment on racial segregation." In fact, I would argue, all scenes in studio-era cinema make a comment on racial segregation, simply in the hierarchies of casting. See James Naremore, *More Than Night: Film Noir in Its Contexts*, 240.

U. *UNION PACIFIC*

1. Warren Sussman, *Culture as History: The Transformation of American Society in the Twentieth Century*, 157.

2. Ibid., 159.

3. Ibid., 149.

4. Pravadelli, *Classic Hollywood*, 30, quoting Christina Simmons, *Making Marriage Modern: Women's Sexuality from the Progressive Era to World War II*, 138.

5. Robert Fyne, "From Hollywood to Moscow," 195.

6. Thomas Doherty makes this point about Hollywood agitprop films in general, "Hollywood Agit-Prop: The Anti-Communist Cycle, 1948–1954," 15.

7. "Reds Extend Demand for Free Screen as colleges Take up Fight," *Motion Picture Herald*, November 1, 1935, 16. *Variety* noted that "it should do fairly as publicity is publicity." Odec, review of *Red Salute, Variety*, October 2, 1935.

8. An ad posted in *Motion Picture Daily* on September 16, 1935, featured praise from one Lucille Sheerwood praising the film as a comedy. Graham Greene also praised the film in *The Spectator* (November 22, 1935), rpt. in Graham Greene and David Parkinson, *The Graham Greene Film Reader: Reviews, Essays, Interviews, and Film Stories*.

9. James Agee, from *Movie Digest*, rpt. in Charles Maland, "The Unpublished James Agee: Excerpts from Complete Film Criticism: Reviews, Essays, and Manuscripts, 26–29.

10. Wilson, *Life of Barbara Stanwyck*, 522.

11. Ibid., 538–39.

12. Laurence Raw, "Deconstructing Political Adaptation: Sean O'Casey's *The Plough and the Stars*," 55.

13. Ibid., 60.

14. Eric Smoodin, *Regarding Frank Capra: Audience, Celebrity and American Film Studies 1930–1960*, 150.

15. Theatre Patrons Inc., *The Movies ... and the People Who Make Them*.

16. Peter Stanfield, *Hollywood, Westerns, and the 1930s: The Lost Trail*, 156.

17. Educational and Recreational Guides Inc. published studies designed for use in junior high and high school film appreciation classes. As Eric Smoodin has noted, these guides included assessments of movies' form and quality alongside their historical content. Smoodin, *Regarding Frank Capra*, 121–23.

18. *Photoplay Studies: A Magazine Devoted to Photoplay Appreciation*, vol. 4, no. 4 (1939): 8, in *Photoplay Studies Group Discussion Guide 1939*, prepared by Maxine Block, *Union Pacific* file, Margaret Herrick Library.

19. A second unit also shot a great deal of landscape footage in Utah, Oklahoma, and around Sonora, California.

20. Wilson, *Life of Barbara Stanwyck*, 756.

21. Ibid., 70.

22. J. P. Telotte, "A Fate Worse Than Death: Racism, Transgression, and Westerns," 124.

23. Ibid., 120.

24. The scene could also be read as a suicidal ménage à trois in which Dick, along with Mollie, submits to Jeff.

25. Telotte, "Fate Worse Than Death," 125.

26. *Photoplay Studies Group Discussion Guide*, 6.

27. Wilson, *Life of Barbara Stanwyck*, 787.

28. Smoodin, *Regarding Frank Capra*, 150.

29. Ibid., 141–51.

30. This point is made by Dudley Andrew, "Productive Discord in the System: Hollywood Meets John Doe," 265; and by Charles Wolfe, "Meet John Doe: Authors, Audiences, and Endings," in *Meet John Doe*, 15.

31. Dudley Andrew, "Productive Discord," 263.

32. Ibid.

33. A full account of the various endings can be found in Wolfe, *Meet John Doe*, 43–185.

34. Wolfe, "Meet John Doe: Authors, Audiences, and Endings," 17.

V. VOICE, BODY, IDENTITY

1. Michel Chion, *The Voice in Cinema*, 13.

2. Silverman, *Acoustic Mirror*; Sjogren, *Into the Vortex*; Lawrence, *Echo and Narcissus*.

3. Sjogren, *Into the Vortex*, 40.

4. Roland Barthes, "The Grain of the Voice," 188.

5. Roland Barthes, *The Pleasure of the Text*, 67.

6. Daphne A. Brooks, *Liner Notes for the Revolution: The Intellectual Life of Black Feminist Sound*, 2021.

7. Klevan, *Barbara Stanwyck*, 21.

8. Ibid., 24.

9. Wilson, *Life of Barbara Stanwyck*, 549.

10. Ibid., 594.

11. Ibid., 50.

12. The app I used for notating dialogue is *ScoreCloud Express* (DoReMIR Music Research AB 2014).

13. Jacob Smith mistakenly associates Stanwyck's radio dramas with "daytime soaps." In fact, *Lux Radio Theatre* and the other programs that she recorded for were broadcast at night as prestige dramas with the imprimatur of Hollywood celebrity. Hilmes, *Radio Voices*, 183–88. Smith compares Stanwyck's radio version of *Stella Dallas* with the film version in order to explain how vocal expressions of emotion are used to replace reaction shots in radio, but he has little to say about her particular performance. Jacob Smith, *Vocal Tracks: Performance and Sound Media*, 101–102.

14. Barthes, "Grain of the Voice," 184.

15. Eidsheim, *Race of Sound*, 8.

W. WORKING WOMEN AND CULTURAL LABOR

1. Wilson, *Life of Barbara Stanwyck*, 550.

2. Roy Grundman, "Taking Stock at War's End: Gender, Genre, and Hollywood Labor in *The Strange Love of Martha Ivers*," 29.

3. Madsen, *Stanwyck*, 235; Grundman, "Taking Stock," 29. Madsen cites Douglas from his first memoir, *The Ragman's Son*, 136.

4. "Here's Hollywood: Gossip by Weston East," *Screenland*, March 1946, 64–65. The production dates for *Martha Ivers* are listed on IMDb as October 2, 1945, to December 1945, so this mention appears three months after the event being reported.

5. Clark, *Negotiating Hollywood*, 15.

6. Ibid., 12.

7. Grundman, "Taking Stock," 28.

8. See "Cultural Labor" at https://wiki.p2pfoundation.net/Cultural_Labor/. See also David Hesmondhalgh, *The Cultural Industries*.

9. Carman, *Independent Stardom*, 101.

10. RKO Radio Pictures Studio Records, UCLA Special Collections., PASC0003.

11. Reviewer pages, RKO Radio Pictures Studio Records, *The Bride Walks Out* production file, Margaret Herrick Library.

12. The two episodes of *The Untouchables* that Stanwyck appears in are "Elegy," season 4, episode 8 (November 20, 1962), and "Search for a Dead Man," season 4, episode 13 (January 1, 1963). Both episodes are available at the UCLA Film and Television Archive.

13. See Desjardins, *Recycled Stars*.

14. "Size Ten" was broadcast on January 16, 1961.

15. "Out of the Shadows" was broadcast on December 19, 1960.

16. Peter Shelley argues that the women in Grande Dame Guignol are either mentally unstable or women in peril. Peter Shelley, *Grande Dame Guignol Cinema: A History of Hag Horror from Baby Jane to Mother*, Kindle loc 152.

17. Edwin Schallert, "*Witness to Murder, Heat Wave* Cause New Crime Stir," *Los Angeles Times*, Thursday, May 13, 1954.

18. *Witness to Murder* production file, Margaret Herrick Library.

19. These reviews are all filed in the clippings file on *These Wilder Years* in the Margaret Herrick Library, from the following publications: *Herald Tribune*, August 18, 1956; Bosley Crowther, "The Scent of Soap: *These Wilder Years* Is Slushy Drama," *New York Times*, August 18, 1956; *Cue*, n.d.; review of *These Wilder Years*, *Monthly Film Bulletin* 23, no. 264 (1956); *Independent Film Journal*, n.d.; *Los Angeles Times*, n.d.

20. *Los Angeles Times*, Sunday, September 9, 1956.

21. Richard Dyer, "Entertainment and Utopia," 19–35.

22. David James, *Rock 'n' Film: Cinema's Dance with Popular Music*, 102.

23. Wilson, *Life of Barbara Stanwyck*, 298.

24. Ibid., 283.

25. Motion Picture Association of America, Production Code Administration Records, Margaret Herrick Library.

26. Cecelia Ager, "Going Places," *Variety*, April 5, 1932, 16; quoted in Wilson, *Life of Barbara Stanwyck*, 296.

27. Wilson, *Life of Barbara Stanwyck*, 197.

28. Toby Miller and Richard Maxwell, "Introduction to the Cultural Labor Issue," 263.

29. Ibid., 265.

X. EXOTICA AND BITTER TEARS

1. Many filmographies date the film as 1933 because its New York premiere was in January 1933, but IMDb and some other filmographies list it as 1932, as it was screened in other American cities in December 1932.

2. Lucille S. Adams, "The Audience Talks Back: Well! Nils Seems Hot!" *Photoplay*, March 1933, 8; Box Office Critics, "Raves," *New Movie Magazine*, April 1933, 78.

3. Ethan, review of *The Bitter Tea of General Yen*," *Variety*, January 17, 1933.

4. Mordaunt Hall, "The Screen: Radio City Music Hall Shows a Melodrama of China as Its First Pictorial Attraction," *New York Times*, January 12, 1933.

5. Review of *The Bitter Tea of General Yen*, *Harrison's Reports*, 1933. This writer also complained that the general is a revolutionary (which he isn't) and noted that the film is not suitable for Sunday screenings.

6. Cecelia Ager, "Going Places," *Variety*, January 17, 1933.

7. Ibid., 13.

8. Isabel O. Santaolalla, "East Is East and West Is West? Otherness in Capra's 'The Bitter Tea of General Yen," 67.

9. David Palumbo-Liu, "The Bitter Tea of Frank Capra," 766.

10. Joseph McBride, *Frank Capra: The Catastrophe of Success*, 281.

11. See Lucy Fischer, *Designing Women: Cinema, Art Deco, and the Female Form*.

12. One of Stanwyck's very few "publications"—perhaps her only one—was a one-paragraph foreword to Joseph Walker's memoir, *The Light on Her Face*.

13. Wilson, *Life of Barbara Stanwyck*, 323.

14. David Palumbo-Liu, "The Bitter Tea of Frank Capra," 759–89 (323); Wilson, *Life of Barbara Stanwyck*, 316.

15. Ethan, review of *The Bitter Tea of General Yen*, *Variety*, January 17, 1933.

16. McBride, *Frank Capra*, 281. (No source provided for the Stanwyck quote.)

17. Palumbo-Liu, "Bitter Tea," 782–85.
18. Smoodin, *Regarding Frank Capra*, 74.
19. Ibid., 67.
20. Ibid., 72.
21. *Photoplay*, April 1933.
22. Sarah Berry suggests that this is the glamourous look that Stanwyck fans may have been expecting, although this film precedes *Baby Face*, and until this point Stanwyck had played many unglamourous working-class women. Sarah Berry, *Screen Style: Fashion and Femininity in 1930s Hollywood*, 139.
23. Gina Marchetti, *Romance and the "Yellow Peril": Race, Sex, and Discursive Strategies in Hollywood Fiction*, 39.
24. Wilson, *Life of Barbara Stanwyck*, 315.
25. Klevan, *Stanwyck*, 81, 108.
26. Wilson, *Life of Barbara Stanwyck*, 325.
27. Steve Neale, "Melodrama and Tears," 6–22.
28. Jane Gaines, "Even More Tears: The *Historical Time* Theory of Melodrama," 333.
29. Ibid., 338.
30. Amanda Anderson, *The Powers of Distance: Cosmopolitanism and the Cultivation of Detachment*, 9.
31. Ibid., 31.

Y. YOU BELONG TO ME

1. *Ever in My Heart* (1932) is also distinguished by the fact that Stanwyck's character visibly shifts from being a "Victorian" blue-blooded matron to a young modern woman in uniform when she signs up for service in World War I.
2. Drew Bernard, "Stanwyck Speaks," 43.
3. "Titles for Pioneer Woman," January 16, 1941, file on *The Great Man's Lady*, Core Collection Files, Margaret Herrick Library.
4. T. S., "At the Paramount," *New York Times*, April 30, 1942.
5. Ibid.
6. David M. Lugowski, "Claudette Colbert, Ginger Rogers, and Barbara Stanwyck: American Homefront Women," 98.
7. Research was also conducted at the archives at the University of Southern California and at the University of Los Angeles, where similar sets of studio memos and clippings are located. At the Museum of Modern Art (MoMA) and New York Public Library, Stanwyck's files consist mainly of clippings from magazines.
8. Mary Ann Doane, "The Woman's Film: Possession and Address," 284.
9. Ibid., 285.
10. Stacey, *Star Gazing*.
11. Amelie Hastie, *Cupboards of Curiosity: Women, Recollection, and Film History*, 32–33.
12. Unfortunately, due to the COVID-19 pandemic, I have been unable to visit this archive in person. However, the library staff have been extremely helpful, and they have inspected the scripts and informed me that they are blank. They have been kind enough to send me digital copies of all the materials referenced

in this book. I have not come across any evidence that Stanwyck annotated her scripts, although that has been a valuable source for many star studies. She memorized them, and had opinions, but may not have made notes.

13. Madsen, *Stanwyck*, 277.

14. The titles added by the secretary include "Concealment," which was the working title for *The Secret Bride* (1934), "I Love Like That," "Private Enemy," and "This Marriage Business." Although the last three may have been working titles, they are not recorded by Victoria Wilson, who includes most of the working titles for Stanwyck films made before 1940. The secretary's note accompanying the cards is dated July 31, 1951, and asks for "forgiveness in the delay getting this information to you" (Pat McMath). Box 48, Barbara Stanwyck Collection, American Heritage Center.

15. I have only the librarian's testimony that none of the books are attributed to an author/collector. See note 9 above.

16. The marriage was motivated by a scandal-mongering article about unwed couples in Hollywood: Kirtley Baskette, "Hollywood Unmarried Husbands and Wives," *Photoplay*, January 1939. Taylor was an MGM star, where there was concern about his reputation. There is no evidence that Taylor was not heterosexual, but before the war he spent inordinate time with his mother, and after the war preferred the company of his male friends. After divorcing Stanwyck, he married and raised a family with Ursula Theiss. See Jane Ellen Wayne, *Robert Taylor: The Man with the Perfect Face*.

17. Joseph McBride, *Focus on Howard Hawks*, 9. Stanwyck was also photographed on a motorcycle in publicity for *Roustabout* (1964), sitting behind Elvis Presley on a large bike.

18. Suzanne Frasuer, "The Barbara Stanwyck Interviews," Barbara Stanwyck Collection, box 50, American Heritage Center.

19. Frasuer's correspondence with the American Heritage Center includes some evidence of contested ownership over Stanwyck with Victoria Wilson, who Frasuer says signed her book contract in 1995, a year after Frasuer had begun collecting materials for the Stanwyck collection, implying that Wilson had begun contacting the same people she was reaching out to. Suzanne Frasuer file, Barbara Stanwyck Collection, American Heritage Center.

20. Dyer, *Stars*, 24.

21. Hastie, *Cupboards of Curiosity*, 78.

22. Jane Wilkie, *Confessions of an Ex–Fan Magazine Writer*, 7.

23. Steedman, *Dust*, 83.

24. Ibid., 69.

Z. ZEPPO MARX

1. Madsen, *Stanwyck*, 154.

2. Simon Louvish, *Monkey Business: The Lives and Legends of the Marx Brothers*, 276.

3. Allen W. Ellis, "Yes, Sir: The Legacy of Zeppo Marx," 25.

4. Barry Norma, "Zeppo's Last Interview," *Freedonia Gazette* no. 7 (Winter 1981): 5.

5. "Zeppo Marx, 77, Loses in Biddy Batter Suit," *Variety*, November 29, 1978, 2.

6. "How Zeppo Marx Ended World War II," https://www.youtube.com/watch?v=uqxTiEaoNZA/, accessed June 24, 2021.

7. Louvish, *Monkey Business*, 301.

8. Tom Kemper, *Hidden Talent: The Emergence of Hollywood Agents*, 125.

9. Ibid., 131.

10. Madsen, *Stanwyck*, 274,

11. Ellis, "Yes, Sir," 18.

12. Wilson, *Life of Barbara Stanwyck*, 435.

13. Ibid., 499. One of Wilson's sources is Tim Marx, the son of Marion and Zeppo, as indicated in her acknowledgments (860).

14. The working title of *Red Salute* was "Runaway Daughter," and the working title of *The Bride Walks Out* was "Marry the Girl," two more titles that cancel out the woman's subjectivity by making her the possession of a man in the first case, and in the grammatical directive to a man in the second case. See chapter Y.

15. Bige, "*Baby Face*," *Variety*, June 27, 1933.

16. Klevan, *Barbara Stanwyck*, 79.

17. Ibid., 68.

18. Ibid., 80.

19. Clippings from the *New York Post, Hollywood Reporter* in *Christmas in Connecticut* production file, Margaret Herrick Library; review of *Christmas in Connecticut, Photoplay*, August 1945; J.R.L., "*Christmas in Connecticut* with Barbara Stanwyck, Opens at Strand," *New York Times,* July 28, 1945.

20. J.R.L., "*Christmas in Connecticut* with Barbara Stanwyck, Opens at Strand," *New York Times*, July 28, 1945.

21. Wilson, passim.

22. *Christmas in Connecticut* production file, Margaret Herrick Library.

23. Kathleen Rowe, *Unruly Women: Gender and the Genres of Laughter*, 118.

24. Wikipedia cites two figures for the box office receipts for *Christmas in Connecticut*, against a budget of $864,000: $3 million, according to Thomas Schatz, *Boom and Bust: American Cinema in the 1940s* (229), or $4,132,000, according to Warner Bros. financial information in the William Schaefer Ledger. See H. Mark Glancy, "Warner Bros Film Grosses, 1921–51: The William Schaefer Ledger," appendix 1, *Historical Journal of Film, Radio and Television* 15, no. 1 (1995) supl., 1–31, p. 25, DOI: 10.1080/01439689508604551.

25. Maggie Hennefeld, "Destructive Metamorphosis: The Comedy of Female Catastrophe and Feminist Historiography," 179.

26. Ibid., 178.

27. Maggie Hennefeld, "Editor's Introduction: Toward a Feminist Politics of Comedy and History," 5.

28. Sara Ahmed describes the feminist killjoy as an "affect alien" that contains " a certain kind of political potential and energy." Sara Ahmed, *The Cultural Politics of Emotion*, 224.

29. Wilson, *Life of Barbara Stanwyck*, 499, citing S. R. Mook, "The Test of a Lady," *Modern Screen,* October 1934, 84.

30. Madsen, *Stanwyck*, 285.

31. Stanwyck won on Emmy for *Big Valley* and was nominated two additional times. The show also won two awards for editing and six additional nominations. *The Big Valley*, "Awards," Internet Movie Database, https://www.imdb.com/title/tt0058791/awards?ref_=tt_awd/.

32. Sara Ahmed, *Willful Subjects*, 17.

BIBLIOGRAPHY

Ahmed, Sara. *The Cultural Politics of Emotion*. New York: Routledge, 2015.

———. *Living a Feminist Life*. Durham, NC: Duke University Press, 2017.

———. *Willful Subjects*. Durham, NC: Duke University Press, 2014.

Alvarez, Al. *The Biggest Game in Town*. London: Bloomsbury, 2009.

Anderson, Amanda. *The Powers of Distance: Cosmopolitanism and the Cultivation of Detachment*. Princeton, NJ: Princeton University Press, 2018.

Andrew, Dudley. "Productive Discord in the System: Hollywood Meets John Doe." In *Meet John Doe: Frank Capra, Director*, edited by Charles Wolfe, 253–68. New Brunswick, NJ: Rutgers University Press, 1989.

Anker, Elizabeth R. *Orgies of Feeling: Melodrama and the Politics of Freedom*. Durham, NC: Duke University Press, 2014.

Austin, J. L. *How to Do Things with Words*. Ed. J. O. Urmson. New York: Oxford University Press, 1970.

Baker, David, and Danielle Zuvela. "Mann and Woman: The Function of the Feminine in the 'Noir Westerns' of Anthony Mann." *Transformations* 24 (2014). http://www.transformationsjournal.org/issue-24/.

Barefoot, Guy. *Gaslight Melodrama: From Victorian London to 1940s Hollywood*. New York: Continuum, 2001.

Baron, Cynthia. *Modern Acting: The Lost Chapter of American Film and Theatre*. London: Palgrave Macmillan, 2016.

———, and Sharon Marie Carnicke. *Reframing Screen Performance*. Ann Arbor: University of Michigan Press, 2008.

Barthes, Roland. "The Grain of the Voice." In *Image/Music/Text*, translated by Stephen Heath. New York: Hill and Wang, 1977.

———. *The Pleasure of the Text*. Trans. Richard Miller. New York: Hill and Wang, 1975.

Basinger, Jeanine. *A Woman's View: How Hollywood Spoke to Women, 1930–1960*. New York: Alfred A. Knopf, 1993.

Becker, Christine. *It's the Pictures That Got Small: Hollywood Film Stars on 1950s Television*. Middletown, CT: Wesleyan University Press, 2008.

Benjamin, Walter. *The Arcades Project*. Trans. Howard Eiland and Kevin McLaughlin. Cambridge, MA: Harvard University Press, [1936] 1999.

———. "The Destructive Character." In [1931] *Selected Works*. Vol. 2, *1927–1934*, edited by Michael W. Jennings, Howard Eiland, and Gary Smith; translated by Jonathan Livingstone and others, 297–98. Cambridge, MA: Harvard University Press, [1930] 1999.

———. "Fate and Character." In *Selected Works*. Vol. 1, *1913–1926*, edited by Marcus Bullock, and Michael W. Jennings, 205. Cambridge, MA: Harvard University Press, 1996.

———. "Notes on a Theory of Gambling." In *Selected Writings*. Vol. 2, *1927–1934*, edited by Michael J. Jennings, Howard Eiland, and Gary Smith; translated by Jonathan Livingstone and others, 297–98. Cambridge, MA: Harvard University Press, [1930] 1999.

———. *The Origin of German Tragic Drama*. Trans. John Osborn. New York: New Left Books, 1977.

———. *Selected Writings*. Vol. 4, *1938–1940*. Ed. Michael W. Jennings. Cambridge, MA: Harvard University Press, 2003.

———. "The Work of Art in the Age of Mechanical Reproduction," Second Version. In *Selected Writings*. Vol. 2, *1927–1934*. [1935].

Berenstein, Rhona. "White Heroines and Hearts of Darkness: Race, Gender and Disguise in 1930s Jungle Films." *Film History* 6, no. 3 (1994): 314–39.

Berkvens, Linda. "No Crinoline-Covered Lady: Stardom, Agency, and the Career of Barbara Stanwyck." DPhil Diss., University of Sussex, 2011.

Berlant, Lauren. *The Female Complaint: The Unfinished Business of Sentimentality in American Culture*. Durham, NC: Duke University Press, 2013.

———. Introduction to "Intimacy: A Special Issue." *Critical Inquiry* 24, no. 2 (1998): 281–88.

Bernard, Drew. "Stanwyck Speaks." *Film Comment* 17, no. 2 (1981): 43–46.

Berney, Adrienne. "Streamlining Breasts: The Exaltation of Form and Disguise of Function in 1930s' Ideals." *Journal of Design History* 14, no. 4, Technology and the Body (2001): 327–42.

Berry, Sarah. *Screen Style: Fashion and Femininity in 1930s Hollywood*. Minneapolis: University of Minnesota Press, 2000.

Bisen, Sheri Chinen. "Censorship, Film Noir, and Double Indemnity." *Film and History* 25, nos. 1–2 (1995): 40–52.

Bjerg, Ole. *Poker: The Parody of Capitalism*. Ann Arbor: University of Michigan Press, 2011.

Bordwell, David, Janet Staiger, and Kristin Thompson. *Classical Hollywood Cinema: Film Style and Mode of Production to 1960*. New York: Columbia University Press, 1985.

Boris, Eileen. "Desirable Dress: Rosies, Sky Girls, and the Politics of Appearance." *International Labor and Working-Class History* no. 69 (Spring 2006): 123–42.

Bronfen, Elisabeth. "Femme Fatale: Negotiations of Tragic Desire." *New Literary History* 35, no. 1 (2004): 103–116.

Brooks, Daphne. *Liner Notes for the Revolution: The Intellectual Life of Black Feminist Sound*. Cambridge, MA: Harvard University Press, 2021.

Brooks, Jodi. "Crisis and the Everyday: Some Thought on Gesture and Crisis in Cassavetes and Benjamin." In *Falling for You: Essays on Cinema and Performance*, edited by Lesley Stern and George Kouvaros, 73–104. Sydney, Australia: Power Publications, 1999.

Brooks, Peter. *The Melodramatic Imagination: Balzac, Henry James, Melodrama and the Mode of Excess*. New York: Columbia University Press, 1985.

Browne, Nick, ed. *Refiguring American Film Genres*. Berkeley: University of California Press, 1998.

Butler, Judith. *Antigone's Claim*. New York: Columbia University Press, 2000.

———. *Gender Trouble: Feminism and the Subversion of Identity*. New York: Routledge, 1990.

Cagle, Chris. *Sociology on Film: Postwar Hollywood's Prestige Commodity*. New Brunswick, NJ: Rutgers University Press, 2017.

Cahill, James. "A YouTube Bestiary: Twenty-Six Theses on a Post-Cinema of Animal Attractions." In *New Silent Cinema*, edited by Paul Flaig and Katherine Groo, 263–93. New York: Routledge, 2016.

Caldwell, John. *Production Culture: Industrial Reflexivity and Critical Practice in Film and Television*. Durham, NC: Duke University Press, 2008.

———. "Industrial Geography Lessons: Socio-Professional Rituals and the Borderlands of Production Culture." In *MediaSpace: Place, Scale, and Culture in a Media Age*, edited by Nick Couldry and Anna McCarthy, 163–89. New York: Routledge, 2003.

Callahan, Dan. *Barbara Stanwyck: The Miracle Woman*. Jackson: University Press of Mississippi, 2012.

Cansler, Sarah. "Annie Oakley, Gender, and Guns: The 'Champion Rifle Shot' and Gender Performance, 1860–1926." *Pursuit: The Journal of Undergraduate Research at the University of Tennessee* 5, no. 1 (2014): 160–87.

Capua, Michelangelo. *William Holden: A Biography*. Jefferson, NC: McFarland, 2010.

Carman, Emily Susan. "Independent Stardom: Female Film Stars and the Studio System in the 1930s." *Women's Studies* 37 (2008): 583–615.

———. *Independent Stardom: Freelance Women in the Hollywood Studio System*. Austin: University of Texas Press, 2016.

———. "'Women Rule Hollywood': Aging and Freelance Stardom in the Studio System." *Celebrity Studies* 3, no. 1 (2012): 13–24.

Carnicke, Sharon Marie. "The Screen Actor's 'First Self' and 'Second Self': John Wayne and Coquelin's Acting Theory." In Taylor, *Theorizing Film Acting*, 184–200.

Cavell, Stanley. *Contesting Tears: The Hollywood Melodrama of the Unknown Woman*. Chicago: University of Chicago Press, 1996.

———. *Pursuits of Happiness: The Hollywood Comedy of Remarriage*. Cambridge, MA: Harvard University Press, 1981.

Chierichetti, David. *Edith Head: The Life and Times of Hollywood's Celebrated Costume Designer*. New York: Harper Collins, 2003.

Chion, Michel. *The Voice in Cinema*. Ed. and trans. Cynthia Gorbman. New York: Columbia University Press, 1999.

Clark, Danae. *Negotiating Hollywood: The Cultural Politics of Actor's Labor*. Minneapolis: University of Minnesota Press, 1995.

Cleto, Fabio, ed. *Camp: Queer Aesthetics and the Performing Subject: A Reader*. Ann Arbor: University of Michigan Press, 1999.

Cohan, Stephen. "Masquerading as the American Male in the Fifties: *Picnic*, William Holden, and the Spectacle of Masculinity in Hollywood Film." *Camera Obscura* 9, no. 1 (1991): 25–26.

Colpaert, Lisa. "Costume on Film: How the Femme Fatale's Wardrobe Scripted the Pictorial Style of 1940s Film Noir." *Studies in Costume and Performance* 4, no. 1 (2019): 65–84.

Cowans, Jon. *Empire Films and the Crisis of Colonialism, 1946–1959*. Baltimore: Johns Hopkins University Press, 2015.

Creed, Barbara. *The Monstrous-Feminine: Film, Feminism, Psychoanalysis*. New York: Routledge, 1993.

Cripps, Thomas. *Slow Fade to Black: The Negro in American Film*. New York: Oxford University Press, 1977.

Day Mitchum, Petrine, and Audrey Pavia. *Hollywood Hoofbeats: The Fascinating Story of Horses in Movies and Television*. Mount Joy, PA: Companion House Books, 2014.

Desjardins, Mary. *Recycled Stars: Female Film Stardom in the Age of Television and Video*. Durham, NC: Duke University Press, 2015.

DiBattista, Maria. *Fast Talking Dames*. Yale Online Scholarship, 2013. DOI: 10.12987/yale/9780300088151.001.0001.

Dietrich, Marlene. *Marlene Dietrich's ABCs: Wit, Wisdom, and Recipes*. Garden City, NY: Doubleday, 1962. Reprint by Open Road Media, 2012.

Diorio, Al. *Barbara Stanwyck*. London: W. H. Allen, 1983.

Doane, Mary Anne. *The Desire to Desire: The Woman's Film of the 1940s*. Bloomington: Indiana University Press, 1987.

———. *Femmes Fatales: Feminism, Film Theory, Psychoanalysis*. New York: Routledge, 1991.

———. "The Woman's Film: Possession and Address." In Gledhill, *Home Is Where the Heart Is*, 283–325.

Doherty, Thomas. "Hollywood Agit-Prop: The Anti-Communist Cycle, 1948–1954." *Journal of Film and Video* 40, no. 4 (1988): 15–27.

———. *Pre-Code Hollywood: Sex, Immorality, and Insurrection in American Cinema, 1930–1934*. New York: Columbia University Press, 1999.

Dombrowski, Lisa. *Samuel Fuller: If You Die, I'll Kill You!* Middletown, CT: Wesleyan University Press, 2008.

Duncan, Aaron M. *Gambling with the Myth of the American Dream*. New York: Routledge, 2015.

Dyer, Richard. "Entertainment and Utopia." In *Only Entertainment*, 2nd ed. New York: Routledge, 2002, 19–35.

———. *Pastiche*. New York: Routledge, 2007.

———. *Stars*. London: BFI Publishing, 1979.

———. *White*. London: Routledge, 1997.

Dyhouse, Carol. *Glamour: Women, History, Feminism*. London: Zed Books, 2011.

Ehrenstein, David. *Open Secret: Gay Hollywood, 1928–2000*. New York: HarperCollins, 2000.

Eidsheim, Nina Sun. *The Race of Sound*. Durham, NC: Duke University Press, 2019.

Ellis, Allen W. "Yes, Sir: The Legacy of Zeppo Marx." *Journal of Popular Culture* 37, no. 1 (2003): 15–27.

Elsaesser, Thomas. "Tales of Sound and Fury." In Gledhill, *Home Is Where the Heart Is*, 43–69.

Enss Chris. *The Lady Was a Gambler: True Stories of Notorious Women of the Old West*. Helena, MT: Twodot/Globe Pequot Pres, 2008.

Esch, Kevin. "The Bond That Unbinds by Binding: Acting Mythology and the Film Community." In Taylor, *Theorizing Film Acting*, 120–34.

Fabian, Johannes. "Theatre and Anthropology, Theatricality and Culture." In *The Performance Studies Reader*, 3rd ed., edited by Henry Bial and Sara Brady, 233–39. New York: Routledge, 2016.

Farmer, Ashley D. "In Search of the Black Women's History Archive." *Modern American History* 1, no. 2 (2018): 289–93.

Feeney, Megan. *Hollywood in Havana: US Cinema and Revolutionary Nationalism in Cuba before 1959*. Chicago: Chicago University Press, 2019.

Finch, Mark. "Sex and Address in Dynasty." In Cleto, *Camp: Queer Aesthetics and the Performing Subject*, 143–59.

Fischer, Lucy. *Designing Women: Cinema, Art Deco, and the Female Form*. New York: Columbia University Press, 2003.

———. "Sirk and the Figure of the Actress: *All I Desire*." *Film Criticism* 23, nos. 2–3 (1999): 136–49.

Fortmueller, Kate. "Gendered Labour, Gender Politics: How Edith Head Designed Her Career and Styled Women's Lives." *Historical Journal of Film, Radio, and Television* 38, no. 3 (2017): 474–94.

Fuss, Diana. *Inside/Out: Lesbian Theories, Gay Theories*. New York: Routledge, 1991.

Fyne, Robert. "From Hollywood to Moscow." *Literature Film Quarterly* 13, no. 3 (1985): 194–99.

Gaines, Jane. "Even More Tears: The *Historical Time* Theory of Melodrama." In Gledhill and Williams, *Melodrama Unbound*, 325–40.

———. "Film History and the Two Presents of Feminist Film Theory." *Cinema Journal* 44, no. 1 (2004): 113–19.

———. *Pink-Slipped: What Happened to Women in the Silent Film Industries?* Urbana: University of Illinois Press, 2018.

———, and Monica Dall'Asta. "Prologue: Constellations: Past Meets Present in Feminist Film History." In Knight and Gledhill, *Doing Women's Film History*, 13–25.

Gledhill, Christine, ed. *Home Is Where the Heart Is: Studies in Melodrama and the Woman's Film*. London: BFI, 1987.

———. Prologue to Gledhill and Williams, *Melodrama Unbound*, xxiv–xxv.

———. "Rethinking Genre." In *Reinventing Film Studies*, edited by Linda Williams and Christine Gledhill, 221–43. New York: Arnold, 2000.

———. "Speculations on the Relationship between Soap Opera and Melodrama." *Quarterly Review of Film and Video* 14, nos. 1–2 (1992): 103–124.

———, and Julia Knight. Introduction to Knight and Gledhill, *Doing Women's Film History*, 1–12.

———, and Linda Williams, eds. *Melodrama Unbound: Across History, Media, and National Cultures*. New York: Columbia University Press, 2018.

Goding-Doty, Christine. "Virtually White: The Crisis of Whiteness, Racial Rule, and Affect in the Digital Age." PhD Diss., Northwestern University, 2008.

———. "White Event Horizon." *Monday Journal* 4. https://monday-journal.com/white-event-horizon/.

Greene, Graham, and David Parkinson. *The Graham Greene Film Reader: Reviews, Essays, Interviews, and Film Stories.* New York: Applause Theatre Book Publishers, 1994.

Grindon, Ledger. "Structure of Meaning in the Boxing Film Genre." *Cinema Journal* 35, no. 4 (1996): 54–96.

Grossman, Julie. *Rethinking the Femme Fatale in Film Noir: Ready for Her Close-Up.* New York: Palgrave Macmillan, 2009.

Grundman, Roy. "Taking Stock at War's End: Gender, Genre, and Hollywood Labor in *The Strange Love of Martha Ivers*." In *The Wiley Blackwell History of American Film*, 1st ed., edited by Cynthia Lucia, Roy Grundman, and Art Simon, 2–35. Malden, MA: Blackwell Publishing, 2012.

Gustafson, Robert. "The Power of the Screen: The Influence of Edith Head's Film Designs on the Retail Fashion Market." *Velvet Light Trap* 19 (January 1, 1982): 8–15.

Hadleigh, Boze. *Hollywood Lesbians.* New York: Barricade Books, 1996.

Halliday, Jon. *Sirk on Sirk.* London: BFI Publishing, 1971.

Halpern, David M. *How to Be Gay.* Cambridge, MA: Belknap Press of Harvard University Press, 2012.

Hampton, Howard. "Extreme Prejudice: Transgressive Cinema from Anthony Mann's Prototypical *The Furies* to the Terminal Postmodernism of *Kill Bill* and *Sin City*." *Film Comment* 41, no. 6 (2005): 50–55.

Hansen, Miriam B. *Cinema and Experience: Siegfried Kracauer, Walter Benjamin, and Theodor W. Adorno.* Berkeley: University of California Press, 2012.

———. "Fallen Women, Rising Stars, New Horizons: Shanghai Silent Film as Vernacular Modernism." *Film Quarterly* 54, no. 1 (2000): 10–22.

———. "The Mass Production of the Senses: Classical Cinema as Vernacular Modernism." In *Reinventing Film Studies*, edited by Linda Williams and Christine Gledhill, 332–50. New York: Arnold, 2000.

———. "Room-for-Play: Benjamin's Gamble with Cinema." *Canadian Journal of Film Studies* 13, no. 1 (2004): 2–27.

Hanson, Helen. *Hollywood Heroines: Women in Film Noir and the Female Gothic Film.* London: I. B. Tauris, 2007.

Harris, Daniel. "The Death of Camp: Gay Men and Hollywood Diva Worship, from Reverence to Ridicule." *Salmagundi* no. 112 (Fall 1996): 166–91.

Hartman, Sadiya V. *Wayward Lives, Beautiful Experiments: Intimate Histories of Riotous Black Girls, Troublesome Women, and Queer Radicals.* New York: W. W. Norton, 2020.

Hastie, Amelie. *Cupboards of Curiosity: Women, Recollection, and Film History.* Durham, NC: Duke University Press, 2007.

Head, Edith, and Jane Kesner Ardmore. *The Dress Doctor.* Boston: Little, Brown, 1959.

Hennefeld, Maggie. "Destructive Metamorphosis: The Comedy of Female Catastrophe and Feminist Historiography." *Discourse* 36, no. 2 (2014): 176–206.

———. "Editor's Introduction: Toward a Feminist Politics of Comedy and History." *Feminist Media Histories* 3, no. 2 (2017): 1–14.

———. "Film History." In *Feminist Media Histories* 4, no. 2 (2018): 77–83.

———, and Nicholas Sammond, eds. *Abjection Incorporated: Mediating the Politics of Pleasure and Violence*. Durham, NC: Duke University Press, 2020.

Hesmondhalgh, David. *The Cultural Industries,* 3rd ed. Thousand Oaks, CA: Sage Publications, 2013.

Hillier, Jim, ed. *Cahiers du Cinéma: The 1950s: Neo-Realism, Hollywood, New Wave*. Cambridge, MA: Harvard University Press, 1985.

Hilmes, Michele. *Radio Voices: American Broadcasting, 1922–1952*. Minneapolis: University of Minnesota Press, 1997.

Hoberman, J. *Army of Phantoms: American Movies and the Making of the Cold War*. New York: New Press, 2013.

James, David. *Rock 'n' Film: Cinema's Dance with Popular Music*. New York: Oxford University Press, 2016.

Kaplan, E. Ann. "The Case of the Missing Mother: Maternal Issues in Vidor's *Stella Dallas.*" *Heresies* 16 (1983): 81–85.

———. "Dialogue." *Cinema Journal* 24, no. 2 (1984): 40–43.

Kemper, Tom. *Hidden Talent: The Emergence of Hollywood Agents*. Berkeley: University of California Press, 2010.

Klevan, Andrew. *Barbara Stanwyck*. London: BFI/Palgrave Macmillan, 2013.

Klinger, Barbara. *Melodrama and Meaning: History, Culture, and the Films of Douglas Sirk*. Bloomington: Indiana University Press, 1994.

Kristeva, Julia. *Powers of Horror: An Essay on Abjection*. Trans. Leon S. Roudiez. New York: Columbia University Press, 1982.

Knight, Julia, and Christine Gledhill, eds. *Doing Women's Film History: Reframing Cinemas, Past and Future*. Urbana: University of Illinois Press, 2015.

Landsberg, Alison. *Prosthetic Memory: The Transformation of American Remembrance in the Age of Mass Culture*. New York: Columbia University Press, 2004.

Lawrence, Amy. *Echo and Narcissus: Women's Voices in Classical Hollywood Cinema*. Berkeley: University of California Press, 1991.

———. "*Sorry, Wrong Number*: The Organizing Ear." *Film Quarterly* 40, no. 2 (1986–1987): 20–27.

Lippit, Akira. "The Death of an Animal." *Film Quarterly* 56, no. 1 (2002): 9–22.

Louvish, Simon. *Monkey Business: The Lives and Legends of the Marx Brothers*. London: Faber and Faber, 1999.

Lugowski, David M. "Claudette Colbert, Ginger Rogers, and Barbara Stanwyck: American Homefront Women." In *What Dreams Were Made Of: Stars of the 1940s*, edited by Sean Griffin, 96–119. New Brunswick, NJ: Rutgers University Press, 2011.

Luhrssen, David. *Mamoulian: Life on Stage and Screen*. Lexington: University Press of Kentucky, 2012.

Madsen, Axel. *Stanwyck*. New York: HarperCollins, 1994.

Maland, Charles. "The Unpublished James Agee: Excerpts from Complete Film Criticism: Reviews, Essays, and Manuscripts." *Cineaste* 41, no. 4 (2016): 26–29.

Maltby, Richard. "*Baby Face*, or How Joe Breen Made Barbara Stanwyck Atone for Causing the Wall Street Crash." In *Screen Histories*, edited by Annette Kuhn and Jackie Stacey, 164–84. New York: Oxford University Press, 1998.

Manon, Hugh S. "Some Like It Cold: Fetishism in Billy Wilder's *Double Indemnity*." *Cinema Journal* 44, no. 4 (2005): 18–43.

Marasco, Robyn. "It's All About the Benjamins: Considerations on the Gambler as a Political Type." *New German Critique* 45, no. 1 (2018): 1–22.

Marchetti, Gina. *Romance and the "Yellow Peril": Race, Sex, and Discursive Strategies in Hollywood Fiction*. Berkeley: University of California Press, 1993.

May, Martha. "From Cads to Dads." *Journal of Popular Film and Television* 25, no. 1 (1997): 2–8.

McBride, Joseph, ed. *Focus on Howard Hawks*. Englewood Cliffs, NJ: Prentice-Hall, 1972.

———. *Frank Capra: The Catastrophe of Success*. Jackson: University Press of Mississippi, 2011.

McComb, Mary. "Undressing an American Icon: Addressing the Representation of Calamity Jane through a Critical Study of Her Costume." MA Thesis, University of Regina, 2016.

McDonald, Paul. "Story and Show: The Basic Contradiction of Star Acting." In Taylor, *Theorizing Film Acting*, 169–83.

McElhaney, Joe. *The Death of Classical Cinema: Hitchcock, Lang, Minelli*. New York: State University of New York Press, 2006.

McGilligan, Patrick. *Cagney: The Actor as Auteur*. Rev. ed. San Diego: A. S. Barnes, 1982.

McGrath, Ann. "Being Annie Oakley: Modern Girls, New World Woman." *Frontiers: A Journal of Women's Studies* 28, no. 1 (2007): 203–231.

Miller, D. A. *Hidden Hitchcock*. Chicago: University of Chicago Press, 2016.

Miller, Toby, and Richard Maxwell. "Introduction to the Cultural Labor Issue." *Social Semiotics* 15, no. 3 (2005): 261–66.

Modleski, Tania. "Editorial Notes." *Critical Inquiry* 17, no. 1 (1990): 237–44.

Morin, Edgar. *New Trends in the Study of Mass Communications*. Birmingham, UK: Centre for Contemporary Cultural Studies, University of Birmingham, 1969.

———. *The Stars*. Trans. Richard Howard. Minneapolis: University of Minnesota Press, [1972] 2005.

Mulvey, Laura. "A Clumsy Sublime." *Film Quarterly* 60, no. 3 (2007): 3.

———. *Death 24x a Second: Stillness and the Moving Image*. London: Reaktion Books, 2006.

———. "Unmasking the Gaze: Feminist Film Theory, History, and Film Studies." In *Reclaiming the Archive: Feminism and Film History*, edited by Vicki Callahan, 474–94. Detroit: Wayne State University Press, 2010.

Naremore, James. *Acting in the Cinema*. Berkeley: University of California Press, 1988.

———. *More Than Night: Film Noir in Its Contexts*. Berkeley: University of California Press, 1998.

Neale, Steve. "Melo Talk: On the Meaning and Use of the Term 'Melodrama' in the American Trade Press." *Velvet Light Trap* no. 32 (Fall 1993): 66–89.

———. "Melodrama and Tears." *Screen* 27, no. 6 (1986): 6–22.

Nottage, Lynn. *By the Way, Meet Vera Stark*. New York: Theatre Communications Group Inc. 2013.

Nugent, Frank S. "Golden Holden." *Collier's*, June 2, 1951.

Olalquiaga, Celeste. *The Artificial Kingdom: On the Kitsch Experience*. Minneapolis: University of Minnesota Press, 1998.

Orr, Christopher. "Closure and Containment: Marylee Hadley in *Written on the Wind*." In *Imitations of Life: A Reader on Film and Television Melodrama*, edited by Marcia Landy, 380–87. Detroit: Wayne State University Press, 1991.

Ortner, Sherry B. *Not Hollywood: Independent Film at the Twilight of the American Dream*. Durham, NC: Duke University Press, 2013.

Palumbo-Liu, David. "The Bitter Tea of Frank Capra." *Positions* 3, no. 3 (1995): 759–89.

Peterson, Jennifer. "Ecodiegesis: The Scenography of Nature on Screen." *Journal for Cinema and Media Studies* 58, no. 2 (2019): 142–68.

Petty, Miriam. *Stealing the Show: African American Performers and Audiences in 1930s Hollywood*. Oakland: University of California Press, 2016.

Polan, Dana. *Power and Paranoia: History, Narrative, and the American Cinema, 1940–1950*. New York: Columbia University Press, 1986.

Porter, Jeff. "The Screaming Woman." In *Lost Sound: The Forgotten Art of Radio Storytelling*. Chapel Hill: University of North Carolina Press, 2016.

Powdermaker, Hortense. *Hollywood: The Dream Factory. An Anthropologist Looks at the Movie-Makers*. London: Secker and Warburg, 1951.

Pravadelli, Veronica. *Classic Hollywood: Lifestyles and Film Styles of American Cinema, 1930–1960*. Trans. Michael Theodore Meadows. Urbana: University of Illinois Press, 2015.

Pribram, E. Deidre. "Melodrama and the Aesthetics of Emotion." In Gledhill and Williams, *Melodrama Unbound*, 237–52.

Rabinowitz, Paula. "Barbara Stanwyck's Anklet: The Other Shoe." In *Accessorizing the Body*, edited by Cristina Giorcelli and Paula Rabinowitz, 185–208. Minneapolis: University of Minnesota Press, 2011.

———. *Black & White & Noir: America's Pulp Modernism*. New York: Columbia University Press, 2002.

Raheja, Michelle. *Reservation Reelism: Visual Sovereignty and Representations of Native Americans in Film*. Lincoln: University of Nebraska Press, 2010.

Rainey, Buck. *Sweethearts of the Stage*, with a foreword by Barbara Stanwyck. Jefferson, NC: McFarland, 1992.

Rancière, Jacques. *Film Fables*. Trans. Emiliano Battista. New York: Berg, 2001.

Raw, Laurence. "Deconstructing Political Adaptation: Sean O'Casey's *The Plough and the Stars*." In *Screening Modern Irish Fiction and Drama*, edited by R. Barton Palmer and Marc C. Connor, 55–72. London: Palgrave Macmillan, 2016.

Ray, Robert. *The ABCs of Classic Hollywood*. New York: Oxford University Press, 2008.

Robertson, Pamela. *Guilty Pleasures: Feminist Camp from Mae West to Madonna*. Durham, NC: Duke University Press, 1996.

Roof, Judith. *All about Thelma and Eve: Sidekicks and Third Wheels*. Urbana: Illinois University Press, 2002.

Rosenthal, Nicolas G. "Representing Indians: Native American Actors on Hollywood's Frontier. *Western Historical Quarterly* 36, no. 3 (2005): 328–52.

Ross, Andrew. "Uses of Camp." In Cleto, *Camp: Queer Aesthetics and the Performing Subject*, 308–329.

Rowe, Kathleen. *Unruly Women: Gender and the Genres of Laughter*. 1st ed. Austin: University of Texas Press, 1995.

Russell, Catherine. *Archiveology: Walter Benjamin and Archival Film Practices*. Durham, NC: Duke University Press, 2018.

———, "*The Barbara Stanwyck Show*: Melodrama, Kitsch, and the Media Archive." *Criticism: A Quarterly for Literature and the Arts* 55, no. 4 (2013): 567–92.

Santaolalla, Isabel C. "East Is East and West Is West? Otherness in Capra's *The Bitter Tea of General Yen*." *Literature Film Quarterly* 26, no. 1 (1998): 67–75.

Savoy, Eric. "'That Ain't *All* She Ain't': Doris Day and Queer Performativity." In *Out Takes, Essays on Queer Theory and Film*, edited by Ellis Hanson, 151–82. Durham, NC: Duke University Press, 1999.

Schackel, Sandra. "Barbara Stanwyck: Uncommon Heroine." *California History* 72, no. 1 (1993): 40–55.

Schatz, Thomas. *Boom and Bust: American Cinema in the 1940s*. Berkeley: University of California Press, 1999.

Sedgwick, Eve Kosofsky. *Touching, Feeling: Affect, Pedagogy, Performativity*. Durham, NC: Duke University Press, 2003.

Shantz, Ned. "Telephonic Film." *Film Quarterly* 56, no. 4 (2003): 23–35.

Shelley, Peter. *Grande Dame Guignol Cinema: A History of Hag Horror from* Baby Jane *to* Mother. Jefferson: McFarland, 2009.

Sheppard, Samantha. "Changing the Subject: Lynn Nottage's *By the Way, Meet Vera Stark* and the Making of Black Women's Film History." *Feminist Media Histories* 8, no. 2 (2022): 14–42.

Silverman, Kaja. *The Acoustic Mirror: The Female Voice in Cinema and Psychoanalysis*. Bloomington: Indiana University Press, 1988.

Simmons, Christina. *Making Marriage Modern: Women's Sexuality from the Progressive Era to World War II*. Oxford: Oxford University Press, 2009.

Singer, Ben. *Melodrama and Modernity: Early Sensational Cinema and Its Contexts*. New York: Columbia University Press, 2001.

Singer, Irving. "*The Lady Eve*." In Singer, *Cinematic Mythmaking: Philosophy in Film*. Cambridge: MIT Press, 2008.

Siomopoulos, Anna. "I Didn't Know Anyone Could Be So Unselfish": Liberal Empathy, the Welfare State, and King Vidor's *Stella Dallas*." *Cinema Journal* 38, no. 4 (1999): 3–23.

Sjogren, Britta. *Into the Vortex: Female Voice and Paradox in Film*. Urbana: University of Illinois Press, 2006.

Smith, Ella. *Starring Miss Barbara Stanwyck*. New York: Random House, 1988.

Smith, Jacob. *Vocal Tracks: Performance and Sound Media*. Berkeley: University of California Press, 2008.

Smoodin, Eric. *Regarding Frank Capra: Audience, Celebrity, and American Film Studies, 1930–1960*. Durham, NC: Duke University Press, 2005.

Smyth, J. E. *Nobody's Girl Friday: The Women Who Ran Hollywood*. New York: Oxford University Press, 2018.

Snyder, Scott. "Personality Disorder and the Film Noir Femme Fatale." *Journal of Criminal Justice and Popular Culture* 8, no. 3 (2001): 162–63.

Sobchack, Vivian. "Lounge Time: Postwar Crises and the Chronotope of Film Noir." In Browne, *Refiguring American Film Genres*, 129–70.

Sontag, Susan. *A Susan Sontag Reader*. New York: Farrar, Strauss, Giroux, 1982.

Stacey, Jackie. *Star Gazing: Hollywood Cinema and Female Spectatorship*. New York: Routledge, 1994.

Stamp, Shelley. "Film Noir's 'Gal Producers' and the Female Market." *Women's History Review* 29, no. 5 (2020): 801–821.

Stanfield, Peter. "An Excursion into the Lower Depths: Hollywood, Urban Primitivism, and 'St. Louis Blues,' 1929–1937." *Cinema Journal* 41, no. 2 (2002): 84–108.

———. *Hollywood, Westerns, and the 1930s: The Lost Trail*. Exeter, UK: Exeter University Press, 2001.

Stark, Cynthia A. "Gaslighting, Misogyny, and Psychological Oppression." *The Monist* 102, no. 2 (2019): 221–35.

Steedman, Carolyn. *Dust: The Archive and Cultural History*. New Brunswick, NJ: Rutgers University Press, 2001.

Steimatsky, Noa. *The Face on Film*. New York: Oxford University Press, 2017.

Stern, Michael. *Douglas Sirk*. Boston: Twayne Publishers, 1979.

Stewart, Jacqueline. "Negroes Laughing at Themselves? Black Spectatorship and the Performance of Urban Modernity." *Critical Inquiry* 29, no. 4 (2003): 650–77.

Straw, Will. "Scales of Presence: Bess Flowers and the Hollywood Extra," *Screen* 52, no. 1 (2011): 121–27.

Sussman, Warren. *Culture as History: The Transformation of American Society in the Twentieth Century*. New York: Pantheon Books, 1973.

Taylor, Aaron, ed. *Theorizing Film Acting*. New York: Routledge, 2012.

Telotte, J. P. "A Fate Worse Than Death: Racism, Transgression, and Westerns." *Journal of Popular Film and Television* 26, no. 3 (1998): 120–27.

———. "Tangled Networks and Wrong Numbers." *Film Criticism* 10, no. 3 (1986): 36–48.

Theatre Patrons Inc. *The Movies … and the People Who Make Them*. New Haven, CT: Theatre Patrons, 1939. https://archive.org/details/moviespeoplewhomoothea/.

Thornham, Sue. *What If I Had Been the Hero: Investigating Women's Cinema*. London: BFI/Palgrave 2012.

Thornton, Edith. "Fashion, Visibility, and Class Mobility in *Stella Dallas*." *American Literary History* 11, no. 3 (1999): 426–47.

Tranberg, Charles. *Fred MacMurray: A Biography*. Duncan, OK: Bear Manor Media, 2014.

Wagner, Robert J. (with Scott Eyman). *Pieces of My Heart: A Life*. New York: HarperCollins, 2008.

Waldman, Diane. "'At Last I Can Tell It to Someone!' Female Point of View and Subjectivity in the Gothic Romance Film of the 1940s." *Cinema Journal* 23, no. 2 (1984): 29–40.

Walker, Joseph B., and Juanita Walker. *The Light on Her Face*. Hollywood: ASC Press, 1984.

Walker, Michael. "*All I Desire*." *Movie* 34/35 (1990): 31–47.

Walsh, Andrea. "Films of Suspicion and Distrust: Undercurrents of Female Consciousness in the 1940's." *Film & History* 8, no. 1 (1978): 1–11.

Wayne, Jane Ellen. *The Life and Loves of Barbara Stanwyck*. London: J R Books, 2009.

———. *Robert Taylor: The Man with the Perfect Face*. New York: St. Martin's Press, 1989.

Westbrook, Robert B. "'I Want a Girl, Just Like the Girl That Married Harry James': American Women and the Problem of Political Obligation in World War II." *American Quarterly* 42, no. 4 (1990): 587–614.

White, Patricia. "Supporting Character: The Queer Career of Agnes Moorehead." In *Out in Culture: Gay, Lesbian, and Queer Essays on Popular Culture*, edited by Corey K. Creekmore and Alexander Doty, 91–114. Durham, NC: Duke University Press, 1995.

———. *Uninvited: Classical Hollywood Cinema and Lesbian Representability*. Bloomington: Indiana University Press, 1999.

Whitney, Alison. "Race, Class, and the Pressure to Pass in American Maternal Melodrama: The Case of *Stella Dallas*." *Journal of Film and Video* 59, no. 1 (2007): 3–18.

Wilkie, Jane. *Confessions of an Ex-Fan Magazine Writer*. New York: Doubleday, 1981.

Williams, Linda. "Melodrama Revised." In Browne, *Refiguring American Film Genres*, 42–88.

———. "Something Else Besides a Mother." *Cinema Journal* 24, no. 1 (1984): 2–87.

———. "'Tales of Sound and Fury . . .' or the Elephant of Melodrama." In Gledhill and Williams, *Melodrama Unbound*, 205–218.

Wilson, Victoria. *A Life of Barbara Stanwyck: Steel-True, 1907–1940*. New York: Simon and Shuster, 2013.

Wojcik, Pamela Robertson. "Mae West's Maids: Race, 'Authenticity,' and the Discourse of Camp." In *Hop on Pop: The Politics and Pleasure of Popular Culture*, edited by Henry Jenkins III, Tara McPherson, and Jane Shattuc, 287–99. Durham, NC: Duke University Press, 2003.

Wolfe, Charles. *Meet John Doe: Frank Capra, Director*. New Brunswick, NJ: Rutgers University Press, 1989.

Wood, Robin. "Screwball and the Masquerade: *The Lady Eve* and *Two-Faced Woman*." *Cineaction!* 54 (2001): 12–19.

Wylie, Philip. *Generation of Vipers*. New York: Pocket Books, [1942] 1955.

Yoggy, Gary A. *Riding the Video Range: The Rise and Fall of the Western on Television*. Jefferson, NC: McFarland, 2008.

Zarzosa, Agustín. "Melodrama and the Modes of the World." *Discourse* 32, no. 2 (2010): 236–55.

———. *Refiguring Melodrama in Film and Television: Captive Affects, Elastic Sufferings, Vicarious Objects*. Lanham, MD: Lexington Books, 2013.

INDEX

212; gaslighting and, 177–78, 253–54, 272; gender norms of, 170; "happy" endings, 153–54; liberal individualism and, 162, 170, 171; melancholia kitsch (Olalquiaga), 35; melodrama theory, 11, 26, 223; motherhood and, 55–56, 57; political discourse and, 162; soap opera and, 31; tears in, 265–66, 267–68; as term, 290n12

Meltzer, Lewis, 93

Menjou, Adolphe, 93–96, 194

Mennen baby oil, 284

Message to Garcia, A (1916), 113

Message to Garcia, A (1936), 111–16, 120–21, 138, 195, 198–99, 226

method acting, 6, 94, 152

Mexicali Rose (1929), 83

MGM, 64–65, 109, 185, 275

Midnight (1939), 140

Mildred Pierce (1945), 32, 130

Milestone, Lewis, 247–48

Miller, D. A., 120

Miller, Nolan, 192

Miller, Toby, 258

Million Dollar Pictures, 216

Miracle Woman, The (1931), 107, 109, 138, 238–39, 245

Misfits, The (1961), 197

modernity, 100–110; acting as shock experience of modernity (Benjamin), 143, 150–52; "cult of true womanhood" vs., 102, 105, 163; New Woman trope and, 13, 39, 43, 46–47, 78, 85, 100–102, 107, 163, 213, 226–28, 232–36, 259–68, 273, 286

Modern Screen magazine, 20, 276

"Momism" (Wylie), 53, 89, 296n19

Monroe, Marilyn, 67, 75

Montgomery, Bob, 85

Moonlighter, The (1953), 146–48, 168, 197–98, 199, 200

Moore, Colleen, 273

Moorehead, Agnes, 176

Morgan, Dennis, 64, 283

Mori, Toshia, 263, 264

Morin, Edgar, 15, 143

Morley, Jay A., 21

Morocco (1930), 224

motherhood/maternal roles, 48–57; "bad mother" trope, 48–57, 210–11;

BS and gossip concerning, 48, 49, 54, 56, 57, 210–11; BS closeness with Sinatra children, 287; BS guardianship for children of Peter Godfrey, 52, 287; BS infertility due to sexual abuse and, 50; BS mentoring and tutoring other actors, 4, 49, 52, 91–93, 94–96, 99, 159, 192; BS sexual orientation gossip and, 1, 48, 49, 91, 98–99, 122–23, 129, 130; BS son (*see* Fay, Anthony "Dion"); invisibility under patriarchy, 204–5, 210–13; "Momism" (Wylie) and, 53, 89, 296n19

mother-in-law trope, 34

Motion Picture Academy, 272, 273

Motion Picture Alliance for the Preservation of American Ideals (MPAPAI), 167, 248–49

Motion Picture Herald (trade paper), 129

Motion Picture Magazine, 276

Motion Picture Production Code Administration (PCA), 39, 46, 81–84, 86, 103–9, 143, 145, 148, 257, 260

Mr. Smith Goes to Washington (1939), 233, 234, 236

Mulvey, Laura, 12, 119

Murphy, Mary, 188

Museum of Modern Art, 98

music/sound tracks: BS singing roles, 220, 239–41, 242, 246; "St. Louis Blues," 211–12, 214, 219–21

My Darling Clementine (1946), 83

My Reputation (1946), 16, 23, 54, 62–64, 129–30, 269

My Three Sons (TV series), 147

Nancy, Jean-Luc, 144

Naremore, James, 161, 212

National Enquirer, 52–53, 56, 98

National Velvet (1944), 197

Native Americans. *See* Indigenous/Native American people

Naturama, 188

NBC, 26

Neal, Patricia, 167–68

neocolonialism, 111–21

Ness, Elliott, 252

New Deal politics, 9, 87, 207–8, 225, 230–33

112–16, 118–19, 259–68; jungle films and, 111–21, 259–68; miscegenation and, 54–55, 72, 261, 263–65; neocolonial settings, 111–21; racial segregation and passing, 211–12; racism and, 13, 54–55, 70–71, 86, 119, 230, 232; "Sambo Art" (Gates) and, 76–77, 79; western cinema and, 69, 70–74, 76–77, 111, 120–21, 268

Raheja, Michelle, 171
Rancière, Jacques, 70–71
Rand, Ayn, 57, 167–68
Randolph, Amanda, 33–34
rape, 50, 54, 151–52, 181
Rapper, Irving, 172
Raw, Laurence, 230
Ray, Nick, 188–89
Ray, Robert, 8, 9
Raymond, Gene, 249
Reagan, Ronald, 168–69, 170–71
realism, 86, 89
Rebecca (1940), 160, 172
Red Headed Woman (1932), 109
Red Salute (1935), 225, 226–28, 230, 281, 282, 317n14
Reed, Donna, 27, 252
Reliance Pictures, 226
Remember the Night (1940), 7, 59, 60, 66, 133, 145, 243
Rennie, James, 103
"reparative reading" (Sedgwick), 12–13, 140–41
Republicanism, 3, 57, 170–71, 230
Republic Pictures, 188–89
Revueltas, Rosaura, 201
Ride Back, The (1957), 119
Riskin, Robert, 104, 235
Ritter, Thelma, 129–30
Rivers, Joan, 243
RKO, 149, 163–64, 185, 195, 229, 249, 280, 281, 289n2
Robertson, Pamela, 189
Robinson, Edward G., 39
Rogers, Ginger, 58, 217, 284–85
Roland, Gilbert, 72, 268
Roof, Judith, 130
Roosevelt, Eleanor, 208
Rorke, Hayden, 253
Ross, Andrew, 184
Roustabout (1964), 67, 68, 248, 255, 287
Rowan, Andrew, 113–16
Rowe, Kathleen, 286

Runbeck, Margaret Lee, 65
Russell, Rosalind, 284–85
Ryan, Robert, 111, 116, 149–50, 152

St. Germain, Kay, 242
St. Johns, Adele Rogers, 271
"St. Louis Blues," 211–12, 214, 219–21
Sakall, S. Z., 283
saloon girls, 82–83, 133, 187–88
Salt of the Earth (1954), 201
"Sambo Art" (Gates), 76–77, 79
Sammond, Nicholas, 173–74, 183
Sanders, George, 254
Savoy, Eric, 125, 126
Sayre, Joel, 163–64
Scheuer, Philip K., 259
Scott, Lizabeth, 241
scrapbooking, 2, 272–78
Screen Actors Guild, 247
Screenland, 51, 111, 248
screwball comedy, 81, 181, 227–28, 236, 284–85; "comedy of remarriage" (Cavell), 54, 66, 131–32, 134–36, 219
Searchers, The (1956), 76, 113
second self, 24–25
Sedgwick, Eve Kosofsky, 12–13, 136, 140–41
Seitz, John, 40
self-alienation, 142–43, 147
sexuality, 89; destructive character/"femme fatale" roles, 38–47, 257; interracial attraction and, 54–55, 72, 73–74, 76, 112–16, 118–19, 259–68; "kept woman cycle," 109–10; kissing scenes, 78, 118, 142–52, 260, 262–63, 295n15; New Woman trope and, 101–2; older woman/younger man, 149, 189–90, 191; party girls/showgirls, 100–101, 129, 256–58; saloon girls and, 82–83, 133, 187–88; sexual innuendo, 76, 130, 133–34; sweater girl/pinup culture and, 62–64
sexual orientation: BS as gay icon, 1, 48, 79, 122, 292n2 (ch. D); BS sexual orientation rumors and, 1, 48, 49, 91, 98–99, 122–23, 129, 130; and "nance"/"poof"/"fairy" roles, 104; queer theory, 11, 13, 125, 136
Shakespeare, William, 130, 131
Shanghai Express (1932), 263–64
Shirley, Anne, 203, 212

Wingate, James, 105–6, 107
Wise, Robert, 96
Witness to Murder (1954), 43, 172, 253–54
Wittgenstein, Ludwig, 8
Wojcik, Pamela, 215
Wolfe, Charles, 236
Woman in Red, The (1935), 66, 195, 199
woman's agency: BS career and, 247–52, 287–88; cultural labor, 5, 42, 249, 257–58; female cosmopolitanism, 259, 263–68; gender performativity and, 5, 22–23, 75, 81, 122, 124–26, 135–41, 163, 166–67, 213; misogyny of American film industry, 1, 2, 11–12, 26–27, 29, 41–42, 46–47, 90, 131, 193, 200, 202, 205; willful subjects, 287–88; woman as hero of her own story, 46, 70, 73, 134–35, 140. *See also* independent woman trope; social mobility
woman's films, 15–25, 34, 53, 100, 105–10, 123, 129–30, 133–34, 156–57, 205, 245, 269, 272–73
Women, The (1939), 224
Wong, Anna May, 28, 263–64
Wood, Robin, 133
Wood, Thomas, 119
Woodward, Joanne, 140
Woolrich, Cornell (aka William Irish), 54, 154–56, 158–59, 269
Worden, Hank, 76
working women, 247–58; anti-union sentiments of BS, 247–49; cultural labor and, 5, 42, 249, 257–58; lack of equity in American cinema, 9, 26–27, 29, 69–70, 202; misogyny in American cinema, 1, 2, 11–12, 26–27, 41–42, 46–47, 90, 131, 193, 200, 202, 205; range of BS roles as, 247, 256–57. *See also* independent woman trope; New Woman trope; professional woman characters
World Animal Jungle Compound (Thousand Oaks, CA), 116–18
World War II, 62–64
Wrong Number (1948), 172
Wuthering Heights (radio show), 245
Wylie, Philip, 53, 89, 296n19

Yates, Herbert J., 189
You Belong to Me (1941), 250–51, 269, 278
Young, Loretta, 2, 26–27, 28, 58, 252, 276–77
Young, Robert, 226, 227, 250, 281
Young, Victor, 189
YouTube, 1, 9, 124
Yurka, Blanche, 73–74

Zane Grey Theatre (1958), 27, 124
Zanuck, Darryl, 75, 103–7, 221, 222, 240
Zarzosa, Agustín, 55–56

CATHERINE RUSSELL is Distinguished University Research Professor of Cinema at Concordia University. Her books include *Archiveology: Walter Benjamin and Archival Film Practices* and *Classical Japanese Cinema Revisited*.

Women's Media History Now!

A Great Big Girl Like Me: The Films of Marie Dressler
Victoria Sturtevant

The Uncanny Gaze: The Drama of Early German Cinema
Heide Schlüpmann

Universal Women: Filmmaking and Institutional Change
in Early Hollywood
Mark Garrett Cooper

Exporting Perilous Pauline: Pearl White and the Serial Film Craze
Edited by Marina Dahlquist

Germaine Dulac: A Cinema of Sensations
Tami Williams

Seeing Sarah Bernhardt: Performance and Silent Film
Victoria Duckett

Doing Women's Film History: Reframing Cinemas, Past and Future
Edited by Christine Gledhill and Julia Knight

Pink Slipped: What Happened to Women in the Silent Film Industries?
Jane M. Gaines

Queer Timing: The Emergence of Lesbian Sexuality in Early Cinema
Susan Potter

Subject to Reality: Women and Documentary Film
Shilyh Warren

Movie Workers: The Women Who Made British Cinema
Melanie Bell

Movie Mavens: US Newspaper Women Take On the Movies, 1914–1923
Richard Abel

The Cinema of Barbara Stanwyck: Twenty-Six Short Essays on
a Working Star
Catherine Russell

The University of Illinois Press
is a founding member of the
Association of University Presses.

Designed by Associés libres, Montréal, Canada
Composed in Minion Pro
with Gill Sans display
at the University of Illinois Press

University of Illinois Press
1325 South Oak Street
Champaign, IL 61820-6903
www.press.uillinois.edu